AT PLAY:

An Anthology of Maine Drama

Preface by Assunta Kent, Ph.D.
[Book Review Editor, New England Theatre Journal]

Levant Heritage Library   Levant, Maine

ISBN 0-9758743-2-2

Library of Congress Control Number: 2004108537

Contents

Editor's Note

I recently proposed staging some scenes from *At Play: An Anthology of Maine Drama* for Tuesday Forum, a Bangor networking group to which I belong. I had settled on Linda Britt's *Let Me Count the Ways* with its witty coven of wronged ex-wives as the ideal selection. As I described the script, I could feel the Tuesday Forum president buy into using this "revenge musical" as a program for working women. Then she posed a question that caught me off guard.

"Are you the editor of the anthology?" she asked.

After some hemming and hawing, I allowed that perhaps I was indeed the book's editor.

Surely, nobody else is acting in that capacity . But "editor" does not quite fit my role either, although my name will be inserted in that space whenever an editor's name is requested. For *At Play* is a uniquely-conceived compendium. This anthology is a spinoff from a monthly series called "Made in Maine Theatre Workshop" that ran from September 2003 to May 2004 at the Bangor Public Library.

Like their co-sponsor, Maine Writers & Publishers Alliance, these readings operated on a shoestring. There were no submission guidelines, no contest rules, no entry fees. Any Maine playwright with a completed script, who was willing to assemble a group of readers on a Saturday afternoon, was eligible to participate.

The readers of *At Play* will encounter the scripts in the same order that the "Made in Maine Theatre Workshop" audience viewed them. The result is an eclectic succession of voices, not all of whose output is destined for Pulitzer consideration.

Still, given the self-selected nature of the works, I believe the collection has considerable literary merit. While only two of us - Sanford Phippen and Carolyn Gage - have built impressive careers as writers, we all brought a publication or production history to the table. I would put this group of scripts up against the winners of any new play festival. The truth is that a complex, competitive process does not always produce excellence. Witness the prime-time television lineup.

I did make suggestions to some of the playwrights. One significant one was implemented, which I found gratifying. But I did not edit the scripts in *At Play*. Nor did I impose a single format upon them - some came to me in "acting edition" style (which is used for submitting scripts), others in some variant of "library edition" style, which uses less paper. Rather, each play represents the writer's original creative vision with little coloration at my hands.

The Bangor series was fun, but I'm glad that the monthly readings have come to an end. As coordinator I had some nervous moments - Do we cancel because of the blizzard warning in the forecast? - and a lot of work to do, much of it admittedly self-imposed. My Jewish mother theory of marketing, "Feed them and they will come" did not prove entirely true. But "Feed them and they will enjoy" was undeniably so. I loved watching strangers strike up animated conversations over my homemade munchies.

As to attendance, it was never awful and sometimes downright respectable. The most meaningful variable proved to be the level of effort put forth by each playwright to bring his or her own people in. Luckily, our biggest crowd assembled in January 2004 to watch *Scribes* of Bucksport High School perform *Oh Grow Up!* and a work in progress called *Dr. Bogtrotter's Secrets for the Comedically Challenged*. That was the day that Channel Seven showed up with a camera. Keith Ludden of the Maine Arts Commission, who was handling *At Play's* then-pending grant application, also chose that day to attend.

The writers have been a joy to work with. Sandy Phippen went to bat when our grant application ran into air turbulence. Assunta Kent rode up from Portland on her motorcycle to meet with me at length before attempting the preface. Hugh Aaron set me straight about print pricing. Carolyn Gage made numerous suggestions and offered me seasoned advice every step of the way.

Rick Doyle wrote a review and got it published in *Wolf Moon Journal*. Catherine Russell provided talented teen actors for several of the readings, including mine. Linda Britt and Peter Lee each drove more than four hours multiple times to attend performances. Caitlin Harrison also came often, and she was eerily convincing when reading the part of Toni, a dysfunctional adolescent bully in *Ugly Ducklings*.

Two other people must be given credit for the success of *Made in Maine Theatre Workshop* and the birth of *At Play.* Annaliese Jakimides, the northern Maine correspondent for *Maine in Print*, attended every single performance. She gave the series major play in her columns and, on a personal level, delivered much-needed pep talks whenever I got discouraged. And the book would have been inconceivable without the friendship and the willingness to crawl *way* out on a limb of John Chisholm. He's the treasurer and the force behind our publisher, Levant Heritage Library, as well as the most driven writer I have ever met.

I believe in the power of theater. Drama has the simple elegance of voice and guitar by starlight. That's how I first heard Bonnie Raitt sing as a no-name warm-up act on the Boston Common. Her low-tech performance was stunningly complete - no mega-million dollar budget required. Likewise, *Hamlet* could be fully realized by a boatloud of castaways on a desert island.

When watching a movie, we the audience demand, "Take me there. The special effects had better be awesome." When watching a play, we the audience allow, "Sure, we'll come along for the ride."

While the stage is every self-respecting play's ultimate destination, a well-written script also makes for a good read. After all, the most engrossing parts of a popular novel consist of dialogue. From opening line to final curtain, a play must be executable in one evening. So the related script can be comfortably absorbed in one sitting.

Enjoy these.

Laura Emack

ABOUT THE CONTRIBUTORS

Hugh Aaron graduated from the University of Chicago, served in the Seabees during World War II, and then became CEO of his own plastics manufacturing firm. He sold his company after twenty years in order to write full-time. His published work includes a book on management called *Business Not as Usual*, several short stories that have appeared in national magazines, and numerous essays on business topics for the *Wall Street Journal.* Hugh Aaron contributed two vignettes to the anthology: ***The Liebestod*** and ***Turned Tables.***

Linda Britt is a full professor of Spanish at the University of Maine at Farmington, where she has taught since 1988. She holds a Ph.D. in Spanish literature from the University of Virginia. She has published two books of translations, numerous articles of literary criticism, and several poems in literary magazines. Her musical *Billionaire Vegans* was staged at the Community Little Theatre in Auburn. Along with her son Colin Britt, who is studying composition at the Hartt School of Music, she penned the only musical in the collection, ***Let Me Count the Ways***. It's a comic, yet edgy portrait of a group of angry ex-wives. The play debuted at the Community Little Theatre in July 2004.

Rick Doyle is a playwright and poet who graduated from the University of Maine School of Law and holds an M.A. in English from the University of Maine. His poetry earned a Grady Award (1994) and a SpiritWord Honors Award (2001) and has appeared in *A Portfolio of Maine Writing* and *Puckerbrush Review.* He currently serves as the staff attorney for the Next Step Domestic Violence Project of Hancock County. ***Regalia***, a winner in the 2001 Maine Playwrights' Festival, highlights the unsettling changes that confront two generations of paper-mill workers.

Laura Emack is a CPA who served as audit partner for a regional firm prior to establishing her own, home-based accounting practice in 1993. She published a quarterly technical newsletter called *Prospects* for four years. Her writings have appeared in *Maine in Print* and *Naramissic Notebook.* Her play *Judith* won the University of Maine's one-act play contest in 1978. *In My Father's House* was a finalist in the Maine Playwrights' Festival in 2001. She created ***Writers Block***, a full-length drama that explores the deep connections that form while six writers from ages twenty-four to seventy-nine tilt at the maddening marketplace.

Carolyn Gage is an internationally renowned lesbian-feminist playwright and performer. The author of four books and forty-five plays, musicals, and one-woman shows, she has been the recipient of numerous awards. Her play, *The Second Coming of Joan of Arc,* was a major hit in South America. She directs Cauldron & Labrys, a women's theatre company in Portland, Maine. ***Ugly Ducklings*** is an ultimately hopeful coming-of-age tale dealing with homophobia and child suicide. Venus Theatre of Washington D.C. gave the play a well-received premiere in April 2004.

Caitlin Harrison is a 2003 graduate of Simon's Rock College of Bard with a B.A. in theater. Her play *Ducttape* was made into a short film for a class. ***Strange Love Triangle at the Children's Theatre,*** a zany comedy about a staged prank that turns into a real murder (or does it?), was presented as a reading at the college. After graduation, she worked on local productions including *The Wizard of Oz* at Bucksport High School and served a summer internship at Mass MoCA. As of the anthology's publication date, she plans to pursue a graduate degree as a playwright.

Dr. Assunta Kent earned her doctorate in Northwestern University's Interdisciplinary Program in Theatre and Drama. She is the Book Review Editor for the New England Theatre Journal and Associate Professor of Theatre History and Dramatic Literature at the University of Southern Maine. At USM she has directed numerous productions that included central female characters, stylized movement, and use of poetic language. She brings an expansive perspective on dramaturgy to the task of composing a preface.

Peter S. Lee graduated from Colby College and the New England School of Law. He is a practicing attorney who has written short stories for twelve years, which he does daily from 4:30 to 6:30 A.M His stories have appeared in *Tenebrus Lux* and *The Licking River Review*. ***Inside Out*** dramatizes the inner struggles of Guy Polatsky, a real estate lawyer who longs to be a writer. The play's characters consist of clashing voices inside Guy's head, one of whom is a John Lennon like incarnation of Jesus Christ.

Sanford Phippen is the author of a novel *Kitchen Boy*, two books of short stories, a book of essays, and a play collection, *Standing Just Outside the Door and Two Other Plays*. His work has appeared in the *New York Times, Maine Times, Portland Monthly Magazine, Down East, Ellsworth American, Bangor Daily News, and Maine Alumnus Magazine*. He hosts the Maine PBS series "A Good Read." He taught high school for over forty years before retiring in 2004. ***Standing Just Outside the Door*** explores how public educators deal with the topic of teen homosexuality. The script is being reprinted in the anthology with the permission of Blackberry Press.

Catherine Russell, leader of **Scribes,** has spent her professional life as an actor, writer, arts critic, editor, researcher, and stage director. She trained at numerous professional venues including the Eugene O'Neill Theater Center. She serves as advisor to the drama programs at Bucksport High school and Bucksport Middle School. Under her leadership, **Scribes** was created by students who wanted to write and perform their own work. Their one-act play ***Oh Grow Up!*** garnered seven awards at the 2002 Maine Drama Festival. The poignant vignettes gently skewer adults for their well-meant, often contradictory advice.

PREFACE

I take great pleasure in sharing my analytic summaries of the fresh new work anthologized in *At Play*. Although replete with double meaning, the title could seem to take the craft of the playwright too lightly. After all, a playwright's keen observation of human interaction, ear for dialogue, and visual/spatial imagination would create nothing more than a phantasm – without plain hard work. However, if "Play" refers to the serious occupation of children becoming fully human, then the title is apt. For only a title so encompassing would do justice to the breadth and depth of the works included here–and to the playwrights' passionate desire to express what they have observed about life–from their peculiar position in Maine, bounded by forest and ocean, on the edge of the country, out of the major airways and airwaves.

Secondarily, *At Play* could refer to the creative use of the playwrights' energies (only one of whom derives her primary livelihood from theatre); all are writing plays in particular for their love and fascination with the power and challenges of this medium.

As I read these plays over, I was reminded how much the reader's associations and notions color a first reading. I encourage you to give these plays a second and third reading, or better a staged reading or full production, in order to plumb the depths and more fully experience the complex visions of contemporary life. Let neither your reactions nor the playwrights' worlds languish for want of a little more work.

Although the subject is as old as humanity itself, only recently has an open and sympathetic treatment of diverse sexual orientations, especially of youth, become commonplace in drama. I am pleased that the two plays leading off this anthology consider the changes in social acceptance of gay teen identity over time, and also seek to expose the forces that maintain inequality and the consequent social and psychological damage.

***Standing Just Outside the Door* is the selective memoir of a teacher's experiences with gay teens "coming out" in his classroom over the past 35 years. We see the progression of Gay Liberation as lived by teens through the eyes of Mr. Harrison, who (like playwright Sanford Phippen) served as a high school English teacher in New York state and then back in his native Maine. It is 1966 and Harrison, only in his second year of teaching, has already established himself as a popular, respected, and demanding teacher. He advises the literary magazine and has instituted creative writing journals, in which his students practice their skills daily, by formally exploring fundamental questions of identity. It is implied here (and corroborated by Phippen's compiled script of student writing, *The Straight and Crazy Doped Up World*) that students trust Harrison enough to chronicle their formative experiences and to share with him their deeper feelings and unedited thoughts about their lives.**

The main story is established within the first few minutes of the play. Wry, "mannish" Doreen stops by Mr. Harrison's office before school, ostensibly to ask for help on her term paper on Edna St. Vincent Millay. But clearly she is as interested in the lives of the authors, particularly gay or bisexual writers, as she is in their works.

Doreen: Tell me, Mr. Harrison, was Millay a little on the funny side? Did she like girls as well as men?

Harrison: Millay? I don't know. Why don't you get some biographies and read about her? Really dig up the dirt on the Pulitzer Prize winner!

Doreen: She liked to be called Vincent. That sounds kind of dikey to me . . .

Harrison: She was a great artist, avant-garde, ahead of her time, a fighter for women's rights, an icon . . . she probably tried everything, but she was also our greatest lyric poet. Don't label her.

But Doreen persists, checking her facts on Walt Whitman, Tennessee Williams and James Baldwin, all the while further testing Mr. Harrison's non-judgmental attitude about sexual diversity. He passes her test with flying colors, and simply takes the opportunity to reiterate his advice not to label and suggests that Doreen might also enjoy reading Carson McCullers. But in mentoring bright teens on their creative writing, this pointed line of inquiry is all in a day's work.

Enter a more unlikely visitor: Paul, the well-mannered captain of the football team. He has come to ask for personal advice: his friend, Bill, has been leaving "gushy and crazy and embarrassing" letters in his locker and he wants him to stop. A gentle and mature young man, Paul hasn't spoken to Bill about it because he doesn't share his feelings but also doesn't want to lose the friendship of this "very bright and funny" classmate. Mr. Harrison is honest in return, saying that he doesn't feel qualified to mediate a meeting between the boys and suggests instead the school psychologist, Mrs. Werner. Although unaware that there is a school psychologist, Paul agrees to let Harrison show some of the letters to her and ask her advice on how best to handle the matter.

At his first opportunity, Harrison meets with Werner, who turns out to be a well-meaning but old-school 'shrink,' whose German-accented English signals her Freudian view that homosexuality is a sickness and her almost prurient interest in the physical descriptions in Bill's love letters. In their rather tense conversation, Phippen includes some very telling details that differentiate the teacher's tolerant openness to his students' individuality from the psychologist's search for treatable symptoms.

Werner manages to elicit a promise that Bill will be sent to her office during his next English class, but Harrison insists that he would feel better if he could "say something to Bill beforehand." Werner quickly cuts him off, "I don't sink zat will be necessary. I just vant to meet him and talk vit him a little." However, she seems to notice Harrison's discomfort at her rush to label Bill's (and possibly Paul's) behavior and desire as aberrant, because she avoids using the label of "mental illness" with him. Instead, she 'reminds' the young teacher that "homosexuality is a very serious condition . . . it's still illegal in many places, you know." In so doing, she exploits the teacher's trustworthiness and sense of responsibility to his students, by implying that if he doesn't go along with her suggestions, he might be placing his young charges at some unspecified medical, or even legal, risk.

The scene in which Bill is 'ambushed' by being the last to know that his locker notes have become the subject of a psychological conference is both more compact and complex than one might imagine. Werner produces the evidence, in D.A. fashion, asking, "Do you recognize zis letter?" And it is Bill who gives voice to society's prejudicial attitude, " So, you probably think I'm perverted and weird, don't you? A real degenerate nut case?" This allows Werner to play the caring professional, pronouncing, "I think you really are in love with Paul. It's rather normal for young boys to fall in love with other fellows . . . ," but then she hits him with the label "homosexual" and recommends testing and weekly appointments. When he resists, she pulls out heavier ammunition, "I'm here as a trained psychologist to help you. Homosexuality is listed as a serious mental illness, you know?" And we almost cheer when Bill retorts that she and his betraying teacher might be the ones who are mentally ill, and denies being "a homosexual." Here, Phippen implies that Bill is correct, if his definition means that he is weird or degenerate to love and admire Paul.

The main plot ends with a couple of confrontations between Bill and Mr. Harrison that leave no real resolution: either to Bill's long-term fate or to the guilt that haunts the teacher.

> **The consequences of what I did could have damaged him for life, but we were all filled with fear and ignorance then. I was torn between what I know in my heart I should do and say, and doing and saying what the school and society sanctioned me to do. . . . it changed me as a teacher and a person. I was determined not to let this happen again.**

The remainder of the play includes a set of "Soliloquies and Colloquies" on students coming out to Harrison in a variety of circumstances over the years–from the first openly gay student body president in the '70s, a lesbian alum who went on to be a female engineer and a pair of gay and straight hunting buddies to a reversal with the gay-bashing of a tranny-boy on the school bus. The script closes with an added scene (that has been omitted from some productions) in which Mr. Harrison shares some comforting closure with

us as he re-encounters Bill as a middle-aged man.

Although the portrait of the German psychologist borders on stereotype, it seems to hold the sort of truth upon which later stereotypes are based. Her scenes with both teacher and student demonstrate the dangerous gap in information and understanding between gay clients and 'trained mental health professionals' with their powerful societal, religious, and 'medical' biases. The play as a whole measures how much things have changed in research on homosexuality but also reminds how recently trained professionals were less open-minded than a caring non-professional (who already knew and cared about the gay student as an individual person), and warns how slowly such attitudes are fully eradicated.

What is most intriguing, however, from a dramaturgical standpoint is the subtle double-plot. The "very emotional and dramatic" young man and his "scholar/athlete" friend draw the attention of teachers, staff and students. But Phippen also includes the (possibly requited) romance of earthy Doreen who imitates her term paper subject, Millay (that "wild Maine woman"), by using her own "passionate and romantic" poetry to court her "feminine and pretty" friend, Linda. When Linda sighs, "I wish someone would write something like this for me;" Doreen admits that it is her writing–and written for Linda. Linda's last lines are simply, "Really? Really?" End of scene.

As a retiring teacher and long-time writer in various genres, Phippen's self-reflection is rich with experience and long pondering. During his career, he has borne witness to the volatile changes in student perceptions and experiences of race, gender, sexuality, and class identity in both urban/suburban (Syracuse, NY) and rural/small town (Orono, Maine) high schools. This play was written in response to a joking request by another teacher/director for a script on a "trendy" social issue to enter into the Maine High School One-Act Festival. But Phippen had been meaning to write such a play and his thinking on the subject is neither new nor faddish. There is a refreshing, non-PC (politically correct) and Maine-ish quality to Phippen's approach: an open-minded decency, an independent spirit, and a willingness to see how things actually are. His play does not preach or pontificate but simply models tolerance and acceptance for gender diversity, where no student is left standing outside the door; it could and should play at every junior and senior high school in Maine and beyond.

Although we can empathize with Bill's defensive response to the school psychologist and few would agree with her approach or her (thankfully outmoded) 'data' on homosexuality, both Mrs. Werner and Mr. Harrison were correct in taking the situation seriously. Not all students are as mature, articulate, and willing to confide in or to confront an adult. Nor are some 'responsible' adults as fair-minded and approachable as Harrison. And Werner was correct that many students who complain of others' gendered behavior may be questioning themselves. Young people need the safety to openly discuss questions of (sexual) identity with peers and adults. The most recent statistics indicate that gay, lesbian, and bi-sexual teens are six times

more likely to commit suicide than heterosexual youth, and that 30% of all teen suicides are committed by homosexual teens. As with most such statistics, given the lingering prejudice and secrecy involving sexual orientation, it is believed that these figures underestimate the actual problem. Plays like these present a range of perspectives from which to begin life-saving discussions.

In her well-crafted drama, *Ugly Ducklings*, Carolyn Gage exposes some of the social conditions and psychological mechanisms that contribute to this inhospitable climate for gender and sexual diversity. The audience still gazes from a voyeuristic position (beyond the imaginary 4th wall), but instead of sympathetically watching the struggles of gay teens from the outside, we are guided into the emotional center of the action by a seasoned playwright who has experienced her own and others' 'coming out,' first hand.

There are several choices of subject position with which the audience member can identify: working and middle class, children of abuse and those of relative privilege, worldly and naive, conscious and unconscious of the 'way the world works.' For example, even the most unaware, blithely heterosexual viewer can follow the awakening of Angie, a 19-year old camp counselor, who discovers, and is able to proudly proclaim by the end of the day, that she is lesbian. Ultimately, the play is about those girls and women who awaken to the workings of the heterosexist world, and still find the strength and support to make their own way; and also sadly, those who passively succumb to social conditioning, or who become active accomplices in indoctrinating or expelling those who don't or can't comply.

Set in a private girls' summer camp on an idyllic lake in Maine, *Ugly Ducklings* presents a spectrum of the coping methods adopted by four groups of females from the youngest girls to the camp's director. The youngest are relatively transparent about their feelings, but the 12 and 13-year old girls, who still have crushes on each other and their counselors, follow the lead of the most physically developed and 'socially precocious' girl in obsessing about their appearance and about boys. Group membership and rules are maintained by name-calling and snubbing anyone who doesn't conform. Two new counselors, middle-class Angie and working-poor Renee, are shyly developing a relationship and begin to pool their knowledge of life from their very different experiences thus far. Renee proclaims her difference by her dress and her unwillingness to "put on an act," but especially since she is the arts counselor, Angie and others who really do not want to know, can more easily ignore her gender signification. Angie's awareness has also been dulled by rooming with Vanessa, a woman seemingly addicted to sex and/or the seeming power of her sex appeal. When Angie asks about her day off, Vanessa reveals that she will be "walking bowlegged for a week" from servicing one of her boyfriends because he had driven all the way up from Boston to see her. In turn, Vanessa is appalled to learn that Angie doesn't have sex with her college "boyfriend." In compressed dramatic style, this day will reveal many more unspoken truths about women and the currency of their personal relationships.

Not surprisingly, Vanessa is the long-time favorite employee of Charlotte, the "deeply closeted" summer camp director, who, in Gage's words, "has sublimated her natural lesbian desires into toxic mentoring of an elite corps of counselors." Wounded as a young woman when her best girlfriend graduated high school and abandoned her for a (puppyish) husband, Charlotte now professes that she might have been spared that "misguided experience [that] left me scarred for life" with "some strong adult guidance during those years . . . someone who had insisted that I spend more time with other girls, and get out and learn how to act around boys." Thus, she makes it her duty "to police same-sex crushes" and to intervene when she deems that they might "get carried too far," enlisting assistants like Vanessa, whose own jealousy and misguided ambitions drive her to play up to the boss and to snitch on the other counselors.

When Angie balks at Charlotte's policy of ignoring any campers or other counselors "who set themselves apart," she identifies herself and Renee as potential threats to the camp's reputation. Charlotte has dedicated her life to carving out an all-too-temporary "oasis of girlhood," the only time and place in the campers' lives "they will ever have the opportunity to experience themselves in an environment apart from their brothers, or their fathers, or their husbands, or their sons. There is freedom here, a safety, that most of them will never know again.' But we will see, as in all abridgments of civil liberties in the name of securing boundaries, the freedom is only for some and comes at a high cost. In the case of gay and lesbian youth, it may cost their lives.

In the opening scene of the play, we meet two campers who will provide the catalyst for the play's crises: lesbian baiting, youth suicide, and 'don't ask, don't tell' employment policies. We discover 12-year old Toni, both street-wise and immature, tying knots (including a noose) on the dock of the waterfront canoeing area. She is soon joined by Lisa, a bright, intense 8-year old, who frankly announces she has been looking for Toni, and assumed she would be down by the water, because Angie, the canoe instructor, seems to be her favorite counselor. When Toni feigns indifference, Lisa tries to gain her attention by demonstrating her own knot-tying skills. But instead of inspecting Lisa's bowline, Toni loops her rope around the younger girl and pulls it painfully tight, making her lose her balance. When Lisa openly complains, "You hurt me." Toni retorts, "If it doesn't show, it doesn't hurt," and goes back to her knotting. Lisa, who has not yet learned to deny her feelings to please others (even the object of her infatuation), maintains, "Yes, it does," but remains watching Toni with interest.

Outspoken Lisa provides a baseline for the play's exploration of the so-called Ophelia Syndrome: the process through which active, forthright, confident pre-pubescent girls become passive, demurring, low self-esteem young women. Here, the continuum of female characters, grouped by age, allows us to see this syndrome in the making, and provides evidence for Gage's thesis that this "precipitous drop in self-esteem" is "the inevitable result of a

colonization process that takes place whenever girls are being groomed" for their limited roles in "heteropatriarchy," the social system under which "girls descend from being the subjects of their lives to perceiving themselves as objects in the lives of others." Clearly, Vanessa has already successfully completed this descent, while Charlotte was so damaged that she is arrested in a permanent state of distorted pubescent girlhood.

We soon learn that Toni has an alcoholic mother, a convict father who probably sexually abused her, and that she is known for lying, spying and almost sociopathic cruelty. While Lisa, her tag-along admirer, appears 'well-adjusted,' she is drawn to Toni's moodiness and resistance to authority. They are allied in knowing that adults are not entirely trustworthy, rules are worth questioning, and also by their knowledge that they are not as "interested in boys" as their cabinmates seem to be.

When Lisa asks her about the noose she has suspended from the camp flagpole, Toni finally tells her it's "to catch the creature that comes out of the lake at night and drowns little girls . . sucks their blood." When in girl-detective style, Lisa expresses skepticism, Toni offers as evidence details of a dead body and a cover-up the previous year by the camp staff: "Don't worry. It was just an old life raft, and the girl just went home early, and the creature doesn't exist." But Toni leaves both the noose and the truth or fiction of her story, hanging–to catch the gullible, the fearful, and at the same time to both raise awareness and to ward off other less tangible fears.

When Angie, the object of Toni's crush, arrives and asks about the noose, Lisa hints at its purpose and "gives Toni a conspiratorial nudge, Toni, embarrassed by the company of an eight-year old," calls Lisa a queer. When Lisa asks what that means, Toni is quick to give the most pejorative definition, " a girl who does nasty things to other girls." Angie cuts them off and as the bell rings, Lisa speeds away to her cabin, but not before the painful shot of doubt and self-loathing has been lodged in her heart. Lisa, who had thus far escaped being labeled and ostracized for "being somebody who likes girls the way they should like boys," will end the day by offering herself up to the lake monster, and when he doesn't take her, attempting to hang herself from the flagpole.

I have room here to address only one more, and perhaps the most powerful, of the many successful devices that Gage employs in this seemingly simple tale: the metaphors of monsters. According to Gage, her script represents an inversion of the traditional treatment of lesbians in mainstream plays. In *Ugly Ducklings*, it is the girls and women socialized to acceptable roles in heteropatriarchy who constitute the vampires and monsters. These are the characters who appear grotesque, exaggerated, two-dimensional. Because they are living out artificial roles and have become traitors to their own sex, they have lost their humanity. It is not the lesbian who is predatory and destructive, who is seducing her victims away from healthy relationships. It is the women who have abandoned their natural same-sex relationships who wreak havoc in the lives of their charges.

And I would add that once we accept that Toni's "monster who drowns little girls," does indeed exist--in society's treatment of females, in the Ophelia Syndrome, with the flashers and rapists that stalk the girls' real world, with the rules and restrictions enforced both by other females and males--then we find that, like the best drama, Gage's play is filled to bursting with sharp-edged double meaning and irony.

Ugly Ducklings exemplifies the original purpose of Realism or modern drama--to illuminate the inherent inequalities underlying the social contract (with all its exclusions, 'sweetheart' deals, and unexamined rules)–by simply showing a day in the life of ordinary people. Like contemporary playwrights Maria Irene Fornes and Wendy Wasserstein, Gage manages the Realist form–criticized for too often naturalizing the status quo–and uses it to 'naturalize' usually marginalized characters and to interrogate 'accepted' social practices and conditions. In a very accessible and engaging format, and with the social consciousness of Ibsen and Shaw, she has made explicit "the connections between homophobia and youth suicides, sexual trauma and aversion to gender roles, and so-called delinquency and resistance to heterosexist social conditioning." By closely observing the interactions of Gage's compelling characters, we can see how natural same-sex attraction is suppressed, expelled, or driven underground by successive groups, but also how we could stand together, tell the truth, and break the cycle of silencing and destruction.

Following these full length plays written from an adult's perspective, with *Oh, Grow Up!,* we hear from actual Maine teens whose ensemble exploration of coming-of-age issues resonates across time and region, sounding universal themes. Catherine Russell advises an improv troupe of Bucksport High School students who periodically perform as "Caught in the Act" at the Alamo Theatre. In 2002, under her tutelage, student "Scribes" devised an award-winning one-act play from a series of comic and dramatic sketches, based on contradictory messages and mixed feelings about growing up. With a target audience of parents, teachers and other teens clearly in mind, their script deftly steers the audience through some of the ups and downs of the maturation process.

During the Prologue, actors illuminate themselves with flashlights in rapid succession, while calling out a dizzying array of one-line instructions--"You'll grow into it. You'll grow out of it. Hurry up! Don't run! Swallow that! Spit that out!"– ending with "Oh, grow up! ... People are watching !" At which point, the ensemble "notices" the audience, and proceeds to 'nonchalantly' ad lib their way into the 'real' start of the show, explaining that "as far as stations in life go, being a kid is really the sticky end of the lollipop" with all that that messy, but somewhat pleasurable, metaphor implies. Before starting the first real scene, they argue (echoing the seeming contradictions of the messages received from adults) whether they are "just kids" and if so, what that means. They conclude: "We can't drive, we can't drink," but we also "don't pay rent . . . we don't have to go to jobs we hate every day . . . and best of all, we don't have kids!"

The first of two (*Saturday Night Live* style) scenarios spoofs *Sesame Street* and lets us in on the 'grown-up' secret that letters are much slippier characters than we were led to believe back in kindergarten. Witness this week's sponsor, "bad boy" X and his backup singers, the "babes," S, E and Y, who get together and introduce SEX(Y) into the youngsters' lives. When W, N, and O push Y aside, the urgency of their dangerous influence is only strengthened (SEXNOW).

We then flash back to a children's 'scary movie,' dramatizing the specters that fertile young imaginations conjure up when parents invoke 'scary monsters' to enforce rules of behavior. In "Monsters in the Closet," as soon as his parents leave the room, the child is assailed by an increasingly threatening parade of ludicrously costumed hobgoblins: from the fairly mild "sugarbugs" (who will get you if you don't brush your teeth) through carnivorous bedbugs to the Devil himself. And, of course, the parents never see the monsters, who may be leering right behind them, but at least this child can rely on his parents to heed his cries and come to the rescue.

But, the narrators ask, what if a child's fears are caused by real hurts or losses, even the loss of the comforting adult who promised to be there always? At this point in the script, the students raise the emotional stakes by introducing the first part of one boy's personal drama. In "Triptych I," little Tommy comes home crying to his Mom, who soon discovers that he has been more wounded by name-calling older children than by the spill he took on the playground.

Tommy: . . . when I fell I cried, an', an', an' I, I said . . . I wanted my Mommy . . . An' they said, only a sissy poophead would cry for Mommy.

Barbara: Oh, now let me tell you something, and you remember this, Tommy . . . It's okay for you to need your mom. . . .

And with a song and a hug and an ice cream cone everything is better—for now.

For the rest of the production, broadly comic sketches are interspersed with serious dramatic scenes as children grow into teens and young adults. Tommy's story provides a chronology upon which to hang the ensemble pieces, lending resonance to both. This dramaturgical method also harnesses the mercurial mix of high school hi-jinx, ingenuous frankness, and unbridled emotion that characterize teens and their writing.

The next ensemble scene is set in a classroom and replays age-old "school myths," such as the "326,475 pages" of homework assigned by one unreasonable teacher, the horrible cafeteria sludge purveyed by diabolical "lunch ladies," and those inane algebra story problems.

But these issues, familiar as they are, pale in comparison to the insoluble problems we face as our family and friends grow older, sicken, and die. In

"Triptych II," the foreshadowed calamity (the loss of Tommy's mom) is presented in a succinct, effective deathbed scene.

Scene 7 offers us comic relief by counterposing the split scene dinnertime of a perfect TV family (*Leave It To Beaver, Father Knows Best*) with that of a scruffy TV-dinner family, who make *Married with Children* seem refined. The contrast comes to a head (underscoring the wide variation within families) when the two groups meet at a mutual family reunion, bearing either store-bought donuts or homemade crème brulée. This provides the perfect segué to "Triptych III" in which we see young adult Tommy at a moment of crisis. Now, a young married father with a stay-at-home wife and child, he has nearly let financial worries overwhelm their young marriage. But, just as his wife is offering to pack up the kids and move out, his mother's memory provides Tom with strength and a saving moment of clarity.

Having brought the "kids" through from pre-school to married life, *Oh, Grow Up!* ends by re-positioning the opening ensemble, as they recap the pros and cons of childhood. This time, however, all but one pair of kids are 'taken over' by the externalized scolding voices, who gang up on the remaining two kids. Finally, the lone boy and girl have heard enough.

Female Victim: **(exploding under the pressure) No! No more!**

Male Victim: **I am just sick and tired of being treated like a child. I can't take it anymore. . . . I'm going to explode, do something radical. I'm gonna, I'm gonna . . .**

Female Victim: **Grow UP!**

The tension released, the former victimizers break from their freeze and join the newly minted 'grown ups' and offer genuine thanks to all those adults who cared enough to yell at them and "held their hand," and who encouraged and paid for and paid attention to them.

***Oh, Grow Up!* showcases young Thespians making use of improvisation and other standard theatrical devices (sketch comedy, satire, ensemble narration and realist scenes) to present a nuanced and entertaining view of issues relevant to teens (and former teens) across generations.**

While the Bucksport Scribes voice the concerns of youth, Rick Doyle focuses on a host of difficulties near the end of life's journey. In *Regalia*, we are left stranded, by pride and a failing memory, with Edgar Dolan who is denied admittance to a special meeting of his Fraternal Order. Although dressed in full regalia and a four-time Past Commander, he is closed out because he cannot remember the current password--which ironically happens to be "regalia," a word derived from "regal" which implies that one's very garments bespeak a royal privilege or at least, for organizations like the Sons of Saul, clearly signal an exclusive membership or office, both of which Edgar has held most of his adult life. The Brotherhood's protocol is rendered even

more hollow since the Order is simply 'following tradition' by holding a mourning ritual ("draping the charter") for a founding member (and Edgar's lifelong work mate) Frank McGinn, who most current members know only as "a nice old gentleman . . . who came to a few meetings."

But Doyle's play begins to reach beyond a poignant and finely drawn character study when we learn that, as young men, Edgar and Frank began cutting firewood together, and then worked their way up to Senior Machine Tender over thirty years in the paper mills. Most Mainers (and indeed most Americans) will immediately sense the parallel between one old man's personal misfortunes and the cultural and economic losses suffered by thousands of workers displaced by the 'outsourcing' of industrials jobs in the U.S.

As Edgar waits out the entire meeting, we learn of his staggering series of losses: a recent life-threatening illness, the death and funeral of his beloved wife, being barred from visiting his old job because of "liability," his son's imminent plan to retire to Florida, his inability to drive safely or to care for himself adequately as well as going unrecognized by his "Brothers" and the death of his closest age mate.

But something else lies festering beneath Edgar's unwillingness to accept help in gaining access to the meeting. His son, Raymond, the current Commander, reminds him that when he had offered him a ride, Edgar had declared that he "wouldn't have anything to do with" honoring Frank. And though Edgar denies "saying such a thing," his deeply mixed feelings about Frank begin to surface. From maddening hints and Raymond's unanswered questions, we can glean that Frank had boarded with Edgar and his wife, May, during the Depression; that Frank had brought in the only cash at one time; that he suddenly moved out of their house right after he "made Mom so mad" that she was "sitting at the table, crying;" and that as a charter member, Frank, would have had the power to "blackball" Edgar from membership in the Order. Although never spoken, one senses that there was some affront to Edgar's manhood or selfhood (sexual, economic, or in terms of status?) that has scabbed over, but never healed. And now that Frank has died, Edgar will never be able to lance the wound by confronting him. Perhaps it is holding in these feelings for a lifetime that has done more damage to Edgar's thought processes than simple aging.

As we now know from studying families of abuse, keeping shameful secrets also impairs the self-esteem of succeeding generations. Doyle's play also intimates that were Raymond given the benefit of understanding the dynamics in his parents' (and perhaps their small town neighbors') relationships from his father's perspective that his life might be more fulfilled; even that he might not be divorced with a son who has formed some sort of rebellious alliance with his grandfather and who has to make a choice which parent to visit on the weekend. Breaking silence about painful but normal occurrences within the extended family might perhaps free all of them from important blocks in memory and understanding.

In terms of his participation in the Order which could have provided Edgar a sense of intergenerational community, his preoccupation with the past coupled with his unwillingness to fully share his experiences has also relegated him to just "an old fool" instead of an elder who could endow their ritual and regalia with a particular history and real meaning. Like so many unskilled workers who have hunkered down in the face of two decades of industrial decline, Edgar clings so tenaciously to his unresolved past that he has lost the capacity to grab onto the present.

But aging need not be all gloom and doom, especially if elders remain "active and alert" (as does Laura Emack's 79-year old, Helen)-- and if they find ways to fully express themselves and to extend their network of friends and confidants beyond their immediate family and age mates. Of course, that is also the prescription for a full and healthy life –no matter what age the character or playwright.

In perhaps the strongest new voice in this anthology, Emack presents an intergenerational group of writers (who wryly call themselves Writers Block), striving to express their peculiar experiences and observations about life, and to share these outside their immediate enclave, preferably with a reading public. Part of the rush of reading this play (I can only imagine how effecting it will be performed) comes because our playwright has succeeded in extending to her audience a network of friends who are handling life's challenges remarkably well, expressing themselves with great wit and wordplay, and sustaining each other (emotionally and intellectually) in the way that all of us wish to be supported. They live and breathe within so vivid and fully realized a world that we feel we could stop by any time to see how they're doing. In the course of one compact play, Emack stirs in us the desire to know her characters personally and to care for them; an elusive achievement sought after by teams of television writers over the course of several seasons. *Writers Block* is both character- and plot-driven. Like Neil Simon and Beth Henley, with a light, sure touch, Emack has created a seamless plot, with no "ribs' showing through, and characters just naturally fleshed out. Rather than unstrand her wonderfully interwoven life stories by giving a synopsis, let me introduce the characters and just some of their many interconnections.

Writers Block consists of five (or six) central Maine writers from all walks of life, who gather to listen to each others' stories, both true and fictional, and to critique and support each others' projects. They are in the habit of meeting at the home of Helen, a frail but spunky retired school teacher, who has taken her place as the 'wise elder' of the group. She explains their procedures to Emily (a new member) thusly,

> **There's one characteristic that distinguishes us from most other writers' groups. We choose one project for special emphasis and we see it through to completion. That writer always reads first with no time limit. Then we divide up the rest of the time, depending on who else**

would liked to read on that particular evening.

In addition to maintaining their traditions, Helen keeps the group on track, gently (but persistently) corrects their grammar, reproves members who 'pop off' while bolstering the less bold, and faces her own challenges (failing health, a decaying home, the prospect of nursing care) with more pluck and aplomb than the younger members of the group. With a keen wit and Zen-like acceptance of life's volatility, she reminds her younger companions, at just the right moments, that "change is inevitable" and that "it's possible for things to go right."

Her most endearing (and closest) companion is Suzanne, a "hyper-sensitive" worry wart, who at 32 is far more hesitant and 'old womanish' than Helen. However, her self-defensive veneer (as well as her frumpy hair style and attire) barely contain the "sea of passion underneath" and her determination to find the truth, however strange and unseemly it turns out to be. Suzanne goes through the most changes and, supported by the extensive contacts and expertise of the group, solves a delicious, salacious mystery about her family and herself, opening floodgates of pent up possibility. At the beginning of the play, Suzanne is characterized by her habitual reaction (especially to change), "I don't like it. I don't like it at all." By the end, she has allowed herself to embrace those she loves, do things she "can't believe I did," and experience "surges of joy."

Big-hearted, 'potty-mouthed' Jim (a 42-year old, twice-divorced divorce attorney) uses coarse language and unbridled humor to cover a 'sea of tenderness' for his fellow writers, his business associates, but most of all, for his perfect opposite. When Helen (his former teacher) pronounces, "It's high time you left adolescence behind, Jimmy," he vows to retain the vitality and freshness (and sophomoric antics) of his 'inner adolescent.' This ornery boy, still fascinated with "bazooms," who "aches to go hang gliding in the Andes instead of report to the office," proves to be, in spirit and in action, much more gallant than his better spoken, professorial rival, Gene.

Professor Gene Cartwright has finally broken into the 'big time' with his novel, after extensive consideration by the group and meticulous (and thankless) typing and proofreading by Suzanne. Although he seems rather ungrateful and even unsatisfied (uncomfortable?) with the reality of his success, he provides a beacon of hope to his as-yet-unpublished peers, and serves primarily as a foil for Jim and Suzanne

Emily is the newcomer, and at 24, the youngest of the group. A local high school and college basketball star, who was drafted by the WNBA, her inner strength was tested to the limit–not by challenges on the court, but by the distorted downside of fame. Her beginning play concerns her horrifying, and unpublicized, experiences as the target of a serial stalker, whose carefully-planned attacks on minor female celebrities embodies one aspect of sexual violence that 'punishes' women who dare to step out of their 'protected' but subordinate positions in society. Despite Suzanne's first defensive reaction to

her admission, Emily fits perfectly into Writers Block and quickly becomes part of the fabric of their mutual friendships. She also presents an amusing counterbalance to Helen's more historical view of things. Witness the following exchange about historical research:

Jim: **Financial records make for some of the most revealing evidence on earth.**

Helen: **That's true. It's how they got Richard Nixon. Deep Throat told the two reporters to follow the money. What were their names again? Don't tell me, I've got it - Woodward and Bernstein. There, Dorothy. I can remember details. Dorothy's my daughter in California, Emily. She's convinced I'm getting senile.**

Emily: ***Deep Throat*. What does that ancient porno film have to do with anything?**

Helen: **Deep Throat was the name used by the anonymous source during the Watergate scandal.**

Emily: **Oh, that's right! Now I remember. I saw that movie, too.**

Jim: **In addition to *Deep Throat*, you mean.**

Helen: **(indignantly) It's not a movie, it's American history!**

Or this interchange, tangentially about the history of women's rights.

Suzanne: **She was an airline stewardess. Back in those days they had to quit their jobs when they got married.**

Emily: **That has got to be majorly illegal!**

Helen: **Not back then it wasn't. You young girls take so much for granted.**

The dramatis personae is rounded out with a 50-something housewife returning to school, a "dirty old man" with a long-repressed secret, a 'big-haired' news anchor, and several surprisingly dimensional off-stage characters.

Thematically, Emack has managed (in one eventful year in the lives of her characters) to stitch together many of the themes introduced elsewhere in this anthology. Into one plausible, cohesive, and thoroughly engaging plot are woven an amusingly lopsided love triangle, a sex scandal, an adult romance, family secrets, male love/sex confusions, crimes and investigations, a funeral, a first date, and stalkers and robbers and television's 'coverage' of all of these. Some of the stories seem to complete scenarios dimly remembered from recent

news: a body mysteriously washes up an island, an up-and-coming star returns home prematurely, local writer makes a national book tour. Others are based on inevitable life passages (the death of a spouse or elder, losing one's job, mid-life relationships) and universal struggles–to find one's voice, to write, to partner, and to grow up and grow old with grace and courage. Again, the fabric of the play is so strong and convincing that I caught myself thinking that Suzanne's story is more central to the play, only because her project is the current focus of Writers Block.

Because her characters and plots seemed so life-like, I assumed that Emack must have written a sort of '*drama a clef*' and that surely her characters were based (perhaps composite and, of course, fictionalized) on members of her own writing group. But, in a funny/wonderful case of life following art, only after she had drafted the play, did she gain the writers' group who would perform the reading and give feedback on her already-completed manuscript. So unlike a Method actor who closely observes and then imitates an actual person (lifting their character from life wholesale), Laura Emack seems to work like a theatre director--observing life as a whole, coming to understand, almost intuitively, how this or that person would think and behave under varying circumstances. In so doing, she has found that place where characters, once set in motion, follow their own internal urgings.

Thus, we find that *Writers Block* belies the creative quagmire implied by its title. Instead, we meet Emack's craftsman-like writers' group just at the moment when life's predictable, but nonetheless shattering, changes propel several of its members through to long-awaited breakthrough–on writing, publishing, and personal fronts. But, for those of us who have experienced the frustration and vulnerability of trying to write, especially in an unfamiliar genre, there is still company for our misery.

Peter Lee's *Inside Out* directly addresses the paradox of trying to plan creative writing, of trying to schedule the Muse's appearance. His nascent playwright, Guy has arranged the perfect setting for writing, "a porch on a cabin in Maine, looking out on a lake." The water is still and the clouds are tinted with early morning reds and yellows." And the perfect time: regularly scheduled early morning writing sessions, from 4:30-6:30, while his family sleeps companionably nearby. And indeed, his perfect set-up does produce a steady, if not very comforting, series of visitations.

Lee's play is a sort of Monodrama, in the vein of experimental Russian playwright, Evreinov's *The Theatre of the Soul*, in which personified aspects of a man's ego (his emotional, spiritual, and rational selves) argue about love and lust within a man's chest cavity. Although less visceral and both more philosophical and whimsical, *Inside Out* allows us to eavesdrop on the internal dialogue of "a middle-aged man, lawyer/writer, who discovers he's a playwright." Although "discover" ironically downplays the ensuing struggles of the lonely would-be writer, beset by angels and devils. Tantalized by the elusive hope of "leaving a lasting impression" on someone else. Cast down by doubts about every aspect of playwriting, from mechanics to metaphysics.

For example, in a randomly chosen game of catch–added to liven up the dialogue-- the word "ball" morphs (in dreamlike fashion) to take on the secondary meaning of "courage," in this case the courage to write seriously, to "break with convention."

In Lee's monodrama, the actor physically portraying the playwright never speaks; all his thoughts are divided between Voices I (his rational mind) and Voice II (a sort of "loyal, but not very interesting" chum) and the various supernatural presences who visit him. In casting the protagonist's thoughts as discreet personalities, Lee fleshes out the sort of schizophrenic condition to which playwrights are instructed to aspire: that creative place when the characters begin to converse among themselves, without conscious direction by the writer. But, once given the stage, these "visitors" confront our writer with the mind-boggling range of considerations that must be handled by a playwright who hopes to be produced. Questions about everything from how the right and left brain interact during the writing process through when to add some "action" to the dialogue to how one might handle the lake setting by projecting a video onto the back curtain.

In Act II, things really heat up when Jesus enters to warn Guy that he is "treading on thin ice (hints of hubris?) by pressing to be made a playwright in addition to having been "saved from cancer."

Jesus: Don't you get it, Pal? You're not even supposed to be here.

Voice I: (pauses, silent) I know you were there both times for my kids. I know you've been there for me.

Jesus: Okay. So you know. Now what? I've got to make you a writer?

Voice I: You know, you don't have to make me anything. It's not ungrateful of me to try and do something with my life besides being a real estate lawyer. You know what? I am more than that, with all due respect to my brethren at the bar . . . I am smarter than that; more clever. I have thought harder, deeper and longer. And you know it.

Jesus: You know, we consider you a problem case.

Through a series of such dialogues, more filled with questions than answers, Lee offers us an absurdly funny meditation on the nagging doubts, the daily grind and the ephemeral highs of being graced with those moments of "peace"--when we"make a connection in a plot, or a narrative twist occurs"-- that most writers crave. And, in the end, Lee's play ponders more than playwriting, for it speaks to all who have the courage to forge a new,

more creative path for themselves.

In a pair of dramatic scenes, Hugh Aaron sets some of these metaphysical questions about how to live properly into a realist frame. In *Turned Tables*, an average, married middle-aged man on a foreign business trip is subjected to an absurd interrogation by a tall thin interlocutor and his silent, but even more infuriating, sidekick. After repeated demands that he come up with the "right answers," the salesman finally turns the tables by swearing and striking his interrogators, upon which they announce that he has become just like them, but worse: "you resort to profanity, and the worst of the worst, physical punishment." However, Aaron's play does not strand us in an endless repetition of existential questions, but breaks the frame to allow the protagonist (and along with him, the audience) to try to make pragmatic sense of his soul-searching. Read on, to see whether our protagonist will find "the courage to look into himself and find the key to his sawdust soul."

In Aaron's second sketch, *The Liebestod*, a middle-aged executive puts the moves on his 20-something secretary, who is just breaking up with her husband. In this classic scenario, there seems to be no sense that sexual harassment in the workplace is now generally understood to be a crime, more and more often successfully prosecuted. However, in this 21st century version, our protagonist, Loretta, is not so easily taken in by Mr. Bronstein's veneer of sophistication, and holds out for her own space and time. After applauding his choice of art prints on musical subjects, Loretta does not miss his lack of genuine response to her expressed interest in the fine arts. In fact, Bronstein does not seem to hear when she says, "I dabble a little in acrylic." Instead he takes the opportunity to distinguish himself from other "insensitive" businessmen because of his self-proclaimed appreciation of art, music and fine wine. His claim, however, is immediately undercut when he exploits these symbols of good taste only to gain access to a beautiful young woman–who is thus relegated to the status of just another "high-class" consumable.

Fortunately, for us and for our damsel in distress, Aaron allows a series of phone calls to expose Bronstein's unvarnished relationships with business and personal associates, chief among them his wife. Although Loretta is in a typically vulnerable position–only recently employed, getting divorced, previously abused–we never see her lose her head. And surprisingly, a moment of missed climax to the stirring music of Wagner's *Liebestod* produces not resolution, but some important realizations for both characters.

Aaron's manipulative and womanizing executive provides the perfect foil for *Let Me Count the Ways*, Linda Britt's musical take on a First Wives' Club–a funny, pointed and ultimately liberating look at six women who fly to the aid of the seventh, and most recent, member of their group of midlife divorcees. The ascerbic jokes and witty lyrics alone are worth the price of admission.

However, you may be surprised at the range and depth of feelings and situations, perfectly matched by musical arrangements from glam rock and tango to plaintive ballads, composed by the playwright's son, Colin Britt. The

audience is taken for the sort of roller coaster ride of emotion that accompanies one of life's top ten stressers: marital breakup.

The play opens with a quick series of monologues introducing the situations under which each of our six now-seasoned divorcees parted from their husbands. In at least two cases, it was the wife who left, so we are clued in right away that this will not be a simplistic male-bashing fest, but neither will our heroine be rescued by falling (too soon) for another "better" man. Although there are several male characters who make cameo appearances, we are firmly in a women's world. Now, we open onto the central plot: Patricia drops by Karen's one morning, to find her sitting in her spotless kitchen, dressed to go out, but staring into space. When Patricia brings in the paper and offers her a cup of coffee, Karen responds, "You get up, take a shower, get dressed, clean the house, pay the phone bill, make your grocery list, put the laundry away . . . and then you notice that none of your husband's clothes are in his closet." To which Patricia responds, "Oh, Karen, I'm sorry. You've become a statistic! Look in the paper. Do you know I only take the paper for one reason any more? To read the divorce log." And she breaks into a patter song, reminiscent of a Gilbert and Sullivan or of Sondheim's mordant little ditties about dysfunctional marriages, called *Why Get Married (in the First Place)*. Not surprisingly, poor Karen (still in shock that Mike has left her, just days after their 14th wedding anniversary party) is not ready to enjoy a comical compendium of marriages that have come apart after "16 or 28 years," or newlyweds who declare their love dead before the year is out. And though, many of us will find the high seriousness of the dirge section pointedly funny, it quickly becomes apparent to Patricia that she will need to call in "reinforcements."

And soon Karen's house is filled with her closest friends, each with her own perspective on this latest domestic disaster. Like many a wake, several friends comfort Karen, while others indulge in the sort of gallows humor that survivors and first responders develop in many dire circumstances that have become almost routine. For example, the second version of a running joke: "How many ex-husbands does it take to screw in a light bulb? None. They don't get the house anyway!"

But all having experienced the trauma before, these ex-wives can also fly into action. Some go out to bring back a chocolate fix, others search for financial documents, and several look for the "farewell note"–surmising correctly, what it will say: "It's not you, Karen, it's me." And in fact, *Dear Karen* expresses Mike's need to "find my future toward the horizon," and mocks the stirring tones of popular WWI-era parlor pieces, like *Keep the Home Fires Burning*. The refrains, complete with a martial beat, are sung by all the women, ending with a repetition of his final instruction to "send the stuff he didn't pack!"

This "considerate" note--and the discovery that Karen's "soulmate" forgot to mention that he had withdrawn the $73,000 in their money market account--sets off another round of jokes and songs, this time centered on

revenge! *Temptation*, a sultry tango, details the "thoughts of sharp objects [that] dance through my head, And pistols, and shotguns and Uzis and cannons" whenever Annie thinks of ex-husband, Billy. While in the self-explanatory ditty, *Lorena Bobbitt*, Rachel (who was left, along with their children, by Phil on Christmas Eve) belts out in 80's "girl rocker" style,

**"But here's the thing about me you should know tonight:
I think Lorena Bobbitt got it right.**

Lest the former wives have the only word; we see a deliciously unconvincing scene in which Billy and Phil, two of the (more callous) ex-husbands try to gain our sympathy on their way to the golf course. In *Our Side*, they lament their lowly status with the former wives and children, in hyperbolic metaphors rendered even more wickedly ironic by the showy stylings of Broadway ballads.

**Phil: If you listened to her and only to her
You'd think I'm the scum of the earth . . .**

**Billy: The scum of the earth, the mud of her shoe
The bacterium on her tooth plaque,
The mold on her bread, already turned blue . . .**

**Duet: If you'd only listen to our side
If you'd please let us have our say
You'd realize then we have nothing to hide
And every dog deserves his day.**

And in a different vein, there is a high tenor solo by Laura's ex; they came apart when she found him in her favorite new outfit from Filene's. Much less bitterly (though no less "irreconcilably") estranged, Laura quips, "I might have handled it differently if he hadn't looked better than I did in my new suit."

In a pivotal scene, Karen has arranged to meet Mike in the park. He arrives first, and then Karen makes her entrance, "looking gorgeous." After complimenting her appearance, he sits and says," So . . . How have you been?"

Karen: (evenly) You bastard. Like you care. Disappear for three weeks and then ask how I've been?

Mike: (standing) I'm sorry, Karen.

Karen: Oh, sit down! And don't come any closer.

Mike: (sitting) . . . Look, I just want us to be civil.

Karen: Let me get this straight. You walk out on me, taking our life savings with you, I have to hire a private investigator to track you down, and you want us to be civil?

The tension escalates; all the while Karen remains "eerily calm;" she has come only to retrieve her portion of their savings, with a "little persuasion," if necessary. Perhaps she has been carried away by her friends' fantasized revenge against their exes or maybe as she says, she simply "didn't want to go alone" to face him, but the sight of the revolver produces first his excuses ("I really need the cash. I had to have a stake, to get a place to live . . .) and then, very quickly: an offer to split the cash immediately. When she cuts off further discussion, he blurts out, "What do you want from me," eliciting a heartbreak duet, *In My Perfect World*, with all the sincerity and wry edges of the best of the genre. Once communication channels are open, Karen's anger begins to flow, but fortunately, Bette "happens upon" them just in time to spirit Karen off for a ladies' day at the museum.

Before coming to as satisfying a resolution of the central story as one might hope, the women friends all gather for the surprisingly tender and nostalgic *Let Me Count the Ways*. Even the playwright was surprised when the lyrics that arose under this rubric ended up "counting the ways" they used to love, rather than the ways they would like to 'disappear," their ex-husbands.

The Britts have created a very do-able musical featuring mature women's voices. If you love musicals with lots of female roles, but are infuriated by the portrayal of women in musicals like *Nine* or *Company*--in which womanizing cads are surrounded by gorgeous women, all cat-fighting among themselves for a chance to be suckered by the male idol–then, Linda Britt has the cure!

If Britt's musical comedy carries too much content to be deemed "purely entertaining," then perhaps the taste for wacky escapist humor will be satisfied by Caitlin Harrison's parody of "slasher" (or shall we say "basher") flicks.

In *Strange Love Triangle at the Children's Theatre*, the words "strange" and "triangle" humorously understate the frenetically twisting interrelationships of the five young actors and technicians. From the opening bow (to which the implied on-stage audience gives a meager response at best), it is clear that most of the "drama" in this second-rate, backwater theatre occurs off-stage.

It seems that the technical director and his unwillingly estranged wife (the leading actress) are in the midst of a trial separation. However, neither has wasted any time in finding new objects for their desires. And, of course, as we might suspect – given the long hours required to eke out a living at a bottom-rung theatre – both have chosen their new romantic partners from within the company.

For Harrison, however, this realistic premise serves only as a throughline on which to hang a series of campy send-ups, leaving virtually no form of popular entertainment unscathed. *Love Triangle* references *Blithe Spirit* (remember the car tampering?), farcical who-dunnits, Bette Davis crime flicks, chainsaw murders, and all those over-the-top macabre Halloween specials (complete with dismembered limbs). And with only five actors, much of the humor resides in the endless permutations of the characters: preening actors versus taciturn techies, vengeful wife against the (seemingly) clueless new girlfriend, the nice guy who (usually) finishes last, vegan serial killers, and android law enforcers. Harrison stops just short of bringing on the Crime Scene Investigator – but that could very well be appended as a sequel! If performed at breakneck speed, this zany romp will leave the audience, along with the poor unwitting accomplice, wondering at the end of the play whether "it's safe to get up now."

I must end this preface with a wish and a warning: that you will read and enjoy the plays anthologized here; and the warning: that having read them, you "may not be safe" from an infectious desire to read them aloud, act out a scene, stage a production, or in other words, to put them 'into play.'

STANDING JUST OUTSIDE THE DOOR

By Sanford Phippen

Reprinted from *Standing Just Outside the Door and Two other Plays*
With the permission of Blackberry Press

SCENES

INTRODUCTION: **Today**

SCENE ONE: **An English Teacher's Classroom**
Old Whiteside, N.Y., 1966

SCENE TWO: **A School Psychologist's Office**
Old Whiteside, N.Y., 1966

SCENE THREE: **Same As Scene One**

SCENE FOUR: **Same As Scene Two**

SCENE FIVE: **Literary Magazine Meeting**
English Teacher's Classroom
Old Whiteside, N.Y., 1966

SCENE SIX: **Soliloquies And Colloquies**
Marsh Island, Maine, 2002

SCENE SEVEN: **Library**
Mount Desert Island, Maine, 2002

CHARACTERS

ANDREW HARRISON, A veteran English teacher who also advises the school literary magazine. In the first scenes he is in his 20s; in the last scenes in his 50s. He's also an author. He's tall and wears glasses.

PAUL DEAN, In the first scenes, he is a handsome and athletic young man of 17 who wears glasses. He wears blue jeans and neat shirts. Of upstanding character and dignity. Mature for his age.

LUISE WERNER, A middle-aged woman who wears women's suits. Her hair pulled back or done up, she wears glasses, is very serious and conservative in both her dress and manner. She talks with a German accent.

BILL KINNEY, A baby-faced, curly-headed boy of 17, who is not effeminate, but he is given to "fluttering about," waving his hands and arms, quite high-strung and very bright and quick with a sarcastic sense of humor. In the last scene he's gray-haired and in his early 50s, an attractive college professor, neatly and stylishly attired.

BOB DAY, A wild-haired, very bright, and electric boy of 18, given to wearing headbands and jewelry, carrying around hand-puppets that he talks with. Proud of being openly gay, he loves being in politics and the theater. Very dramatic, he's always putting on shows. He wears tight bell-bottom jeans with wild shirts and belts. He loves disco.

DOREEN MCINTIRE, A heavy-set earthy girl with a wild sense of humor, mannish, usually wearing a winter coat. Bright, but not particularly studious. Interested in creative writing, she has her own agenda.

TUCKER SHERMAN, A handsome Maine boy with strong Maine roots. Likes to go fishing and hunting. Wears jeans, hunting jackets, and boots. Of average height, decent and sensitive.

FLETCHER COOMBS, Sporting blue and spiked hair, he's a sensitive-looking boy of 17 who wears jeans and colorful tee-shirts and sports a wiseguy attitude. Of average height, and bright, but because of his gayness, and a difficult home life, he's not a very good student, always getting into trouble.

ANITA PLOURDE, A librarian who wears glasses, prim and proper, intelligent, all business. Well-dressed and neat.

LAURA FENNELLY, An athletic, somewhat mannish young woman of 22. A former basketball star, she's attractive in pants and blouses. Of sharp intelligence and quick wit.

LINDA COVERLY, Doreen's classmate and friend. Very feminine, warm and friendly. Wears dresses.

TONY, Bill Kinney's close friend. In his late 40s [similar looking to Paul Dean, as an older version, may be played by the actor who plays Dean earlier.]

INTRODUCTION

ANDREW HARRISON: In the nearly four decades that I have been a public school teacher, I have been privy to many scenes such as the ones about to follow. My career began in the 1960s amidst race riots and anti-Vietnam War demonstrations. In an age of revolution, I have witnessed not only the liberation of Black people, Native Americans, Chicano migrant workers, and women; but also homosexuals – and right in my classroom! However, as a young English teacher of 24 in my second year of teaching at a suburban school in upstate New York, I was not prepared for the "coming out" of one of my students …

SCENE ONE

A typical teacher's classroom with his desk piled high with books, papers, etc. On the wall behind the teacher's desk is a blackboard and to the right a door to the classroom. There are a few student desks in front. Probably, there should be an American flag off to the side. MR. HARRISON, the teacher, is at his desk, trying to correct papers early in the morning before school, when a knock comes at the door.

HARRISON: Yes? Come in!

[*DOREEN MCINTIRE enters. She is a heavyset girl, very bright, and witty. Loves literature. Unusual for the time, she wears slacks and blouses, affects a rather mannish persona. Her hair is cut short*]

DOREEN: Oh, I'm so sorry to disturb you, Mr. Harrison; but I'm all alone in the cafeteria and I need to know about the homework for English.

HARRISON: Good morning, Doreen! Now, there's a first – you never do homework for me!

DOREEN. Oh, I just love the way you say that! It must mean you really care about me!

HARRISON: Oh, Doreen, of course, I care about you. But right now, I've got to get these papers done before period one.

DOREEN: What were ya – out all night? Couldn't get <u>your</u> homework done?

HARRISON: Yeah, right ... go now back to the cafeteria and write me that essay on Edna St. Vincent Millay.

DOREEN: Tell me, Mr. Harrison, was Millay a little on the funny side? Did she like girls as well as men?

HARRISON: Millay? I don't know. Why don't you get some biographies and read about her? Really dig up the dirt on the Pulitzer Prize winner!

DOREEN: She liked to be called Vincent. That sounds kind of dikey to me ...

HARRISON: She was a great artist, avant-garde, ahead of her time, a fighter for women's rights, an icon ... she probably tried everything, but she was also our greatest lyric poet. Don't label her.

***DOREEN [walking around looking at the picture of American and British writers over MR. HARRISON's desk]:* Now, Walt Whitman, he was on the funny side too, wasn't he? And Tennessee Williams? James Baldwin? Didn't you tell us they were homosexuals?**

HARRISON: I may have, but I also told you not to label. We're all many people; we're mixtures of things ... do you know Carson McCullers? Have you ever heard of a book called *A Member Of The Wedding*?

DOREEN: Nope.

HARRISON: I think there are some copies of it over there on the back shelf if you'd like to look ... *[But they are interrupted by a knock on the door. It's DOREEN's friend and classmate LINDA COVERLY, who enters.]*

LINDA: Doreen! I've been looking all over for you. Where have you been?

DOREEN: I came up to talk to Mr. Harrison about um ... uh ... the homework. That's it – I came to ask about the homework.

LINDA: Oh, O.K ... Well, I thought we were gonna work on some stuff for the literary magazine. Do you still want to work on it?

DOREEN: Oh, that's right. We have ten minutes till homeroom. Do you want to do it now?

LINDA: Yeah, sure. I have the stuff in my knapsack in the cafeteria.

DOREEN: O.K., let's go.

[PAUL DEAN knocks at the door and steps in.]

PAUL DEAN: Hey, Linda ...

LINDA: Well, the captain of the football team ... Hi, Paul.

PAUL: How's it going?

LINDA: I'm go ...

DOREEN: Hi, Paul.

PAUL: I was wondering what you were doing at lunch today. I thought it would be cool if ...

DOREEN: We're busy ... Mr. Harrison, see you in class ...

[DOREEN and LINDA exit.]

HARRISON: O.K., now, Paul, what can I do for you?

PAUL *[who has a handful of letters with him]*: Uh, good morning, Mr. Harrison ...

HARRISON: Good morning. What brings you to school so early?

PAUL *[nervously]*: I get up early, and I'm usually downstairs studying in the cafeteria, but I needed to see you this morning about something that's been happening this fall. After school, I go to football practice as you know, and it's hard to see you alone during school.

HARRISON: Oh, I know. It's a madhouse once first period begins. But I've meant to tell you how great you were in last Saturday's game. It's easy to see why the boys elected you captain, even though you're only a junior.

DEAN: I'm glad you enjoyed it, and yeah, I'm really happy that our team is doing so well ... but I have this problem that I wanted to ask you about.

HARRISON: It can't be English class, since you're getting an A ... one of my best students – my scholar-athlete! So, what is it? What could possibly be troubling you?

DEAN: It's personal. I wish you'd look at these letters. I've been getting them almost every day since school started. He's been putting them in my locker; and, thank God, it's my regular hall locker and not the gym locker ... *[PAUL hands the letters to HARRISON.]*

HARRISON: Who is it? *[as HARRISON begins to open one of them] [HARRISON scans the letters as DEAN talks.]*

DEAN: Bill Kinney, who's also in our English class. He has this crush on me, and it's getting worse. I just brought a sample of the many he's written me. He's a very bright and talented writer, of course; but I don't feel the same about him, and these letters are so gushy and crazy and embarrassing that I cringe when I see the latest one in my locker ... I'm afraid he's telling other people and it will get around. I like him as a person; but I don't know what to do about this ... and I thought you might have a suggestion about what to do since you know both of us ...

HARRISON: I'm not sure if I do, Paul ... this is a first for me in my teaching career ... have you tried talking with Bill?

DEAN: No, and he doesn't say much to me. Everything in school during the day seems normal. We talk and joke with each other, as we always have ...

HARRISON *[reading one of the letters]:* He is funny! And flattering ... it's obvious that he thinks a lot of you, comes to all your games ...

DEAN: Oh, yes, he is funny and he does make me laugh ... I do love that about him; of course, it's flattering, except when he's talking about how I look in my jeans and football pants and his wanting to be a football in my hands ...

HARRISON: Footballs are for kicking, too ... he also berates you for wearing the wrong sweater ...

DEAN: Oh, yes, he has definite ideas about what I should be wearing and how my hair should be. He's like my secret fashion consultant ...

HARRISON: Somehow, I think you two need to get together and talk; but I'm not sure if I should be the mediator. ... How about one of the guidance counselors?

DEAN: No, I don't think so ... we have the same counselor; and she's too cold a person. Neither of us would feel comfortable with her. It would be better with you.

HARRISON: How about the school psychologist? Do you know her?

DEAN: No, I didn't even know we had one.

HARRISON: Yes, we do. Do you mind if I go to her about this and see what she thinks? Then I'll get back to you as soon as possible?

DEAN: O.K., do you want to show her the letters?

HARRISON: Yes, if that's O.K. with you. But as soon as we can, I think we need to meet, or at least you and Bill need to meet ...

DEAN: I just want him to stop the letters. I still want to be friends with him. We've known each other since junior high. He's a bright, creative person who should probably become a writer. He's on the literary magazine that you advise, isn't he?

HARRISON: Oh, yes, he is; and he is everything you say. But this is a delicate situation. I don't want him to get hurt; but I also sympathize with you. I promise you I'll do what I can today. I'll try and get an appointment with Dr. Werner right away ...

DEAN: Thanks, Mr. Harrison. I'm sorry to bother you with this ... *[He gets up to leave.]* I'll see you in English class.

HARRISON: Today we're doing *Macbeth*, you know; and I want you to play the king ...

DEAN: As long as you don't get Bill to play the queen!

HARRISON: With his sense of drama, he'd probably be great! ...incidentally, Paul ...

DEAN: Yes?

HARRISON: You're handling this matter very well, very maturely. This could have been very ugly with another guy ...

DEAN: Don't think that some days I don't want to punch him out and scream at him!

HARRISON: I know, but don't ...

DEAN: No, I won't. Thanks, Mr. Harrison...

HARRISON: You're welcome ...

SCENE TWO

A small dark narrow office with one window. DR. LUISE WERNER is at her desk reading a movie magazine. MR. HARRISON knocks at her door. MRS. WERNER speaks with a German accent.

WERNER: Come in, please.

HARRISON: Hello, Dr. Werner ...

WERNER: *[she gets up to greet him and shakes hands]:* Hello, Mr. Harrison. You're early.

HARRISON: I guess I am a little. Thank you for your immediate attention to this matter.

WERNER: *[removing the packet of letters from her desk drawer]:* Vell, of course. Now, before ve discuss this case, I vanted to tell you how nice it is to get to meet you. You are one of the new young teachers vith whom I've never spoken. I know that you're from Maine ...

HARRISON: Yes, I am.

WERNER: Now, I believe from your note you told me that you had spoken vith Paul Dean but not vith Villiam Kinney.

HARRISON: That's right. I feel guilty about not talking with William before coming to you. I tried to encourage Paul to approach William about this, but he didn't want to.

WERNER: He impresses me as a very mature young man, very thoughtful and kind ...

HARRISON: Have you spoken to him already?

WERNER: Yes. I vent over a few of ze letters vith him. I may vant to see him again later, maybe test him.

HARRISON: Test him? Why him?

WERNER: Vell, in zese cases of young homosexuals just beginning to realize zeir nature, it is often true that one claiming to be the object of attention may himself harbor homosexual feelings.

HARRISON: All Paul wants is for Bill to stop writing him letters. Have you seen Bill, too?

WERNER: No, but I vant to see him tomorrow during your English class, if zat's all right. You could send him to me vith a note, O.K.?

HARRISON: Yes, I guess so; but I feel as if I should say something to him beforehand ...

WERNER: I don't sink zat vill be necessary. I just vant to meet him and talk vith him a little. I'll have to test him, of course, to see if he should be referred to a psychiatrist ...

HARRISON: Well, let me tell you, he can be very emotional and flighty. He has outbursts in class sometimes. He's quite dramatic ... but he's a good kid with a lot of talent. He has a wonderful sense of humor.

WERNER: Does he? Vell, I can tell from these letters that he has a flair for the dramatic and romantic. He may also suffer from an anal fixation ... the vay he describes Paul ...

HARRISON: Well, I hope he can be helped ...

WERNER: Mr. Harrison, homosexuality is a very serious condition ... it's still illegal in many places, you know.

HARRISON: Yes, I know; well I hope you'll do everything you can to help him.

WERNER: You like him, don't you?

HARRISON: Yes, I like both the boys very much.

WERNER: Yes, I can see zat ... zey are both lucky to have you as a teacher ...

SCENE THREE

The psychologist's office, same as Scene Two. DR. WERNER is at her desk when BILL KINNEY knocks at the door.

WERNER: Come in, please.

[BILL KINNEY comes in holding a pass, which he hands to DR. WERNER.]

KINNEY: I'm William Kinney, and Mr. Harrison gave me a pass to come and see you.

WERNER: Yes, I've been expecting you, Villiam. Please have a seat. Mr. Harrison has been concerned about you and he came to see me the other day. Ve had a good talk; and now I hope zat you and I may do the same.

KINNEY: I'm afraid I don't know what you're talking about. I just went to English class as usual, and Mr. Harrison made out this pass and told me that you wanted to see me. I didn't even know we had a school psychologist.

WERNER *[chuckling]:* Vell, I'm afraid ve have not been very good vith our publicity. Only the most serious cases get referred to me.

KINNEY: So, I'm a serious case?

WERNER: I'm afraid you might be, Villiam. *[She takes the packet of letters out of her desk drawer and hands one of them to him.]* Do you recognize zis letter?

KINNEY: Yes, where did you get it?

WERNER: Mr. Harrison gave me several of these vich had been given to him by your classmate Paul Dean.

KINNEY: Oh no! These were only for Paul, not for anyone else!

[KINNEY becomes very agitated and upset at this point.]

KINNEY: So, you probably think I'm perverted and weird, don't you? A real degenerate nut case?

WERNER: No, I think you are really in love vith Paul. It's rather normal for young boys to fall in love with other fellows ... you obviously admire him very much ... and I'm not sure vat can be done about your homosexuality. There are those who believe this to be an emotional condition that one eventually grows out of, and others who think it goes much deeper. Vat I can do for you, if you are

villing, is to explore. There are a number of tests you can take ... you can have a veekly appointment vith me ...

KINNEY: I don't need to take any tests or have appointments. I do think a lot of Paul, but that's nobody else's business.

WERNER: Vell, it becomes other people's business when Paul is asking others for help ... he vent to Mr. Harrison to see if he's talk vith you about these letters, vich upset Paul ...

KINNEY: Why didn't Paul tell me he didn't like the letters?

WERNER: Perhaps he was scared to?

KINNEY: Paul scared?? I can't imagine Paul too scared to talk to me.

WERNER: Villiam, do you vant me to analyze your letters for you? To tell you vat I see in them?

KINNEY: What? Do you tell fortunes? Read tea leaves?

WERNER: No, I'm here as a trained psychologist to help you. Homosexuality is listed as a serious mental illness, you know?

KINNEY: I'm not mentally ill, but I think you and Mr. Harrison might be! I'm not a homosexual! And I'd like my letters back!

WERNER: I'm sorry, Villiam, the letters are not yours. They belong to Paul. How about if I set up a meeting between you and Paul?

KINNEY: What for?

WERNER: So ve can resolve this situation to the best of our abilities ...

KINNEY: I would prefer to talk to Paul by myself.

WERNER: All right; but if Paul comes to me about this, ve may have to get together, O.K.?

KINNEY: Maybe.

WERNER: Let me have the letter back. *[He gives it to her.]* Vould you like a pass back to class now?

KINNEY: I need a pass, but not back to Harrison's class. Paul's in there. Just give me a library pass, please. I'll see Mr. Harrison, and maybe Paul after school.

WERNER: All right. I think you should at least apologize to him; and please realize, Villiam, zat I am here to help you. You can talk to me about anything and it vill stay right here. Now, I also have some booklets for you zat may prove helpful.

[She hands him the booklets, and he reluctantly accepts them.]

WERNER: I hope you vill consider seeing me again soon. *[She writes him a pass and gives it to him.]*

KINNEY *[trying to contain his anger and taking the pass]*: Maybe. *[He walks to the door.]*

WERNER: I vish you vell, Villiam ...

[KINNEY walks out. He doesn't respond to her.]

SCENE FOUR

HARRISON's classroom, the same, except it's after school with MR. HARRISON picking up, trying to find stuff he will need to take home with him, when DOREEN MCINTIRE enters [wearing her coat and hat]. Since the door is ajar, DOREEN sticks her head in before entering.

DOREEN *[knocking]:* Oh, I'm so glad you're still here!

HARRISON: Yes, Doreen, I'm still here ... I live here!

DOREEN *[waving a paper]:* I wanted to show you the beginning of my paper on Vincent Millay! I'm finding out all kinds of juicy stuff on this wild Maine woman!

HARRISON: I'll be glad to check out the beginning, Doreen. Let me see ...

[She hands him the paper, and as he's reading it, she talks.]

DOREEN: I see what you mean about her lyrics ... I just love her! *Renascence* is a wonderful poem ... I wish I could memorize it and recite it dramatically in front of the whole school ...

HARRISON: Why don't you?

DOREEN: Oh, Mr. Harrison, everyone would laugh at me – look at me! I'm hardly romantic looking!

HARRISON: Well, it would help if you'd take that off coat and hat ...

[LINDA walks in on MR. HARRISON and DOREEN]

LINDA: Hey, um ... I thought we were having the meeting for the literary magazine now ...

DOREEN: Oh! Um, uh, urr ... I was just showing Mr. Harrison the beginning of my paper...

LINDA: Oh, all right ...

HARRISON: I'm sorry, but I don't have time for the meeting today. It will have to be tomorrow ...

[Suddenly, they are all interrupted by BILL KINNEY, who, without knocking, flies into the room in a wild fury.]

KINNEY *[screaming]:* Get out of here, Doreen and Linda!

[KINNEY stands there wild-eyed while DOREEN, scared, takes her paper from MR. HARRISON and starts out the door with LINDA.]

DOREEN: Wow, Bill, for God's sake! What's the matter with you? You've really lost it this time!

[DOREEN and LINDA exit. KINNEY slams the door behind them, and turns to face HARRISON.]

KINNEY *[screaming and tears streaming down his face]:* How could you? How could you?! *[He knocks stuff off HARRISON's desk, rips things off the wall, throws chairs around, etc.]* Who gave you the right to interfere in my life? What business is it of yours? How could you do this to me????

[HARRISON grabs KINNEY and sits him down.]

HARRISON: Stop it! Stop it! Give me a chance to explain myself before you wreck the room and have the janitors in here!

[KINNEY does sit, but he's sobbing and heaving, very upset.]

HARRISON: I take it you've just come from Mrs. Werner's?

KINNEY: Yes!

HARRISON: So tell me what happened?

KINNEY: I don't know if I should tell you anything ever again ... You went behind my back ...

HARRISON: I'm sorry, I truly am. I should have spoken to you right after Paul came to see me with your letters ... I'm sorry!

KINNEY: You gave that bitch my letters?! She had them and she analyzed them in her Nazi spy fashion. *[Imitating MRS. WERNER]* Vat's your problem? She called me a homosexual!

HARRISON: What did she say you should do?

KINNEY: Stop writing Paul letters and come and see her on a regular basis and she'll test me to see how queer I am, or what kind of queer I am, or to what degree queer I am! Jesus, Mr. Harrison! You're my favorite teacher and you do this to me! Turn me in to the Queer Police!

HARRISON: I think you should try and see Paul and the two of you talk this over.

KINNEY: How could I approach him after this? I may have to change out of your English class ... change schools maybe ... leave town!

HARRISON: Don't be crazy! How about simply apologizing to him?

KINNEY: That's what Dr. Nazi said. She said I should apologize to him and stop sending him letters. She gave me booklets to read and a list of books to read ... all about coming to terms with one's homoness!

HARRISON: That all sounds all right to me. Paul doesn't want you to send him the letters anymore, but he still wants to be friends with you. I think he's been quite a gentleman about this matter. Other guys in his position would have pushed your face in or worse ...

KINNEY *[looking directly at HARRISON]:* Why didn't you talk to me first before going to her?

HARRISON: I said I'm sorry. Will you accept my apology? I had never dealt with a situation like this before, and I didn't want to hurt you ... I also want to help you if I can ...

KINNEY: I don't want your help! I don't need your help! You were my favorite teacher, but now I'll never trust you again!

HARRISON: What did you think would happen writing letters like that every day to Paul? Did you think he'd ultimately come around and be your fantasy pal? Didn't you expect him to react somehow, sometime?

KINNEY: I don't know.

HARRISON: Will you speak to him soon on your own?

KINNEY: I don't know, I don't know ...

HARRISON: You didn't ask, but we started doing *Macbeth* in class while you were with Mrs. Werner.

KINNEY: So, I should take my book home and read the first part?

HARRISON: Yes, I think that would be advisable ... I'd like you to play a part in our class reading ...

KINNEY: Doesn't someone get stabbed to death in the play?

HARRISON: Yes ...

KINNEY: Good! I feel like stabbing someone!

HARRISON: I hope not for real ... why don't you keep a journal, Bill? For yourself as well as for me and write out all your feelings about all of this?

KINNEY: So you can show my journal to Mrs. Werner? And you two can have fun examining how queer I am?

HARRISON: You are a very creative and clever person; you should be writing, I think, all the time ... I'll give you extra credit in class.

[KINNEY gets out and walks around dramatically gesticulating.]

KINNEY: Instead of a journal, I think I'll make a big map of the world of this high school. There will be countries like Wernertania which will be big and Militant and war-mongering; and then there will be small countries like Harrisonistan, insignificant and of limited importance on the world scene ... I'll bring you a copy!

[KINNEY goes to leave...]

HARRISON: Are you leaving now, Bill?

KINNEY: Leaving all right... we're finished, Mr. Harrison ...

HARRISON: Are you going to drop my class?

KINNEY: I don't know yet ... I just know now I'm going home.

HARRISON: Would you like me to drive you? Will you be O.K.?

KINNEY : I'll be able to make it home all right, despite the forces of Werner and Harrison always there to meddle and protect me from myself ... it's only five blocks ...

HARRISON: I hope you'll stay in my class ...

KINNEY : Don't hold your breath!

[KINNEY bolts from the room.]

SCENE FIVE

It's a few weeks later in MR.HARRISON's classroom after school. DOREEN and her friend and classmate LINDA COVERLY are getting set up for the weekly literary magazine session before the other members and MR. HARRISON arrive.

[DOREEN and LINDA enter an empty classroom.]

LINDA: I don't think Mr. Harrison is here.

DOREEN: Let's go ...

LINDA: Well, let's just see what's here anyway. Well, these look like the poems he wanted us to go through, but ... uggh, it doesn't look like much of a selection. I mean, how can he expect us to do anything with this?

DOREEN: I don't know.

LINDA: For once, I wish he'd be on time; he could at least tell us what he wants.

DOREEN: Um, well, how about this one? Uh, I liked it a lot and I wanted to know what you think.

LINDA: Wow, this is really good! This is exactly what we're looking for. Where did you get this?

DOREEN: I found it in a book by the library.

LINDA: Oh, well, we should publish this, but we need to know who wrote it.

DOREEN: It was anonymous.

LINDA: This is really good!

DOREEN: Really? You like it? Well, what do you like more? This? Or this down here?

LINDA: I like them both so much. I mean, the whole thing is just so passionate! And look at how descriptive it is. The way this guy is describing this girl. It's just so romantic ... I wish someone would write something like this for me...

[MR. HARRISON hurries in ...]

HARRISON: Hello, girls, sorry to be a little late … I see you've found some of the stuff for today … any more submissions? There's more, too, in this manila folder …

[HARRISON opens the folder and starts flickering through it.]

HARRISON: Here, for instance, is another anti-war poem …

DOREEN AND LINDA: Groan …

HARRISON: Actually, it's not bad – and here's a new story by Bill Kinney!

DOREEN: No! Let me see it! *[She grabs the paper.]*

HARRISON: It's angry and funny …

LINDA: Surprise! Surprise!

[At this point, PAUL DEAN enters the room.]

DOREEN: Paul what are you doing at a literary magazine gathering?

DEAN: I've got a couple of poems, Doreen, for your expert scrutiny; but I can't stay for the meeting. I've got football practice.

[He hands the poems to her.]

DOREEN: Oh, Paul, what a thrill. Poems from you – our star jock! Our poetic quarterback! Or are you a fullback?

DEAN: Quarterback, and I'm not just a jock, Doreen.

DOREEN: I know …

[Then, BILL KINNEY appears, wild-eyed in the doorway, clutching his drawing of the world.

LINDA: Bill! You've returned to the literary scene!

HARRISON: Bill, I'm glad to see you here …

KINNEY: I'm sure you are, Mr. Harrison!

DEAN: Hello, Bill …

[BILL just looks at PAUL without speaking and then looks away.]

DEAN: Well, gotta go to practice …

LINDA: Bye, Paul. We'll let you know tomorrow what everyone thinks of your poems.

DEAN: Great.

KINNEY: Poems? *[and PAUL leaves]* What the hell is this?

HARRISON: So, Bill, what have you got with you – another darkly comic tale?

KINNEY *[handing HARRISON the map of the world]:* No, it's my map I told you about.

HARRISON: You want us to try and reproduce this?

KINNEY: Yes, if possible, if it's acceptable ... You might not like it. Some, you especially, may find it offensive ...

DOREEN *[reading the map]:* "McIntire – a small island, thinly populated! Deanland, a rugged and cold, inhospitable place! Old Whiteside, the lost continent ... Oh, Bill, you are funny – even if you think I'm thinly populated!

KINNEY: It's because you are, Doreen ...

DOREEN: Aren't you sweet!

HARRISON: Bill... *[trying to get BILL to leave the room with him so they can talk privately]*

KINNEY: What, Mr. Harrison?

HARRISON: How about we go across the hall for a talk?

KINNEY: What? We can't talk about it now here? It's not as if they aren't going to find out about it!

HARRISON *[coming from around his desk towards BILL]:* I don't think you'll be comfortable ...

KINNEY: How do I know I can trust you?

HARRISON: Let's go in the other room and talk alone ... I don't think you'll be comfortable in front of your friends ... let's go ...

[He leads him out off the room.]

KINNEY: Friends?! ... O.K ....

[The girls are alone.]

LINDA: What was that all about? I mean, he just came in here and started losing it. What do you think is going on with him? What were they talking about? That was so weird ...

DOREEN: I don't know. That's just Bill. He freaks out about five times a day ...

LINDA: Well, anyway, I wonder.

DOREEN: So, what did you really think of that poem?

LINDA: It was so good! I really loved it. We definitely have to publish it, if only we know who wrote it ...

DOREEN: I wrote it ...

LINDA: Really? Wow, this is so good! I had no clue you could write like this ...

DOREEN: For you.

LINDA: What?

DOREEN: I wrote it... for you.

LINDA: Really?

DOREEN: Yep.

LINDA: Really?

SCENE SIX

SOLILOQUIES AND COLLOQUIES

HARRISON: That happened over thirty years ago, and I'm still haunted by it. A day doesn't go by that I don't think about that young man. The consequences of what I did could have damaged him for life, but we were all filled with fear and ignorance then. I was torn between what I know in my heart I should do and say, and doing and saying what the school and society sanctioned me to do. Because of what happened, it changed me as a teacher and a person. I was determined not to let this happen again.

In 1969, the Stonewall Riot occurred in Greenwich Village that gave the modern Gay Liberation movement its name and energy. Over the next thirty years the culture changed; and the attitudes of my students and myself along with it. In 1975, in Syracuse, New York, I had a student named Bob Day, who came out of the closet with a vengeance ...

[BOB DAY appears, attired in a colorful headband, bright shirt, with tight bell-bottom jeans, jewelry, etc. – the outfit of the 1970s. He has a hand puppet with him. He talks half the time as if imitating an American Black "cool dude" type.]

BOB DAY: Hey, there, Mr. Har'son! Thought you might be hidin' in your classroom when you should have been down at the big assembly listening to me take this education factory by storm! You missed my triumph, dude! Well, I came out to them big time! And most of the Blacks liked me. The Hispanics loved me. The cool whites seemed appreciative, too ... so much so that you are looking at the first openly gay student body president! The press has been calling me, man! With my little puppet pal here, Cool Breeze, he and I had a conversation about the prejudice and putting people down and so on ... we talked about who's most despised in this school and culture, and how it ain't Blacks, it ain't women, it ain't even Indians, it's GAY PEOPLE! I also, of course, mentioned my record as a natural student leader who's been involved; and how I'm extra sensitive to all their needs because I'm a goddamn queer! I've had to fight 'em all! Right Cool Breeze?

BOB DAY AS COOL BREEZE: Right on, man! I wish you could have been there, Mr. Harrison. It was great. I didn't even hear any boos ... there was great applause at the end of my speech; and you know, the Black kid, Candy, the football player star? He came out and hugged me right in front of everyone and said, "Bob Day, you might be gay, but you O.K.!" And that became something of a chant!

BOB DAY AS COOL BREEZE: Bob Day, You are Gay, but you sometimes O.K.! The principal was there, and even shook my hand! But I'm pissed that you

weren't there! One of my prime supporters! What were you too scared for me, or something? We're beyond Stonewall now, ya know ... Gay Liberation has reached the outskirts of Syracuse in the middle of New York State farm country! I'll be marching in the homecoming parade ... and I'll be sporting the greatest outfit yet ... Gotta go! My public awaits me! Time's are a-changing, Mr. Harrison. I may become New York's first gay governor!

HARRISON: And then there was the time, one night after school, when one of my former students Laura Fennelley came to see me.

LAURA *[knocking on MR. HARRISON's classroom door]:* Guess who? Hi, Mr. Harrison. I thought since I'm now a senior in college about to leave my native state that I'd drop by to see you ... I want you to know that when I was fifteen, I wasn't ready for the likes of you. You and your classes seemed crazy to me, not like those of an ordinary teacher. The things you'd say! You scared me. But now that I'm 22, have had a few experiences, grown up a bit more, and have realized some things about myself, I don't see you as I did before; and I want to thank you for making me think, not just about literature and writing, but about who we really are and what life's all about ... Say, did you know I was a lesbian when I was in your classes?

HARRISON: No, not really. That didn't show up on too many vocab. quizzes ...

LAURA: Well, I am; and I'm proud of who I am. I like myself a lot better now that I did in high school. And I've been offered a job next semester in Texas. I'm in engineering, you know. I'm a top notch female engineer. Companies are begging for my talent from coast to coast ... I'm hoping my girlfriend will go with me ...

HARRISON: Good luck to you, Laura!

HARRISON: If I've had 8,000 students in my teaching career, then maybe 800 or more of them were gay ... of course, most of them never told me about themselves; but the ones who did I remember vividly ... for instance, there was a handsome outdoors boy named Tucker Sherman ...

TUCKER *[knocking at MR. HARRISON's door]:* Mr. Harrison, I need to talk to you about something that's been going on ... You know my good friend Vinnie O'Toole? He brought you some deer meat last hunting season? Well, this year we went hunting again, as usual, just like always ... and Vinnie got another deer. He always does. He's a great hunter. We grew up together, ya know? And we both love the outdoors. We've been in Boy Scouts together, went fishing and hunting all the time ... but last week, when we were coming back from his father's hunting camp ... we were in his pick-up truck with all our gear, music playing, joking with each other the way we've always done, when all of a sudden he grabs my leg and tells me how much he loves me and he wants us to live together when we get out of high school ... Well, I think the world of him. We're

best friends ... but I don't think I want to be lovers with him ... but, at the same time, I wouldn't mind living with him ... it's a good deal, you see. He's going to have this really nice apartment all furnished ... what would you do?

HARRISON: And then, just recently, there was this scene, not before or after school, but just as school had begun.

[Suddenly, the door to MR. HARRISON's classroom bangs open, and without knocking, in comes FLETCHER COOMBS, with his spiked blue hair and earrings, but looking beat-up and disheveled ...]

HARRISON: Fletcher! What happened to you?

FLETCHER: I was gaybashed on the school bus! It's not safe coming to school on the bus anymore!

HARRISON: Who did this to you?

FLETCHER: One of your favorite students – the basketball champ! He kept calling me a fag and a queer just as I got on the bus, first thing in the morning!

HARRISON: What did you do? Didn't you fight back?

FLETCHER: Of course, but he's a lot bigger than I am! And his friends, if you could call them friends, just laughed!

HARRISON: Well, you need to go to the nurse first, and then you should go to the office and report this.

FLETCHER: O.K., I will. He's not getting away with this hate crime! Can I be late to class?

HARRISON: Yes ... of course!

[FLETCHER leaves.]

HARRISON [alone at his desk and to the audience]: How come with every student who comes to me like this I see Billy?

HARRISON: Leaving New York and coming back home to Maine to teach, I also began a writing career, which often led to scenes like the following:

SCENE SEVEN

The Acadia Library on Mount Desert Island where MR. HARRISON, the author, is giving a reading and book signing.

HARRISON: I would like to conclude with a quotation from Kenneth Eble who wrote this wonderful book *A Perfect Education*, in which he wrote: "To learn is to love. Any sound education must grow from this principle … education is personal. At its best, it is intensely personal … we make a joke of pupils falling in love with teachers. It is no joke – it is the way of learning. That is the advantage of live teachers and live books. They can be fallen in love with, possessed … teachers and books, then, and someone to love them, to use them, to cherish them. These come first …"

LIBRARIAN: Thank you so much Mr. Harrison, for that lovely reading and talk. I'm sure anyone who ever went to school or taught school will be interested in your new book. Now, if anyone here would like to purchase a signed copy, please step over here to the table where the books are. Now, don't forget, also, next month in our series we will be having another wonderful writer, Bettina Jane Quigley, whose 30th book *Forever Astonished* has just been published to rave reviews. She was the best-selling author, you must remember, of such books as *Heavens, Mr. Evans!*, and *Downeast Utopia* … Thank you all for coming!

***[MR. HARRISON and the LIBRARIAN shake hands and MR. HARRISON walks over to the chair for him at the table. The audience lines up to speak to him and purchase his book. First in line is the older – and now gray-haired – BILL KINNEY; but MR. HARRISON doesn't recognize him. KINNEY hands him a copy of the* new book.]**

HARRISON: To whom should I sign this?

BILL KINNEY: To Professor William Kinney …

HARRISON: Bill? Is that you? Oh, for God's sake!

BILL KINNEY: It's been a while … I'm here in Maine on vacation with my good friend Tony here …

TONY: Hello, Mr. Harrison. Nice to meet you. Bill has talked about you often…

HARRISON: He has? Nice to meet you, Tony … so what happened to you, Bill?

BILL KINNEY: Oh, I went to college at Syracuse University, majored in English, enjoyed it so much, I went on and on. Decided to get my Ph.D. in California where I still am teaching at San Diego State.

HARRISON: I bet you're a fine teacher.

BILL KINNEY: I enjoy it.

HARRISON: Well, I hope you enjoy my book.

BILL KINNEY: I've enjoyed all of them.

HARRISON: You've bought the other ones? How did you know about them? They don't go much beyond New England ...

BILL KINNEY: Remember Doreen McIntire?

HARRISON: Yes! Doreen stays in touch ... Does she with you, too?

BILL KINNEY: Yes, ever since I went back to Old Whiteside for a class reunion ... she's a regular correspondent. She keeps our class in touch ...

HARRISON: Look, Bill, why don't you and Tony hang around after the signing. We can go somewhere and have dinner or a drink?

BILL KINNEY: I'd like that very much ... we have a lot to catch up on ...

HARRISON: We certainly do ...

UGLY DUCKLINGS

A Play in Two Acts

Cast of Characters

Toni: A twelve-year-old camper.

Lisa: An eight-year-old camper.

Angie: The nineteen-year-old canoeing instructor.

Sherlock: A twenty-five-year-old counselor.

Renée: The nineteen-year-old arts-and-crafts instructor.

Vanessa: The twenty-year-old swimming instructor.

Charlotte: The director of the camp, in her fifties, deeply closeted.

Michelle:
Sarah:
Jennifer:
Rita:
— Twelve- and thirteen-year-old campers.

Stephanie:
Laurie:
Susan:
— Eight- to ten-year-old campers.

Scene

The waterfront dock of Camp Fernlake, a private girls' camp in Maine.

Time

Mid-July, the present.

ACT I

SETTING:

The scene is the waterfront area of Camp Fernlake, a private camp for girls on a small lake deep in the woods of southern Maine. A dock runs across the front of the stage, jutting out over the lake with ells at the left and right extremities of the stage. There is a rough wooden bench on the dock.

The dock is built up on pilings. A three-foot area under the dock is visible. On the dock is a flagpole nailed to the side of a pier piling. It flies the flag of Camp Fernlake. Upstage right of the dock is the entrance to the canoe shack. In the center of the stage is a campfire circle.

AT RISE:

It is a hot July day, mid-way through the camp session. It's the period of free time after lunch, before the bell for rest hour.

TONI is seated on the dock. She is practicing tying knots with varying lengths of rope. TONI is twelve years old. In some ways she is old and wise beyond her years, but in other ways she could be judged immature for her age. She has the suspicious nature of a child accustomed to abuse. She forms passionate, possessive attachments.

LISA enters. She is eight. LISA is bright, intense, and fond of girl-detective fiction. She has a fierce desire to live life on a more dramatic plane than that laid out for a middle-class, eight-year-old. She is attracted to TONI's dark and turbulent moods.

LISA

Hi, Toni. I was looking for you.

(TONI doesn't look up.)

I figured you'd be down here. You're always down here.

(She sits next to TONI.)

We're going to be late for rest hour if we don't leave now.

(TONI ignores her, but she persists.)

It takes ten minutes to walk back up to the cabin from here, and the bell's going to ring any minute.

TONI

I don't have to go.

LISA

How come?

TONI

Angie said I could stay down here and practice tying knots. I'm going to help her teach knots to her canoeing class this afternoon.

LISA

Angie's your favorite counselor, isn't she?

TONI

She's okay.

LISA

You like her. That's how come you're always down here at the waterfront.

(TONI is ignoring her. LISA picks up a piece of rope and crosses to a pier piling.)

I know how to do a bowline. Watch.

(TONI doesn't look up.)

Watch me! Toni!

(TONI looks up. Slowly LISA executes a bowline knot around the piling. She makes a mistake and has to back up. TONI goes back to her knot.)

There. Is that it? Toni!

TONI

(Looking up)

What?

LISA

Is that a bowline?

(TONI gets up, carrying her rope, as if to examine the piling. Suddenly she loops the rope over LISA and pulls it tight. LISA screams and loses her balance.)

TONI

That's a bowline.

LISA

What did you do that for?

TONI

You wanted to see a bowline.

LISA

You hurt me.

TONI

Where?

LISA

It doesn't show where.

TONI

If it doesn't show, it doesn't hurt.

(TONI goes back to her knot.)

LISA

Yes, it does.

(She starts to untie herself. She watches TONI.)

What's that?

TONI

A noose.

LISA

What are you going to do with it?

TONI

Something special.

LISA

What?

TONI

I can't tell.

LISA

Yes, you can. You can tell me.

TONI

No.

LISA

Toni!

TONI

Look, quit bothering me. Why don't you hang out with the kids from your own cabin?

LISA

They're babies.

TONI

And you're not.

LISA

No, I'm not. And why don't you hang out with the kids from your cabin?

TONI

Because all they want to do is talk about their stupid boyfriends.

LISA

See . . . Age has nothing to do with it. A lot of girls older than me act more babyish. What are you going to do with your noose?

(In response to this question, TONI gets up and climbs onto the pier piling next to the flagpole. She begins attaching the noose to the Camp Fernlake flagpole.)

Why are you putting it on the flagpole?

TONI

(Looking at LISA)

To catch the creature.

LISA

(Challenging her)

What creature?

TONI

(Dead serious)

The one that comes out of the lake at night and drowns little girls and dissolves all their bones and then sucks them out with their blood.

LISA

There's no such thing.

TONI

Right! Of course not! It's just a ghost story. It's just something people say to scare you. I wouldn't believe it either.

(She jumps down)

Except I saw the body.

LISA

What body?

TONI

(Going back to her knots)

The body of the girl who disappeared last summer.

LISA

A girl disappeared?

TONI

Oh, well, the counselors will tell you she got homesick and went home early. Only I saw the body.

LISA

(Still challenging her, but with less conviction)

Where?

TONI

Right there. Washed up under the pier. Of course, everyone said it was just an old life raft that had been at the bottom of the lake, that's all. And then they took it away, so it wouldn't scare the other girls . . . only I saw the face . . .

LISA

The face!

TONI

I turned it over with a stick, and there it was . . . her nose all folded over like a flap, and her mouth all smushed up next to her ear.

(LISA is wide-eyed.)

But don't worry. It was just an old life raft, and the girl just went home early, and the creature doesn't exist. This noose is probably just going to hang here.

(She goes back to her knots.)

This is a half-hitch.

LISA

(Crossing to the noose)

The thing is, why would the creature just come up and put its head in the noose?

(She studies the flagpole.)

No, what we're going to have to do is lay a trap. You and me are going to have to come down here after dark, and one of us is going to have to be the bait. We're going to have to lure the creature up to the dock, so we can get the noose around its neck.

TONI

It's just a story.

LISA

It's going to take both of us pulling at the same time to break his neck.

TONI

I told you, it's just a story.

LISA

You don't have to tell me that. I'm not like the other girls. I know a lot of things they don't. I've see a lot of things people pretend not to see. There's a lot of things grown-ups don't want us to know, but some of us find out anyway. And it's up to the ones like you and me to take care of these things, because nobody else is going to do it.

(TONI is taken aback by the intensity of this speech. She can't figure LISA out.)

You can trust me, Toni. You're my best friend.

Just then the door of the canoe shack opens and ANGIE enters. ANGIE is a nineteen-year old college student. She is the canoeing instructor. ANGIE has grown up surrounded by middle-class privilege, and she has never had cause to

question her entitlement or the cost of it.

ANGIE

Hi, guys.

LISA

Hi, Angie.

(TONI, who is in love with ANGIE, pretends not to see her.)

ANGIE

(To TONI)

And how are you, Toni?

TONI

(Without looking up)

Fine.

ANGIE

Look at all these knots! Toni, you know them better than I do.

(She sees the noose.)

Is that yours too?

LISA

It's ours.

ANGIE

Is it a warning to trespassers?

LISA

Sort of.

(She gives TONI a conspiratorial nudge. TONI, embarrassed by the company of an eight-year old, ignores her.)

ANGIE

You're going to scare off hunters with it?

LISA

Sort of . . . Aren't we, Toni?

(She nudges TONI again.)

TONI

Hey, get away from me! What are you . . . some kind of queer?

ANGIE

Toni!

TONI

Well, she is. She's all the time trying to hang on me.

LISA

What's a queer?

ANGIE

Never mind. Toni, you need to untie all these knots, because I'm going to use these ropes for my class.

TONI

(Getting back at ANGIE, she turns to LISA)

I'll tell you what a queer is.

LISA

What?

TONI

It's a girl who does nasty things to other girls.

LISA

(Excited)

Like putting snakes in their bed?

ANGIE

Toni, you don't need to be worrying about "queers" now. You and Lisa get those knots out.

(The bell rings.)

LISA

(Jumping up and handing her ropes to ANGIE)

That's rest hour! I gotta go! See you later, Toni!

(She takes off running.)

ANGIE

You better get going too, or you're going to be late.

TONI

I don't have to.

ANGIE

(Suspicious)

You don't?

TONI

Sherlock said I could stay down here and help you get ready for your class.

ANGIE

I don't need any help.

TONI

(Ingenuous)

It's part of this new program she's got. I think she called it a "mentorship" or something . . . Where every rest hour she's going to send a different camper to help a different counselor. I think it's supposed to teach us responsibility. Anyway, today I'm supposed to work with you.

ANGIE

Well . . . In that case, take down that noose before it scares the younger campers. I'll finish the knots.

(TONI crosses to the flagpole. She watches ANGIE closely as she sweeps. Finally, she gets to her point.)

TONI

So . . . Angie . . .

(ANGIE looks up.)

I saw on the bulletin board at the lodge that tomorrow's your day off.

ANGIE

That's right!

TONI

Does this mean you're taking off tonight?

ANGIE

(Checking her watch)

Six hours and counting.

TONI

Where are you going to go?

ANGIE

Well, I'm going to take one of the canoes tonight and paddle across the lake to Fern Island, and then tomorrow morning I'm going to sleep in, and have a big pancake breakfast - all that I can eat, and then I'm going to spend the whole

ANGIE (Cont'd)

day doing nothing but reading and eating and laying out in the sun.

TONI

It might not be safe.

ANGIE

I think I can handle it.

TONI

I heard there's rapists on the island sometimes.

ANGIE

They better not try anything on my day off.

TONI

I could go with you.

ANGIE

I don't think so.

TONI

Why not?

ANGIE

For one thing, because I'm already going to ask someone to go with me.

TONI

(A violent reaction)

Who?

ANGIE

Lisa's counselor. Renée.

TONI

(Exploding)

That's not fair! How come Renée gets to go and not me?

ANGIE

Because she's a grown-up and you're a kid.

TONI

That's no reason. I can do everything she can.

ANGIE

And she's got a day off.

TONI

How come us campers don't get days off?

ANGIE

Because every day is your day off.

TONI

That's bullshit!

(ANGIE is surprised by TONI's vehemence.)

You think it's fun to get stuck in a camp all summer you didn't even want to come to, and then get stuck in a cabin with a bunch of girls you can't stand and have to listen to them talk about themselves and their stupid boyfriends all day, and to have to do everything together like some kind of herd of cows or something --- "Girls! Sit over here!" "Girls! Time for lunch!" "Girls! Lights out!" You wouldn't like it either. It's degrading as hell, and it doesn't have anything to do with how old I am.

ANGIE

(Taking her seriously)

Well, I'm sorry, Toni. But you can't come.

TONI

Yes, I can. I can sneak out after lights out. I've done it before. We can take two canoes. I can spend the night, and then paddle back before it's light and be back at camp before anybody wakes up.

ANGIE

No.

TONI

Why not? It would work.

ANGIE

Because I don't want you to.

TONI

You don't want me to come?

ANGIE

No. I'm going to ask Renée.

Just then SHERLOCK appears.

SHERLOCK is twenty-five. She is the counselor in charge of TONI and LISA's cabin. She also teaches team sports at the camp. SHERLOCK is a large, athletic girl. She has a kind heart, but it is concealed under a rough, unsentimental style of dealing with the campers.

SHERLOCK

Hey, Toni! I figured I'd find you down here. Get your butt back up to the cabin!

TONI

Angie said I could . . .

SHERLOCK

Don't give me that stuff! You heard me . . . Get moving! Now!

(TONI turns to say something.)

I said now!

(TONI turns and exits.)

ANGIE

She told me you gave her permission to be down here.

SHERLOCK

Oh, she did?

ANGIE

Actually, it was a pretty good story. She told me you had this new mentorship program during rest hour . . .

SHERLOCK

(Cutting her off)

Mentorship! Oh, give me a break! Where does that kid come up with this stuff? And the stories she tells the campers! Summer before last, it was getting AIDS from going barefoot. Last year it was rapists in the woods. This year she's got all the little kids believing there's some kind of monster in the lake.

ANGIE

Oh . . . That explains the noose.

SHERLOCK

The noose?

(ANGIE points.)

SHERLOCK (Cont'd)

Oh, Jeez . . . Mind if I have a smoke? If I light up in front of those little snitches, I'll never hear the end of it. They'd threaten to report me. They would too.

ANGIE

Be my guest.

SHERLOCK

(She proceeds to pack and light her pipe.)

Toni's been coming here the last three summers, and every year she's got bigger stories. I've never seen such a born liar. I suppose you've heard the one about her dead mother and her dad, the man who programs Bill Gates' computer?

ANGIE

First thing she told me.

SHERLOCK

Yeah, well, her mother's an alky in and out of treatment centers, and her dad's doing twenty years in the state pen. Church group sends her here.

ANGIE

What did he do?

SHERLOCK

Her father? I don't know. Charlotte won't tell any of us counselors, but if you ask me, Toni knows an awful lot about sex for her age.

ANGIE

You think she was sexually abused?

SHERLOCK

Who knows? Something happened to her. Kids like Toni don't just grow on trees. She's one in a million, and wouldn't you know . . . of all the cabins in all the summer camps in the world, she'd have to end up in mine. You and Vanessa are lucky. All you have to take care of is a bunch of canoes and life jackets. Be glad you don't have to sleep with a cabin full of girls.

ANGIE

I am.

SHERLOCK

They drive you nuts. Twelve and thirteen-year old girls - the oldest girls in the

SHERLOCK (Cont'd)

camp, right? Wouldn't you think they'd set an example for the other kids? But no . . . They're always the worst. Look at Renée's cabin - the eight-year olds? Sweet, thoughtful, homesick - like that kid Lisa. They do whatever you tell them. They want to be helpful. They want you to like them. But my kids? All they want to do is sit around and talk about their boyfriends. Their boyfriends or their hair. Jeez. And then, there's Toni . . . Four bimbos and a psychopath!

ANGIE

I take it you don't like kids.

SHERLOCK

Whatever gave you that idea?

(She laughs.)

No, I love 'em. That's why I come back here every year. Either that or I'm a glutton for punishment. What about you?

ANGIE

Vanessa was my roommate last year at Boston University, and she told me she had a job here as the swimming instructor, and that they were looking for someone to teach canoeing. Sounded pretty nice . . . spending the summer on a lake in Maine.

SHERLOCK

Disillusioned yet?

ANGIE

No, but then, I don't have to sleep with them.

SHERLOCK

Speaking of Vanessa, where is she? Shouldn't she be out here working on her tan?

ANGIE

She probably won't be back until after dinner. Today is her day off.

SHERLOCK

You mean one of her boyfriends came up last night from Boston.

ANGIE

How did you know? It's supposed to be a secret. She doesn't want Charlotte to find out.

SHERLOCK

Figures. Vanessa and her boyfriends. The second hottest topic of the twelve-year olds.

(She looks at her watch.)

Well, I better get back before Toni ties up the girls and burns down the cabin. Oh, I didn't tell you . . . I'll be back tonight. I'm bringing my cabin and Renée's down here for a campfire. It's Cabin Night.

ANGIE

Sounds like fun.

SHERLOCK

Toni with all her monster stories, will have those guys so scared they'll be peeing in their pants . . . waiting for some clammy hand to reach up and pull them into the lake.

ANGIE

I'm afraid they're going to be disappointed.

SHERLOCK

Hey, wait a minute! I just had an idea! Let's really scare those guys! They'll all think you've gone already, and you could hide back in the woods and make noises or something.

ANGIE

I could hide under the dock, because I'm leaving in a canoe anyway. I'm going to Fern Island.

SHERLOCK

That'd be even better! Boy, I'd love to see old Toni's face when she gets a taste of her own medicine!

Just then RENÉE appears. RENÉE is also nineteen. Her clothing is very "street," she wears her hair in a highly eccentric, radical-dyke "do," and sports multiple piercings.

SHERLOCK

Hey, Renée! You playing hookey too?

RENÉE

I just came down for a minute.

SHERLOCK

What do you have to worry about? You got the eight-year olds!

(She passes the flagpole as she heads up the path.)

See this? You know what my kids would call this? Decorative macrame.

(She exits.)

ANGIE

See you, Sherlock.

(SHERLOCK disappears into the woods. ANGIE and RENÉE are suddenly very shy together.)

RENÉE

Well, so . . . in the arts-and-crafts class, I was showing the kids how to make beaded earrings, and, uh . . . I thought maybe you'd like them . . . since I had to make them anyway.

(She hands her an exquisite pair of beaded earrings.)

You've got pierced ears, haven't you?

ANGIE

Yeah.

(Looking at them)

Oh, these are beautiful, Renée. They're just beautiful.

RENÉE

It won't hurt my feelings if you don't like them. Like I say, I had to make them anyway. You can just give them to somebody else.

ANGIE

No, I love them.

(Putting them on)

How do they look?

RENÉE

Yeah.

(There's an awkward silence.)

At lunch you said you had to ask me something?

ANGIE

I'm taking my day off tomorrow, and I saw on the schedule that tomorrow was your day off too, and so I was wondering if you'd like to go with me. I'm taking a canoe out to Fern Island, and I thought I'd just hang out for the day.

RENÉE

I was going to catch a ride into North Conway and spend the day looking around. Being a tourist, you know.

ANGIE

Why don't you go with me instead? You could bring your sketchbook and do a lot of drawing. I'm going to be reading a lot. I talked to the kitchen staff, and they're going to let me take whatever I want, so we can have some great meals.

RENÉE

Thanks for asking, but I got some stuff to do in town.

ANGIE

Like what?

RENÉE

Just some things I gotta buy.

ANGIE

Like what?

RENÉE

Some art supplies.

(A long silence)

ANGIE

You know what? I don't believe you.

RENÉE

What?

ANGIE

I don't believe there's anything you really have to do tomorrow. I think you just don't want to go with me. And if that's the case, you should just tell me, so I won't waste my time asking you again. People should say what they really mean. Everyone wonders why kids tell so many lies, but if you ask me, they get it from the adults.

(She gets up and starts to leave.)

RENÉE

Wait, Angie! I don't mean that. I mean, you're right . . . I don't have to go to town, but you're wrong that I don't want to go with you.

ANGIE

I don't understand.

RENÉE

(Uncomfortable)

I . . . it's just that I'm used to doing things by myself. It's a habit, I guess.

ANGIE

Then I won't ask you again.

RENÉE

People who ask me to do things, they usually don't know me too well. I don't like having to put on an act . . . so it's just easier to say no.

ANGIE

You don't have to put on an act for me. I don't care. You can go to the other side of the island and sketch all day. I just thought you might like some company, that's all. Frankly, I'm not used to being turned down.

RENÉE

Yeah, okay. What the hell . . . I'll go.

ANGIE

Really? You want to?

RENÉE

Yeah . . . Yeah.

(There's a moment of awkward silence, then they both speak at once.)

What . . .

ANGIE

So . . .

RENÉE

(Laughing)

Go ahead.

ANGIE

I was going to ask you what you're going to teach your arts-and-crafts class next hour.

RENÉE

I'm going to show them how to dye.

ANGIE

That ought to make Sherlock happy.

RENÉE

(Laughing)

Tie-dye. I told them to bring their sheets. Hope their parents don't care. Oh, well, by the time they go home and their parents find out about it, I'll be long gone. What are you going to do?

ANGIE

Oh, I've got a free period. My next canoeing class isn't until two. It's your cabin.

RENÉE

Nice girls, aren't they?

ANGIE

Yeah. Very polite. Especially that Lisa

RENÉE

First time away from home.

ANGIE

Really?

RENÉE

Yeah. She doesn't let on, but sometimes I can hear her crying at night.

ANGIE

Oh, that poor kid.

RENÉE

She'll get used to it. Where'd you learn to canoe?

ANGIE

Family vacations. Do you know how?

RENÉE

Me? No. I don't even know how to swim.

ANGIE

You're kidding!

RENÉE

It wasn't a survival skill where I came from.

ANGIE

Where's that?

RENÉE

New Orleans.

ANGIE

People swim in New Orleans.

RENÉE

Yeah.

ANGIE

So how come you didn't learn?

RENÉE

I just didn't.

ANGIE

Look, this really pisses me off. You say something, and then you don't finish it. And then you act like I'm prying. Don't start something you don't want to finish.

(RENÉE gives her a funny look and laughs.)

What's so funny?

RENÉE

"Don't start something you don't want to finish."

ANGIE

What's funny about that?

RENÉE

Nothing. Absolutely nothing. It's the must unfunny thing I've ever heard.

ANGIE

You just want to talk to yourself, don't you?

RENÉE

No. Not at all. What do you want to know? Why I don't swim? Okay. Because, like I said, but you weren't listening, it wasn't a survival skill. Ever since I can remember, I had to take care of myself. No, I didn't take family vacations, no, I've never been to Disney World, no, I hardly ever went to the movies . . . I never canoed, I never learned to swim, I never went ice skating, I never went skiing, I never rode horses. I survived. Okay?

ANGIE
How come you had to take care of yourself?

RENÉE
Because no one else would do it.

ANGIE
What about your mother?

RENÉE
My mother. I had to take care of her, too.

ANGIE
Was she sick?

RENÉE
Depends on whose version of "well" you use.
(ANGIE doesn't understand.)
I mean, if you think it's normal to need to be around a man, any man, all the time, even if he's a drunken sadistic bastard . . . then, you could call her the healthiest woman alive. Personally, I thought she was sick.

ANGIE
What about your father?

RENÉE
Good question.

ANGIE
You mean he wasn't there?

RENÉE
No, he wasn't there. But nobody missed him. Like I say, there were always plenty of men. Can't have too much of a good thing, can you? One morning, when I was about fourteen, I was in the bathroom brushing my teeth. In my own bathroom, brushing my own teeth, and this asshole I've never even seen before comes in without knocking, stark naked . . . like he owns the goddam place, and the next thing I know he's standing behind me looking at me in the mirror, while I gotta mouth full of toothpaste, and he's putting his hands on my breasts.

ANGIE
You're kidding!

RENÉE

No. It gets better. The next thing I know the asshole has his elbow across my neck and he's fucking raping me. In my own bathroom, right in the middle of brushing my teeth.

ANGIE

Did you tell your mother?

RENÉE

There's no point in telling people what they can't handle.

ANGIE

(In disbelief)

So you didn't say anything?

RENÉE

Oh, I said something all right. I said, "He goes or I go." I moved out that afternoon.

ANGIE

Your mother chose a strange man over her own daughter?

RENÉE

You seem to think that's unusual.

ANGIE

I'm sure if you'd told her ---

RENÉE

(Cutting her off)

Look! My mother was into men the way some people are into alcohol. Like a disease. It's pretty common. They ought to have something like Heterosexuals Anonymous for people like her.

ANGIE

Where did you go when you left?

RENÉE

I moved in with my grandmother, but she was a real bitch. Here I am . . . been taking care of myself since God knows when, and all of a sudden it's, " Renée! Where are you going?" and "Have you done your homework, Renée?" and " Renée, you be back here by nine o'clock!" So I moved in with a friend.

ANGIE

Someone from school?

RENÉE

No. It was an older woman.

ANGIE

Like a foster mother?

RENÉE

(Snorting)

Not hardly.

ANGIE

I don't understand.

RENÉE

It was a friend.

(She changes the subject.)

She was an artist. She taught me how to work with all these different things. Living with her was when I figured out that I wanted to be an artist too. Before that, I felt like I just had to keep moving out of people's way. I mean, you know, always having to sleep in the living room of my own house . . . that kind of thing. But living with her, and she was real independent, I got some idea of where I was going. She helped me get the loan to go to BU. In fact, she's responsible for my getting the arts and crafts job here. She knew one of the board members.

ANGIE

She must be a very good friend.

RENÉE

Was.

(ANGIE looks at her.)

We don't see each other too much anymore.

ANGIE

How come?

RENÉE

That's just the way it goes. What about you?

ANGIE

Pretty boring, I guess. I've got two parents who love me, a brother, and a dog. Lived in the same suburban split level all my life. Normal.

RENÉE

You got a boyfriend?

ANGIE

Yeah.

(She backtracks.)

Well . . . not really.

(RENÉE looks at her.)

I mean, there's this guy at school I go places with, but I'm not in love with him or anything. How about you? Do you have a boyfriend?

RENÉE

(Snorting)

Not hardly.

ANGIE

(Embarrassed that she asked)

Yeah.

RENÉE

(Breaking the awkward silence)

So . . . What time you want to leave?

ANGIE

Some time after supper. Oh! That reminds me . . . Sherlock's bringing her cabin and yours down here for a campfire tonight . . . .

RENÉE

Yeah, she told me.

ANGIE

And she wanted to do something special to scare the kids. Toni's been telling all these stories about some kind of monster in the lake. So I promised her I would dress up and act like a monster for the campfire.

RENÉE

(Shocked)

You're kidding!

ANGIE

(Surprised at her reaction)

What?

RENÉE

You're really going to do that? In front of the kids?

ANGIE

Why not?

RENÉE

Well, I don't know. It's so dumb.

ANGIE

So? A lot of things are dumb. In fact most of the fun things I ever did were dumb.

RENÉE

I mean, in front of the kids.

ANGIE

Why not? It's going to be the highlight of their summer . . . "The Night I Saw the Monster."

RENÉE

But they'll know it's you.

ANGIE

That's part of the fun. They'll know, but I won't admit it, so they'll never really be sure. Why don't you dress up too? We could be two monsters.

RENÉE

(Quickly)

Me? No way!

ANGIE

Why not?

RENÉE

I couldn't do that.

ANGIE

Why not?

RENÉE

I just couldn't.

ANGIE

Oh, come on . . . It'll be fun.

RENÉE

No way.

ANGIE

I can't believe it! The tough kid from New Orleans - scared to put a pillowcase over her head.

RENÉE

You got it.

ANGIE

I don't understand, Renée. How come you . . .

Just then CHARLOTTE arrives. She is the Director of Camp Fernlake. A woman in her fifties, she has been running the camp for fifteen years. CHARLOTTE genuinely cherishes the culture of girls and, aware of how endangered it is, she has made it her lifework to protect and build up the camp. She is a lesbian who is closeted even to herself, and it is problematic for her that the very passion behind her life work would, if known, also destroy it.

CHARLOTTE

Girls . . .

RENÉE

Hi, Charlotte.

ANGIE

Hi.

CHARLOTTE

(Seeing the noose)

And what is the meaning of this?

ANGIE

Oh, one of the campers put it there for a joke.

CHARLOTTE

Toni.

ANGIE

I'll take it down.

CHARLOTTE
I understand Toni has been spending all of her free time and some of her not-so-free time down here with you.

ANGIE
Well, yeah. She's here a lot.

CHARLOTTE
(Smiling)
Apparently she has a crush on you.

ANGIE
Oh, I don't think that's it. She just likes boats.

CHARLOTTE
She didn't seem to care for them last year, or the year before.

ANGIE
Oh, I'm sure that ---

CHARLOTTE
Angie, this is your first summer here, but if you'd been here as long as some of the counselors, like your roommate Vanessa, you would know that most of the girls have crushes on their counselors. It's normal and healthy for us to be a little infatuated with our role models. It's part of growing up. I always considered it part of the magic of camp. But these crushes can get carried a little too far ---

RENÉE
How far is that?

CHARLOTTE
I beg your pardon?

RENÉE
I said, "How far is that?"

CHARLOTTE
I think a girl's crush has gone too far when it reaches the point where it becomes destructive
(She turns back to ANGIE.)
So, Angie ---

RENÉE
Excuse me, but what point is that exactly?

CHARLOTTE

What?

RENÉE

That point . . . where the relationship becomes destructive?

CHARLOTTE

I believe we were talking about crushes, not relationships.

RENÉE

Well, at what point do they get destructive?

CHARLOTTE

Renée, I'm not sure I understand the point of this test, but I assure you I'm qualified to speak on the subject. I've been involved with Camp Fernlake for four decades now. I was a camper here in the sixties, a counselor in the seventies, and for the last twenty years I have been the director. With all due respect for your five weeks at camp, I have to say there are just some things you will have to take my word for.

(She turns abruptly back to ANGIE)

Now, Angie, I'm going to ask a little favor from you. I'm going to ask you to discourage Toni from coming down here outside of her scheduled class times. She needs to spend more time with the girls in her cabin. Toni is at that critical age where some firm boundaries could make all the difference. A little guidance from someone like you, an older girl she respects, could just keep her from heading down the wrong path.

RENÉE

What path is that?

CHARLOTTE

(She pauses and then looks at her watch.)

It's still rest hour, Renée, and I believe counselors are required to supervise their cabins during that time.

RENÉE

(RENÉE just looks at CHARLOTTE for a minute.)

See you later, Angie.

(She exits.)

CHARLOTTE

(Turning back to ANGIE with a friendly smile)

So, Angie, I can count on your cooperation, can't I? I know you want what's best for Toni, don't you?

ANGIE

Yeah . . .

CHARLOTTE

Good! Oh, look! Here comes Vanessa!
(Calling out)
How was Kennebunkport?

VANESSA enters carrying a large shoulder bag. A year older than ANGIE, she is a very beautiful, in a mainstream-media sense. She is very tired, but she puts on a good front for CHARLOTTE.

CHARLOTTE

(Beaming)
Welcome home! We have all missed you so much.
(Making a fuss over VANESSA)
Vanessa's one of our veterans. I remember her first summer here. She started coming to Fernlake when she was thirteen, didn't you? And the next two summers she came back to work in the kitchen. Then we made her a counselor. The youngest counselor we've ever had. But she's so responsible, aren't you? I don't know what I'd do without her.
(VANESSA gives ANGIE a wan smile. CHARLOTTE turns to VANESSA.)
I was just explaining to Angie about the crushes these girls get on their counselors.
(Back to ANGIE)
Vanessa knows all about these. The older girls always get crushes on her. They all want to wear their hair like her, and they argue over who's going to sit at her table. It happens every year.
(She puts her arm around VANESSA's waist.)
So tell us, how was your Aunt Alice and how was Kennebunkport?

VANESSA

(Flashing ANGIE a quick look)
It was a lot of fun.

CHARLOTTE

So where did you go?

VANESSA

Well, actually, we never got to Kennebunkport.

CHARLOTTE

You didn't?

VANESSA

We stopped at a barn auction on the way, and we spent the whole day there. My aunt collects antiques.

CHARLOTTE

Oh? Isn't that wonderful? And did you buy anything?

VANESSA

I didn't, but Aunt Alice bought a Bentwood rocking chair.

CHARLOTTE

Oh, those are wonderful ---

VANESSA

(Smiling conspiratorially at ANGIE)

And a braided rug --- a really large one.

CHARLOTTE

I'd love to see it!

VANESSA

And an old copper tea kettle with the handle missing. Oh, and she bought some quilts.

CHARLOTTE

Quilts! Well, I wish I'd known about this auction. You know, I collect quilts. Sometime you and I will have to steal away to one of the auctions around here.

VANESSA

(Yawning)

Excuse me, Charlotte, but I need to get ready for my class. It's almost time.

(Smiling)

I came back early so I wouldn't miss it.

CHARLOTTE

(To ANGIE)

Look at that --- always thinking of the girls!

(To VANESSA)

I tell you what - Why don't you and Angie come up to my cabin tonight after lights out, and we'll have a special treat. I'll get some brownies from the kitchen, and maybe we'll even have a little glass of sherry, if you won't tell anybody.

(To ANGIE)

I have these little soirees every now and then for some of the "old-timers" like Vanessa. I have a feeling you're going to become part of our little Fernlake family too. Vanessa has told me so many wonderful things about you ---

ANGIE

(Breaking in)

Thanks for the invitation, but tonight is the beginning of my day off, and Renée and I have made plans to go camping.

CHARLOTTE

Renée? Well, that's very nice of you to go with her. She doesn't seem to have made many friends among the staff.

ANGIE

Actually, she's going with me. I asked her.

CHARLOTTE

(Not pleased)

You asked her? Well, wasn't that thoughtful?

(A pause)

You know, Angie, I've seen a lot of girls and young women pass through these gates, and if you don't consider it intrusive of me, I would like to share a little something I have learned over the years. May I?

ANGIE

(Uncomfortable)

Sure.

CHARLOTTE

(Putting an arm around ANGIE)

There are some girls --- and young women --- Toni's one of them, and so is Renée --- who set themselves apart. They let the world know they are different, and after they've run themselves up a tree socially, they expect other people to come and rescue them. But just like the cats who do that --- for all their crying, they really have no intention of coming down, and they'll hurt anyone who tries to help them. The best thing you can do for your friend Toni and for Renée is to ignore them ---

ANGIE

I don't think it's really fair to talk about Renée when she isn't here.

CHARLOTTE

I'm not talking behind her back, if that's what you're trying to accuse me of.

(ANGIE tries to protest, but CHARLOTTE cuts her off.)

CHARLOTTE (Cont'd)

I was advising a new counselor about a situation that pertains to the welfare of the camp. Like it or not, we have a structure here --

ANGIE

I don't see what this has to do with Renée.

CHARLOTTE

Tolerance of other people's antisocial habits is a noble philosophy, but I am afraid it is only practical where every person can afford to operate independently. At camp that is a luxury we cannot afford.

(She sighs.)

You young women don't realize how rare, how precious this summer camp experience is for these girls. For some of them, this may be the only time in their lives they will ever have the opportunity experience themselves in an environment apart from their brothers, or their fathers, or their husbands, or their sons. There is a freedom here, a safety, that most of them will never know again. We must do everything in our power to protect this little oasis of girlhood. It's little enough we can give them, and it will be over for them all too soon.

(VANESSA yawns audibly. CHARLOTTE responds to the hint.)

Well, we've wandered rather far afield, haven't we? I tell you what --- You just tell Renée to take a rain check on that camping trip, and we'll go ahead with our little soiree just like we planned.

ANGIE

(Stunned by the suggestion)

I couldn't do that.

(CHARLOTTE looks at her.)

We've already made plans.

CHARLOTTE

(A gentle smile)

Plans can be changed.

ANGIE

But I don't want to change them.

CHARLOTTE

I see.

(She turns to VANESSA)

Your roommate certainly does have her own agenda, doesn't she?

(Back to ANGIE, very gay)

We'll just have to get together another time, won't we?

CHARLOTTE (Cont'd)

(She doesn't give ANGIE time to answer.)

So . . . Vanessa, I'll see you at nine?

VANESSA

(Mustering a bright smile)

I'll be there.

CHARLOTTE

Good.

(To ANGIE)

Sorry you won't be joining us, Angie.

(She exits. As soon as she is out of sight, VANESSA drops her polite facade.

VANESSA

Oh, Jesus, what a windbag!

(She flops down on the dock.)

God, Angie . . . Why didn't you just agree with her?

ANGIE

Because I don't.

VANESSA

Well, argue with her on your own time. God, I thought I was going to die. I didn't get any sleep last night. I'm so sore I'm going to be walking bowlegged for a week.

ANGIE

You're back early. You don't have to be here until dinner.

VANESSA

I told Rick I needed to be here after lunch. God, I was afraid I wasn't going to make it to dinner.

ANGIE

Doesn't sound like much of a day off.

VANESSA

Day off? Whose talking about a day off? I didn't even get a night off. One thing's for sure --- Rick hasn't been screwing anyone else while I'm gone, unless the guy is some kind of sexual triathelete. God, I almost wish he would.

ANGIE

Why didn't you just tell him you wanted to do something else?

VANESSA

Well, Angie, he came all the way up from Boston just to see me. I don't think he drove two hundred miles to play Trivial Pursuit.

ANGIE

But it was your day off. You only get one every two weeks. You ought to at least be able to do what you want to do.

VANESSA

Well, I mean, it's not like I don't like sex.

ANGIE

So why didn't you just tell him you'd had enough?

VANESSA

Is that what you tell Mark?

ANGIE

Mark and I don't have sex.

VANESSA

Oh, come on. I'm your roommate. Last year you guys slept together all the time.

ANGIE

Not "all the time," and when we did, we didn't have sex.

VANESSA

Come on.

ANGIE

It's the truth.

VANESSA

You and Mark sleep together and you don't have sex?

ANGIE

Would you like to tell the whole camp?

VANESSA

Angie Barrett, you mean you've been my roommate for a whole year, and all this time you and Mark have been sleeping together and not doing it, and you didn't tell me?

ANGIE

It isn't any big deal.

VANESSA

I bet it's a big deal to Mark.

ANGIE

(Defensive)

If it is, it's his problem. I have a right to control my body.

VANESSA

God, Angie --- if you don't want to fuck, why do you have a boyfriend?

ANGIE

I hate that word.

VANESSA

"Boyfriend?"

(ANGIE gives her a look.)

Well, excuse me. If you don't want to "engage in intercourse," why do you have a boyfriend?

ANGIE

I like Mark.

VANESSA

Yeah, but you go around pretending he's your boyfriend.

ANGIE

He is my boyfriend. He's a friend . . . He's a boy . . . He's a boyfriend.

VANESSA

Well, all I can say is, not for long.

ANGIE

Not all guys are like Rick. Mark enjoys my company.

VANESSA

Just try telling him there's no hope, and see how long he sticks around. You didn't ever tell him that, did you?

ANGIE

Neither one of us wants to do it until it feels right for both of us.

VANESSA

So you're just waiting till it feels right for you?

ANGIE

Yeah.

VANESSA

Girlfriend, I've got news for you. If you are waiting for your first time with a man to feel right, you might as well enter a convent.

(ANGIE turns away in disgust with the whole conversation.)

But I gotta hand it to you --- you sure figured out a way to get yourself a free escort service.

ANGIE

(This hit a nerve.)

We're friends.

VANESSA

Right.

ANGIE

At least I don't have to spend my one day off counting spiders on the ceiling of some cheap motel.

VANESSA

No --- You'll just be off sharing a tent with a lesbian.

ANGIE

(Turning around quickly)

Renée's not a lesbian.

VANESSA

Oh, yeah, sure. And Madonna's a virgin.

ANGIE

What makes you think she's a lesbian?

VANESSA

Oh, come on, Angie! Are you really that naive? Just look at her! The woman's got "dyke" written all over her. It's coming out of her ears . . . and her nose and her eyebrows --- literally.

ANGIE

What do you mean?

VANESSA
That haircut, and all those piercings? You don't think that's dykey?

ANGIE
No. I think it's artistic.

VANESSA
And a tattoo? I suppose you think that's artistic too?

ANGIE
Yeah.

VANESSA
And how about those books she brought with her? Stone Butch Blues? Dykes to Watch Out For?

ANGIE
I've read those.

VANESSA
I'm not surprised.

ANGIE
Just because you read a book doesn't mean you're a lesbian.

VANESSA
Ever hear her talk about a boyfriend?

ANGIE
I don't talk about mine.

VANESSA
I'm not surprised.

ANGIE
(Exploding)
Just because not everybody wants to broadcast their sex life all over camp, doesn't mean they ---

VANESSA
(Rising)
Okay! Okay!
(Just then the bell rings, signaling the end of rest hour.)
Aw shit, the end of rest hour. Look, Angie, I'm dead. Will you take my class? You don't have one this hour, do you?

ANGIE

Didn't you tell Charlotte that's why you came back early --- to teach your class?

VANESSA

Yeah, but she's never going to know. Will you teach it?

ANGIE

(She turns away.)

I need to pack for my trip.

VANESSA

(Rising to leave, she gives ANGIE a meaningful look.)

I hope you've got two tents.

She exits down right towards the swimming area. ANGIE turns and exits into the canoe shack.

Voices of twelve- and thirteen-year old girls are heard off left. These are the voices of SHERLOCK's cabin.

RITA

Then how come no one else has ever seen it?

JENNIFER

Yeah, Toni! How come no one else has ever seen it?

TONI

Because it just washed up yesterday.

SARAH

Oh, barf.

MICHELLE

Hey, come on! We're going to be late for swimming!

The girls enter from up left. They are all wearing bathing suits and carrying towels. MICHELLE's body is more mature than the others, and she has leadership status because of this. JENNIFER is her groupie. RITA is bouncy and outgoing. She teases a lot, but

it's always good-natured. SARAH is very preppie. She has adopted certain mannerisms and inflections to make herself appear sophisticated.
TONI is leading the girls. She marches onto the left ell of the dock.

RITA
So how come the fish haven't eaten it, if it's been in the lake for a year?

JENNIFER
Yeah, Toni! How come the fish haven't eaten it?

TONI
Because fish don't like skin.

(As the others gather at the end of the ell, MICHELLE walks deliberately past them, heading down right.)

SARAH
Hey, Michelle, aren't you going to look at it?

MICHELLE
I'm going to swimming class. I know there isn't any dead body. Toni's just making it up, just like she always does.

TONI
(Angry)
No, I'm not!

MICHELLE
What about those men you saw in the woods last year?

SARAH
What men?

MICHELLE
Go ahead, Toni.

TONI
They were there --- two of them!

MICHELLE
Oh, sure.

RITA

Where?

MICHELLE

Over by the archery range. Only nobody except Toni ever saw them.

TONI

So?

MICHELLE

Good excuse for not going to archery, wasn't it? She'd go into this big act, like this.

(MICHELLE opens her eyes wide, raises her eyebrows, hunches her shoulders, and withdraws into a ball. She imitates a "psycho" voice:)

"No! No! I can't go! I can't go to the archery range today!"

TONI

You'd have been scared too, if you'd seen them.

SARAH

Did they have guns?

MICHELLE

Toni said they weren't wearing any pants.

(JENNIFER snickers.)

TONI

It's not funny.

RITA

I saw a man like that one time in a park. He had his pants down around his knees, and he was playing with himself.

TONI

Yeah, see?

MICHELLE

Yeah, but nobody else ever saw these guys by the archery range, and nobody ever found them when they organized a search party. Toni just wanted to get some attention, like she always does.

(She starts to walk off. JENNIFER joins her.)

JENNIFER

You're right, Michelle. There's no point in even looking. There's nothing there.

TONI

Okay, look.

(She crosses to the downstage edge of the ell. SARAH and RITA join her.)

SARAH

Where?

TONI

(Pointing)

See where the end of that sunken log is?

RITA

Yeah, I see it.

SARAH

Where?

RITA

There. Look.

(She stands next to SARAH and points.)

JENNIFER

Come on, you guys! We're going to be late!

TONI

(Ignoring her)

Okay, look halfway down the log, just next to it. What do you see?

SARAH

(Jumping)

Oh, my God!

JENNIFER

(Running back over)

Where? Where?

SARAH

(Quiet horror)

Oh, my God . . .

JENNIFER

Where?! Sarah!

SARAH

I don't believe it.

JENNIFER

(Grabbing TONI)

Where's the log? I don't see it.

TONI

(In triumph)

Okay . . . Stand here and follow my arm.

(She positions JENNIFER and points. During this time, MICHELLE is watching from the other side of dock. RITA is studying the site.)

JENNIFER

(A long, piercing scream)

Ahhhhhh! I see it!

SARAH

(Slow)

Oh-h-h-h-h, m-y-y-y-y God-d-d-d-d-d.

JENNIFER

(In awe)

I don't believe it.

TONI

(Turning triumphantly to MICHELLE)

I guess you better get to swimming class, Michelle.

JENNIFER

I'm never going to swim in this lake again, so help me God.

(She crosses herself.)

SARAH

Wait! Look! You can see her tee shirt!

RITA

What are you guys looking at?

SARAH

It's a little over to the right, kind of underneath the log.

JENNIFER

Was she wearing a tee shirt, Toni?

SARAH

It's got letters.

JENNIFER

I can read it!

(She reads)

"Umbo Family Pack"

SARAH

It's one of those big wrappers the hot dog buns come in.

JENNIFER

Why was she wearing one of those?

RITA

Oh, I see what you're looking at. The scummy part is just the other end of the bag.

MICHELLE

Maybe the monster was having a weenie roast?

TONI

(Furious with RITA)

You just don't want to see it!

SARAH

Oh, come on, Toni . . . It's just an old plastic bag.

JENNIFER

I knew it all the time. I was just going along with it for a joke.

RITA

Hey, what's the difference between a dead camper and a plastic bag?

JENNIFER

What?

RITA

If you're Toni, nothing!

(They all laugh.)

MICHELLE

Come on, guys, we're going to miss swimming.

(They all troop over.)

JENNIFER

I knew she was lying. I just went over to see what everybody was looking at.

SARAH

Hey, Toni --- I wouldn't eat hot dog buns anymore. I hear they wrap them in the skin of dead campers.

(They all laugh.)

We should just call her "Hot Dog Buns" from now on.

JENNIFER

Hey, come on, Hot Dog Buns! You're going to be late!

RITA

This is Toni's mother --- "How many times do I have to tell you, Toni --- 'hot dog buns.' Now what am I going to do with another box of dead camper skins?"

(The girls exit in hysterics. After they have left, TONI turns and calls after them, but not loud enough for them to hear.)

TONI

Fuck you, you bitches!

(She crosses to the canoe shack and knocks on the door. She calls softly.)

Angie . . . Angie . . ..

ANGIE

(Calling from inside)

Just a second.

Suddenly RENÉE appears. She has a bundle in her arms. It's the monster suit. TONI, scared of being sent to class, ducks behind the canoe shack. RENÉE knocks on the door.

ANGIE

I'm coming! I'm coming!

(She opens the door and steps out. She is surprised to see RENÉE.)

I thought you were Toni.

(She looks around.)

Was she here?

RENÉE

I didn't see anybody.

ANGIE

I could have sworn I heard her voice.

(She calls.)

Toni!

RENÉE

Boy, Charlotte's sure got you paranoid about Toni, hasn't she?

ANGIE

(Looking at RENÉE)

I heard her voice. And I don't like what you're trying to say.

RENÉE

What?

ANGIE

That I kissed Charlotte's ass.

RENÉE

You sure didn't call her on any of her shit.

ANGIE

I was trying to hear what she was saying.

RENÉE

She wasn't saying anything!

ANGIE

It was hard to tell whether she was or she wasn't, because she kept being interrupted.

RENÉE

Take my word for it, she wasn't saying anything.

ANGIE

I don't take anybody's word for anything.

RENÉE

So you think Charlotte has a right to judge other people's relationships?

ANGIE

I think she likes to have her way ---

RENÉE

That's the understatement of the century!

ANGIE

. . . but I also think she's got the best interests of the girls at heart.

RENÉE

Oh, come on, Angie! Gimme a break! The woman's on a power trip. She's a frustrated old bitch.

(ANGIE laughs.)

It's not funny. People like her are very dangerous.

ANGIE

Hey, come on, lighten up, Renée. It's only a summer camp.

RENÉE

(RENÉE looks at her for a minute. She becomes very businesslike.)

Here's the monster costume.

(She gives the bundle to ANGIE.)

I came down here to tell you I changed my mind about the camping trip. I'm not going with you after all.

ANGIE

Oh, you're not?

RENÉE

(Delivering her speech)

Don't take it the wrong way. I just . . . I 'm just more comfortable by myself, that's all. Sorry if this messes up your plans.

ANGIE

Renée . . .

RENÉE

(Raising her voice to finish the speech)

I didn't really want to go, but I let you kind of talk me into it --- which isn't your fault. That was real nice of you, but, really, I just enjoy being by myself better. So . . .

(She looks up and waits for ANGIE to say something. ANGIE has decided not to. They stand there looking at each other. Finally ANGIE does speak.)

ANGIE

Oh, is it my turn? Did I miss my cue or something? Let me see if I can

ANGIE (Cont'd)

remember the lines . . .

(With fake cheerfulness)

"Gee, that's too bad, Renée, but I understand."

(She breaks character.)

No?

(Same business)

"Oh, okay. Well, maybe we can do something else together sometime." How about, "Well, really, it's no bother. I was planning to go by myself anyway, and I know I asked you at the last minute."

(She turns to RENÉE.)

Tell you what --- you just pick the one you like.

RENÉE

(Uncomfortable)

Angie . . . don't . . .

ANGIE

Oh, I didn't say them right? Well, you'll have to excuse me . . . You had more time to practice your lines.

RENÉE

I should never have said I would go in the first place.

ANGIE

Well, you've unsaid it. You're safe.

She crosses to the canoe shack, enters, and closes the door. RENÉE stands outside, uncertain what she should do. TONI peers around to see if the coast is clear. She sees RENÉE and ducks back behind the shack. RENÉE starts to go. She hesitates, and turns back. She knocks on the door. ANGIE opens the door. Her face is expressionless, and she waits for RENÉE to speak.

RENÉE

Angie . . . I don't want you to think I'm not going because I don't like you.

ANGIE

Did you knock on the door to tell me you liked me?

RENÉE

The reason I'm not going has nothing to do with that.

ANGIE

Oh. So you don't like me, but you want me to think you do?

RENÉE

(In agony)

That's not what I said.

ANGIE

What do you want, Renée?

RENÉE

I don't want you to be mad.

ANGIE

Then why did you cancel the trip?

RENÉE

(Becoming angry)

I told you --- I'm just real uncomfortable with people.

(ANGIE stands there. This is not enough.)

And I'm real uncomfortable right now.

RENÉE

(With rising anger)

And you're enjoying that, aren't you? Look at you --- standing there like Charlotte the Second, looking at me like I just peed on your rug. Who do you think you are? I told you I had other plans. That wouldn't have hurt your feelings. That would have been good enough for most people. Why didn't you just let it go at that? But, oh no, you had to have more. It was "Trust me," "Tell me the truth." So I trust you. I tell you the truth --- and what do I get for it? A load of shit dumped on my head. I should have known you were lying. People only want you to say what they want to hear.

ANGIE

What about you? Can you listen to what you don't want to hear?

RENÉE

Yes.

ANGIE

Good, because I'm going to tell you what I think, and I don't think you're going to like it.

RENÉE

(A challenge)

Go ahead.

ANGIE

I think you got mad because I didn't take sides with you against Charlotte. You just couldn't stand that, could you? And so to punish me, you're not going camping. You know what I think? You're on a bigger power trip than Charlotte.

RENÉE

(Cutting in)

That's not ---

ANGIE

I thought you were going to listen . . .

(She changes tack.)

You know what else I think? I think there's a hurt little girl named Renée who wishes her mother would stop picking fights so she could go on a camping trip. It's always the kids who have to suffer . . . That's just the way it is, isn't it?

RENÉE looks down. This has hit her hard. She crosses to the bench and sits. ANGIE crosses next to her and sits also. She puts her hand over RENÉE's. Surprised, RENÉE turns and looks at her. ANGIE meets her eye. Embarrassed, RENÉE withdraws her hand.

RENÉE

I'm sorry.

(They sit in silence for a moment.)

I can borrow Sherlock's tent.

ANGIE

You don't need to. Mine's big enough for two.

RENÉE

What do you want me to bring?

ANGIE

Whatever you want. It's your day off.

RENÉE

(Getting up uncertainly)

I gotta go . . . get things ready.

ANGIE

Meet me down here after dinner.

RENÉE

Okay.

(She starts to go.)

ANGIE

Renée!

(She turns.)

I'm glad you changed your mind.

RENÉE gives her a shy smile and stumbles off. ANGIE picks up a piece of rope and begins to knot it.

TONI sneaks out from behind the canoe shack and tries to head back towards camp without being seen. As she crosses up left, ANGIE suddenly stands up and sees her.

ANGIE

Toni!

(TONI turns.)

What are you doing here?

TONI

(Startled)

Vanessa sent me to get some extra life jackets.

ANGIE

The life jackets are that way.

(She points down right.)

In the canoe shack.

TONI

No, but there's two of them on the path up to camp.

ANGIE

On the path?

TONI

Yeah. Some of the little kids forgot to take them off, and then when they remembered, they just took them off and left them . . .

(ANGIE doesn't believe her.)

. . . right there on the path. So Vanessa sent me to get them.

ANGIE

Toni, don't lie to me.

TONI

I'm not. Honest.

ANGIE

You're cutting class again, aren't you?

TONI

No.

ANGIE

Toni, I can live with the fact you don't trust me, but it kills me how stupid you must think I am.

TONI

What?

ANGIE

Lying to me all the time. It's an insult.

TONI

I'm not lying! That's an insult! If I was Renée I bet you wouldn't say I was lying. I bet I could tell you the biggest lie in the world if I was Renée, and you'd believe every word.

ANGIE

(Evenly)

That depends on whether or not she had lied to me before. You lied to me about being down here during rest hour.

TONI

No, I didn't!

ANGIE
Toni! Sherlock told me you made that whole thing up about "mentorships."

TONI
Sherlock's a queer.
(This stops ANGIE cold.)
She smokes a pipe.
(TONI is watching ANGIE closely.)

ANGIE
I don't want you spending any more time down here away from your cabin.

TONI
Why not?

ANGIE
Because none of the other girls do it.

TONI
What's that got to do with it?

ANGIE
Well, Toni, like it or not, this is summer camp, and summer camp has classes and bells, and whether or not you like it, that's the system around here, and you're just going to have to follow it.

TONI
And what if I don't?

ANGIE
If you don't, then I guess that will have to be between you and Charlotte.

TONI
Oh, so you're going to turn me in?

ANGIE
If there is some problem at the camp, it's my responsibility to let the director know about it.

TONI
And if there's some problem at the camp, is it my responsibility to tell the director?

ANGIE

(Evenly)
If you felt that you had to.

TONI

Good.

(She sits.)

ANGIE

Toni, go back to your swimming class.

TONI

(Dangerous)
What if I don't want to? What if the "hurt little girl named Toni" wants to stay here with you?

ANGIE

(A long pause)
Suit yourself.

She turns and exits into the canoe shack. TONI takes one of the ropes and begins beating on a pier piling. LISA shows up. She's wearing a bathing suit and carrying a pine cone and an envelope.

LISA

Hi, Toni.

(TONI turns her head, and then turns back to her pier piling without acknowledging LISA's greeting. LISA approaches her gingerly.)

Hi, Toni.

(TONI continues whipping.)

TONI

(Not looking)
What are you doing down here?

LISA

I'm going to canoeing class.

TONI

I didn't hear the bell. Where's the rest of your cabin?

LISA

I'm early.

TONI

You're going to get in trouble.

LISA

I brought you a present.

TONI

(Still not looking)

What is it?

LISA

It's a bird feeder. I made it out of a pine cone.

(She holds it out. TONI stops whipping and reaches out to take it.)

TONI

(She drops it and looks at her hands.)

What is this shit?!

LISA

It's peanut butter. That's what holds the sunflower seeds on it.

TONI

Shit. Look at this.

(She wipes her hands on the dock.)

LISA

You're supposed to hang it up in a tree, and then the birds come and eat off it.

TONI

You think the birds are going to starve or something if you don't feed them?

LISA

No.

TONI

Then why make a stupid feeder for them?

LISA

It's just . . . something to do.

TONI

And what's this?

(She points to the envelope in LISA's hand.)

LISA

Nothing . . . It's a poem I wrote last night.

(She gives it to her.)

TONI

(Stuffing it into her pocket)

Yeah, well, I got better things to do than read poetry and take care of birds who can already take care of themselves.

LISA

You mean like catching the monster?

TONI

(Yelling)

There isn't any monster!

LISA

(Disappointed)

Sure, Toni.

TONI

And you can just stop following me around and giving me stupid presents I don't want.

(She kicks the pine cone into the woods.)

LISA

(Looking down)

Sure, Toni.

TONI

And the only time I want to see you is when the whole camp is together, like at campfires or at dinner. You got that?

LISA

(Very quiet)

Yeah.

TONI

Good, because that's the way it ought to be.

(LISA is struggling with tears.)

Get out of here! Get out of here!

She lashes the rope like a whip. Frightened, LISA takes a few steps back, and then she runs off right, towards the swimming area. TONI watches her. After she has left, TONI takes the envelope out of her pocket. She opens it and begins to read the poem, as the lights fade.

(BLACKOUT)

(END OF ACT I)

ACT II

SETTING: **The same as Act I. It is after supper, but not yet dusk. A canoe is tucked up under the dock, visible to the audience, but not from the top of the dock. It is packed with camping equipment.**

AT RISE: **Voices are heard from the canoe shack.**

RENÉE

I can't see! Wait!

ANGIE

Come on! We have to practice.

RENÉE

Wait! I'm going to break my neck! Wait! Where are you going?
(The door of the canoe shack opens a crack.)

ANGIE

I have to make sure the coast is clear.

The door opens wider and ANGIE enters. She is wearing a pillowcase which has been painted with a monster face. The pillowcase is pulled down snug, so that only her hands extend out the bottom.

ANGIE

(Beckoning with one of her hands)
They're all still at dinner. Come on!
(She turns back to the canoe shack.)
Renée, come on!

RENÉE

(Offstage)
I can't see anything! The eyeholes are in the wrong place.

ANGIE

Then, move your eyes!

RENÉE

Funny . . .

ANGIE

Here. Here's my hand. We have to see if we can get into the canoe like this.

RENÉE

I don't know about the canoe, but I'm sure there are a few state institutions we could get into.

ANGIE

Come on! Quick, before somebody comes down here and sees us.

(She reaches in and takes RENÉE's hand. RENÉE enters. Her costume is even more fantastic than ANGIE's.)

Come on, Renée! Trust me.

RENÉE

Oh, yeah, sure. I've already lost my pride, my eyesight . . .

ANGIE

Okay, now look, here's the edge of the dock. Just sit down, here . . . like this.

(She sits, taking RENÉE down with her.)

See --- you can feel the edge with your hands. Now just ease yourself over the edge. The sand is only three feet below.

RENÉE

I can't believe I let you talk me into this. You know, I never would have made this costume if I thought I'd be the one to end up wearing it.

ANGIE

Well, I already made one for myself. Besides, it suits you better. Now, look . . . It's only three feet to the ground, so just jump.

RENÉE

Just jump she says.

(She does.)

ANGIE

Now, all you have to do is step into the canoe.

RENÉE

Where's the canoe?

ANGIE

Here! Listen . . .

(She thumps the side of the canoe.)

Just step over it and sit.

(RENÉE misses and falls over.)

RENÉE

Oh, shit!

ANGIE

Come on! No big deal! Here it is. Here. Touch the gunwale. Okay. Now, over.

(RENÉE finally makes it into the canoe.)

There --- piece of cake.

RENÉE

I can't believe I'm doing this.

ANGIE

You did it.

RENÉE

No, I can't believe I'm doing this in front of a cabin of little girls who used to look up to me.

ANGIE

Oh, come on. Pretend it's Halloween.

RENÉE

(Taking off her pillowcase)

I never did Halloween.

(ANGIE looks at her.)

I'm the kid with no childhood, remember?

ANGIE

(Taking off her case)

Well, take my word for it. This is not that big a deal.

RENÉE

For you, maybe.

ANGIE

I can't believe you're worried about what people will think if you put a pillowcase over your head and act a little bit silly at a campfire one night.

RENÉE

Yeah, well, I am.

ANGIE

I mean, to me --- Renée --- look at you! You've got this haircut wilder than anybody I've ever seen, a ring in your nose, a ring in your eyebrow, and a tattoo. I mean, it's like you're in costume every day.

RENÉE

(Touchy)

This is me.

ANGIE

I didn't mean it like that. I just wouldn't have the nerve to dress like you in real life.

RENÉE

I wear what I feel like.

ANGIE

But it's so different.

RENÉE

(Defensive)

So what? I like the way I look.

ANGIE

But other people are going to make judgements about you because of the way you dress.

RENÉE

I want them to. That way they leave me alone.

ANGIE

Now, see, that would scare me to death.

RENÉE

(Irritated)

That's because you're "normal." I'm not. When you're normal, it's okay to put a pillowcase on and act like an idiot once in a while. That's normal deviation. But it's pretty scary for me, because underneath the costume, I really am different.

ANGIE

(Angry)

I didn't say I was normal. I said I had a normal family. That's not the same thing.

RENÉE

Yeah, but it gives you membership privileges. And if you want to know the truth, the way you dress would scare me.

ANGIE

Why's that?

RENÉE

Because if I dressed like that, it would be because I wanted to make other people think I was just like them, and if I dressed that way long enough, I probably would be just like them.

ANGIE

Believe it or not, I dress the way I do, because I like it.

RENÉE

Yeah, well, so do I.

(They don't say anything.)

ANGIE

You're wishing you weren't going, aren't you?

RENÉE

I can think of better ways to spend my day off.

ANGIE

Is that your solution to people who don't agree with everything about you? Just get rid of them?

RENÉE

Is that your solution? To pretend you don't mind?

(Suddenly CHARLOTTE's voice is heard off left.)

CHARLOTTE

You see, Vanessa, the trouble with Angie is, she doesn't have enough experience to understand a child like Toni.

ANGIE

It's Charlotte! She's coming!

RENÉE

Shhhh! Let's hide.

They duck further under the dock out of sight. CHARLOTTE and VANESSA enter. CHARLOTTE has her arm linked through VANESSA's. They cross onto the dock, unaware of the two women under the dock.

CHARLOTTE

A child like Toni needs to know exactly where the limits are.

VANESSA

I don't think Angie knows exactly where they are.

ANGIE

(Whispering)

Me? What?!

RENÉE

Shhhh!

CHARLOTTE

Oh? She seems to be a responsible girl to me. Maybe a little over-protective …

VANESSA

Angie is really naive about the world.

CHARLOTTE

Really? She seems so mature to me.

ANGIE

(Whispering)

That little bitch . . .

RENÉE

Be quiet!

VANESSA

I don't think she understands the difference between the grown-up world and the child's world.

CHARLOTTE

Then she's letting herself in for a lot of pain.

VANESSA

That's what I tried to tell her.

ANGIE

She couldn't tell me anything!

RENÉE

(Putting her hand over Angie's mouth)

Shhhh!

CHARLOTTE

Sit down, Vanessa. I have a story I want to tell you. It's about a young woman much like Angie. She thought things would always stay the same for her even after she grew up. It's a sad story.

(She indicates the bench. VANESSA sits. CHARLOTTE sits also.)

This woman . . . she was always a loner, off by herself. Quiet, rebellious girl. And of course, she wasn't very happy that way. And then one day a new girl showed up at school. And the new girl didn't know how to meet people. Pretty soon the two of them began to get together, and the next thing you knew, they were best friends. You never saw closer friends. They went everywhere together. And that's how it was all through high school for them. They just weren't interested in boys.

VANESSA

Sounds kind of strange.

CHARLOTTE

(Defensive)

I don't know about that. You know, boys in high school aren't always the most stimulating companions for girls.

VANESSA

Depends on the boy.

CHARLOTTE

(Miffed)

It's a fact that many high school girls are simply more mature than the boys, and it takes several years for the boys to catch up to their level. I'm sure you had trouble finding boys which were up to your speed in high school.

VANESSA

(Smiling)

Well, yeah, you might say.

CHARLOTTE

Exactly. And that was the case with these girls. They never dated.

VANESSA

They never dated at all?

CHARLOTTE

Not while they were in school. You see, they found they enjoyed being with each other more than being with boys. They even went bowling on prom night.

VANESSA

With each other?

CHARLOTTE

And they had a wonderful time.

(VANESSA shakes her head.)

Anyway, my friend was the younger one, and so when her best friend graduated, she still had another year of high school. Her friend went away to college and so, suddenly, after four years of doing everything together, the friends found themselves hundreds of miles apart living in two different worlds.

VANESSA

Probably good for them.

CHARLOTTE

Painful, Vanessa, painful. They wrote a lot, of course, as girls do, but it wasn't until Christmas vacation they would be together. My friend was just counting the days. She had made all these plans for things they would do together. I think secretly she was hoping that her friend would decide not to go back to college.

VANESSA

That was pretty naive.

CHARLOTTE

She was naive. Well, anyway, to make a long story short, her friend called and asked her to meet her at the train station. She said she had a surprise. So my friend borrowed a car and drove to the station, which was in another town,

CHARLOTTE (Cont'd)
and waited two hours because the train was late. And finally it pulled in. And do you know what that surprise was?

VANESSA
(Yawning)
A box of candy?

CHARLOTTE
A boyfriend. The friend had brought a boyfriend with her from college to spend the vacation with her. And she expected that her best friend would be as delighted with him as she was.

VANESSA
And she wasn't?

CHARLOTTE
(Irritated at VANESSA's insensitivity)
No, of course she wasn't. She didn't want to have to share her vacation with this eager little tail-wagging cocker spaniel of a boyfriend following them around everywhere, pawing and sniffing at everything. But you know how it is with other people's pets. They just can't see it.

VANESSA
Sounds like a real drag.

CHARLOTTE
A real drag. That would describe this man. He was a real drag. So my friend cancelled all her plans and stayed in her room. She wouldn't even answer the phone calls from her friend.

VANESSA
Sounds like she was jealous.

CHARLOTTE
(Distressed by VANESSA's narrow interpretation)
I don't know that I would say she was jealous. I would say she was disappointed in her friend's taste - and justifiably so. She felt let down. No, I would not call her jealous. She was not a petty person, and he was certainly not anything she would compare herself to. No, not jealous. Definitely not jealous. But, getting back to the story --- they never really did get together after that. There were a few letters, very superficial. And then in the spring, my friend received the wedding announcement. In fact, she was asked to be the maid of honor. She sent a present, of course, but she didn't go.

VANESSA

That wasn't very nice.

CHARLOTTE

No, it wasn't, but it wasn't all her fault. You see nobody had seen what she was headed for. She had built up this big daydream in her mind of rooming through college with her friend, and taking classes with her, and then after college they would go to Europe together, and then they would run a summer camp together, the two of them. Of course, this was all completely unrealistic, but how was my friend to know that? Who was going to tell her that women don't grow up and do these kinds of things together? You see, she had never gotten her little-girl picture of life out of her head.

VANESSA

God, I guess not. Didn't she want a boyfriend?

CHARLOTTE

It never even occurred to her.

VANESSA

Weird.

CHARLOTTE

Well, don't be too harsh on my friend, Vanessa, because that young woman was me.

VANESSA

(Shocked)

You?

CHARLOTTE

Sad, but true. Yes, I was that naive young woman who let her friendship get a little too carried away. You know, it took me years to get over it.

VANESSA

But you started going out with guys didn't you?

CHARLOTTE

Oh, yes. But they never meant as much to me. I never really gave them a chance to. That's why I've never married. No, Vanessa, that misguided experience left me scarred for life. If I had just had some strong adult guidance during those years . . . someone who had insisted that I spend more time with other girls, and get out and learn how to act around boys . . . Well, I just don't think things would have gotten so . . . out of balance.

VANESSA

I'll say.

CHARLOTTE

But, you see, Vanessa, this is why when I see a child like Toni who has a tendency towards these kinds of attachments, I see it as my responsibility to step in and do something. And it isn't easy. These things start out very subtly, but by the time they become obvious, it's too late to stop them, without a great deal of pain on all sides. So, really, it's kinder to intervene in the initial stages. It's difficult to be in my position, Vanessa. No one understands me. The girls are afraid of me, or they think I am too strict, when all that's in my heart is to save them from pain, to help them have a girlhood they will remember forever. It's all too short, Vanessa . . . this precious period of life called girlhood. All too soon, these girls will go off and get married, and devote themselves to raising a family. These are precious, precious days, Vanessa. We must make sure that nothing takes their girlhood away. It's the best time of their lives. You don't think unkindly of me, do you, Vanessa?

VANESSA

Me? No. I was just thinking about Angie.

CHARLOTTE

What about Angie?

VANESSA

Well, I was thinking that she might be forming one of those unhealthy attachments.

CHARLOTTE

Oh? With whom?

VANESSA

Renée.

(ANGIE begins to get out of the boat, but RENÉE stops her.)

RENÉE

(Whisper)

Don't! I want to hear this.

ANGIE

(Whisper)

But she has no right ---

RENÉE

Shhhh!

VANESSA

And I think Renée's interest in her is definitely unhealthy.

CHARLOTTE

Really?

VANESSA

To tell you the truth, I think Renée's coming on to her.

ANGIE starts up again, but this time RENÉE grabs her violently, concentrating on what is being said. Frightened by RENÉE's fierce expression, ANGIE returns to her seat.

CHARLOTTE

I'm not sure I understand what you're saying, Vanessa.

VANESSA

Coming on to her --- You know --- making passes, flirting --- sexual energy --- you know.

CHARLOTTE

This is very serious.

VANESSA

Yeah, it is. I don't like to see my friend hustled by a lesbian.

CHARLOTTE

Vanessa, that is a very serious charge to make against someone.

VANESSA

But it's true.

CHARLOTTE

But can you prove it?

VANESSA

Oh, I don't think she hides it. Ask her. She'll probably just come right out and tell you.

CHARLOTTE

(In shock)

I can't believe it.

VANESSA

It's very "in" in some circles to be a dyke. Some women even try to pretend they are when they aren't.

CHARLOTTE

(The foundations of her world are crumbling.)

I don't believe it.

VANESSA

I just wish she'd lay off Angie. But I guess that's better than having her hitting on little girls.

CHARLOTTE

(Jolted back to her position)

Vanessa, are you sure about what you're telling me?

VANESSA

Ask her.

CHARLOTTE

All right. I'll have to talk to her.

(She turns, and then turns back.)

Vanessa . . . I'll talk to Angie too.

VANESSA

I wasn't going to say anything to her.

CHARLOTTE

Well, I'm sure it's going to come as a shock. It's very painful when we find out that our friends are not what they appear. I think it will be best if she hears it from me.

VANESSA

Oh, yeah.

CHARLOTTE

This is the kind of thing that needs to be handled very carefully. Rumors like this can ruin a camp. It could take years and years to live it down. And, of course, my not being married . . . I would be an easy target. You won't

CHARLOTTE (Cont'd)
mention this to the other counselors, will you?

VANESSA
No, but I don't think anybody would be surprised.

CHARLOTTE
Oh, this is terrible. Vanessa, I appreciate your telling me.
(She turns again to leave.)

VANESSA
Where are you going?

CHARLOTTE
I'm going to see if Renée has left yet for that camping trip. I want to speak to her as soon as possible.

VANESSA
Good.

CHARLOTTE
Thank you for your support, Vanessa. You know, it's trials like this, that test the true mettle of a counselor. The kind of loyalty and discretion you have shown me here today are the kind of qualities I would take into consideration when I was hiring an assistant director. I won't forget this.

VANESSA smiles, and CHARLOTTE exits up left. VANESSA crosses and exits off right. RENÉE, a look of cold determination on her face, climbs out of the canoe. ANGIE, stunned, follows.

ANGIE
Renée! Wait! Where are you going?
(RENÉE doesn't answer. She starts to climb up on the pier. ANGIE grabs her leg.)
Wait!

RENÉE
(Turning violently on her)
Don't touch me!

ANGIE

(Still holding on)

Renée ---

RENÉE

Don't touch me..

ANGIE

(She lets go.)

Then don't leave. Tell me where you're going.

RENÉE

I'm going back to my cabin to meet with Charlotte.

ANGIE

Don't do that! You don't have to. We could still leave right now. She won't know.

RENÉE

Oh, great. And how long do you plan to stay on the island? Or do you think Charlotte is going to have an attack of amnesia in the next twenty-four hours? Or maybe you think she'll just wake up tomorrow morning, look in the mirror and say, "You know, I believe I'm a dyke," come out to everyone at breakfast, and lose her job before I have to quit mine?

ANGIE

But you're not a lesbian!

(RENÉE looks at her in disbelief.)

You're not.

RENÉE

Of course I am.

ANGIE

But . . . I mean, you don't have to . . . Nobody really knows for sure here . . . I mean, you could just . . .

RENÉE

(Cutting her off)

I love women. I love them better than men do. I'm proud of that. I would be insulted if anybody believed I was straight.

ANGIE

But it isn't anybody's business who you sleep with.

RENÉE

(With a bitter laugh)

Oh, give me a fucking break! It's everybody's business. It always was and it always will be. As if you didn't make it your business who I slept with! As if that wasn't the main reason you've been so interested in me! You straight girls are always cruising me, looking for a thrill --- until your mother comes to get you. Looks like Mommy's here, Angela --- better tell Renée to go home.

ANGIE

That's not true! I didn't know!

RENÉE

The hell you didn't! You know something? I never met a straight woman who wasn't schizophrenic - and you are no exception. You've all got this lesbian half that you let out of the closet for pajama parties, or late nights in the dormitory, or for those drinking bouts with your best friend. But you don't ever let your straight side meet that other half. Let me tell you something, Angie --- You straight women are easier than any dyke I could pick up in the bars. You're just not worth the trouble.

(She gets up and leaves. ANGIE is stunned for a moment, but then she leaps onto the dock and runs after RENÉE, who is offstage by now.)

ANGIE

Renée!

(Suddenly TONI steps in front of her path.)

TONI

Are you looking for somebody?

ANGIE

You're not supposed to be down here.

TONI

I'm here with my cabin. We're going to have a campfire. Hear them?

(The sound of the girls is heard off left. TONI smiles.)

Why don't you and Renée come too? It's important for us young girls to have the right kind of role models.

Frightened, ANGIE looks at TONI, turns, and exits abruptly into the canoe shack. TONI slips into the bushes.

SHERLOCK enters with her cabin: RITA, MICHELLE, JENNIFER, and SARAH. She also has with her RENÉE's

cabin: LISA, STEPHANIE, LAURIE, and SUSAN. These younger girls are considerably more subdued in the presence of the oldest cabin.

During this scene the sun is setting, and the stage begins to get dark. The campers are all carrying their blankets. Some of them carry wood.

SHERLOCK

Okay, girls! Here we are! This is the place!

(The girls are all excited. Some of them dump their blankets down. The older girls run out onto the dock.)

RITA

(To MICHELLE)

Hey, you wanna show Renée's cabin the dead camper?

SHERLOCK

Hey! Come back here! Nobody out on the dock!

MICHELLE

Aw, come on, Sherlock!

JENNIFER

(Holding onto MICHELLE)

Look! The sun's setting!

SHERLOCK

It's going to be dark soon. I'm not going to dive into the lake after one of you girls.

RITA

Why not? Scared of Toni's monster?

(The older girls laugh.)

JENNIFER

Yeah, Sherlock! Scared of Toni's monster?

LISA

(To JENNIFER)

Shut up! What do you know about it?

JENNIFER

I know she's lying.

LISA

How do you know?

JENNIFER

Because we came down here today, so Toni could show us the body of the dead camper, and it was nothing but an old hot dog bag.

LISA

Maybe you weren't looking in the right place.

SARAH

We were looking where Toni was pointing. Maybe she wasn't looking in the right place.

JENNIFER

Yeah, maybe Toni isn't looking in the right place.

LISA

You shut up!

STEPHANIE

Lisa, don't fight with them.

JENNIFER

Hey, where is Toni anyway?

SHERLOCK

(Looking around and calling)

Toni! Has anybody seen her?

LISA

She was just ahead of us on the path.

MICHELLE

Toni's scared of the dark. She won't go far.

LISA

(Getting up)

Toni! Toni!

JENNIFER

(To SHERLOCK)

You going to organize a search party?

SHERLOCK

Let's give her a chance to show up. Who's going to help us build a fire here? Stephanie? How about you and Lisa? The rest of you, come over here and get in a circle. We're going to play a game.

(LISA and STEPHANIE move to the center and begin to lay the fire. The others sit down. JENNIFER starts to sit down between SHERLOCK and SARAH.)

JENNIFER

I want to sit next to Sherlock.

SARAH

What are you, some kind of queer?

(The older girls laugh.)

RITA

Jennifer has a crush on Sherlock.

JENNIFER

No, I don't! I just don't want the smoke to blow in my face, that's all.

SARAH

She's queer. Jennifer likes girls. Ooo-oo.

JENNIFER

(Frightened)

No, I don't.

SARAH

Yes, you do. You're always trying to hang on my arm.

(JENNIFER moves away from SARAH to sit in a different spot.)

RITA

Don't sit next to me! Help! Faggot!

(They scramble to get away from her.)

SHERLOCK

Sarah! Rita! Jennifer, sit down. We're going to play a game.

SARAH
Not here! Don't sit here!

SHERLOCK
Sarah! Jennifer . . . Here's a place.
(She indicates a seat between herself and MICHELLE.)

SARAH
Watch out, Michelle!

JENNIFER
I'm not queer! You're the queers! I saw you chasing each other in the showers!

SARAH
Me? We were playing swat tag.

RITA
Yeah, Jennifer, why were you looking?

JENNIFER
You're queer.

SHERLOCK
Okay! Okay!

MICHELLE
What kind of game are we going to play?

SHERLOCK
We're going to go around in a circle, and take turns telling part of a story, and when the person says "Beep," that means the next person has to finish it. Who wants to start it . . . Michelle?

MICHELLE
Somebody else.

SHERLOCK
Sarah?

SARAH
What kind of story?

SHERLOCK

Any kind.

RITA

Tell us about that book you're reading.

(SARAH starts to laugh uncontrollably.)

JENNIFER

What book?

RITA

Tell her, Sarah.

SARAH

(Through her self-conscious laughter)

Rita! Shut up!

JENNIFER

What? Tell me!

SARAH

(Sneaking a look at SHERLOCK)

I'll tell you later.

JENNIFER

Tell me now.

RITA

Yeah, Sarah . . . Tell her about the scene on the beach when the lifeguard finds her alone on the beach . . . The one you read to me . . .

SARAH

You tell.

SHERLOCK

Okay, Rita. You start.

RITA

Okay . . . There's this lifeguard, and he's named Brad.

(SARAH is hysterical with laughter.)

And when he sits on top of the lifeguard chair he looks like a bronze god on a pedestal . . . (SARAH starts to wrestle with her, trying to cover her mouth.) . . . And he sees Marlene . . . But Marlene doesn't know he's there . . .

SARAH

Stop it!

RITA

It's your book!

SARAH

No, it isn't.

RITA

Yes, it is. You brought it to camp.

SHERLOCK

Okay. I'll start. Once upon a time there was a . . . a . . . . man who went fishing.

RITA

Brad.

(Gales of laughter)

SHERLOCK

A boy. It was a little boy, and one day he woke up real early in the morning and he got his rod . . .

RITA

(Bursting out laughing)

His rod!

SHERLOCK

He got his fishing gear and took a boat and went out in the middle of the lake. And he sat there a long time, when all of a sudden he saw the line move, so he grabs his rod.

(RITA and SARAH explode into laughter again. SHERLOCK tries to ignore them.)

And he reels in the line, and . . . Beep!

(She points to MICHELLE.)

Your turn.

MICHELLE

Me? No!

SHERLOCK

(Prompting)

He reels it in and . . .

MICHELLE

It's an old tennis shoe.

SARAH

A Reebok.

MICHELLE

Yeah, a Reebok.

JENNIFER

With orange laces.

MICHELLE

I'm telling it! So it's a Nike. And it smells bad.

(They laugh.)

And he looks inside and . . . . Beep!

(She points to SARAH.)

SARAH

And there's somebody's foot still in it.

JENNIFER

That's how come it smells.

SARAH

And so he puts it in the boat to take it to the police and suddenly . . . Beep!

(She points to RITA.)

RITA

And suddenly he notices this little hole in the bottom of the boat and the water is coming in faster and faster, and beep!

(She points to JENNIFER.)

JENNIFER

(Very excited)

Me? I don't know what to say! And he takes the foot out of the shoe, so he can use it to bail out the water, but just when he does that . . . beep!

(She points to SHERLOCK.)

SHERLOCK

Let's give the other cabin a turn.

LISA

The fire's done.

SHERLOCK

Great. We'll light it in a minute. You and Stephanie join the circle.

LISA

Toni's not back yet.

SHERLOCK

She'll be here.

LISA

What if she's lost?

SHERLOCK

She's not lost. She's probably watching us right now. Lisa, why don't you take a turn?

LISA

I wasn't paying attention.

SHERLOCK

Okay - Susan. How about Susan?

SUSAN

(Very intimidated by the older girls)

I forgot. What happened?

JENNIFER

(Always willing to pull rank)

He was bailing the water out of the boat.

SUSAN

Oh, yeah . . .

(She talks very slowly to stall for time.)

He's bailing the water out of the boat and . . . he's bailing and he's bailing . . .

(A long pause)

I can't think of anything.

JENNIFER

Just say anything!

SUSAN

I can't think of anything.

LAURIE

Just say he heard a noise.

SUSAN

And he heard a noise.

(Another long pause)

JENNIFER

What was it?

SUSAN

It was . . .

(Long pause)

Beep!

(She points to LAURIE.)

LAURIE

(Picking up the cue)

It was this deep slimy breathing.

(She illustrates, very seriously, trying to scare the girls.)

RITA

It's Brad!

(The older girls laugh.)

SHERLOCK

It's Laurie's turn, Rita. Let her tell the story.

MICHELLE

Come on. Let her finish.

LAURIE

(Again, very serious)

And so the boy starts to turn around to see who it is, when suddenly he sees this hand reaching up on the side of the boat . . .

RITA

Groping for his rod!

(Laughter)

SHERLOCK

Rita!

RITA

Sorry.

LAURIE

And so this hand reaches up and it starts to tip the boat back and forth, back and forth.

She puts her arm around her companions and begins to lean from side to side. It catches on and soon the whole circle is laughing and swaying. LAURIE's voice becomes very singsong. TONI has crept out of the bushes and is standing behind LISA.

LAURIE

And it's going back and forth, and back and forth, and the boy is getting seasick, but the hand just keeps rocking . . . back and forth and back and forth and back and forth. And then suddenly the hand reaches up and grabs him!

(At this point in the story, TONI reaches out from behind and grabs LISA by the neck. LISA screams and screams. TONI does not let go immediately. The group freezes.)

TONI

(Finally releasing LISA)

It's only me.

SHERLOCK

(Angry)

Toni, is that your idea of a joke?

TONI

What? What did I do?

(To LISA)

Did I scare you? Did I?

(LISA, still in shock, shakes her head.)

See, she's not scared. It was just a story.

(TONI sits.)

Whose turn is it? Mine?

(Nobody says anything.)

What's the matter? Laurie started it. She was rocking everybody. Come on, Lisa, tell them it was a joke.

LISA

(Miserable)

It was a joke.

TONI

See? It was a joke. So . . . Whose turn is it? Is it my turn? Can I go?

SHERLOCK

All right.

TONI

So he pulls the fingers back one by one, breaking them like match sticks, and the hand goes back in the water. And he looks over the side of the boat to see what it was, only he sees this piece of paper floating on the water. He pulls it out and unfolds it.

(At this point, TONI takes out LISA's poem and unfolds it.)

And it reads:

"When I lie in bed at night and look at all the stars,
I like to think about you, what a special friend you are ---"

LISA

(Horrified, she pleads with TONI.)

Toni . . .

TONI

(Giving LISA a big smile, she continues to read. LISA, mortified, shrinks back.)

"I think about how strong you are and brave and funny too,
And wish that you were here right now, and I could sleep with you."

RITA

Did you write that?

TONI

Nope. What do you think I am, queer?

SARAH

Who wrote it?

TONI

Some queer.

JENNIFER

I bet I know. I bet Lisa wrote it.

SHERLOCK

(Rising)

Okay, Toni. Give me that.

TONI

No, it's mine. Some queer gave it to me. I'm going to finish reading it.

SHERLOCK

(Crossing to her)

Give it to me.

TONI

(Standing up)

No.

SHERLOCK

Did you hear what I said?

TONI

Did you hear what I said?

SHERLOCK

(Snatching the paper)

Sit down.

TONI

Give me back my poem, bitch!

SHERLOCK

Sit down!

TONI

You sit down!

(She gives her the finger.)

Sit on this!

(SHERLOCK grabs her hand as she makes the gesture and twists her arm into a hammerlock.)

Ow! You fucking bitch! You queer! Let go of me!

SHERLOCK

Michelle, will you take everyone back up to their cabins. I'll be up in a minute.

MICHELLE

(Springing into action)

Okay. Everybody get with a buddy. Stay on the trail.

(The girls, wide-eyed at TONI's action, pair off quickly.)

Okay, let's go!

TONI

(She has been struggling through all of this. Now she begins to scream.)

Fuck you! Fuck you! I'll kill you! You fucking bitch! You faggot! You smoke a pipe! I've seen you! Sherlock smokes a pipe! You're going to die for this!

(As the girls head off, ANGIE, hearing TONI scream, comes out of the canoe shack.)

ANGIE

(To SHERLOCK)

What's going on here?

TONI

Angie does it with girls! Angie does it with Renée! Angie's a homo!

(Turning to SHERLOCK)

You fucking queer!

(She slugs SHERLOCK in the face and runs off. SHERLOCK staggers.)

ANGIE

Are you okay?

SHERLOCK

I don't know. My nose.

ANGIE

Did she break it?

SHERLOCK

I don't know.

ANGIE

You better go up to the infirmary.

SHERLOCK

What's wrong with that kid?

ANGIE

You want me to go with you?

SHERLOCK

No, I'll be okay. Stay down here. See if Toni comes back.

ANGIE

You sure you're okay?

SHERLOCK

Yeah. I'm going to break that girl's neck.

She exits. ANGIE crosses to the bench. She sits. RENÉE enters. She doesn't look at ANGIE, but crosses right in front of her, headed for the canoe. ANGIE watches her. She crosses to the edge of the dock and watches RENÉE, who is gathering up her gear.

ANGIE

(Quietly)

What are you doing?

RENÉE

(Not looking up)

Getting my stuff.

ANGIE

You're leaving . . . ?

(RENÉE doesn't say anything.)

Need a hand?

RENÉE

Nope.

RENÉE carries her gear to the edge of the dock. ANGIE reaches out for her to hand the bundles to her. RENÉE ignores the gesture and slings them up on the dock. She climbs up on the edge and begins to pick them up. ANGIE takes the sleeping bag. RENÉE looks at her for the first time. She holds out her arms for the bag.

ANGIE continues to hold it.

RENÉE

My sleeping bag.

(ANGIE still doesn't move.)

My sleeping bag.

ANGIE

I'll carry it for you.

RENÉE

(A flash of anger)

The hell you will. Give it to me.

ANGIE

No.

RENÉE

(Recovering her composure)

Then keep it. Whatever turns you on.

(She begins to cross up left. ANGIE drops the bag with a thud. RENÉE turns around. She crosses back to pick it up, but as she reaches for it, ANGIE grabs it again.)

What is this? Let me guess . . . You don't want it, but you don't want anyone else to have it either? Typical closet game.

ANGIE

Why are you blaming me?

RENÉE

Because if it weren't for you, I wouldn't be having to quit.

ANGIE

That's not true.

RENÉE

Angie, grow up. Your hopelessly heterosexual roommate, believe it or not, is jealous of you. If it hadn't been for our camping trip --- the one I said I didn't want to go on --- Vanessa would have been too busy chewing gum to ever think of discussing my sexual orientation with Charlotte.

ANGIE

I'm sorry. What happened?

RENÉE

Well, I went up to my cabin, and I met with Charlotte, and she asked me to step into her office, and I did. And she tells me to sit down, and she closes the door, and she comes around and sits behind her desk. Like it's a fucking movie or something. And she puts her hands together like this, and she leans forward, and she gives me that Christ-on-the-cross look of hers, and she says, "Renée, I have heard something about you that concerns me very much." And I smile back and say, "Oh?" And she gets a little nervous now, because I was supposed to flinch, and she pulls back and puts her hands in her lap. She's looking out the window now. And she says, "Renée, I have been told that you are a homosexual." And I sit there smiling at her, you know, still waiting to hear what it is that concerns her. And this really throws the old bitch. Her face kind of twitches and she says, "Do you have anything to say about that?" And I said, "Well, yes. I really resent anyone using that word to refer to me." She looks a little more relaxed, and she starts to say something, but I cut her off. I say, "I prefer to be called a lesbian." Well, old Charlotte just about dropped her teeth on that one. She gets all flustered, and she walks over to the window and her hands are just going a mile a minute. So I say, "Well, if that's all --- I have to get back down to the waterfront. Angie and I are leaving for an overnight camping trip." And I'm at the door. Well, she really springs into action now. She says, "Renée!" and I say "Yes?" and she says, "Would you sit down please. I'm afraid we're going to need to discuss this." And then of course it's the song and dance about personal lives being kept personal, but once they become public then it becomes her business to guard the reputation of the camp. The usual hypocritical double-standard bullshit. And I just sit there. And she starts to get a little angry, like I should be agreeing with her that I'm a pervert. And she tells me I should know that it's not something people want to know about. And so I ask her why. And she says because they find it disgusting. So I say, "Why is it disgusting for one woman to love another, to want to hold her in her arms all night, to want to touch her the way only another woman can . . . ?" And Charlotte interrupts me. She's got her checkbook out. She tells me she's going to give me the rest of my salary, and enough money to pay for the trip back to Boston. She tells me I will have to leave tonight. She holds out the check and says she doesn't have to do this, but she wants to, just as she knows I will not want to leave in a fashion that will upset the camp. So I ask her, "Is this hush money?" And she says, "This is money in recognition of your concern for the welfare of the girls at Fernlake. Many of them might never get to go to camp again over a thing like this. They may never see the friends they met at camp again." And we look at each other. And then I take the money. That's what happened.

ANGIE

Don't go, Renée.

RENÉE

I should stay and fight? Let's see . . . I could ask Vanessa to recruit the other counselors . . . Or maybe I should organize the eight-year olds . . . ? I know ... their parents!

ANGIE

I'll support you.

RENÉE

(Snorting)

You want to support me? Come out of the closet.

(She takes the sleeping bag out of her arms and starts to leave. Just then CHARLOTTE appears. She is out of breath.)

CHARLOTTE

Oh, there you are, Renée! I wanted to tell you I'd be happy to give you a lift into town to the bus station tonight.

RENÉE

(Brusquely)

Thank you, Charlotte. That would be helpful.

CHARLOTTE

Certainly. Just come by my office when you're ready.

(She turns to leave, but ANGIE intercepts her.)

ANGIE

What are you talking about? Why should Renée leave?

(CHARLOTTE and RENÉE exchange looks.)

RENÉE

(Smiling at CHARLOTTE)

I'll be ready in about fifteen minutes.

CHARLOTTE

(Returning the smile)

Fine. I'll be waiting.

(RENÉE exits. ANGIE, who has not understood the dynamic she has just witnessed, wants to confront the issue.)

ANGIE

(To RENÉE)

Wait! Don't go! You don't have to go!

ANGIE (Cont'd)
(To CHARLOTTE)
She hasn't done anything! Why is she leaving? Renée!

CHARLOTTE
(A hand on ANGIE's shoulder)
I know you'll miss your friend. We all will, but, you see, she understands this is best for the camp too.

ANGIE
But she hasn't done anything!

CHARLOTTE
Angie, today I was told that Renée was a lesbian. I asked her if it was true, and she admitted it.

ANGIE
So what? That doesn't mean she can't be a camp counselor.

CHARLOTTE
Angie, girls like Renée are different. And they know it. She understands why she has to leave. That's part of the choice she has made about the way she lives her life.

ANGIE
No, it isn't.

CHARLOTTE
Well, perhaps I'm not the one in this situation to explain it to you. But I need to tell you that someone at camp has also accused you of being a lesbian.

ANGIE
Who?

CHARLOTTE
I'm not going to tell you who it was, but this person reported to me that she saw you holding hands with Renée.

ANGIE
Toni!

CHARLOTTE
I'm not going to say who it was.

ANGIE

It was Toni.

CHARLOTTE

The point is, the accusation has been made, and now it must be dealt with. Since Renée has agreed to leave, all I need is for you to tell me that it wasn't true.

(ANGIE says nothing.)

The individual who made the report does not have the reputation of always telling the truth, and this is something we can just put behind us right now, just between ourselves. It isn't true, is it, that you were holding Renée's hand? Or, perhaps it was just a little gesture of friendship that was misinterpreted ... ? That was it, wasn't it?

(ANGIE says nothing.)

You know, Angie, if you're trying to protect your friend, it's a little too late for that.

(ANGIE says nothing.)

This is a very serious charge, and even though I am not inclined to believe the person who made it, still, as director of Camp Fernlake, I must follow it up. All you have to tell me is that the girl who reported it was mistaken. You don't even need to go into any details. I am willing to take your word for it.

(ANGIE says nothing. Charlotte walks a little apart from her.)

I know how summer camps are. There's a certain magic about them, the excitement of being away from home, out in the woods, in a very special community. I know how easy it is to get carried away . . . even for you older girls. I understand that.

(Turning to ANGIE)

Really, I do. I was your age once too.

(She turns away again.)

Things happen. Sometimes things we're not even aware of. Things we didn't even want to happen. But let's not hang onto them and let them ruin our lives.

(She turns crisply back to ANGIE.)

So . . . The girl who reported you was mistaken, wasn't she?

(ANGIE still says nothing. CHARLOTTE's expression becomes hard.)

All right, Angie. These heroics of yours are not going to help anyone, and they are going to hurt many, many people. I will have to assume that you are not going to deny the accusation of homosexual behavior. Is it also correct for me to assume that you are not going to resign from your position?

(ANGIE says nothing.)

Well, then, I will have to telephone your parents tomorrow and discuss the charges with them. And I am afraid that it's my duty to dismiss a counselor who exhibits inappropriate sexual behavior in front of the campers. You leave

CHARLOTTE (Cont'd)
me no choice.
(She turns to leave, but turns back again.)
If you do change your mind, leave a note in the office before nine o'clock tomorrow morning.
(She starts to exit. Just then VANESSA enters from the path.)

VANESSA
Hi, Charlotte. Angie.

CHARLOTTE
Vanessa, it seems you're going to be losing your little cabinmate.

VANESSA
Angie?

CHARLOTTE
I'm afraid her loyalty to Renée is greater than her loyalty to Camp Fernlake.

VANESSA
God, Angie, you don't even know her.

ANGIE
If it hadn't been for you, none of this would have happened.

VANESSA
(Looking innocent)
What?

ANGIE
Don't act dumb with me, Vanessa. You know what I'm talking about. You told Charlotte, Renée was a lesbian, and now she's had to quit her job.

VANESSA
Me? Everyone knows Renée's a dyke!

ANGIE
Don't give me that look! Renée and I were under the dock. We heard every word.

VANESSA
Oh, so now she's got you eavesdropping on your roommate!

ANGIE

We were packing for our canoe trip - a trip that's been cancelled thanks to you.

VANESSA

Yeah, thanks to me. Why do you think she was so hot to go out and spend the night on the island with you? God, Angie, would you grow up!

ANGIE

You grow up, Vanessa! Not everybody is obsessed with sex the way you are.

VANESSA

I am not!

ANGIE

Oh, right. You can't even spend a day off without checking into some sleazy motel in Kennebunkport

VANESSA

(Glancing over at CHARLOTTE)

Angie! What are you talking about?

ANGIE

Oh, so I'm supposed to protect your sexuality now, is that it? Everybody else gets reported because you think they're perverted, but the fact you spent the last fourteen hours flat on your back letting some big hairy ape grind away on you, when you didn't even want to, when you didn't even like it . . . I'm supposed to respect that? I'm supposed to consider that normal or something?

VANESSA

God, Angie! I'm sorry you're so upset about Renée, but that's no reason to start making up things like this about me. I'm sorry Charlotte, but I'm not going to stand here and listen to it.

(She starts to exit.)

CHARLOTTE

Wait, Vanessa!

(VANESSA turns.)

You didn't meet a boyfriend yesterday did you?

VANESSA

Charlotte, if you choose to believe what Angie says right now when she's so upset, go ahead. I'm not going to call my roommate a liar.

(She exits.)

CHARLOTTE

(CHARLOTTE makes up her mind.)

Well, Angie, I don't know what you're trying to prove. I really don't. But I have to do my job, which is to run a summer camp. You'll just have to work out your problems in another environment. And I don't mean that harshly. I really don't.

(She looks off in VANESSA's direction.)

You've got some fine friends here.

CHARLOTTE smiles and squeezes her shoulder and exits after VANESSA. ANGIE turns and begins to walk back to the canoe shack. Suddenly SHERLOCK rushes on. It's quite dark now.

SHERLOCK

Angie!

ANGIE

Sherlock! How's your nose?

SHERLOCK

(Breathless)

Never mind my nose . . . Lisa's . . . run away!

ANGIE

What . . . Lisa?

SHERLOCK

She must have run back to the cabin before the others could get there. She left this note on Toni's bed.

(She hands ANGIE a piece of paper like the one on which the poem was written.)

ANGIE

(Reading)

"Dear Toni . . . I'm sorry I'm such a bad person and you don't want to be my friend anymore. I never knew before I was a queer. I'm going away, but I don't think anybody will miss me . . . Lisa."

SHERLOCK

When Michelle and the girls got to the cabin, Toni was already there with the note. She had a knife and was threatening to kill anyone who tried to come in. The nurse had to call the hospital for an ambulance to come get her.

ANGIE

Do you think Lisa's note is serious?

SHERLOCK

I don't know. She's a funny kid. I'm going to check the archery range and the soccer field. The other counselors are checking the cabins and up by the road. Will you keep an eye on the waterfront in case she's headed back down here?

ANGIE

Sure.

SHERLOCK

What a night!

SHERLOCK exits. ANGIE jumps into the canoe and gets a flashlight out of her bag. She hears someone enter above her on the dock, and shines the flashlight in that direction. It's RENÉE.

ANGIE

Who is it?

RENÉE

It's me. Renée. I heard about Lisa. I thought I'd stick around and help look for her. She trusts me. I thought maybe she'd want to talk to me.

ANGIE

I'm leaving camp tomorrow too. I'm quitting my job.

RENÉE

Whatever. Don't think it makes any difference to me.

ANGIE

I don't. I just wanted to tell you.

RENÉE

Fine. You've told me.

ANGIE

Why don't we go around the lake? You go that way, and I'll go this way ---

RENÉE

Fine.

They part awkwardly. ANGIE heads off right towards the swimming area. RENÉE heads off left.

The stage is dark for a minute. A little figure appears from the bushes. It's LISA. She is scratched and disheveled from her flight, and her eyes are wild. She is very, very scared and crying a little. She crosses down to the edge of the dock. She stands there and and sniffles. After a moment she speaks quietly.

LISA

Okay, monster . . . Here I am.
(A pause)
You can come and get me now.
(Nothing happens. She crosses out to the end of one of the ells.)
Here I am. I'm eight years old and nobody else is here.
(A pause)
Right here on the end of the dock.
(Pause)
Not doing anything.
(Pause)
All by myself.
(Pause)
Full of blood.
(When nothing happens, she picks up a rock and throws it into the lake. She yells.)
Hey, monster! Monster!

LISA looks around. She sees TONI's noose on the flagpole and crosses over to it. Slowly she climbs up onto the pier piling. She takes the noose in her hands and looks at it carefully. Then she slips it on over her head.

Just then ANGIE appears down right. She has heard the yelling. She shines the flashlight around the dock. It picks up LISA on the piling with the noose around her neck. LISA freezes. ANGIE,

realizing the gravity of the situation, begins to talk very carefully as she moves towards LISA.

ANGIE

Hi, Lisa.

(LISA doesn't respond.)

Boy, I'm glad we found you. You know everybody at camp is wondering where you are. Everybody's really worried about you.

(LISA still doesn't move.)

We sure missed you. I know your cabin is going to be so happy to see you again.

(She takes a step towards LISA, but LISA pulls back. ANGIE stops and backs up. She turns off the flashlight.)

Why don't we just talk a little bit? There's been a lot going on, hasn't there? Maybe there's something that's been bothering you?

(RENÉE appears down left. LISA has her back to her, but ANGIE can see her. RENÉE takes in the situation immediately. She begins very quietly to sneak up to the flagpole while ANGIE talks.)

Camp is pretty intense sometimes. You know us counselors, we get days off, but you kids don't get any. That's not really fair, is it? It gets pretty exhausting being around so many people all the time, doesn't it? And being away from home. This is your first time away from home, isn't it? I bet you miss your family, don't you?

LISA

No.

ANGIE

Well, sometimes people do. And sometimes they don't. Maybe you're having some trouble with some of your friends here . . . You like your cabin?

LISA

Yes.

ANGIE

You like your counselor?

LISA

Yes.

ANGIE

How about those older girls?

(LISA says nothing.)
Sometimes they play a little rough, don't they?

LISA

No.

ANGIE

I've had a hard time with some of those older girls. That Toni has really hurt my feelings. Did she hurt yours too?

LISA

No.

ANGIE

Well, good. I like Toni. It's been very hard to be her friend, but I like her. You can say it's hard to get along with someone, and still be their friend.

LISA

It isn't Toni's fault.

ANGIE

What isn't Toni's fault?

LISA

That I'm a queer..

RENÉE has gotten to the flagpole. She begins slowly and quietly to uncoil the rope where it's looped around the cleat.

ANGIE

Who says you're a queer?

LISA

That's what I am.

ANGIE

And what is a queer?

LISA

Somebody who likes other girls the way they should like boys.

ANGIE

I see.

LISA

I'm a queer.

ANGIE

I see.

(LISA says nothing.)

The word for what you're talking about is "lesbian." And there's nothing wrong with it.

LISA

If there's nothing wrong with it, how come everybody acts like there is?

ANGIE

Because it's different. Like being left-handed. Most people are born right-handed, but a certain number of people are always going to be born left-handed. Even if they learn to write with their right hand, they're still left-handed. It doesn't mean they're bad or wrong. It just means they're different. And being lesbian doesn't mean you're bad. It just means you would rather be with girls.

LISA

They how come everybody talks about it like it's a bad thing?

ANGIE

Because a lot of people are scared of anything that's different. But that doesn't mean you have to be.

Just then RENÉE hands the end of the rope to LISA and holds out her arms for her to jump down. LISA takes the rope and looks at it. Then she holds out her arms and allows RENÉE to lift her down from the piling. She hugs RENÉE.

RENÉE

I'm really proud of the way you stood up for your friend Toni.

ANGIE

You were braver than I was. I'm the one who let her down.

(ANGIE takes the noose off her neck.)

LISA

Angie, do you know any lesbians?

(ANGIE looks at RENÉE. RENÉE lets go of LISA.)

ANGIE

Some.

LISA

Are there any at camp?

ANGIE

Yes.

(RENÉE, bracing for another betrayal, steps away, her back to ANGIE.)

LISA

Who?

ANGIE

(A pause)

Me. I'm a lesbian.

(Surprised, RENÉE turns to look at her.)

LISA

You are?

ANGIE

Yes. I'm a lesbian.

LISA

Really?

ANGIE

Really. Cross my heart.

(LISA is staring at her. ANGIE makes a monster face.)

Boogah, boogah, boogah!

LISA laughs. She crosses to ANGIE and puts her arms around her. ANGIE looks at RENÉE for the first time since she came out. RENÉE smiles and holds out her hand. ANGIE reaches out and takes it as the lights fade.

BLACKOUT

THE END

WRITERS BLOCK

A Play in Two Acts

by

Laura K. Emack

Cast of Characters

Helen: A retired schoolteacher, SHE is seventy-nine. SHE walks with a cane that she hates. Mentally, SHE is energetic and alert.

Suzanne: Age thirty-two, SHE is attractive, but goes to great lengths to look frumpy. SHE has large breasts and a rich, throaty laugh.

Emily: Age twenty-four, SHE is tall and blonde. SHE spent one season playing in the WNBA. SHE is a fading local celebrity.

Jim: Age forty-two, HE is an affluent divorce lawyer with two failed marriages. Still handsome, HE is developing middle-aged spread.

Betty: Age fifty-eight, SHE is a petite woman working toward a college degree. SHE spent thirty years as a conventional homemaker raising five children.

Gene: A college professor, HE is fifty-three. HE is distinguished-looking in a pallid and ascetic way.

Reporter: SHE is twenty-nine and wears heavy makeup. Her hairdo changes from scene to scene.

Gerald: HE is a sixty-five-year old, wheelchair-bound diabetic with a muscular upper body.

Voices of Dorothy (Helen's daughter) and Joe (Helen's son-in-law)

Scene

Act I: HELEN'S living room near Middleton, a small city on the East Coast.
Act II, Scenes 1-3: BETTY'S living room in Middleton.
Act II, Scene 4: Outdoors on JIM'S wooded, riverfront land.

Time

The present (2004).

ACT I

Scene 1

SETTING: We are in HELEN's cluttered and dusty living room. A front door with a peephole leads to the outdoors. A willow tree overhangs the house. A doorway leads to the kitchen. Most of the room is occupied by a couch and soft chairs. A snow globe sits on the coffee table. Incongruously, a big-screen television dominates the stage rear wall. Two dinner places are set at a card table. A meal has just been eaten. A cane leans against the wall.

AT RISE: HELEN is seated at the table. The other chair is pushed back from the table. HELEN puts sugar and cream into her coffee and stirs it.

SUZANNE

(calling from the kitchen)

Well, I don't like it. I don't like it at all.

(HELEN blows on the coffee to cool it, then coughs.)

SUZANNE

Are you all right, Helen?

HELEN

I'm fine, Dear. What is it that you don't like now?

(SUZANNE enters from the kitchen carefully carrying a cup of tea. SHE sits in the other chair.)

SUZANNE

Betty bringing some stranger here tonight.

HELEN

Bet*ty's* bringing some stranger. The possessive is proper, you see, for it's not Betty herself but the action she took that you dislike. I can't help correcting your grammar, Dear. It's an old habit.

SUZANNE

I don't mind that. It's very important to follow rules. I'm just saying we don't need any newcomers in Writers Block.

HELEN

Well, I don't see it that way. The chances are that Gene won't be coming to meetings for very much longer. And some of us are getting on, Dear.

SUZANNE

That's not true. Gene won't desert us no matter how successful he becomes. Besides, if he ever does leavc, then we especially won't want another female. We'd be four to one if what's her face -

HELEN

(interrupting)

Emily. Her face is Emily.

SUZANNE

If Emily was in and Gene was out.

HELEN

If Emily *were* in and Gene *were* out - oh, never mind. Wouldn't Jim be happy as a raccoon in a corn patch, surrounded by all women!

SUZANNE

We'd be way out of balance. Betty should have checked with the group first.

HELEN

And she did. She tried you several times, but the phone just rang and rang. She stopped by the bookstore too, but it was buttoned up tight.

SUZANNE

That's because Fred decided to close early this year. He says it costs too much to heat the building. I don't really mind. I hate driving in the wintertime. The ice is downright treacherous. I don't venture forth any more than necessary.

HELEN

So you *were* home when Betty called. I told her she should pound relentlessly on your front door. I said "Don't assume, just because she doesn't answer the phone -

SUZANNE

(interrupting)

When I do, it's just some telemarketer.

HELEN

Suzanne Dear, I don't see why you refuse to use an answering machine, especially after your brother bought you one. As to our membership, Gene was out of town and Jim had no objection to adding Emily, so -

SUZANNE

(interrupting)

He knew I didn't want one.

HELEN

What's that now?

SUZANNE

My conceited brother. He's just like my father buying me what he thinks I ought to own instead of something I actually want for my birthday.

(The doorbell rings.)

Shall I get that?

HELEN

Come right in. It isn't locked.

SUZANNE

What do you mean it isn't locked? Helen, what were you thinking?

(SUZANNE rushes to the door. EMILY - tall, blonde and young - pushes it open from the other side and enters. SUZANNE and EMILY collide. After they separate, SUZANNE locks HELEN'S door indignantly.)

EMILY

I'm so sorry! Are you all right?

SUZANNE

I was about to open that door.

EMILY

I'm really sorry.

(EMILY raises her hand, as if she has committed a foul on the court.)

EMILY

My fault.

HELEN

Nonsense! I said to come right in. Emily, I'm Helen and that's Suzanne. She means well.

SUZANNE

The point is, you have to lock your door. We don't live in Leave-it-to-Beaver land. Promise me you'll lock your door from now on.

HELEN

The point is that suppertime is over and meeting time is here. Emily dear, can I offer you a cup of coffee or tea? I have Girl Scout cookies as well. I buy enough to last all year. I stick them in the freezer along with the vegetables from the garden, the little patch I can still manage. I have plenty of room for cookies nowadays. Jim adores the shortbread ones.

SUZANNE

I prefer the mints. They're the originals. But I can't believe how expensive they've gotten! And they put all of eight cookies in a box nowadays. Helen, people on a fixed income can't afford to throw away their money like that.

HELEN

Nonsense! The Girl Scouts are a worthy cause. Would you like coffee or tea, Emily?

EMILY

Just a glass of water, please.

HELEN

No wonder you stay so fit and trim. I'll put ice and a slice of lemon in the glass to liven it up.

SUZANNE

Are you sure? I can do it.

HELEN

I'm entirely sure.

(As HELEN reaches for her cane, SUZANNE rushes to hand it to her. HELEN uses the cane to walk to the kitchen. SUZANNE and EMILY face off in awkward silence. The sound of ice clinking is heard. HELEN returns and hands a glass to EMILY.)

HELEN

There, now. Perhaps you girls can fold up that table and put it away before the others get here.

(EMILY AND SUZANNE clear the dishes, then fold the table and chairs and remove them to the kitchen. HELEN heads toward the couch and sits. SUZANNE brings a plate of cookies from the kitchen and sets it on the coffee table. The doorbell sounds. SUZANNE goes to the door and stares through the peephole. SHE unlocks and opens the door. BETTY - a petite 58 - and JIM - portly, bearded, 42 - enter. SUZANNE re-locks the door.)

SUZANNE

Where's Gene? I thought he was riding up with you.

JIM

Hello to you too, Suzanne. He's not coming. He's doing a reading.

SUZANNE

But Gene never misses a meeting of Writers Block!

BETTY

Well, there's a first time for everything. Hi, Emily. I see you found the place. Have you met Jim?

EMILY

I don't think so.

JIM

Well, I remember seeing you play. Those two free throws at the state championship were awesome. Your composure was amazing.

EMILY

That was a long time ago.

SUZANNE

Gene never misses a meeting. Never!

JIM

If it helps any, Gene said he felt very bad about not being here.

SUZANNE

Badly.

HELEN

No, Suzanne, Jim is right. Gene felt bad.

JIM

(miming a basketball shot.)

So there! Score one for me.

HELEN

Ah, but do you know why you're correct?

JIM

Because feel is an intransitive verb which takes an adjective, not an adverb. Am I right, Teach?

HELEN

You remember so well!

JIM

(giving HELEN a quick, fierce hug.)

Everybody needs one good English teacher in his life. You were mine, Helen.

SUZANNE

Where is Gene reading tonight?

BETTY

At Borders.

EMILY

Like wow!

JIM

You'd think he'd be thrilled, but no. He got miffed at being a last-minute substitution. He made the poor woman at Borders wait all morning while he confirmed the arrangement with his New York agent.

BETTY

I told him he was foolish to jeopardize his chances - they could have opted to find somebody else. I told him nobody minds if he misses a session of Writers Block once in a while.

SUZANNE

Speak for yourself, Betty.

HELEN

No squabbling, boys and girls, or I'll make you stay after school.

JIM

What would we do without you to keep order, Helen?

HELEN

Oh, you'll learn to manage without me.

BETTY

God forbid!

SUZANNE

I like the way we do things now.

HELEN

Speaking of which, it's time to get started.

(EVERYONE sits on the couch and chairs with SUZANNE in an armchair somewhat apart from the others. All take out some typed pages except Suzanne. During the ensuing several speeches, SUZANNE surreptitiously tries to figure out what she's been left out of.)

HELEN

Emily, for your benefit, I'm going to review our procedures here at Writers Block. We meet every other Thursday from seven thirty to ten o'clock. And

HELEN (Cont'd)

I'm a stickler about punctuality. Now, there's one characteristic that distinguishes us from most other writers' groups. We choose one project for special emphasis and we see it through to completion. That writer always reads first with no time limit. Then we divide up the rest of the time, depending on who else would like to read on that particular evening.

BETTY

It's a fair system. Nobody gets neglected and everybody gets to stand in the spotlight.

JIM

Eventually.

HELEN

Now, Gene volunteered to sit this round out in light of his recent success. Betty tells me she offered you a chance to get in on our little competition. It's a play you're writing?

EMILY

I only have like a scene and a half written down.

HELEN

Well, it takes time. Now here's a bit of our history. My memoir - good grief, that has such a sound of finality to it - my "Recollections of a Country Schoolteacher" was our most recent project. Before that we did Gene's novel called *Island Treasure*.

JIM

Which took forever.

BETTY

Any luck finding a publisher yet, Helen?

HELEN

Never mind that. Emily, when a project is finished, that writer is privileged to make the next selection. I made mine and sent the opening pages along to each of you. We begin with a reading aloud by the chosen author.

SUZANNE

But I didn't get a copy! You told me Betty was bringing the copies tonight.

HELEN

Just a little white lie, Dear. Congratulations, Suzanne. The floor is yours.

SUZANNE

But I didn't submit anything to you!

HELEN

Yes, you did.

SUZANNE

I told you I wasn't ready to show that to the group yet!

HELEN

Yes, you did tell me that. Many times. I thought the lady did protest too much.

SUZANNE

Helen, how could you?

HELEN

Because I have your very best interests at heart. I truly do. It's high time you got up and danced.

JIM

Hear, hear!

SUZANNE

I don't like it. I don't like it at all

EMILY

I'm not okay with it either. We should respect each other's choices.

SUZANNE

What's her f-, Emily's right. At least somebody understands how I feel about being set up.

HELEN

Just stand up and read, Dear. Deep inside, I know you want to.

SUZANNE

Well ...

EMILY

Do you want that, Suzanne?

BETTY

Come on. For once in your life, don't be a wallflower.

HELEN

Here's your copy, Dear. Betty did make them for me. I didn't lie about that part.

SUZANNE

Well, I don't like the way it happened, but oh all right.

(SUZANNE stands up and accepts the pages from HELEN.)

JIM

(mimics bugle)

Pah pa pa pah!

BETTY

What in the world was that?

JIM

A bugle, of course. Sorry, but I don't have the real thing handy. It's her first time up. That was the special ritual salute for virgins.

SUZANNE

I can't do this. No, I really can't.

(Gasping, SUZANNE collapses in the chair and buries her face.)

JIM

Oh God, don't tell me.

HELEN

Jimmy, please! Don't make it any worse than it already is.

EMILY

Come on, Suzanne. Never mind him.

JIM

For Christ's sake, we've seen the manuscript. Your underthings are already flapping in the summer breeze.

BETTY

Jim, you're not helping.

JIM

No? Well, try this. Suzanne, I'm jealous of you. Helen picked your novel over mine.

SUZANNE

It's not a novel. It's more of a true history. Actually, it's more of a persistent pipe dream.

JIM

As I was saying, I'm bitter that I lost out yet again. But I can see why it happened. The fact of the matter is that I'm intrigued. I'm dying to find out what's inside that old trunk that arrived at your door. I really am.

HELEN

It's now or never for you. Can't you see that, Dear?

BETTY

Everybody deserves a turn. It's your turn now.

SUZANNE

I suppose.

(SUZANNE heaves a grand sigh and starts reading.)

SUZANNE

This is the story of my grandmother Elsa Higgins who died over fifty years ago. A scandal was involved, one that caused Elsa's husband George to whisk his only daughter away to the big, anonymous city. My mother was too young to remember more than a sense of profound upheaval. When I ask, she claims she truly doesn't know what took place. She also says I shouldn't ask such questions.

People say I look just like Grandma Elsa. Her portrait used to hang in my parents' guest room. It was my job at dinner parties to stand by the front door, to smile sweetly and collect coats. I carried them upstairs and laid them on the tufted beige bedspread that was never pulled back. Later, long after my brother and I were supposed to be asleep, the guests would ascend the stairs two by two to fetch their own things.

My brother Brian would be in his room listening to records. But I would crouch in the guest closet, well hidden by dresses and skirts that no longer fit my mother. I loved to hear what the grownups had to say outside my family's

SUZANNE (Cont'd)

presence. About the coquilles Saint Jacques they'd just eaten. About whose dye job looked phony. About Brian's buck teeth. About me.

They meant it as a compliment when they stopped to stare at Grandma Elsa's portrait and point out the uncanny resemblance. I couldn't see it. My grandmother had sweeping dark tresses and a Mona Lisa smile. My hair was just plain brown, my smile full of metal and not a bit sublime.

In the end, they turned out to be half right. I'm not flamboyantly beautiful, far from it. But I do share Elsa's plump arms - hers were bared for the artist - and all the accursed swells of a full figure. Some say you are what you eat. My wise friend -

(looking up)

Helen, that is -

(continuing to read)

says you are what you read. Perhaps it is so for those whose bodies don't betray them by emerging, fully formed, ahead of the proper season. Grandma Elsa, were you still a little girl who dressed dolls and skipped rope when it happened to you? I knew from the age of ten that first and foremost, negating all else that might follow, I was and would always be a set of bold, protruding ... I can't do this. I really can't!

(SUZANNE throws her papers down and runs to the front door. SHE tries to pull it open. Flustered, SHE manages to unlock it, then run out and offstage.)

HELEN

Oh, dear. Perhaps I did misjudge the situation.

(HELEN reaches for her cane.)

HELEN

Damn these old legs! Emily, you run after her. Make her wait for me. Go on now, go!

(At first reluctant, EMILY rises and runs out. BETTY helps HELEN to her feet. They follow SUZANNE out. Alone, JIM paces.)

JIM

Shit! Me and my big mouth, me and my gigantic trap. She can't possibly be a ... in this day and age -

JIM (Cont'd)

(turn to audience)

Can she?

(JIM picks up the snow globe and plays with it, then sets it down. HE switches on the TV.)

JIM

I wonder what the score is.

REPORTER

Thanks, Bart, for that update on the other conference games. The action here at George Mason Arena will resume in just a few minutes. But first, here's a preview of tonight's "Who's Who in Middleton."

(The screen switches from the broadcast booth to the studio. GENE - pale, thin, age 53 - and the REPORTER sit in armchairs.)

REPORTER

Local author Gene Cartwright joined me in the studio earlier today. Unless you've been dwelling under a rock, you already know that his debut novel ISLAND TREASURE is causing a stir nationwide. Gene, I understand that you worked on your book for over a decade. Is that right?

GENE

Thirteen years, not to put too fine a point on it.

JIM

So you made it to our little gathering after all, Gene old boy.

REPORTER

My, what dedication! What kept you at it for so many years?

GENE

It wasn't easy, and there were long lapses when I wrote nary a word. But characters can be oddly insistent. They will speak their piece. Still, I suppose it is hard to labor alone day after day, month after month, without a scrap of encouragement.

JIM

What about Writers Block?

REPORTER

I can only imagine. What finally allowed you to break through?

GENE

My agent. I owe it all to my agent Elizabeth Hill.

JIM

What about Suzanne, you prick? She agonized over every comma with you.

REPORTER

***Island Treasure*. What a clever title.**

(JIM picks up the snow globe. He winds up to deliver a pitch at GENE on TV. Panting, EMILY reenters.)

EMILY

Christ! She practically ran me over.

(JIM attempts to disguise the pitching motion by fiddling with the channel knob.)

JIM

I, I was trying to catch the score. You probably wish you went to that Middle U game instead of hanging out with this bunch of freaks.

EMILY

(laughing)

The thought did cross my mind.

JIM

(flipping channels)

Our meetings are not normally filled with histrionics. We're not really like this. Aw, I missed the damn score.

(JIM shuts off the TV. He turns to the audience.)

JIM

No. We're not like this at all.

(BLACKOUT)

END OF SCENE 1

ACT I

Scene 2

AT RISE: **HELEN and BETTY are seated at opposite ends of the couch. JIM and EMILY carry a large, old trunk onto the stage and toward the front door. JIM is walking backward at his end. SUZANNE follows them, hovering.)**

SUZANNE

Be careful, Jim. There's a big crack in the floor there.

(SUZANNE darts ahead to open the door. JIM backs into SUZANNE. For a second his body presses hers against the wall. EMILY backs up at her end of the trunk. JIM and SUZANNE take a moment longer than needed to separate.)

SUZANNE

Sorry. I'm such a klutz.

JIM

Hell, I'm not sorry.

EMILY

Get the door already, Suzanne. This mother is heavy.

SUZANNE

Oh. Right.

(SUZANNE opens the door, JIM and EMILY set the trunk down in the middle of the seating area. Everybody sits.)

HELEN

Good. We're all here.

SUZANNE

Except Gene.

HELEN

Now, before we begin, I need to apologize for what took place last time. You must have gotten a frightful first impression of us, Emily. Apparently you're not easily discouraged. I had no right to circulate Suzanne's material without her permission. On a happier note, Betty has managed to persuade Suzanne to share her project with us after all. I don't know how she did it.

BETTY

I suggested we try a different approach. It she's not comfortable reading out loud, we can allow for that.

SUZANNE

I thought we might paw through these things that belonged to Grandma Elsa instead. This trunk sat up in my parents' attic for years until they sold the house. My mother thought the bookstore might be interested in the old papers. I told her to go ahead and send everything of Grandma Elsa's to me. I didn't ask for anything else from the house I grew up in.

EMILY

What happened to that portrait you mentioned?

SUZANNE

The picture? I have no idea. These old magazines, I don't know if they're worth anything or not. I'll take them into the store for Fred to look at when he comes back from Florida. I sure wish Gene was here - I bet he'd know.

HELEN

You wish Gene *were* here.

JIM

What, and miss a stop on his book tour?

SUZANNE

I couldn't ask that of him!

HELEN

Why don't you start by telling us all the things you know for certain about your grandmother's life and death.

(JIM sticks a pencil in his mouth and pretends to smoke his "cigar.")

JIM

Just the facts, Ma'am.

(The women all giggle.)

SUZANNE

Well, there's this newspaper article that was on top of everything else. I'll read it to you.

JIM

Are you sure you can handle reading aloud?

(SUZANNE gives JIM a dirty look, then opens the lid of the trunk and removes a yellowed newspaper.)

SUZANNE

Sure, when they're not my words. "The body of twenty-eight year old Elsa Higgins was discovered by a clam digger early yesterday morning on Porcupine Island. Elsa Higgins went missing eight days ago when she failed to return from making deliveries. State medical examiner Alfred Jebley has determined that the death was accidental, caused by exposure to the elements. Elsa Higgins is survived by her husband, businessman George Higgins and the couple's five-year old daughter Sally. Funeral services will be held at the Blain Memorial Chapel on ... it gives the details for the service and the burial. That's it. The photo of Elsa is from her high school yearbook. It's kind of grainy.

EMILY

(taking the paper from SUZANNE)

She does look like you, Suzanne. I mean you look like her.

JIM

Does it say what she was delivering?

SUZANNE

It says exactly what I read aloud to you.

HELEN

What's the dateline?

SUZANNE
It doesn't say that either, but I do know that Elsa died in 1949.

BETTY
What else have you got?

SUZANNE
Class photos. First through twelfth grade, all neatly labeled. There's her future husband George Higgins. Here, look at the one second from the left in the back row.

EMILY
He's a hunk, isn't he? I mean "wasn't he." Are any of these people, like, still alive? Or would they be a hundred ninety years old?

HELEN
Hardly!

SUZANNE
I do have all their names because my grandmother wrote them on the back of each picture, along with an occasional snide comment. It seems that Elsa wrote lots of details down. If only she'd kept a journal!

BETTY
What are those? They look like passbooks.

EMILY
They look like what?

BETTY
You know, old-fashioned savings account books. The kind you had to bring with you so the teller could write in the deposit or withdrawal.

HELEN
And they'd bring the interest up to date at the same time. Sometimes they'd have to enter six months or more at once.

EMILY
They wrote numbers in by hand?

HELEN
Yes, Dear. In ink. And they hardly ever made a mistake.

SUZANNE

What good are some moldy old bank books? I want to know who my grandmother was.

JIM

Financial records make for some of the most revealing evidence on earth.

HELEN

That's true. It's how they got Richard Nixon. Deep Throat told the two reporters to follow the money. What were their names again? Don't tell me, I've got it - Woodward and Bernstein. There, Dorothy. I can remember details. Dorothy's my daughter in California, Emily. She's convinced I'm getting senile.

EMILY

Deep Throat. What does that ancient porno film have to do with anything?

HELEN

Deep Throat was the name used by the anonymous source during the Watergate scandal.

EMILY

Oh, that's right! Now I remember. I saw that movie too.

JIM

In addition to Deep Throat, you mean.

HELEN

(indignantly)

It's not a movie, it's American history!

JIM

Both Deep Throats made history. The country never was quite the same after Linda Lovelace. A woman of stupefying oral capacity.

SUZANNE

I don't think that's funny at all. Movies like that are offensive to women.

JIM

I admit "Deep Throat" was not much of a chick flick.

HELEN

That's enough, Jimmy.

JIM

Shall I go stand in the corner? Or maybe you should paddle me.

BETTY

I recommend scotch-taping his mouth closed.

HELEN

Let's just get back to business, shall we? What else is in the trunk?

SUZANNE

Clothes. Some dresses and lots of weird undergarments.

(SUZANNE removes a dark red, low-cut dress with a full skirt.)

SUZANNE

This is the dress she had on in the portrait.

BETTY

(stroking the material)

Isn't that a lovely color! Why, it's real velvet!

(EMILY takes the dress, stands, and holds it up to herself. The dress was made for a shorter, fuller woman.)

EMILY

Very hot. I bet it would fit you, Suzanne.

SUZANNE

But it wouldn't suit me one bit.

(JIM takes the dress from Emily, holds it in front of himself and does a few pirouettes)

JIM

You think?

(The women titter. SUZANNE removes and sets aside some lace garments with distaste.)

BETTY

What are those ledger books at the bottom?

SUZANNE

I think they pertain to George's store - he owned a general store, I do know that much - though they're all in a flowery handwriting.

BETTY

Oh, wives have kept the books for their husbands forever and ever. I used to keep Harry's accounts before his firm got so big. And Jim's right. Financial records can be full of telling details.

SUZANNE

About George, not about Elsa.

JIM

Use what you have, Woman. Betty, do you suppose Harry might take a look at the ledgers and bank books? It would be helpful to get his take.

SUZANNE

Oh, I wouldn't want to bother him.

BETTY

Nonsense. Tax season's almost over. I'll be glad to ask him.

JIM

Meanwhile, I'll get one of our paralegals to check the probate records. Let's see which of these folks are still breathing.

EMILY

And not drooling.

HELEN

Really now! They're right around my age.

SUZANNE

They are, aren't they? That means we can still find them!

JIM

Quite possibly, but don't get your hopes up sky high. It's tough enough to get at the truth in a case that's fresh in people's minds. This information is half a century old.

SUZANNE

The truth is what I'm after. I'm only going to write what's absolutely true.

HELEN

That's a tall order, truth.

JIM

More like mission impossible.

EMILY

But a noble goal for a writer, don't you think?

JIM

Not necessarily.

SUZANNE

And why not?

JIM

Because truth is too constraining. Too mundane, too crowded with irrelevancies.

SUZANNE

Well, I'm not about to make Elsa's story up. Either I find out what happened to her or I don't. It's that simple.

HELEN

It's rarely that simple, Dear.

SUZANNE

I think it is and no offense, but it's my book. Gene says not to let outsiders interfere with the essence of your art. He says to trust your own voice.

BETTY

Yes, but you do want our help. You haven't changed your mind about that, have you?

SUZANNE

No, of course not.

BETTY

So I'll take the ledgers and the bank books with me for Harry to put under the microscope.

JIM

And I'll take the class pictures with the names on the back.

EMILY

What do I get, the retro underwear?

SUZANNE

Well, I don't have any use for it. Or for that slutty red dress.

HELEN

Just put the clothes away then, Dear. But let me see that article first.

(SUZANNE hands her the newspaper article and begins repacking the trunk.)

HELEN

People must learn to put labels on such things. If it's important enough to keep, it's important enough to identify. Otherwise, these old snippets are practically useless. Betty, perhaps you could try the Middle U Library. I know they have newspaper archives on some sort of plastic sheets you squint at with a funny viewer.

EMILY

You mean microfiche.

HELEN

Precisely. See if you can identify what newspaper this came from.

JIM

Good idea. Perhaps there are related pieces around the same date.

EMILY

Actually, I could do that. I'm on campus four days a week.

SUZANNE

If it's not too much trouble.

BETTY

Well, I'll take Harry's homework out to the car. No Jim, I've got it. Just get the door for me.

(JIM rises and opens the door for Betty, who exits.)

HELEN

Good. Now perhaps you and Emily can take that trunk and set it on the floor in the storeroom for safekeeping.

JIM

(to EMILY)

Ready, Muscles?

EMILY

(from her end)

Oh, the beast is much lighter now!

SUZANNE

It certainly is.

(JIM and EMILY exit to the kitchen with the trunk.)

SUZANNE

You know what, Helen? This could actually work.

HELEN

Yes, Dear. It's possible for things to go right.

(SUZANNE gets a dreamy look on her face. HELEN watches her with a smile of satisfaction.)

(BLACKOUT)

END OF SCENE 2

ACT I

Scene 3

AT RISE: **HELEN is lying on the floor. HER wooden cane, broken in two, lies beside her. The wall phone is dangling by the cord. Various pieces of furniture have been overturned with knick knacks and books strewn about the floor. The snow globe lies shattered on the floor. An annoyed female voice says "Hello, hello" through the receiver. Panting, JIM comes rushing through the wide-open front door. He shuts it and kneels beside Helen.**

JIM

Helen! What happened? I got here as quickly as I could.

(HELEN is slow to open her eyes. At first dazed, she rapidly regains her composure.)

HELEN

Jimmy. You're here.

JIM

I'm here.

HELEN

Hang up that phone for me. Your girl is going bonkers on the other end.

JIM

Oh, screw the telephone. And the girl.

(HELEN lets out a startled laugh, then "tut tuts.")

HELEN

I'm cold, Jimmy. I'm so cold.

(JIM takes an Afghan and puts it around HELEN's shoulders. HE helps her sit up.)

JIM

You should have called 911. They would have gotten here much quicker, I mean much more quickly than I did. Why didn't you?

HELEN

Because I'm not the sort of woman who depends on the kindness of strangers.

JIM

Paramedics don't act out of kindness. They get paid.

HELEN

They make a pittance compared to you lawyers.

JIM

Guilty as charged.

HELEN

And they would have insisted on dragging me off to the hospital.

JIM

Or you could have called Suzanne. Her apartment can't be twenty minutes away, even at the snail's pace that she drives.

HELEN

She doesn't answer her telephone And she'd insist on a trip to the emergency room, during which she would lecture me endlessly about locking my door.

JIM

Maybe you *should* go to the hospital and get checked out.

HELEN

Nothing's broken, I tell you. Nothing but my old cane. And that phone will be if I have the strength to yank the damn thing from the wall.

JIM

(gets up, speaks into phone)

Marcy, are you there?

JIM (Cont'd)

(When there is no response, HE shrugs and hangs up. HE helps HELEN to her feet and to the couch. HE sits beside her, after turning the heat up.)

JIM

Now tell me what happened.

HELEN

Well, I was in the kitchen when I heard somebody moving around in my living room. I thought perhaps it was Gilly, the boy who delivers my groceries. Then I remembered that Bob Haskins called last week and told me Gilly took a job in Middleton and I'd have to make other arrangements. I still don't know what I'm going to do about getting my groceries. I peeked around the corner and saw this boy - I think he was just a boy - in a ski mask. He was over in that corner.

(HELEN points to the corner furthest from the front door, from which it is necessary to pass by the kitchen to get to the front door.)

HELEN

I decided to hide in the storeroom and let him go about his business. I tried to back away without making any noise at all, but he turned around and caught sight of me.

JIM

You must have been terrified.

HELEN

He was as surprised as I was. He must have thought that nobody was home. Then his eyes narrowed - I could see that right through the ski mask - and he came toward me. That's when I got scared. At the last second I thought to trip him with my cane. He sprawled face first onto the floor.

JIM

Bravo, Helen!

HELEN

I did try to call 911 at that point. I stepped toward the telephone, but the boy started to get up. I swung at his head with my cane. He cried out and fell back again. Then he stumbled to his feet. He said, "You're f-ing loco, Lady." On his

HELEN (Cont'd)
way out he turned and looked right at me. In the most contemptuous tone imaginable he said, "Nothing but junk anyway."

JIM
So he didn't get any of your things.

HELEN
No, I don't think so.

JIM
That's good. How did you end up on the floor yourself?

HELEN
My cane betrayed me. It must have cracked when I knocked him on the noggin. The very first step I took, I went kerplunk. Then I simply could not make it back onto my own two feet. I became that helpless crone in the commercial who croaks, "I've fallen and I can't get up." Fortunately, after a good panic, I figured out that I could scooch over to the telephone, knock the receiver off the wall with the handle of my cane, and dial for help.

JIM
You sounded terrible when you called. You sound like yourself again now.

HELEN
After I let go of the telephone, I closed my eyes to rest for just a second or two. Twenty minutes later I woke up freezing to death. But I couldn't find the strength to crawl to the front door and shut it against the cold. Fortunately, you rode gallantly to my rescue. And there you have it.

JIM
Well. That's quite a story.

HELEN
With a happy ending. Turn the heat up a little more for me, Dear. And put the books back where they belong.

(HE turns a switch on the wall.)

JIM
The mess I'm going to leave intact for the authorities.

HELEN
No police. What's the point? Nothing was taken.

JIM

What's the point of enforcing the law? That doesn't sound like the Helen I know.

HELEN

Jimmy, my house embarrasses me. I saw it through a young person's eyes today. I saw dust. I saw clutter. I saw water stains on the ceiling. I saw holes in the carpet.

JIM

Every old house has flaws. They add character.

HELEN

My son-in-law Joe says that one of the main sills is rotting. And he says I've got to cut down that old willow tree, but I love the way it shades the porch in the summertime. Rotting sills. That's a serious problem, isn't it?

JIM

Sills can be replaced. It's an expensive undertaking, but it can be done.

HELEN

But it's a serious, structural problem.

JIM

Yes.

HELEN

This is an old person's place. Does my house stink, Jimmy? Tell me the truth. Does it reek of imminent decay?

JIM

That kind of talk gets us nowhere.

HELEN

You evaded my question.

JIM

I'm not a lawyer for nothing. And speaking of the law, we need to report this break in.

HELEN

They'll never catch him.

JIM

Actually, most small-town crimes do get solved. Matt McCrae may not be a brain surgeon, but the sherriff's a hell of a lot brighter than the punks. Helen, you heard this one's voice. He left blood behind. They'll catch him and you'll help them put the asshole away. Then you'll be able to relax in your home again.

HELEN

I don't know it that's possible anymore.

JIM

Do it for the sake of his next, not-so-feisty victim.

HELEN

Hush, Jimmy, I know what I have to do. It's the schoolteacher in me that wants to think I already taught that boy a lesson to last a lifetime. I like to think I affect my students, even though they forget all about me.

JIM

After Matt and his deputy are done poking around here, I'm taking you out to dinner. Then we'll pick you out a brand new shelali.

HELEN

But the stores will be closed.

JIM

The pharmacy at Walmart stays open all night.

HELEN

It does? All night long? I'm sorry, Jimmy. I've had a rough day and C-Span is doing an interview with ... with an author that I'm fond of. Perhaps tomorrow.

JIM

Don't turn me down, Helen. I can't take any more rejection right now. My novel came back again yesterday.

HELEN

Oh Jimmy. I'm so sorry.

JIM

That's the fourth fucking time! Only this flaming asshole tied up my manuscript for nine months. That's long enough to hatch a kid, for God's sake. The idiot sent me a form letter that wasn't even signed. He sounded so

JIM (Cont'd)

enthusiastic when he called and asked to see the manuscript. Nine months he keeps me hanging on the edge of heaven or hell and he can't spare me one lousy parting thought.

HELEN

You're a talented writer, Jimmy.

JIM

I must be nearing some sort of record. Do you suppose Guinness gives credit for the planet's largest collection of rejection letters?

HELEN

Oh dear.

JIM

I don't know if I can keep trying anymore. I'm not used to being treated like a nobody. At times like this my heart pumps pure poison. I'd strangle that arrogant bastard of an agent if I could get away with it. I would!

HELEN

Now you're the one with thoughts that lead nowhere.

JIM

I'm a selfish pig, Helen, for depressing you with my same old shit after what happened to you. We'll go anyplace you like, my treat. I absolutely promise to put a happy spin on our dinner conversation.

HELEN

No swearing at the dinner table, either.

JIM

You got it. Scout's honor.

HELEN

Well, I do need another cane. Dinner in Middleton it is. At least I'll come home with fresh senses. Since you won't tell me, I can find out for myself whether my house stinks to high heaven.

JIM

What a gracious acceptance. Today, I'll take it.

HELEN

Jimmy, as long as your words are special, does it matter how many people hear them?

JIM

Damn right it matters. I'll go make that call.

(JIM goes to the phone.)

JIM

The number for the Middleton County sheriff. No, it's not an emergency. Anymore.

(JIM reaches into his shirt pocket. HE searches for something to write with.)

JIM

Thirty-five cents? Yeah, go ahead and connect me. ..... Suzanne would scold me if she were here, Helen, I just wasted your money.

(HELEN isn't paying attention. JIM waits to be connected while HELEN peers around the room as though she has never been there before.)

JIM

I remember when a boy could buy seven candy bars for thirty-five cents. A whole gallon of gas.

HELEN

Nothing but junk, you say.

JIM

Three phone calls with a nickel left over . ... Yes, I'm here. I want to report a break in.

(JIM turns his back to the audience and speaks inaudibly into the telephone.)

HELEN

Junk. Nothing but junk.

(BLACKOUT)

END OF SCENE 3

ACT I

Scene 4

AT RISE: **HELEN stands, leaning on a new cane, by the front door. SHE opens it with a key. Once inside (which has been put to rights), SHE locks the door, producing a loud click. SHE sniffs and switches on an inside light. A car horn beeps and a vehicle drives off.**

HELEN

Humpf! Could be worse. Could be better, too.

(SHE walks over to an end table, picks up a stack of magazines, dropping a few on the floor. SHE plops the remaining stack into the wastebasket. SHE sits on the couch.)

HELEN

Oh dear! I suppose I've missed Gene's interview.

(SHE reaches for the remote. SHE flips through channels and stops at the local news.)

REPORTER

Now, here's a case of turnabout is fair play. Sheriff Matthew MacRae told me about an elderly woman who foiled a robbery attempt in her home today.

(A tape of a much younger Helen in a crowded gymnasium begins to play on the screen.)

REPORTER

Shown here at her retirement party in 1984, Helen Cloutier taught English at Loon Lake High School for forty years. Seated next to her at the table is Attorney General Todd Harris. He told me, when I spoke with him earlier this evening, that he owes his career to the years he spent on Helen Cloutier's state-champion debating team. Long widowed, Helen lives alone. But she's far from helpless. At age eighty I'm told she still grows and cans her own vegetables.

HELEN

I don't can them, I freeze them. And I'm seventy-nine. Get your facts straight.

REPORTER

Anything but helpless, as one hapless lawbreaker discovered.

HELEN

Oh, good grief!

(SHE flips through channels and is astonished to find the story playing on several. SHE flips some more and finds GENE on screen.)

HELEN

There you are, Dear! My luck is finally turning.

(The telephone rings.)

Turning worse, that is.

(HELEN mutes the TV, then uses the cane to hobble over to the telephone. The silent TV screen shows an animated interview between GENE and a female reporter.)

HELEN

Hello.

(DOROTHY's excited voice comes through over the phone in the ensuing conversation.)

DOROTHY

Mom! Are you all right? I've been trying to get you for hours and hours.

HELEN

Yes, Dear. I'm perfectly all right.

DOROTHY
Thank God! What did Dr. Frobisher say? You must have gone to see him, that's what Joe said when I couldn't reach you. Does *he* think you're perfectly all right?

HELEN
I was having dinner with a friend in Middleton, if you must know. And I'm not damaged goods.

DOROTHY
They say the creep trashed your living room. I can only imagine what it looks like, with all those magazines that you never throw away. This is the last straw, Mom. Let Joe and I help you.

HELEN
Joe and me, Dear. Actually, there is one thing I do need. Gilly Haskell took a better-paying job in Middleton. So I need to find somebody else to fetch my groceries once a week. Can you do that?

DOROTHY
Don't start in with me, Mom. You're the one who insists on living all alone in the backwoods.

HELEN
How ever did you about know this way out in California?

DOROTHY
It was all over the evening news.

HELEN
I made the national news? Good lord, it must have been a slow day in America.

DOROTHY
You should view this as a wakeup call, Mom. You simply can't stay alone in that decrepit old place anymore. There are alternatives.

HELEN
Dorothy, please, I don't hear from you for six months and now you declare yourself my keeper.

DOROTHY
I just want you to face reality.

HELEN

I won't discuss this. Not tonight.

DOROTHY

That's what you always say. If not now, when?

HELEN

When I'm good and ready, that's when!

(HELEN angrily hangs up the telephone. SHE tries unsuccessfully to shut a drawer that is slightly ajar. SHE yanks the drawer out and dumps it in the overflowing wastebasket.)

HELEN

Damn you, Dorothy! Damn you.

(SHE sits back on the couch and turns the sound on. GENE and the REPORTER immediately disappear. A screen advertising the next event comes on.)

HELEN

Now it really is over.

(HELEN flips channels idly, then shuts off the TV. SHE leans back and closes her eyes. The radiator emits a loud hiss, making HELEN jump. She settles back again)

BLACKOUT for several seconds.

(HELEN is sprawled on the couch and snoring. SHE shifts position and accidentally hits the remote control. Guns go off. HELEN lets out a strangled cry and sits up.)

HELEN

Who is it? Who's there?

(SHE realizes that the television is making the noise.)

HELEN

Oh, how stupid of me!

(SHE shuts the TV off.)

HELEN

Now calm down, Fool.

(The telephone rings. HELEN tenses, then gets up to answer it. JOE's voice comes through the telephone in the ensuing conversation.)

HELEN

Dorothy, it's very late and you should mind your own business.

JOE

(interrupting)

Simmer down, Helen. You know what? I almost feel sorry for that poor, dumb kid. He sure picked the wrong house to rob.

HELEN

Oh it's you, Joe!

(HELEN bursts into tears.)

JOE

Aw Helen, I'm sorry. I shouldn't be joking about what happened. It's way too fresh in your mind.

HELEN

Oh, it isn't that. It's just a relief to hear your deep voice. My nerves are truly on edge tonight.

JOE

No wonder. You should be very proud of how you handled yourself today. We certainly are.

HELEN

Dorothy's proud of me?

JOE

You bet. And she feels just terrible about getting into an argument with you tonight. She wanted me to tell you how sorry she is.

HELEN

Then she should apologize to me herself.

(The blare of a car horn, followed by a distant crunch of metal, sounds. HELEN gasps.)

JOE

Helen! What's going on there?

HELEN

It's, it's nothing. Something happened outside, that's all. At that four corners over on Route One Eleven, I imagine. They simply must trim those trees that obscure the stop sign. Oh God, Joe. I'm scared of my own shadow tonight.

JOE

That's perfectly understandable under the circumstances.

HELEN

It may be understandable, but it's not acceptable. Not to me. I simply must get my act together, as you young folks like to say. Only ...

(HELEN' voice breaks.)

I just don't know that I will. I don't know anything anymore.

JOE

Take it easy, Helen. Nothing needs to be decided now in the dead of night. Try to get some rest, if that's possible.

HELEN

I, I'll try.

JOE

I'll say good night now.

HELEN

Wait! Joe, are you still there?

JOE

I'm here. You want me to get Dorothy?

HELEN

No, but tell her something for me. Tell her that I'll consider what she said.

JOE

You will? You mean that?

HELEN

I said it, didn't I?

JOE

Yes, but I never believed in miracles before.

HELEN

I suppose I deserved that.

JOE

Not really. Change is difficult for all of us.

HELEN

And inevitable. I will think about it. I promise.

(HELEN turns away from the audience. Her shoulders slump in defeat as she says goodbye to Joe and hangs up.)

(BLACKOUT)

END OF SCENE 4

ACT I

Scene 5

AT RISE: The card table is set for dinner for three. SUZANNE is lying on her back on the couch with a wet washcloth across her forehead. JIM enters, tries to push the front door open and finds it locked. HE knocks.

HELEN

(calling from the kitchen)

I'm coming. Hold your horses, I'm coming.

(HELEN walks slowly, but without the use of the cane, to the front door and opens it.)

HELEN

Good, you're here at last. I was afraid we wouldn't have time to talk before the others arrived.

JIM

I had a closing that ran late. What's with her?

HELEN

Fred Forester has decided to close the bookstore once and for all. She just found out she's losing her job, poor thing. Then while she was driving over, she felt a migraine coming on. I suggested she lie down while we waited for you. I was going to tell both of you my news at the same time. Now I'm not sure I have the heart to tell her at all.

JIM

Tell her what?

HELEN

Come. Sit with me.

(HELEN and JIM sit at the card table.)

HELEN

As you know, it's been four weeks since the break-in. I didn't want to make a major decision while I was still in a tizzy over it. But now it's time.

JIM

I'm not going to like what's coming, am I?

HELEN

I'm moving, Jimmy. I'm selling this old house and everything in it. I know there are services for the elderly around here, that they would send some social worker to assess my needs. But I can't abide the thought of becoming somebody's cantankerous case.

JIM

You could give the local do-gooders a chance before you write them off. I have a few contacts in the care business. If you'd like me to try -

HELEN

(interrupting)

I always lock my front door now and not just to appease Suzanne. I lock it because I'm terrified of the next intruder. Then I wonder if I'm sealing my own fate when I give that dead bolt a turn. What if I can't get to the telephone next time? I'm bound to slip and fall again.

JIM

My offer stands - say the word and I'll make some calls.

HELEN

Stop it, Jimmy. All it would buy me is a little stitch of time. Then I'd have to face the music all over again. Best to get it over with at once.

JIM

Oh, Helen. You'll be missed more than you can imagine. Tell me what your plans are.

HELEN

I'm going to move into an assisted-living facility in California near Dorothy. I insisted on speaking at length with Joe to make sure he was truly agreable. He's such a lovely man. He's the one who bought my satellite dish, you know. I never even see the monthly bill. He turned a deaf ear to all my protests. "I'll never watch it," I told him. That was four years ago - now I don't know how

HELEN (Cont'd)

I ever lived without the history channel and C-Span. I remember when all we could get out here were two grainy channels.

JIM

It was still that way when I was growing up.

HELEN

I won't interfere in their marriage. I swear I won't. It may be decades ago, but I still remember. My mother-in-law lived with us when Sol and I were first married. I know exactly what not to do.

JIM

Back in school you taught us that there are two kinds of role models, positive and negative, and that both can be put to good use.

HELEN

You remember that after all these years?

JIM

I most certainly do. So you haven't told Suzanne yet.

HELEN

Not one to embrace change, Suzanne, but she'll manage. She'll simply have to.

JIM

She'll be heartbroken, as close as the two of you are. First Gene goes AWOL and now you.

HELEN

Stop it. You're making me feel guilty.

JIM

Join the club.

HELEN

Why, what did you do?

JIM

You know, that wisecrack about virgins the other night. I never felt like such a buffoon in my entire life.

HELEN

Well, you had no way of knowing. I always wondered how that store made ends meet. There's so little market for historical titles these days.

JIM

No, they crank out the newest crap on masse, then dump it onto the bargain table a month later. A novel has a shorter shelf life than a carton of milk.

HELEN

She's a sweet girl, Suzanne.

JIM

She's a royal pain in the ass.

HELEN

Why, I always thought that you had a crush on her. Do they still use that expression?

JIM

They do and this teacher doesn't miss a trick. Truth be known, I do find Suzanne attractive. If a man ever made it through all that weather proofing, he'd find a sea of passion underneath. Not to mention an amazing pair of bazooms. But she'll never let the likes of me near them. Suzanne worships at the shrine of Gene Cartwright. Surely you've noticed that as well.

HELEN

Quite so.

JIM

For all the good it does her.

HELEN

I do wish she'd blossom. That year she student taught with me, she showed such promise. She was hyper-sensitive to criticism, mind you. Still, I was sure she'd find her voice in the classroom. Maybe when the bookstore closes and change is forced onto her, she'll, she'll ... she'll probably fall completely apart. Oh Jimmy, I do have to leave. I've made up my mind.

JIM

For what it's worth, Helen, I admire your gumption. I really do. Most people refuse to face such things.

HELEN

It does feel good to look forward to something new again. It's the right decision. And if not, it's still a decision.

(HELEN stands up.)

I can warm up the corn chowder. Are you hungry?

JIM

Not at all, truth be told. I just wolfed down four bowls of pretzels - the bar wench kept refilling the damn thing. My client insisted on having a drink at Gibelli's after the closing.

HELEN

John Gibelli's no fool. He knows people will drink more if he feeds them something salty for free.

JIM

Worked like a charm on me.

HELEN

Do you suppose we should wake Suzanne and see if she's hungry? No, it's getting late. She can eat after the meeting. I'll just clear the dishes away.

JIM

Can I help?

HELEN

No thank you, Dear. My legs are working today and it's sheer joy to move about. You can fold up the table when I'm all done.

JIM

I'll step out for a breath of air, then.

HELEN

Don't tell me you started smoking again.

JIM

Fine. I won't tell you.

(JIM stands on the porch. A gust of wind comes up, to which JIM turns his back to light up.)

HELEN

Such a nasty habit.

(HELEN carries dishes to the kitchen. SUZANNE moans, shifts position, and draws the covers over her head.)

BLACKOUT for several seconds.

(SUZANNE is standing in the middle of the room. A blanketed figure is still lying on the couch.)

SUZANNE

Daddy, is that you?

(SUZANNE stares at a spot in the distance, then walks toward it. She moves in slow motion with great effort. A spotlight shines on GENE who has materialized.)

SUZANNE

Gene? I thought you couldn't come to meetings anymore.

(GENE turns toward SUZANNE and folds his arms.)

SUZANNE

I keep seeing you on television. You always look so thin, just as thin as reality.

(SUZANNE tries to approach him, but her legs don't work. Meanwhile, GENE's gaze has shifted toward another corner of the room. SUZANNE looks and sees EMILY. EMILY is wearing sneakers, basketball shorts, and a sports bra. GENE leers at EMILY.)

SUZANNE

Gene! Look at me!

(SUZANNE's dress drops to the floor, leaving her in a plain white bra and cotton underpants. GENE looks briefly at SUZANNE, then turns disdainfully away. HE strides off in the direction where EMILY stood a moment earlier. EMILY has disappeared.)

SUZANNE

Come back!

(SUZANNE realizes that SHE is indecent. SHE crosses her arms over her chest. SHE tries to scream, but no sound comes out.)

BLACKOUT for several seconds

(A light rain begins. JIM struggles to relight his cigarette. When the lights come up inside, SUZANNE is back on the couch. She thrashes wildly and emits a strangled cry. JIM stubs out his cigarette and rushes to her side. He leaves the front door slightly ajar.)

JIM

Sweetheart, what's the matter?

(As SUZANNE opens her eyes, SHE crosses her arms across her chest.)

SUZANNE

Where'd you go? Gene? Oh, it's just you.

JIM

Yup. It's just Jim. You were having a bad dream, weren't you?

SUZANNE

You could say that.

JIM

Do you want to talk about it?

SUZANNE

Talk about that kind of dream with you? Not for all the tea in China.

JIM

Well, I hate tea. I'll just leave you alone then.

(JIM starts to get up.)

SUZANNE
No! I'm pretty shaken, actually. Please don't go.

(JIM sits down closer to SUZANNE.)

SUZANNE
My dreams never end in triumph. Do yours?

JIM
Not usually. What went wrong this time?

SUZANNE
He wanted Emily. Even though I was ... I can't say it.

JIM
You were naked.

SUZANNE
Just about. Don't you laugh now.

JIM
(in a husky tone)
Quite the contrary.

SUZANNE
It was humiliating! The tall blonde beckoned and away he went. I hate his guts! They all crave the skinny twenty-two year old with the teeny weeny tits.

(JIM puts his arm around SUZANNE.)

JIM
Believe me, not all men think that way. And those that do are seriously misguided.

SUZANNE
They are?

JIM
Damn right. Curves rule!

SUZANNE
They do?

JIM

You betcha.

(JIM kisses SUZANNE on the cheek.)

SUZANNE

Kiss me for real, Jim.

JIM

Lady, I thought you'd never ask.

(JIM and SUZANNE kiss with increasing passion. HE puts his hand on her breast. SUZANNE moans with pleasure, then stiffens and pulls away.)

SUZANNE

Don't ever do that again!

(BETTY and EMILY arrive together. It is raining steadily now, weather for which neither woman is dressed. They dash up the steps, laughing. They enter dripping as JIM and SUZANNE leap to opposite ends of the couch. HELEN comes in from the kitchen carrying a plate of cookies.)

HELEN

I didn't know it was doing that outside. How's your headache, Dear?

SUZANNE

I, I guess it's gone.

HELEN

Splendid news. We're all here, except Gene of course, so let's begin.

(THEY sit and ready themselves for the evening's discussion.)

HELEN

Suzanne, the floor is yours.

SUZANNE

What's that? I'm not ready yet. I had a horrid day.

BETTY

Really? Me too. I just found out that Middle U won't take some of my credits from twenty years ago. I'm going to have to spend another whole semester to get my bachelor's degree. And they just raised the tuition.

EMILY

Betty, you're worth it. God, that sounded like a hair dye commercial, didn't it? But it's true.

BETTY

Harry made quite a fuss, but he'll get over it. Business at the firm is positively booming. I hardly see him at all, even though tax season's come and gone.

JIM

Harry's a fucking workaholic all right.

HELEN

Language! Really, Jimmy, there's no need.

JIM

Right. Use profanity sparingly to preserve its impact. The hell with your rules, Helen. I don't even know why I come here anymore. All I write these days are legal briefs.

HELEN

Your opening chapter about the boy hiding in the barn, what's his name again? Don't tell me, don't tell me.

JIM

His name is Jason and he's the first fresh character I've invented in years. But my project didn't get your vote. Remember? Even you rejected me.

HELEN

You shouldn't look at our process that way. Besides, you can all change the group protocol soon, anyway.

SUZANNE

What's that supposed to mean?

HELEN

Nothing. Jimmy, you simply can't stop writing because you haven't been published yet. You know how tough the market is.

JIM

I can't find a publisher. I can't find an agent. I can't get a magazine to accept a short story. Even the ones that don't pay a red cent won't print my shit. It's time I faced reality. It ain't gonna happen for me. Hell, maybe my novel sucks out loud. I don't know anymore. But it wasn't just me. All of you thought my book would sell. A tense courtroom drama with quirky but lovable characters. What could be more marketable? What?

HELEN

The new book you're working on. What did Jason witness while he was hiding in the barn? That's what I want to hear about later tonight instead of the foul mouth and the whining.

JIM

Hell if I know what he saw.

EMILY

But you wonder about Jason. He inhabits your mind.

JIM

Not very often.

EMILY

Not never.

JIM

Look. You all mean well, but you can't fix what's wrong with my life. Just ignore me. I'll shut up and quit bellyaching sooner or later.

HELEN

Emily dear, since we're digressing anyway, how about telling us about the play you're working on. Writers Block never had a playwright before.

EMILY

It's about a young woman with sky-high expectations placed upon her. Only, instead of soaring like everybody assumes she'll effortlessly do, she crashes and burns. This play is about getting knocked back by adversity and then learning how to move on after experiencing failure.

JIM

What does a kid like you know about failure? You're still shitting yellow.

HELEN

No need, no need at all.

JIM

No, really! Everybody in the state knows her name. First Middle U player to be rated number one nationwide.

EMILY

In one poll for one week.

JIM

Nationwide! What the hell do you know about toiling in oblivion? About falling miserably short?

EMILY

I'll tell you exactly what I know about failure. Once upon a time this girl was a star basketball player. She broke all kinds of records in high school and the very same thing happened in college. She got drafted by the WNBA and her mother was ecstatic. It was a rude shock when the girl discovered she was just an ordinary talent after all. Barely that and nowhere near as aggressive as the big, black girls from the ghetto.

BETTY

Oh come on. You were ferocious on the court!

EMILY

She scored some free throws in her first professional game and our heroine blithely assumed she was on her way to stardom. Then she committed six turnovers in her second game and the coach benched her. She tried to cheer from the bench like a true team player. She was the only white girl on the squad.

SUZANNE

Why did that matter?

JIM

Reality, Woman. Reality.

(EMILY stands and looks out the window as she continues her story. She speaks with little emotion, as if in a trance.)

EMILY

Then I met him. He had memorized all my stats. I wasn't used to adulation anymore. So I let him undress me on our first date. It took just two more dates, both of which included rough sex, to know that I wanted nothing to do

EMILY (Cont'd)

with him. I told him so in no uncertain terms. But he had secretly copied the key to my apartment. One night he entered my bedroom. I used to think I was powerful like Xena. Not anymore. I mean, he wasn't even as tall ... He stuffed a balled-up pair of socks in my mouth, then he raped me.

(A chorus of gasps and "Oh my's" comes from the women. JIM makes a sound of disgust.)

SUZANNE

How degrading!

BETTY

Did the police catch him?

EMILY

Of course I should have called the police, but I was too ashamed. After all, I was dumb enough to go out with the creep in the first place.

BETTY

You didn't even call the police?

EMILY

No, I packed up my things and moved across town. I didn't leave a forwarding address. I got an unlisted phone number.

SUZANNE

But he found you.

EMILY

He broke in and trashed my new place. Then I called the police.

HELEN

Thank God!

EMILY

Only they let him out on bail three days later. I moved again to a more expensive apartment with security. Now I had to drive forty minutes to and from practice. One day I actually played a few totally spastic minutes. It was all I could do not to burst into tears as I took my customary seat on the bench. When I looked up, I saw him in the stands. He wasn't supposed to be there - the judge had issued a restraining order. I completely freaked out, much to the disgust of my coach.

BETTY

Why? It wasn't your fault.

EMILY

Then he grabbed me in the parking lot at the 7-11. I would have screamed, but he held a knife to my throat. This time he took me to his place and kept me prisoner. It took three days for the coach to send the police looking. This time the judge said "no bail."

BETTY

I should say not.

EMILY

I was determined to get on with my career. But I had two broken ribs courtesy of him. I tried to play through the pain, but there was no way. I expected the coach to put me on the injured reserve list. Instead, she sent me packing. So I came home. To Middleton.

(JIM walks over to Emily and touches her gently on the shoulder. EMILY tenses, then shakes off the reaction with a self-conscious laugh.)

JIM

I'm so sorry, Emily. I'm a flaming ignoramus sometimes. Tell me they put that scumbag away for a good, long time.

EMILY

(rejoining the group)

Not yet.

HELEN

You'll go back and testify, of course.

EMILY

I will if they need me. But the D.A. decided to prosecute him on a similar case instead. Better facts, he told me. I don't care as long as they get him. I just want it to be over and done with.

SUZANNE

Yet you're writing about it.

EMILY

I know. I can't help myself.

BETTY
You can try out for another professional team, can't you?

EMILY
See, it wasn't just the wrong team I was on. It was the wrong path. While I was licking my wounds in my old bedroom, I got to thinking. I realized that I used to want something else with all my heart before basketball took over my life. In the seventh grade I was thrilled when I got the lead in the school play. All the popular girls auditioned for it. We were doing "Sarah Plain and Tall. I won the lead."

HELEN
A marvelous role! I bet you were terrific.

EMILY
The rehearsal schedule conflicted with basketball practice, so I couldn't do both. My mother was really into women's lib and she wanted me to play sports. I said I'd think about it. A couple days later, I said "Mom, I want to do the play." Somehow, she misunderstood and thought I said I wanted to play. I don't know, maybe she tricked me on purpose. She called the coach and told him I'd decided to stay on the team after all.

HELEN
(with a dismissive snort)
There's way too much emphasis on sports in our public schools.

EMILY
Now people tell me I should capitalize on my pro experience, such as it is, and go into coaching. But I decided not to listen to everybody else this time. I decided to go back to college and get another bachelor's degree. In theater.

HELEN
Good for you. I have an excellent book you should look at - it's a collection of interviews with famous playwrights. I'm sure it's back here somewhere. Oh dear. I used to be so organized.

(HELEN rummages for a book on the back shelf. SHE knocks an envelope onto the floor. BETTY picks it up.)

BETTY
Where do you want me to put this, Helen?

HELEN
A lady doesn't say where I'd like you to put that letter. It's from that obscure little press in Mississippi that Gene recommended, the one that specializes in memoirs. Unfortunately, they're not interested in mine. My efforts didn't even merit a passing comment with the form letter.

JIM
I thought I'd cornered the market on those.

SUZANNE
I've never gotten a rejection letter, boiler plate or otherwise. Then again, I've never submitted anything.

HELEN
Gene certainly got his share over the years. It took him a long time to break through.

JIM
(sighing)
I know.

HELEN
Suzanne, are you ready to proceed now?

SUZANNE
I'm still thinking about Emily. How do you carry on? I would crawl in a hole and die after what you went through. My will would be completely broken.

EMILY
Maybe playing basketball all those years did me some good after all. You certainly learn how to get up, dust yourself off, and try again.

BETTY
Sounds like good advice for a writer.

SUZANNE
Geez, Emily. I feel so awful.

HELEN
In spite of that, we must get on with our business. Suzanne?

SUZANNE

Well, I didn't get much written this past week. But I did hear from Jim's paralegal. Four of Elsa Higgins' former classmates are living in various corners of the state. I suppose I should say thank you to Jim. For that part, anyway.

JIM

My pleasure. All around.

SUZANNE

Anyway, I have married names for two girls in Elsa's class. One of them is a resident at the Cromwell Nursing Home, which is only an hour and half's drive away. I plan to interview her. I'll have to write to her first, though. I can't just show up out of the blue. Her name is Mavis MacGraw.

JIM

Why not? The old lady's probably bored to tears. Anyway, I doubt if the staff would deny her a visitor. You could imply that you're a distant relative.

SUZANNE

I won't lie just to get inside.

JIM

I forgot. You're pure in thought, word and deed.

HELEN

Stop it, Jimmy. Let her proceed at her own pace. Betty, what does Harry have to say about George Higgins' account books?

BETTY

He says he'll get to them in a few weeks.

SUZANNE

See, he's too busy. I shouldn't have bothered him.

BETTY

Nonsense! If he says he'll get to them, he'll get to them.

SUZANNE

I just don't like to impose on other people.

EMILY

Can I say what I found out now?

HELEN

Please. Go ahead, Emily.

EMILY

That article in the trunk came from a weekly called "The County Record". I found another article from the week before. There was a man who went missing at the same time as Elsa Higgins. Only he was found clinging to his overturned boat a day later.

BETTY

Hmm. I wonder if there's a connection.

EMILY

Here, Suzanne. I made a copy for you. His name was Carl DiCenza, the one who went missing.

(SUZANNE takes the article from Emily. SHE sets it aside.)

SUZANNE

Just what I need. Another mystery.

(SUZANNE hesitates, then picks up some typed pages and clears her throat.)

SUZANNE

I guess I did write four pages. It's not very much to show for two whole weeks' work, but I could -

HELEN

(interrupting)

Let's hear it.

(The lights dim as SUZANNE begins to read to the group. The wind and rain intensify, drowning out SUZANNE's words. Thunder rumbles. Lightning flashes in the sky. The lights in the house flicker off and back on.)

HELEN

That storm is not letting up. I think we should call it a night. Suzanne, I need to speak with you briefly after the meeting.

SUZANNE
Does it have to be now? My headache is coming back.

HELEN
Yes Dear, it simply cannot wait.

(JIM, EMILY and BETTY gather their things and get ready to leave. HELEN and SUZANNE sit at the card table. HELEN reaches across the table and clasps both SUZANNE's hands.)

JIM
(to EMILY)
I was way out of line tonight. I don't even know what to offer up as a defense.

EMILY
How about temporary insanity?

JIM
No, with me the condition is permanent.

(JIM, EMILY and BETTY banter as they exit. The storm intrudes loudly into the room while the front door is open. Meanwhile, HELEN is talking to SUZANNE who stiffens and shakes her head vigorously. Several cars are started and drive off. SUZANNE pulls her hands away and stands up.)

SUZANNE
But you'll hate Los Angeles. It's nothing but triple-decker freeways. Your life is here, Helen.

HELEN
I'm sorry, Dear. My decision is made.

SUZANNE
You don't get along with Dorothy. You always side with Joe against her and then you feel awful. You told me so yourself.

HELEN
Nevertheless.

SUZANNE

I can't let this happen, Helen. You're my best friend in the whole, wide world.

HELEN

Suzanne, that's not healthy. You're still young and I'm decidedly not. You have your whole life ahead of you.

SUZANNE

I have a past, a present and a future just like you do.

HELEN

(laughing)

You're so stubborn. Perversely, it's the trait I like best in you.

SUZANNE

Writers Block will fall apart. Don't you even care about Writers Block anymore?

HELEN

I simply must face the reality of my own inevitable decline. I can't go on living alone. Someday you'll understand what I'm going through.

SUZANNE

There has to be a better answer.

HELEN

I want to know my only grandson while he's still a child.

SUZANNE

Denny can visit you here. It will be good for him and for Dorothy and Joe. I'm right about that and you know it.

HELEN

Please, Dear. I'm in no condition to run after a small child.

SUZANNE

But you just made it through another winter. At least wait until fall.

HELEN

That's enough now.

SUZANNE

Promise me you won't go right away.

HELEN

I said that's enough and I meant it. Try to be happy for me, Dear.

SUZANNE

I won't be. I can't be.

(A popping sound is heard as the wind gusts. A large tree limb crashes through the ceiling in the far corner. HELEN gasps. SUZANNE screams.)

HELEN

You see, Dear? It really is time.

SUZANNE

It is not time! N-o-o-o-o!

(BLACKOUT)

END OF ACT I

ACT II

Scene 1

SETTING: **We are at BETTY's house. The living room has a modern, minimalist decor that contrasts with HELEN's clutter. A big-screen TV is part of an entertainment center. The room opens onto a wooden deck which holds a porch swing.**

AT RISE: **EMILY is sitting on the edge of the deck. GENE occupies the swing. HE wears half glasses and is reading SUZANNE's work. Ill at ease, EMILY fidgets and watches for the others to arrive.**

GENE

(more to himself than to EMILY)

I say! This is quite engaging, if a bit rough around the edges.

(The sound of a car approaching is heard, followed by brakes and a slamming door. JIM enters. HE spots GENE and frowns. Then he forces a smile and steps forward. EMILY visibly relaxes when she sees JIM approach.)

JIM

Gene, good to see you again.

(JIM extends his hand which GENE shakes without getting up.)

JIM

How was the book tour?

GENE

Quite grueling. I'm very glad it's over with.

JIM

Right.

GENE

Oh, don't misunderstand me. I'm grateful for my good fortune. But I did miss the comforts of home. Astoundingly, I even missed teaching "Survey of American Literature" to Middle U freshmen. Imagine that!

JIM

I might miss pontificating in front of a jury myself. I'd sure like the chance to find out, though. On a brighter note, I see you've met Emily. The WNBA's loss is our gain.

EMILY

I hope so. Where do you suppose Betty can be? And Suzanne's usually the first one to arrive.

JIM

I know Betty is expecting us. I saw Harry at Rotary yesterday morning. He said Betty went on a mad cleaning binge in preparation for our first meeting here. Harry also gave me his executive summary on the Elsa Higgins matter. Suzanne isn't going to like what he has to say.

GENE

And what is it that Suzanne does like?

JIM

Well, she's certainly devoted to Helen. That's blindingly clear.

EMILY

And to you as well, Gene, the way I hear it.

GENE

I suppose that's so.

(The sound of a car approaching is heard. A car door slams. BETTY hurries onstage with her arms full of grocery bags.)

BETTY

I'm here. I'm here. There was an accident on the bridge. I thought traffic would never move again.

JIM

Let me get those for you.

(HE takes the bags from BETTY who gets a key out of her purse.)

BETTY

Come in, come in. Don't mind the mess.

(Carrying the bags, JIM follows BETTY into the offstage kitchen. GENE and EMILY stand awkwardly in the spotless living room. BETTY reappears, carrying a fancy hors d'oeuvres tray. JIM follows carrying two full pitchers.)

BETTY

Sit. Help yourselves.

(JIM and EMILY sit down. SUZANNE and HELEN enter and ascend the stairs to the deck. They walk slowly with HELEN leaning on SUZANNE's arm. Before they can ring the bell, BETTY runs to the door and flings it open. BETTY sings the next line off key.)

BETTY

Hail, hail, the gang's all here. How's the repair work coming, Helen?

HELEN

Don't ask. Don't even ask.

SUZANNE

It's terribly inconvenient, but we know it will be worth it in the end.

HELEN

You see, I'm replacing the defective sill at the same time.

SUZANNE

And half the clapboards were rotten, so she's getting aluminum siding put on.

BETTY

My, that sounds expensive.

HELEN

Well, insurance will cover the damage from the willow tree. As for the rest, I have a nest egg. Joe says I'll get some of it back when I do finally sell the place. Meanwhile, Suzanne insists on paying me rent. I feel guilty taking her money with all that she does for me, but she won't take no for an answer.

(BETTY turns to whisper to HELEN. SUZANNE's gaze is focused intently on GENE, who is still perusing her manuscript.)

BETTY

But she's not even working!

SUZANNE

Yes, I am. I'm doing some tutoring.

GENE

That does not sound like a lucrative occupation.

HELEN

But she's using her education. And she's very good at it.

SUZANNE

I do like working one on one with each student. And I don't need a lot of money.

HELEN

And I adore having a roommate! I feel like a young girl again.

BETTY

I wonder if I'll ever get my roommate back. Harry's forever working late these days.

SUZANNE

That must be awful for you.

BETTY

It wasn't a problem for me until the last of the kids moved out. He was supposed to cut back when he turned sixty, but he hasn't. Not one bit.

JIM
You don't go into the office at all anymore yourself?

BETTY
The girls are all so young. And they're wearing those mini-skirts again.

JIM
They are? Tell Harry I need an appointment.

SUZANNE
You shouldn't call them girls, Betty. It's disrespectful. They're full-grown women and some of them have college degrees.

BETTY
They do have several female accountants, but no female partners.

EMILY
Not yet.

JIM
(with a snort)
Right.

EMILY
I am right. They may not have any yet, but they will before long. It's inevitable.

JIM
And two women will compete for U.S. president in the next election cycle.

HELEN
You're so cynical, Jimmy.

JIM
Show me a reason not to be.

BETTY
Well, here's a small one. My husband did find time to look at those financial records. He just handed me a written report this morning.

SUZANNE
Harry wrote a whole report? Just for me?

BETTY

Yes, he did. I suggested he come tonight, but he had a board presentation to do. He'll be glad to answer your questions later, Suzanne. It starts with a summary letter.

HELEN

(interrupting)

Let's get started. Read the letter aloud, Suzanne.

SUZANNE

No, Betty. You go ahead. I'd rather listen to this.

BETTY

All right, if you like. "Dear Suzanne. I apologize for the long delay in responding to you. Here are the facts as revealed by the financial records. Your grandfather George Higgins operated a retail store that was chronically insolvent. As shown in Attachment A, sales did not keep pace with expenses in any of the seven years for which records are available. At the start of the period, a deposit of approximately seven thousand dollars was made into the business checking account. That took place on April 25, 1942."

SUZANNE

(interrupting)

That's the year George and Elsa were married. Sorry, go on.

BETTY

"That money was quickly expended. Moreover, that deposit precisely matches a withdrawal which nearly depletes savings account number 11-411, which then becomes inactive, except for occasional postings of interest. That account was opened sometime prior to January 1942 in the name of Elsa Greenfield. During 1943 and 1944 three other savings accounts were opened in three separate banks located in surrounding towns. These accounts were in the names of George and Elsa Higgins. There is a pattern of matching withdrawals from the new passbooks and deposits into the business checking account beginning in 1943. These deposits are entered into the store's daily sales journal as 'bakery receipts.' Once a week a deposit is made into each of the three out-of-town accounts. Each deposit, without exception, is in an even dollar amount with minimal variation from week to week. No pennies appear, except as postings of interest." That's the end of the first section. Shall I go on?

SUZANNE

Yes, please.

BETTY

"Speculations." This section is labeled speculations. "I believe that savings account 11-411 represented funds that Elsa Greenfield brought into the marriage, a sort of dowry if you will. I surmise that the Greenfield family did not have prior knowledge that George's store was experiencing financial difficulties."

SUZANNE

That pig stole her money.

JIM

Legally it was his money.

EMILY

Really?

HELEN

Absolutely. You young girls have no idea what it used to be like. No idea at all. Please continue, Betty.

BETTY

"The question that looms large is 'What was the source of the three revenue streams?' You see, I'm convinced that there was no bakery operation of substance, for I saw no bulk purchases of flour and eggs and the like. Some other form of goods or services must have been involved, but what? A bootleg liquor business might have generated such a revenue stream during Prohibition. But Prohibition had already ended by the 1940's. Any legal business involving merchandise would have required purchases that went through the books. I found no evidence of such expenditures. So, I asked myself, 'What form of service would generate a steady income week after week in each of three outlying locations?' There is only one answer that seems to fit the fact pattern. I hesitate to offer it to you. I ask that you bear in mind that I am speculating in the absence of clear evidence. Rather, it is the very lack of documentation combined with the dearth of resources available to your grandmother that leads me in one particular direction."

SUZANNE

The first part of the report made perfect sense. But what is Harry trying to say now? Why can't he spit it out?

GENE

Sweet, naive Suzanne. My dear, Harry thinks your grandma was engaged in the world's oldest profession.

SUZANNE

No!

EMILY

What does that mean?

HELEN

Don't you know that expression? Explain it to her, Jim.

JIM

Why me?

SUZANNE

No, I don't believe it. I don't believe it for a minute.

JIM

Elsa Higgins was selling her body.

EMILY

I was kind of thinking that.

SUZANNE

Well, I wasn't. I bet you weren't either, Helen.

HELEN

Actually, Dear, it does sound rather logical, certainly more so than any alternative explanation I can think of.

SUZANNE

This can't be happening to me.

GENE

Nor is it. It either happened to your grandmother long ago, as Harry thinks, or else it did not. What you choose to believe and what you choose to shut out of the realm of possibility, that's another matter altogether.

BETTY

The really intriguing question, to me, is why would a wife do such a thing. Why would she sleep with other men in order to secretly generate enough money to keep her husband's business afloat?

GENE

To keep up appearances, I suppose. She apparently came from a family of means. She'd have wanted to keep the truth from them.

JIM
I wonder if she transferred all her earnings into the store. Maybe she kept something in reserve.

BETTY
Like mad money? I don't know.

JIM
Can I have a look at that report?

(HE takes the report from BETTY and flips to the back.)

JIM
Nope. Not growing. She transferred it all to the store account.

SUZANNE
I bet George squandered every penny.

JIM
Well, it certainly does look that way.

BETTY
Harry told me that, for a lawyer, you grasp financial matters extremely quickly.

JIM
I'm not sure if that's a compliment or a slur.

GENE
A bit of both, I suppose.

JIM
Harry could tell you all kinds of things about the lives the two of them led, Suzanne. You should take him up on his offer to meet with you.

SUZANNE
I wouldn't feel comfortable.

JIM
Damn it, Suzanne! You claim you want to get to the truth of the matter. Do you or don't you?

SUZANNE
I guess I do. I mean yes. I'm just ... not fluid around people the way you are.

JIM
(suddenly gentle)
Would you like me to come with you? I could call Harry to set it up.

SUZANNE
God, yes! Thank you, Jim.

JIM
You're welcome.

HELEN
I thought the words "you're welcome" had vanished from America forever, like Jimmy Hoffa. On TV they just keep parroting "thank you, thank you, thank you" back and forth.

EMILY
Who's Jimmy Hoffa?

JIM
You are a child. He was the president of the teamsters' union. He vanished back in the sixties. Nobody knows what happened. Perhaps Suzanne can solve that mystery when she's through with this one.

EMILY
Don't make fun of her. Or me.

GENE
Well, the trail's certainly cold on that mystery. Suzanne, any luck setting up your interview with the old lady at the nursing home?

SUZANNE
I wrote to her a couple weeks ago and said I was coming. I didn't ask if it was all right. I just announced my arrival time. I tried to talk Helen into coming with me. She can relate to Mrs. MacGraw better than I can.

HELEN
Because I'm frightfully old as well?

SUZANNE
I didn't mean it like that. Now I've offended you.

HELEN

Nonsense. You worry too much.

JIM

Hear, hear.

BETTY

Does anybody need a refill on iced tea or lemonade?

EMILY

(to SUZANNE)

You look like you could use something a lot stronger than that.

SUZANNE

To think that my own grandmother was a ... I can't even say it.

JIM

Do you suppose George suspected?

GENE

Not likely. Never underestimate the power of denial. But after Elsa died, you say George moved away.

SUZANNE

A thousand miles away. He remarried six months later. He sat my mother down the night before his second wedding - she had just turned six - and told her she was never to speak about Elsa again. He told her, "Sally, you've got a brand new mother now. Let bygones be bygones."

BETTY

How cruel! Is George Higgins still alive?

SUZANNE

No. He died about twenty years ago.

JIM

What about his second wife?

SUZANNE

Gayle? She's around someplace, but my family doesn't have anything to do with her.

JIM

If I were you, I would definitely talk to the second wife. If anybody knows a man's deepest secrets, it's wife number two. Boy, doesn't the poor slob regret his wagging tongue when divorce number two rolls around. I insisted on learning that lesson the hard way. It wasn't sufficient to watch my clients screw up.

EMILY

So you don't plan on telling wife number three anything.

JIM

Name. Rank (Lord of the Manor). And social security number, since there will be a directory of those on the internet soon anyway. Anything else she'll have to coax out of me with gourmet meals and virtuoso blow jobs.

HELEN

Jimmy, you're incorrigible.

JIM

Thank you.

HELEN

You're not welcome.

BETTY

How are you doing, Suzanne?

SUZANNE

I was doing better until that disgusting last comment of his.

BETTY

I do hope you can cope with this turn of events. Your grandmother no doubt had her reasons. If Harry's right about her.

SUZANNE

Well, it's hardly what I expected from my own flesh and blood. Still, I have to admit I see the makings of one wild tale.

JIM

Hell of a fucking story.

HELEN

No need. No need at all. I'm certain that Betty doesn't appreciate hearing a string of four-letter words spoken in her living room any more than I did in mine. It's high time you left adolescence behind, Jimmy.

JIM

Never.

(HE sings a la Peter Pan..)

"I won't grow up, I won't grow up. I refuse to act my age, So put me in a cage."

SUZANNE

That's not how the song goes.

JIM

It isn't? You sing it for us, then. Sing it the right goddamn way.

HELEN

Please! Somebody put a leash on him.

JIM

Hey Suzanne, you want me on the end of a short leash? Where's that studded leather collar of yours, Betty?

(JIM, on all fours, rubs against SUZANNE's leg.)

JIM

Woof, woof.

SUZANNE

I think this dog needs a certain operation. For the good of society.

JIM

I'd rather go to hell. Shoot me now.

BETTY

Only a man would say such a foolish thing.

SUZANNE

(pointing her finger at JIM.)

Bang, bang.

(JIM, still on all fours, staggers. HE drags himself over to an empty chair in the corner and

lifts his leg. Everybody laughs, even HELEN. JIM collapses in a heap.)

(BLACKOUT)

END OF SCENE 1

ACT II

Scene 2

At Rise: **HELEN is seated in the living room, marking a manuscript with a red pen. BETTY enters with a pitcher and glasses. SUZANNE follows a moment later. Her hair is down and has been professionally set. SHE is wearing a severe, navy-blue suit. The trunk is out on the floor.**

BETTY

I just can't get over how wonderful your hair looks tonight, Suzanne.

HELEN

Yes, I told her it was extremely becoming.

SUZANNE

It's just to please my brother. Brian said if I showed up at the wedding in a pony tail, he would personally chop if off. I don't know what the big deal is. It's not like I'm in the wedding party or anything. She has three sisters.

(BETTY bustles about, arranging trays of hors d'oeuvres.)

BETTY

Who has three sisters?

SUZANNE

My brother's fiancee. They're getting married in St. Andrews at the crack of dawn.

BETTY

Oh, that's so romantic! Such a beautiful beginning. Don't you be a wallflower now. Weddings are wonderful occasions to meet, shall we say, members of the opposite sex.

SUZANNE

Actually, I have a d - , I'm bringing a guest. I invited Gene.

HELEN

That's right, Betty. Suzanne and Gene are going to hie tail it north right after our meeting.

SUZANNE

After I drop you off at home, that is.

BETTY

How did this come about? You and Gene going on a date.

SUZANNE

It's not really a date. The other morning I met with Gene so we could go over the first chapter of his new book. I always have questions - words I can't decipher and arrows that point off the page - before I type up his stuff. I'd just gotten the wedding invitation in the mail that morning. It said I was supposed to bring a guest. And I thought to myself, "I never asked anything of Gene before. Not one single favor. Famous or not, he owes me." I think he was dumbfounded when I invited him, but then he murmured 'I suppose so.' I was so relieved. I know they'll all be impressed when I show up with Gene Cartwright. Even my father will have to notice.

EMILY

(enters through the front door.)

Sorry I'm late. Wow, Suzanne. Your hair looks great!

SUZANNE

I wish everybody would stop talking about my hair.

HELEN

Dear, the proper response to a compliment is "Thank you."

SUZANNE

(mumbling)

Thanks, Em.

EMILY

You're welcome. There, Helen. The younger generation isn't completely illiterate.

(JIM enters. HE does a double take when he sees SUZANNE, but decides not to say anything about her hair.)

JIM

Greetings, fellow troubadours. Don't those munchies look fabulous! I'm famished.

(HE puts a large quantity of food on a small plate and sits down with the plate in his lap. HE begins to talk with his mouth full.)

BETTY

Glad you're here, Jim. Now we can get started.

SUZANNE

Shouldn't we wait for Gene? He's going to be here for sure tonight. We're leaving together from here.

JIM

What's this?

BETTY

They're going to her brother's wedding. I'm sure Gene will be here soon. But perhaps we ought to go ahead without him.

JIM

So what else is new?

HELEN

Already you start in.

JIM

I'm sorry, Helen. I lost a big case today. And I desperately need to get laid. That would help immensely. Suzanne, how did it go with the old crone?

BETTY

That's an insensitive choice of words.

JIM

Suzanne, how did it go with the elderly Mrs. MacGraw?

SUZANNE

She was a chirpy, blue-haired lady who smelled like a perfume factory. She couldn't remember Elsa Greenfield or George Higgins, not even when I showed her the class pictures.

JIM

A complete waste of time, then.

SUZANNE

Not exactly. She told me there was a man in the nursing-care section from their high school. My ears really perked up when she told me his name. Gerald Dicenza.

EMILY

Like the man who went missing, the one who drowned! Gerald must be Carl DiCenza's brother.

SUZANNE

His nephew, actually. Gerald's not all that old. He's just ... in a bad way.

BETTY

Well, what did he tell you?

SUZANNE

A lot, actually. I wrote a whole chapter. Here goes nothing.

(SUZANNE stands to read.)

Sickness scares me. I have never been one to face fear head on. Better to be judged a wimp, I say, than to step into the path of trouble. So I avoid hospitals. I send flowers and cards to people who get ill, but I don't visit them. The glass doors snapped shut on the nursing care building. A medicinal aura closed in on me. I wasn't prepared for this place - Mrs. MacGraw's little white room with the kitchenette had misled me. Here nurses in turquoise pajamas bustled about and aides in funny, flowered shirts pushed carts down corridors. The building housed patients, two to a room, tethered to IV bottles. Shrunken limbs jutted from sleeves. Vacant eyes half noticed me as I passed in the hall. I made myself forge ahead because my friends at Writers Block would be so disappointed if I faltered. Room 217, when I found it, reeked of ammonia. In fact, the chalky tile floor was slick from a recent mopping. I slid once, after

SUZANNE (Cont'd)
which I took mincing penguin steps toward the nearer bed. Next to it sat a bald man in a wheel chair with a blanket on his lap. In sharp contrast to the others I'd glimpsed, Gerald DiCenza's arms exuded strength. At least I hoped this was Gerald DiCenza, for the room's other occupant was dead to the world.

(GERALD wheels himself onto the edge of the stage. SUZANNE half-turns toward him as SHE continues reading.)

SUZANNE
"Mr. DiCenza?" I said uncertainly. No reply. So I came closer and deliberately spoke louder. "Mr. DiCenza, the lady at the front desk said it was okay to come to your room."

(GERALD turns his chair toward SUZANNE as she steps nearer.)

SUZANNE
When I caught sight of his face, I gave up all hope. I saw the gleam of madness in his eyes. He mouthed the name twice before he managed to utter it aloud, his voice a quavering croak.

GERALD
Elsie.

SUZANNE
Then, to my surprise and relief, he recovered his senses.

GERALD
(in full voice)
But that's impossible. You must think I've gone bonkers.

(SUZANNE addresses Gerald directly.)

SUZANNE
(after giggling nervously)
No! You're not crazy because I'm her granddaughter. My mother kept a portrait of Elsa Higgins -

GERALD
(interrupting)
He called her Elsie.

SUZANNE

In the house I grew up in. Of course I couldn't tell for myself, you never can, but everybody said the resemblance was uncanny. You see, I never met my grandmother and I'm hoping you can answer some questions about her.

GERALD

Oh.

(GERALD draws a sharp breath, then fidgets. SUZANNE shifts from foot to foot nervously.)

SUZANNE

You, you said he called her her Elsie. Who did? Is that what she went by? You see, I don't even know if she had a nickname.

GERALD

Elsie.

SUZANNE

(turning to group)

He fell maddeningly silent. Well, I thought, two can play at that game. My friend and mentor Helen, who will turn eighty next month, and I share many languid hours. Our house is a chatter-free zone. I never had that before, the comfortable quiet of two companions. I sat down beside him and waited.

(SUZANNE sits down in a ladderback chair that has been set beside GERALD. There is a pregnant pause. JIM helps himself to more food. The spotlight switches between the speakers in the ensuing exchange.)

GERALD

I wish I knew, Lady, whether you were sent from heaven or hell. Look. I know it's in vogue these days to get in touch with your feelings. But there's a wise old expression: let sleeping dogs lie. God knows it would do me good to spit it all out. Do you know how hard it is to keep a secret from everybody for all time? It changes you inside, to have such knowledge.

SUZANNE

What knowledge?

SUZANNE (Cont'd)

(facing the group)

I listened to the hum of machinery, punctuated by the distant ring of the telephone and the occasional, falsely cheerful human voice. Female, always female. Where were the men in charge, the doctors and the administrators? My father's image came to mind. I thought how impossible it was for him to talk about sex to anybody, let alone to a strange young woman. Gerald was probably around the same age as my father. Perhaps his paternal instinct formed the barrier between us. Perhaps if he understood how much I already knew or at least suspected, perhaps ... And so I began to talk. You know me. I mostly listen. But I made myself tell him all about Writers Block, how Jim and Betty's husband Harry did specialized research I could never have afforded otherwise. I told him about Elsa's mysterious finances just like Harry told me. Finally, I explained how Emily discovered that a man named Carl DiCenza had gone missing at the same time that my grandmother did. Apparently my strategy was the right one, for Gerald took over the narrative. And once he began, he could not stop himself.

GERALD

Uncle Carl. That lecher. They're all gone now. All the players are dead. I don't know whether that makes it acceptable to tell you what happened. I just don't know. Actually Annie, that's my cousin, is technically still alive. She's Carl and Aunt Eileen's kid. She's the only one I ever really cared about protecting. Annie lives in a place like this in a state like that.

SUZANNE

He gestured toward his insensate roommate and went on. It so happened that one October day Gerald played hooky from his job at the lumber mill to go fishing. Come lunchtime, he decided to dock on Porcupine Island and visit Uncle Carl's camp. The place was never locked and Gerald had permission to use it. He opened his lunch pail and ate at the rustic kitchen table, then headed up to the loft for a nap. He awoke to the sound of female laughter. The next day, Elsa Higgins was waiting for Gerald in the mill parking lot at the end of his shift. She grabbed him by the forearm. "I saw you." Like most men, he lied. He said he had no idea what she was talking about. He only abandoned the pretense when she began to cry. "We don't actually do it, you know. We never do." "It's none of my business, Mrs. Higgins," he muttered in response. What he really wanted to say, to shriek, was just how much worse that made it. If only Uncle Carl had just done her like a man instead of ... Gerald shuddered as the picture replayed. There was Uncle Carl stroking his own nipples. There was Elsie on all fours with her skirt bunched above her waist and no panties on.

(SUZANNE turns toward GERALD.)

GERALD

When he was done, Uncle Carl reached into his wallet. He extended a wad in his sticky right hand. Elsie crawled forward and took the money with her teeth. Then she reached up to brush a sheaf of hair from her cheek. We made eye contact, her on the plank floor and me up in the loft. At the time I wasn't absolutely certain. Out in the mill parking lot the next day's when I found out for sure. "You can't tell George." she begged me. "Why would I do that?" I asked. I never liked George Higgins. He was a braggart who threw money around. Turned out it wasn't even his money. She told me "He's really very kind-hearted, your uncle. You mustn't tell his wife either." "Kind-hearted," I echoed stupidly, thinking of what I'd witnessed. No, I would not be telling Aunt Eileen about Uncle Carl's perversions. "Why do you do it, Elsie?" I grew bold and addressed her by her first name. She ignored the disrespect. "Because I can't afford to stop." It was the only answer I ever got.

SUZANNE

Did George know what was going on?

GERALD

He didn't have a clue till the state cops figured it out. They made Elsie's rounds, those imaginary bakery deliveries that George had bought into. Of course George was mortified. Any husband would be. Uncle Carl was devastated too. You know what really did my uncle in, if you ask me? He got over the loss of his live pinup. Hell, all he ever did was watch anyway. See, he thought he was her one and only sugar daddy. Uncle Carl never was the same afterward. People attributed the change to forty hours of floating in the cold ocean, but I knew better. It was finding out about the two other men. That and the guilt.

SUZANNE

You mean for cheating on his wife?

GERALD

Hell, no! That's commonplace. I mean for not telling the cops where to look for Elsie. He didn't realize that she'd made it back to Porcupine Island alive. See, the coroner determined that the cause of death was exposure, not drowning. But Uncle Carl never said a word about any passenger when the Coast Guard rescued him.

SUZANNE

Why didn't you say something yourself?

GERALD

I didn't know they were together that day. I didn't connect the dots till they found Elsie's body on the island.

SUZANNE
Did you ever confront your uncle? Did he admit to any of this?

GERALD
He didn't have do. Uncle Carl's marriage fell apart right after the boat accident. Aunt Eileen moved out. I was engaged to be married at the time - that ended, too. See, watching Elsie had pumped me up in a way my girlfriend couldn't come close to. Nipples like red rosebuds she had. Lord, the things I'm telling you! Perhaps you are Elsie Greenfield after all, returned from the dead to put a curse on me.

SUZANNE
Hardly!
(turning toward the group)
We fell silent again. "Is there anything I can do for you before I go?" I asked naively, never suspecting what would follow. Gerald laughed out loud. He had trouble stopping.

GERALD
(laughing maniacally)
Nah. Never mind.

SUZANNE
Never mind what?

GERALD
Oh, what the hell? Our paths will never cross again. What I'd really like, Lady, is to get a gander at your bare knockers. There.

(SUZANNE gasps. She stands and backs away.)

GERALD
Yeah, I'm a dirty old man.

SUZANNE
I took a step backward. He leaned toward me and the blanket slipped from his lap. I saw then that Gerald DiCenza was a double amputee.

GERALD
Diabetes.

SUZANNE
He spit the word out like a bug in a forkful of salad. "It's a killer," I remarked.

GERALD

If only!

SUZANNE

I was repulsed and embarrassed and ashamed. "I guess I'll be going," I blurted. "I have a long drive back. I go Route eighty-nine to the interstate, where there's all kinds of construction going on." I couldn't stop babbling.

GERALD

(with transparent agony)

Please.

SUZANNE

We both heard the desperation. For the first time I vacillated, but just for a second. "No," I said. "It would be wrong."

GERALD

I won't ask again.

(GERALD picks up the blanket and covers his stumps. He wheels himself off stage. SUZANNE stares after him, then walks slowly toward the group.)

SUZANNE

Back on the road, I went over all the reasons I was right to refuse Gerald DiCenza's outrageous request. Thirty minutes into my return trip, I let out a string of swear words worthy of Jim and turned around. Gerald was lying on the bed, attended by a battle axe of a nurse. I stood in the doorway feeling mighty foolish. If it meant that much to him, why the hell not? But my timing was bad. Disappointment assailed me, surprising me with its force. Did I actually long to perform this whorish act? I started to leave. The motion caught Gerald's attention. He saw me and his eyes lit in recognition. I vaccilated yet again. I shrank back into the hallway. No way, I couldn't do this. So sorry, Gerald. You dared to frame and (gasp!) speak a wish in this moribund place. A vital man's wish. The nurse turned and bent her broad back over Gerald. Suddenly resolute, I stepped back into the doorway. Just perceptibly, I saw Gerald nod. The last of the three hooks proved extra stubborn. It finally gave way. In one swift motion I peeled both sweater and bra skyward. Gerald stared, his jaw agape. Then he grinned like the Cheshire cat and mouthed, "Hallelujah!"

(SUZANNE looks at her feet.)

SUZANNE (Cont'd)

That's it. It only lasted a couple seconds. You probably don't believe I did it. To tell you the truth, neither do I.

BETTY

You didn't really! It's a story.

EMILY

Did you?

(SUZANNE blushes and nods her head.)

EMILY

Way to go, Girlfriend!

BETTY

(to HELEN)

Did you know about this?

HELEN

No, but I'm impressed.

BETTY

(to JIM)

What do you think?

JIM

(HE sings, a la Bob Dylan.)

They stone you when you speak your thoughts aloud. They stone you when you hide them in a shroud.

That's no answer.

SUZANNE

Did you like the writing?

JIM

Yes. In fact I did. There's a bit of throat clearing at the start that ought to shrink. I heard a couple rough transitions. Otherwise, I was right there in that rustic cabin, right there in that dreary nursing home. Horny as hell both places. Anyway, you don't give a damn what I think. You want to know what Gene thinks.

SUZANNE

Don't presume to know what I want. Where the ... where the fuck is Gene, anyway?

JIM

No need for such language. No need at all.

SUZANNE

I'm sorry, but I'll die if he stands me up tonight. I will.

HELEN

No you won't, Dear. Gene is the one who will die. I'll kill him myself with my bare hands.

(SUZANNE goes over to HELEN and hugs her.)

SUZANNE

That's so sweet.

BETTY

I say it's time for a break. I need a moment to to take in what I just heard. It's the same way for me at Middle U. I'm bowled over by the things the young people have already experienced. My word!

EMILY

You can't shelter us. It's foolish to try.

SUZANNE

(through clenched teeth)

Where - is - Gene?

BETTY

Perhaps he'll get here by the time we reconvene.

(SHE rises.)

I'll go refill the pitchers.

JIM

Good. I need a smoke break.

(HE goes out the front door and onto the deck. SUZANNE follows him outside. JIM lights a cigarette. SUZANNE coughs and moves away.)

JIM

Sorry. I'm toxic.

SUZANNE

Jim, I need a really big favor. I mean, just in case - God, I can't ask it this way, can I? It isn't fair to you. But I have to be at my brother's wedding and I just can't go alone.

JIM

You want me to be your backup date.

SUZANNE

Well yes, to put it bluntly. Oh, this is really awful of me. Just forget about it. Forget I even came out here. I'm leaving now.

(SUZANNE turns to re enter the house.)

JIM

I accept.

SUZANNE

Did I hear you right?

(JIM shrugs his shoulders and nods.)

SUZANNE

Now that is truly sweet. It's way better treatment than I deserve.

(SHE impulsively goes over to JIM and kisses him on the cheek.)

BETTY

(calling)

Time to get back to work, everybody.

(JIM stubs out his cigarette. The group gathers in the seating area. The lights dim for long enough to signify the passing of the remaining meeting time. The group puts away their papers and gets ready to disband. HELEN picks up a magazine and sits in a chair in the corner. BETTY and EMILY carry empty dishes to the kitchen.)

SUZANNE

(to JIM)

Well. You ready? It's a long drive, but they have two rooms reserved for us. We can rest before and after the ceremony. You'll want to stop at your house and pick up a few things, I imagine.

JIM

I carry a spare suit in the car. Anything else I'll just pick up along the way.

SUZANNE

This is so good of you.

JIM

Thank me later. Get your things.

SUZANNE

(SHE picks up a cloth tote bag.)

This is all I'm bringing.

JIM

So that's what you're wearing to the ceremony?

SUZANNE

Yes. This is my interview suit!

JIM

Exactly.

SUZANNE

What's wrong with it?

JIM

Nothing, if you're planning to testify before the Securities and Exchange Commission. It's just not very festive.

SUZANNE

It's all I have with me.

JIM

What about Elsa's red dress? That trunk's in Betty's guest room, isn't it?

SUZANNE

I could never wear that.

JIM
Why not? At least see if it fits. Come on. Try it on and then decide.

SUZANNE
(mumbling)
It fits.

JIM
Oh really? What if I refuse to go with you unless you change clothes?

SUZANNE
If I wear that dress, I might end up in bed with you.

JIM
Whatever I say next you'll take the wrong way.

(SUZANNE leaves the room. JIM paces. EMILY comes in and out, clearing dishes, glancing at JIM with curiosity. SUZANNE reemerges wearing the red dress.)

JIM
Hallelujah indeed! Let's hit the road.

(SUZANNE does a pirouette and laughs coquettishly. Meanwhile, GENE has entered through the front door. EMILY stands in the kitchen doorway.)

GENE
Why, I hardly recognize you tonight, Suzanne. I apologize for my extreme tardiness. I hope you weren't overly concerned.

SUZANNE
I was a little. What happened to you?

GENE
I was writing. I got into the zone and lost track of the time.

JIM
You missed the entire meeting.

GENE
I suppose I did, despite the best of intentions. So, Suzanne, are we ready to fly?

SUZANNE
(SHE looks sadly at JIM.)
I, I guess I'm ready.

GENE
Come along, then.

SUZANNE
I have to drop Helen off at home. Can you follow behind me?

BETTY
(entering from the kitchen)
Oh, hello Gene. You needn't bother with all that. I can give Helen a ride home. Just leave your car here, Suzanne, and come by for it later.

SUZANNE
Well, all right I guess. Good night, everybody.

BETTY
Have a wonderful, wonderful time!

(JIM collapses in a chair and puts his head in his hands as GENE and SUZANNE leave together.)

EMILY
Well, that sucks. Do you want to go out for a drink with me instead?

JIM
Thanks, but I wouldn't be very good company.

EMILY
That's all right. You don't have to make small talk.

JIM
Maybe some other time.

EMILY
No really. You'd be doing me a favor. There's a band I promised to go hear, and I hate walking into a bar alone.

JIM
Oh, what the hell?

(EMILY and JIM exit together. JIM puts his hand on EMILY's back. SHE leans toward him. BETTY drops into a chair near HELEN.)

HELEN

Now there's a twisted turn of events. As Suzanne would say, I don't like it. Poor Jimmy!

BETTY

Why? He looked quite content to me when he left. You don't suppose he and Emily ... Or Gene and Suzanne? No, not Suzanne. Still, after that story she wrote ... Speaking of Suzanne, how are the new living arrangements really working out?

HELEN

Absolutely swimmingly. I speak the truth.

BETTY

And that week with the grandson, how did that go? I imagine Suzanne got pretty rattled, set in her ways as she is.

HELEN

No, she was marvelous with Denny. Absolutely marvelous. As a matter of fact, his visit was mostly her doing. She demanded that I promise to take him for a week every year. That way she doesn't feel so guilty about keeping me away from my family.

BETTY

Really? I wouldn't have expected that.

HELEN

And I demanded a promise of Suzanne as well.

BETTY

What was that?

HELEN

I made her promise that, if ever she has a chance to -

(The telephone rings.)

BETTY

What awful timing! Excuse me a moment. It's probably Harry.

(BETTY leaves the living room to answer the phone. SHE screams and cries out, "Oh no!")

HELEN

What is it, Dear?

(BETTY rushes back into the room.)

BETTY

It's Harry! He's in the emergency room. The doctor thinks he had a stroke. I have to go now. Oh, but you need a ride home. You're on the way, more or less. I'll, I'll drop you off.

HELEN

Nonsense. I'm going to the hospital with you.

BETTY

That isn't necessary.

HELEN

(interrupting)

Nonsense, I said.

BETTY

But I don't know how long, I don't know whether -

HELEN

(interrupting)

You don't know whether you're coming or going. Believe me, this is no time for a woman to be alone. No time at all.

(BETTY and HELEN exit together. HELEN hangs onto BETTY's arm while murmuring comforting words in her ear.)

(BLACKOUT)

END OF SCENE 2

ACT II

Scene 3

At Rise: **The spotlight is on the TV screen. The rest of the room is in shadow. The reporter appears on the screen. The lights rise to reveal the six writers sitting and watching.**

REPORTER

We end tonight with this. Traffic became snarled on both sides of Royal River, as Middleton hosted the largest funeral in recent memory. CEO's from businesses statewide, political leaders past and present, joined family and friends in saying farewell to CPA Harry Sable yesterday. A moving tribute was offered by one of the deceased's business associates. Let's listen.

(JIM appears momentarily on the TV screen, wearing a dark suit. A lectern is brought onto the edge of the stage. JIM, still in a suit, gets up from the seated group and walks to the lectern. As JIM speaks, the screen shifts among various views of the ongoing funeral.)

JIM

Some of us were born to bellyache. We bitterly resent every obligation and commitment. Wives, children, and in my case clients who have the nerve to demand my close attention. Each morning drive is the same. I ache to go hang gliding in the Andes instead of report to the office. Then I might, for a split second, be content. Or not.

Harry Sable wasn't like that. Harry was grounded and focused and, dare I say, ennobled by his work. A noble accountant? Go ahead and snicker. Harry appreciated a good laugh. But it's true. Harry was born to translate the Internal Revenue Code into plain English the way Mozart was born to make

JIM (Cont'd)

music. Harry and I worked on a lot of cases together. One time I sadly shook my head as I watched him patiently explain an arcane Code provision to a mutual client. I knew that business owner to be number than a garden hoe. Then he asked Harry an astute question that proved he'd absorbed all the nuances.

You didn't even have to be a client to command Harry's full efforts. Another time I was sitting in his reception area. Marlene, that's Harry's secretary, kept apologizing and glancing nervously at his closed door as my appointment time came and went. "Big client?" I asked. "Oh no," she replied. "My son's struggling this semester. They're in there discussing inventory valutation." Frankly, I was surprised when Betty asked me to speak today.

(At this point BETTY leans toward JIM. A spotlight shines on her as she pays close attention.)

JIM

For Harry and I were not close friends. We never met for drinks. We never played golf. I thought, "Gee, wouldn't somebody else have more anecdotes to share about his good buddy Harry?" Well, perhaps not. For if Harry had a wild or sentimental side, it faced away from prying eyes like the dark side of the moon. And for that reason I used to view Harry Sable as an under-developed person.

That changed recently. The last stretch of time I spent with Harry, he was right in his element. We sat in his conference room, Harry and I and Suzanne from my writing group.

(A spot shines on SUZANNE.)

JIM

Harry had just completed, pro bono, a detailed report on some old business records for Suzanne. The way he unraveled that fifty-year old mystery was mind-boggling. He never once glanced at the clock while Suzanne plied him with questions. He didn't begrudge two and a half hours of lost billable time. Harry actually thanked Suzanne afterward. And meant it. He said, "I rarely get to wiggle my toes in it anymore." Then he grinned and added, "I cost too damn much."

Under-developed? Instead, I have begun to see Harry's methodology as mature and whole. As something to aspire toward in my own professional

JIM (Cont'd)

practice. And in my empty personal life. Betty, he may not have sent you roses or recited sonnets in the moonlight, but he kept a picture of you on his computer screen. It's not a sterile, posed photograph either. You're wearing an apron with a spot of flour on your left thigh. Your hair is tied back with a blue bandanna. You're frosting somebody's birthday cake. It's a perfect emblem of what Harry came home to, albeit very late, each and every night.

Harry did not forget occasions, though with such a large family he had literally dozens of dates to keep track of. He even sent a fruit basket when my law partnership turned ten years old - we'd have completely missed the milestone otherwise. I would bet the farm that Harry Sable never had an extramarital affair. But he left his affairs in order. A cogent will, plenty of life insurance to fund his firm's succession plan, college accounts for the grandchildren, money for his alma mater Middleton University.

What I have belatedly come to admire most about my friend Harry is that he did not rail against the indifferent world. He never once said, "Poor me!" or wondered what to be when he finally grew up. Instead, he stepped into his chosen vocation, he picked his spot on the planet, he fell irretrivably in love, all at a very young age. Then he played his role with intense energy and without hesitation right up until, sadly, the curtain suddenly fell.

(The spotlight returns to the TV. JIM rejoins the group as the lectern is removed from the stage.)

REPORTER

Harry Sable was a frequent commentator on the WBSK morning news. Everyone in the WBSK family extends our deepest sympathies to Harry's widow Betty and their five children. We hope they are among friends tonight.

(The lights rise upon the group. BETTY is seated in the middle of the couch with HELEN on one side and SUZANNE on the other. EMILY is cross-legged on the floor. JIM and GENE sit in armchairs that flank the ends of the couch.)

BETTY

I certainly am. Thank you all for coming. Even though I wasn't up to holding a real meeting, I wanted some semblance of normalcy on a Thursday night. It's been such a madhouse here the last few days.

SUZANNE

Have your kids all gone home?

BETTY

Yes, thank God. I shouldn't say such a thing, but they took energy from me when I had none to spare. Then there were the grandchildren running wild in a pack. I'm not used to such bedlam anymore. Harry would be home by now. He always got home in time to watch the eleven o'clock news.

EMILY

We'll stay as long as you like.

GENE

Just tell us, each of us, what to do. Please don't stand on ceremony.

BETTY

It's not like Harry would be paying a bit of attention to me, except perhaps during a commercial. He always focused intently on the news. He'd be sitting in that chair where Gene is, his mind far away from me. But he would be here.

GENE

If it's aloof and inaccessible you're seeking, I can supply that.

(BETTY laughs, then begins to cry.)

BETTY

I do miss him so much.

(JIM can't control his emotions. HE gets up and goes onto the deck. He leans against the railing and sobs. SUZANNE follows him out.)

SUZANNE

Are you all right?

JIM

I'm peachy.

(HE blows his nose into a handkerchief, his back to SUZANNE.)

JIM

Give me a second, will you?

SUZANNE

There's nothing wrong with crying over somebody you loved. Take all the time you need. Do you want me to leave you alone?

JIM

No, not really.

(SUZANNE walks over to JIM. SHE leads him to the porch swing. THEY sit down together. SUZANNE takes the handkerchief from JIM's hand and wipes off his cheek.)

JIM

What was that? A booger?

SUZANNE

As a matter of fact.

JIM

How dashing.

(SUZANNE laughs.)

SUZANNE

The eulogy was really beautiful. It meant a great deal to Betty.

JIM

I hope so.

SUZANNE

You transformed Betty's thinking about her entire marriage. I saw it happen.

JIM

Bullshit! What difference can a speech make when somebody loses a spouse of forty years? Not one microscopic speck.

SUZANNE

Most words don't matter, they're just platitudes. Yours were different. What you said about Harry, it helped Betty to accept the distance, to see that it was never meant to go away. Harry's lack of overt emotion, do you really admire that quality as much as you implied?

JIM

Yes and no. Right now I think it's the noblest endeavor on earth just to get up every day and do your job without kvetching. To excel at it. You see, I'm sick of self pity. I'm giving it up cold turkey.

SUZANNE

How will we know you?

JIM

Touchee.

(There is a pause, during which the porch rocker's squeak is the only sound heard.)

JIM

I'm serious, Suzanne. Something happened while I was composing that eulogy. The words started flowing. You know how Betty always quotes that professor of hers who says no word a writer puts forth is wasted. Sometimes I'd hear her say that - me with my eighty-seven rejection letters - and I'd explode inside. But last night I realized the old prof was right. Every time I ever reached for the right metaphor or agonized over sentence structure was part of the process. From all those struggles came the skill to form sentences that resonated and provided a measure of comfort to a grieving friend. For the very first time, even if I never do publish a single work of fiction, I felt grateful for my talent and proud of the hard work that honed it.

SUZANNE

So you know the speech was good.

JIM

Parts of it. You don't think it was too much about me and too little about him?

SUZANNE

You let people see him through your eyes. You made him sound very special, but I still wouldn't want to marry a man like Harry.

JIM

No? That surprises me. I thought you craved an orderly world.

SUZANNE

Don't tell me what I crave. Men always think they can read your mind.

JIM

Especially men who write. But I'll quit psychoanalyzing you. We ought to go back inside before they start talking about us.

SUZANNE

I guess. Only, only not quite yet. I want to apologize to you for what I did the other night. You know, about Gene and my brother Brian's wedding.

JIM

Why? Your date showed up. He had an excuse.

SUZANNE

A piss-poor one. He could have called to say he'd be late instead of making me sweat.

JIM

He could have.

SUZANNE

I heard you left with Emily that night.

JIM

True. God, you looked hot in that red dress. Did you sleep with Gene?

SUZANNE

Did you sleep with Emily?

(THEY move apart and glare at one another.)

JIM

No. No, I didn't.

SUZANNE

Why not?

JIM

You are a piece of work. "No" isn't good enough for you. I'm not going to submit to some inquisition.

SUZANNE

I know she likes you. I bet she wanted to.

JIM

No comment.

SUZANNE

Well, I didn't sleep with Gene either. But you already know that because, well, you know me. The subject never even remotely came up.

JIM

Did you have a good time, at least?

SUZANNE

Gene did, once we got there. Everybody fawned over him and begged him to sign copies of his book which, by the way, he remembered to bring plenty of. I made small talk with my invalid Aunt Ada.

JIM

So your family was impressed.

SUZANNE

Very. Mission accomplished. Except ...

JIM

Except what?

SUZANNE

I wanted to be with you instead. There, I said it. Jim, I really would like - if you're not too mad - to go out with you sometime.

JIM

Look, the other night was unfortunate, but it happened. I don't want us to go out on a pity date just to assuage your guilt.

SUZANNE

It isn't like that at all.

JIM

So you do want to play "hide the baloney" with me.

SUZANNE

Eewwww! That's disgusting. I don't want anything to do with you anymore.

JIM

I don't know what to make of you, Suzanne. One minute you shriek, "Don't ever do that again!" when I get a little friendly. Then you flutter your lashes and say, "Gosh, I'll just have to sleep with you if I put on that red dress." Which you proceed to do. Only then you waltz off on the arm of another man. It's too damn hard on me. Believe it or not, men have feelings.

SUZANNE

You think it's hard on you? I'm so confused I can't think straight. Maybe I'm making way too big a deal over sex. I should just pick up some jerk and get it over with. Except I'd freeze up with a stranger, I know I would. I'm a goddamn mess, aren't I?

JIM

No argument there.

(SUZANNE reacts as if JIM has struck her.)

JIM

Shit, Suzanne. I didn't mean to be flippant. It's obvious that writing about Elsa Higgins has set loose certain demons.

SUZANNE

And how!

JIM

Most of us just deal with them, however imperfectly, much earlier in life.

(raising his arm, then hesitating)

Is it okay to touch you right now or will you freak out on me?

SUZANNE

I promise not to go berserk.

(JIM puts his arm around SUZANNE. THEY sit together for a minute. The singing of crickets and the creak of the swing are heard.)

JIM

We should go in now. Betty needs us.

SUZANNE

I know. It's so sad.

JIM

No argument there.

(THEY go inside. The television has been turned off. A lit candle is burning on the coffee table. HELEN is holding BETTY's hand. Otherwise, nobody has changed position. SUZANNE and

JIM take their former places. SUZANNE takes BETTY's other hand.)

(BLACKOUT)

END OF SCENE 3

ACT II

Scene 4

Setting: **A picnic table sits in front of the closed curtain.The image of a resplendent fall forest is displayed. A flowing stream sounds throughout the scene.**

At Rise: **BETTY enters pushing HELEN in a wheelchair. HELEN has a Tupperware container and a cake dish on her lap. EMILY and SUZANNE follow. SUZANNE is blindfolded and being led by EMILY.**

SUZANNE
I don't like it. Where are you taking me? You know I'm in no mood to go anywhere today.

HELEN
Nonsense! Brooding all alone just makes a person feel worse.

SUZANNE
It's my right to be miserable. I'm the one who got rejected. My book will never, ever get published.

BETTY
Of course it will.

HELEN
Believe me, Dear, I know exactly how you feel.

BETTY
Emily, did you hear about that internship at the Middleton Mirror yet?

SUZANNE

Where are you two taking me?

(SUZANNE reaches for the blindfold. EMILY slaps SUZANNE's hand.)

HELEN

Emily, you were saying.

EMILY

I don't know what to do. They only want me as a sportswriter. On the other hand, it is a writing job. And my adviser's okay with it even though it's kind of unrelated to theater.

BETTY

A writing job. That's a major accomplishment.

EMILY

I guess. Plus I can keep looking for something better.

HELEN

Discreetly, Dear, if you must.

EMILY

I would really miss Writers Block if I had to move away.

SUZANNE

The group wouldn't be the same without you.

HELEN

My, my. I didn't realize that the birches had turned already. Look at that rich, golden glow.

SUZANNE

I would if I could see anything.

BETTY

(laughing)

Patience. All will be revealed. Is this the path, Helen? What do you think?

SUZANNE

Oh goody, now we're lost in the woods. Let's just turn around and go home. All I want is a cup of tea and a hot bath.

EMILY

I see the beaver dam. This has to be it.

SUZANNE

This has to be what?

(JIM enters from the fold in the curtain carrying a picnic cooler. HE unpacks food and utensils onto the picnic table. EMILY unties SUZANNE's hair from its habitual rubber band and arranges it about her shoulders.)

EMILY

There. That looks much better.

SUZANNE

Ouch!

(EMILY unties the blindfold.)

SUZANNE

I still don't know where you've dragged me off to, but it is pretty out here. Jim! You're here too.

(JIM wheels HELEN to one end of the table, as BETTY begins to fuss over the table.)

JIM

Emily, take care of the guest of honor. You too, Betty. Never mind where the salad fork goes.

(EMILY places a garish, jeweled crown on SUZANNE's head.)

EMILY

Courtesy of the Middle U Theater department.

HELEN

For you, Dear.

(HELEN hands SUZANNE an elegant Japanese fan.)

SUZANNE

This makes absolutely no sense.

(BETTY distributes party hats and puts one on. JIM dons his and bows to SUZANNE with a flourish.)

SUZANNE

(laughing)

You are very weird.

JIM

Thank you. I take that as a compliment. Sure beats being dismissed as ordinary.

SUZANNE

Is that lobster salad? And Helen's homemade cole slaw and, my God, that's a German chocolate cake! My favorite cake in the whole wide world.

BETTY

I was going to make a lemon chiffon, but Jim insisted.

JIM

Upon Helen's advice, with which I wholeheartedly concurred.

SUZANNE

This table is just right for Writers Block - it has room for exactly six people. Except Gene's not here.

JIM

He sends his regrets.

HELEN

Don't be sarcastic, Jimmy. It doesn't become you.

JIM

I'm not. Gene sounded genuinely upset he couldn't be here today. I mean, where would you rather head on a gorgeous fall day, to a picnic with friends or to the goddamn airport? You know how Gene hates to fly, especially nowadays. He said your book is good enough to be published, Suzanne, but that it's hard to categorize. Even less suited for the cookie-cutter market than his fiction.

HELEN

Speaking of *Island Treasure,* I don't understand how they can make a movie out of it. The strength is in the subtle interplay of the quirky characters. There isn't much of a rip-roaring plot.

BETTY

I saw Gene on Good Morning America the other day. There were no scenes from the film, though. I was quite disappointed. They usually show a little excerpt, don't they?

JIM

A trailer. They say it's a bad sign if there's no trailer. It means the studio lacks faith.

BETTY

You don't suppose they're waiting to see how the film does before they print the paperback edition. Do you?

JIM

Could be. If the movie bombs, the publisher can cut its losses. If the movie's a hit, then they've created a well of pent-up demand. It sounds quite possible to me. Hell, it even sounds like a brilliant marketing strategy.

SUZANNE

You'd think, once you found a publisher, that they would stick with you.

EMILY

Yeah, right. And I had a three-year contract to play in the WNBA.

BETTY

No more negative thoughts, everybody. Let's eat.

(THEY do so. Nobody says anything except to make various satisfied sounds over the food.)

HELEN

Well, this is quite the intellectual conversation.

SUZANNE

Everything tastes so good. We're all concentrating on that.

JIM

Hear, hear.

SUZANNE

And it's so pretty and peaceful here. Where are we, anyway?

JIM

On five acres that came on the market at a price I couldn't pass up. The couple that used to own the property cleared space for a cabin, but all they ever finished was the outhouse. I put a camper in the clearing for now. After I retire, if I live that long, who knows?

SUZANNE

Well, I like it. I like it a lot. And this food is fabulous. I'm completely stuffed, but I can't wait to bite into that cake. Isn't that sinful?

JIM

In that case -

(HE gets up and fetches a bugle from the picnic basket.)

JIM

Betty, light her up.

BETTY

Oh dear, I forgot to bring any matches. Harry would have reminded me.

(JIM takes a cigarette lighter from his pocket.)

JIM

Never fear. A Boy Scout is always prepared.

EMILY

They let you in the Boy Scouts?

JIM

I was an Eagle Scout, I'll have you know.

(BETTY lights the sparkler on the cake. JIM plays Reveille.)

SUZANNE

That doesn't make any sense either. It's late in the afternoon.

HELEN

We're heralding a new beginning for you. Now be quiet and listen. He's very good.

(JIM finishes. A few seconds of silence follow while the sparkler burns down.)

SUZANNE

What do you mean, a new beginning?

HELEN

Well, Dear. You're a real writer now that you've been officially rejected. What I don't understand is how it happened so quickly. You must have sent your query letters out before you even finalized the manuscript.

SUZANNE

I sent one letter out right after last Thursday's meeting. You know, when we went over my last chapter.

JIM

Ah, you got a ricochet. They're quite frequent. It's a dead certainty that nobody but the receptionist considered it before dismissing it. Unless somebody with clout recommends you, many agencies do exactly that.

SUZANNE

Really? How idiotic! Well, I thought this agent would be just perfect for my book. I know you're supposed to send multiple queries. Only I thought I would be different, that my manuscript's excellence would be self-evident. What an idiot!

JIM

No more than the rest of us. We all think we'll be the cream that rises to the top. It's a humbling experience to have your most intimate thoughts dissed by strangers. Perhaps it's His plan.

(HE looks skyward, then hands SUZANNE a knife.)

But thank you for inventing cake. Here. You do the honors.

SUZANNE

With pleasure.

EMILY

Think how much further along you are in your career than me.

HELEN

Than I am.

EMILY

Whatever.

BETTY

Suzanne, you're an inspiration to me. I'm going to start my Comp Litt seminar project tonight.

SUZANNE

You decided to go back this semester after all.

BETTY

That's right. And for the same reason we insisted you come out and be with Writers Block this lovely fall afternoon. You have to keep on moving forward. Harry would be ashamed of me if I did anything less.

SUZANNE

I wish I didn't always dwell on the negative.

JIM

You simply mustn't waste time wallowing in it. Believe me, I've been there, doing that for way too long. Do you remember how you felt when you finished your manuscript?

SUZANNE

It felt amazing. There was an even bigger surge of joy during the writing process. It came right after I flashed Gerald DiCenza, believe it or not.

JIM

Lucky guy.

SUZANNE

He's a geriatric double amputee.

JIM

Good point.

BETTY

I still can't believe you did that.

SUZANNE

Well, it gave me the key to my protagonist. There was an element of triumph to her. Up until then I assumed Elsa felt nothing but crushing shame all the time. Suddenly it hit me that being with the, the johns I guess they were, that was the only time she felt in control. There was Carl DiCenza, big-shot owner of the lumber mill, slobbering and drooling over her. Gerald too, from his secret perch in the loft. She had a whole bunch of men lusting after her. I wanted to experience the same ecstatic power.

BETTY

Well, I don't know about that.

SUZANNE

The meeting with my grandfather's second wife was pivotal, too. Gayle raised my mother all right, but they were never close. She felt it was her duty. Now Gayle views her marriage to George as a mistaken interlude. You see, George was a handsome and charming man. But he was terrible, just terrible when it came to money. And so Gayle quickly realized that she couldn't afford to leave her job. She was an airline stewardess. Back in those days they had to quit their jobs when they got married.

EMILY

That has got to be majorly illegal!

HELEN

Not back then it wasn't. You young girls take so much for granted. Go on, Suzanne Dear. Tell them what happened next.

SUZANNE

Gayle kept a secret just like Elsa did. Only one person at work knew she'd gotten married, her supervisor. She took Gayle aside one day and suggested she'd best act the part of the single girl a bit more convincingly. So, as Gayle continued to fly for American Airlines, she sometimes said yes to a traveler in a suit.

EMILY

Wow. George's second wife screwed around on him too.

SUZANNE

Dating strange men in faraway cities became Gayle's way of temporarily escaping her life with George. My mother learned to stay out of her parents' hair. That's why she became such a mouse. She never felt she deserved a place at the table. But I'm not going to live like that anymore. Jim is absolutely right. I learned so much while I was writing my book. I won't let the bastards spoil it for me. I won't.

JIM

You know what? I had this totally insane thought the other day. Nobody knows where publishing is headed. All we can reasonably expect is that the future will be different from the present. Maybe, just maybe, conditions will improve for writers. Maybe what we ought to do is pack our very best work into a time capsule and sink it somewhere to be opened in, say, a hundred years. Or a thousand years even.

HELEN

Eternal possibility. How intriguing.

JIM

I swear our work would stand a better chance of avoiding obscurity in a goddamn time capsule. Even Gene's book will be out of print in ten years. Hell, maybe in two years. This way we would always have an outside shot at reaching an audience.

BETTY

Well, I think it's a fabulous idea. I'm going to pursue it with the folks at Middle U. Harry left them a substantial sum, so I have a rare bit of clout. I might as well use it before it fades away.

JIM

I know one thing. That crime novel I've been hawking forever, I still think it's good enough to get published. But it's definitely not great enough for the ages. So, if my work is to be included in the time capsule, we'll have to hold off while I do a proper job of completing JASON'S REGRET.

SUZANNE

Which I decree shall be Writers Block's next project.

JIM

Oh yeah? Well, I have something to say about that.

(JIM pauses dramatically, then lets out a triumphant whoop. HE does a football player's end-zone victory celebration.)

EMILY

That's a fifteen yard penalty for excessive celebration, Asshole.

JIM

(HE flips her the bird.)

Screw you, Ref. God damn, I'm psyched.

HELEN

Such language! Everybody pipe down and pay attention to nature. Just look, there, across the river, at the red sun peeking through the fir trees.

EMILY

It is awesome.

SUZANNE

Mmmm. Play taps for us, Jim. It's such a sad and simple song.

(The sun sets as JIM plays taps. A bird call provides a two-note echo to the song.)

SUZANNE

This party has been so wonderful. Thank you, Helen. This had to be your idea.

HELEN

Think again.

SUZANNE

Okay then, it was Betty's idea.

BETTY

Not mine.

SUZANNE

Emily?

(EMILY shakes her head no.)

HELEN

It was his idea. Yes, I called Jim and told him you were down in the dumps over your first rejection letter. But that's all I did.

(SUZANNE gets up and goes to JIM, who is still holding the bugle. SHE throws her arms around HIM and kisses HIM. JIM is too stunned to reciprocate. Then, after SUZANNE starts to walk away, HE sets the bugle down on the picnic table and grabs HER by the arm.)

JIM

Come back here, you.

(JIM kisses SUZANNE at length.)

HELEN

I'd love to get a closer look at that beaver dam down the road. Wouldn't you, Betty?

BETTY

Yes, I would. And then I need to get home and wash my hair. Help me with the chair, Emily. Leave the goodies for the love birds.

(As HELEN, BETTY and EMILY proceed toward the edge of the stage and exit, SUZANNE and JIM kiss.)

HELEN

Remember your promise, Dear.

JIM

What promise was that?

(JIM and SUZANNE sit down next to each other on the picnic bench facing the audience. The curtain behind them opens slightly. A car starts and is heard driving away.)

SUZANNE

It's way too personal to - No, it isn't. It was about the right man and the right setting and not letting a crotchety old lady - her words - stand in the path of progress. Also her words.

JIM

Which she never minces. Does she use the wheelchair a lot now?

SUZANNE

When we go for long walks. For some reason she doesn't hate it like she does the cane. Growing old is awful, isn't it?

JIM

It beats the alternative. How did you ever persuade that stubborn old woman to change her mind and stay put? She was bound and determined to move after the break in. Talk about a way with words.

SUZANNE

Actually, my words failed completely. Then Dorothy flew east to make the arrangements. The two of them clashed over every little thing, without Joe in between to keep the peace. Plus Helen learned that the "facility," as Dorothy referred to it, was forty-five minutes from their house. Helen saw that she wouldn't become part of their daily life. She would be someone to fetch at holiday time, someone they'd feel obligated to visit.

JIM

Somehow, I can't picture Helen in California. She'd lose that frosty edge.

SUZANNE

I hope she never, ever moves away.

JIM

Hear, hear.

(SUZANNE puts her hand on JIM's thigh.)

SUZANNE

I think I'd like a tour of that camper of yours now.

JIM

(chuckling)

Is that right?

(SUZANNE leaps to her feet. She throws her arms in the air.)

SUZANNE

I feel positively exuberant! Come and get it while you can.

(SUZANNE unhooks her bra and lifts up her sweater as, giggling, SHE runs toward the exit at stage right. JIM catches up, grabbing the back of her sweater.)

JIM

This way, if you please. That is, unless I've sadly misinterpreted the lady's intent. That there is the path to the privy.

(SUZANNE laughs throatily.)

SUZANNE

You show me the way.

(JIM turns SUZANNE to face him. HE gently eases her sweater down.)

JIM

But first I need to know how you really feel about me. I happen to be very fond of you.

SUZANNE

I see that now. Nobody ever threw such a perfect party before. And to think you did it for no other reason than to lift me from the slough of despond.

JIM

That's true. Scout's honor, I hadn't a clue I'd discovered the way into your pants at last.

SUZANNE

That's so crude! You'll never change. Not that I ... exactly ... want you to.

JIM

Suzanne. Sweetheart. Much as I'm dying to dive between the sheets, it would be wrong to alter the dynamics of Writers Block for anything less than ... well, less than love. So what do you say? Are we ready to walk Helen's path of progress?

SUZANNE

Yes!

(SUZANNE throws her arms around JIM. THEY embrace. Hand in hand, the two walk through the separation in the curtain.)

(BLACKOUT)

END OF PLAY

Strange Love Triangle at the Children's Theatre

A Play in One Act

Scene: A small theater. There is a stage, possibly a house. The stage is set for a children's show. The set is cutout trees and the like. It is brightly colored to the point of being obnoxious. The only "real" set piece is a large staircase.

Actors enter. They line up for curtain call. They are wearing obnoxiously bright mismatched costumes and overly done makeup. They stand nervously for a moment before bowing. They rise and look at each other, wait for audience reaction. It does not come. There is maybe scant clapping. The actors bow again and exit the stage. The lighting shifts. The stage lights go out. Work lights come up. SAM the stage manager enters, presumably from the booth. He has an air about him of being in charge. He wears a single dog tag around his neck. Sam is followed by ED, another technician. He is somewhat intimidated by Sam. They begin their post show duties, removing props and putting them backstage, resetting any set pieces, etc. Enter MITCH, one of the actors from before, now out of costume and in street clothes. He goes to Sam.

MITCH

Um. Sam I have a question. The special on the secret door seemed a little slow. Do you think you can do it little quicker next time?

(Sam doesn't stop moving the whole time he is talking to Mitch. Mitch follows him around the stage. Sam occasionally exits off stage to return a prop. Mitch does not follow him off, instead he follows Sam to the exit and simply raises his voice until he sees Sam has reentered at which point he

runs to where ever Sam has entered from.)

SAM

I'll take a look at it. But I honestly don't know if there is much I can do about it. It is a manual cue so the timing will change a little every day.

MITCH

OK. But it just feels like I am out there all alone without any lines or anything for a really long time before anything happens. You know, like dead time.

(Enter TESS, another actor, she has a wild mane of what would be curly hair if she took better care of it. She is also dressed in street clothes. She crosses to Ed. He smiles at her as she approaches and stops in his work. He kisses her on the cheek.)

ED

Hey babe. We going out tonight?

TESS

I don't know, Ed. I think I really want to just stay in and rent a movie.

ED

Alright. Tess, I am up for anything as long as I get to do it with you.

SAM

I'll take a look at it. But I can't promise you anything.

MITCH

I just don't want any of it to look stupid. You know? I feel it is dragging the show down. But you take a look at it and see if you can do something about it.

TESS

You're sweet, Ed.

(Mitch exits. He says good night to Ed

and Tess as he leaves. He does not say anything more to Sam. Sam has stopped moving. He watches Mitch leave in disbelief.)

SAM

That fucking dick! Can you believe that! Ed, can you fucking believe that? Talking to me like that. Christ!

ED

Yeah man, some people.

TESS

He is a fucking punk kid.

SAM

When he gets his lines right then he can talk about the god damn lights. This job would be perfect if the actors didn't get in the way.

(Sam returns to resetting the stage. Ed returns to resetting the stage. Tess crosses to Sam.)

TESS

Have you had anything to eat today, Sam?

SAM

What? Oh, yeah. I had lunch. Why Tess?

TESS

What did you eat? (Pause) Sam, what did you have for lunch?

SAM

I had a Cliff Bar and a soda.

TESS

Shit Sam. That is not a lunch. I'll cook you dinner. What do you want?

SAM
Tess, I am perfectly capably of feeding myself. I don't need you to nor do I want you to make me anything to eat.

TESS
I worry about you. That's all. I don't want to see you waste away and starve to death.

ED
Honey, Sam is not going to starve from eating Cliff Bars for lunch a couple of times. He is a big boy. He doesn't need you to take care of him, he can take care of himself.

TESS
Let me make you something to eat.

SAM
I don't need you to make me anything. I am fine. Look. Look.

(He shows her how healthy he is by running around the theater.)

SAM
See. I didn't pass out. I didn't die.

TESS
Why are you fighting me on this? This is because of her isn't it? You wouldn't be fighting me on this if it weren't for her.

SAM
Why do you have to do that? This has nothing to do with her. We had an agreement. You can't keep coming over and making me dinner. I wouldn't mind going out and spending time with you but I want some space right now. I thought that was what you wanted too?

TESS
Fine. If that is what you want, have fun with your little whore.

(Tess exits angrily)

SAM
Tess. Tess that is not fair.

(Ed starts to follows Tess. He turns back to Sam but is still moving to the exit.)

ED

Sam, are we all set here? I think...

(Ed gestures to where Tess exited.)

SAM

Yeah. Get out of here Ed.

(Enter KRISTEN, a young woman, she wears a single dog-tag around her neck. She is looking around, unsure if this is where she should be. Ed in his hurry backs up in to Kristen.)

ED

I'm sorry.

(Ed quickly exits before Tess can get too far ahead of him. Kristen looks around. She sees Sam. Smiles at him. He walks toward her.)

KRISTEN

Hi. I am sorry I'm late. I --

SAM

Late? You were supposed to be here two days ago. Where the hell have you been?

KRISTEN

I can explain. You see --

SAM

I don't want to hear your excuses. What possibly could have happened to make you two days late?

(Kristen is silent, Sam stares at her)

SAM
Well?!

KRISTEN
I am confused. Do you want me to tell you what happened or not?

SAM
Of course I want you to tell me.

KRISTEN
OK. My car broke down. (Beat) Twice.

SAM
Twice? As in two times? Why didn't you call?

KRISTEN
The first time I couldn't find a phone. The second I dropped my phone card down a sewer grate and didn't have enough money to call you and feed myself. I couldn't even get something decent, I had to eat at all those burger joints along the interstate.

SAM
Ew! Kristen!

KRISTEN
Oh Mr. High-and-Mighty Vegan Man doesn't approve. Like you have never used my shampoo made from animal fat. If it makes you feel better I didn't enjoy the burgers.

SAM
Yes, actually that does make me feel better. I am glad you didn't like them. I have to go upstairs to write up a report and lock up. Then we can get out of here. You hungry?

KRISTEN
Starving.

SAM
Great. I'll be back in a minute.

(Sam exits. Kristen alone wanders the stage. Enter Tess.)

TESS

So you finally showed up.

KRISTEN

Hi Tess. How have you been?

TESS

You had us all very worried there for a little while. So good to see you got here safe and sound.

KRISTEN

Oh, yeah. Good. I heard you have a boyfriend.

TESS

Ed is nice enough. But once Sam is done with this soul searching business I'll have to let him go. Shame, he really is a nice guy.

KRISTEN

How can you do that to a person?

TESS

Oh, like Sam isn't using you until he is ready to come back to me.

KRISTEN

Tess, Sam isn't your husband anymore. You aren't getting back together.

TESS

We shall see. Oh and Kristen I hope that car of yours gets back to Massachusetts in one piece.

(Tess exits. Suddenly the lights go out.)

KRISTEN

Great. Just what this day needs. A blackout.

(A spot comes up on a Masked Man on the top of the stairs. He has a deep

bellowing voice and is holding a sheet of paper.)

MASKED MAN

Kristen. Are you Kristen Gallium?

KRISTEN

Yes, can I help you?

MASKED MAN

You must be judged.

KRISTEN

Judged? You have got to be joking.

MASKED MAN

You must pay for your crimes.

KRISTEN

Crimes? What crimes have I committed? So I sped half way here. Most of the people on the road were going faster -

MASKED MAN

Hey, hey. I don't need your life story here. Today we are focusing on one small aspect of it. Now may I continue?

KRISTEN

By all means.

MASKED MAN

Now, you need not be concerned with what exactly your crime has been, only know that you did not violate the laws of man. Your crimes are against the laws of the heart.

KRISTEN

What laws of the heart?

MASKED MAN

Do you mind, it is hard enough to remember this speech without you interrupting all the time. Where was I? Did I do the part about "crimes of the heart?" Oh, forget it. Let's just skip to the end. The time has come. You must be judged.

(Masked Man pulls out a knife. He

lunges at Kristen. She tries to escape, but he is faster. He corners her. They struggle. Kristen is stabbed. She falls to the ground, dead. The Masked Man kneels over the body and removes his mask. He is Mitch. He screams.)

MITCH

Shit! Tess! Tess, get out here!

(The lights come back up. Tess and Ed enter. Tess examines the body.)

ED

Oh my God! She's dead.

MITCH

I didn't know the blade was real. I thought it was from Props.

(He tests the blade with his hand. It is indeed a fake knife.)

ED

I think I am going to throw up.

MITCH

I just killed someone. I'm never going to get work again. I'll be banished to regional theater and summer stock and nothing with more than 150 seats.

ED

We committed conspiracy. We are all going to jail. For a long time.

TESS

No one is going to jail.

MITCH

I hope you're right. I couldn't survive in jail. Imagine it, doing some musical for the inmates. Giving head to some guy named Bubba to secure the lead. The other inmates will be jealous and I'm not pretty enough to be someone's bitch, so they'll beat me up. I bruise easily.

TESS

Will you two shut up. Get a grip. She's dead. It's not the end of the world. We just need to think of a new plan.

ED

Oh God, I can't do this. Maybe we should call the police. Maybe they'll go easy on us.

TESS

No. No police. We can handle this. Nothing has changed.

ED

Everything has changed. The girl is dead! She wasn't supposed to die.

MITCH

Right, she is supposed to be in Massachusetts. You said we were going to scare that little bitch cheerleader back—

TESS

Shut up Mitch. We have to hide the body. In the staircase. Ed, pull off that facing. First, this is mine!

(Tess rips the dog tag necklace off Kristen's body. Tess, Ed and Mitch try and shove the body into one of the stairs.)

TESS

Damn. She won't fit.

MITCH

There's a chop saw down in the shop. We could cut her up.

TESS

Perfect. Mitch, you and I will take the body downstairs. Ed you stay up here and keep watch for Sam.

(Tess and Mitch exit with the body. Ed paces nervously.)

ED

Oh God. This is bad. This is really bad. I killed my boss's girlfriend. It will be on next week's "Law and Order."

Ripped from the headlines. This is so bad.

SAM
(Entering behind him)
What is bad?

ED
Ahhhh! Hi Sam.

SAM
Is everything alright, Ed?

ED
Yes, everything is fine. Great in fact.

SAM
Then what is so bad?

ED
Nothing. It's nothing. (Beat) How are you doing, buddy?

SAM
OK.

(Pause. Ed smiles a big fake smile. The kind you flash at a ravenous dog when it is trying to bite your leg off.)

SAM
Have you seen Kristen?

ED
Um, no, I-I can't say I have.

SAM
Are you sure? She was just here. She said she'd wait.

ED
Now that I think about it, she said something about car trouble. Brakes or something. Or you could check the bathrooms.

SAM
Thanks Ed. You look kind of sick maybe you should get some

rest.

(Sam exits. Ed sighs and relaxes. Tess enters caring the dismembered parts of Kristen. Arms, legs, thighs etc. These body parts should be humorous, not gory. Tess drops the limbs in a pile. Tess is not covered in blood.)

TESS

We got her cut up easily. She went through the saw like butter. But everything's a mess down there. It's beautiful. The bright red against gray concrete floor. And that smell of life escaping. It reminded me of this time when I was 14. I woke up one morning to find my thighs covered in blood. Warm and sticky and half dried. And that same smell hung in the air. At that moment I felt powerful for the first time, like I could do anything.

(During this speech Ed has begun putting the body parts in the staircase.)

ED

Tess could you possibly stop talking about blood for five minutes.

TESS

Men are such babies. Downstairs Mitch made me wear gloves and trash bags as a dress so he wouldn't touch the blood. Killing someone is ok but if you have to touch their blood ...

(Mitch enters carrying more of the body, interrupting Tess. He is still wearing his trash bag dress. They all are putting body parts in the stairs.)

MITCH

I got most of the blood out. What's left on the floor could be mistaken for paint.

TESS

So, Ed, after this, do you want go out and get something to

eat?

ED

OK. Chinese?

MITCH

Oh, can I come too? There is this new place that just opened up around the corner.

ED

I heard about them. They are supposed to have really good General Tso's Chicken.

TESS

I can't believe you would kill an innocent chicken like that. Do you have any idea what kind of conditions that chicken lived in? Or was killed in. It probably soaked in its own vomit and shit for several hours before it was packaged and shipped.

SAM (o.s.)

Kristen! Kristen!

ED

It's Sam.

TESS

Oh no. We missed one.

(Tess picks up an arm. The boys block the stairs. Tess hides the arm behind her back. Enter Sam.)

TESS

Hi Sam.

ED

Hey.

MITCH

What's up.

SAM

Have you seen Kristen? I've looked everywhere for her and I—What's that?

TESS

What's what?

SAM

What are you hiding behind your back?

TESS

Nothing.

SAM

It looks like a severed arm.

(He grabs the arm from her.)

TESS

It's nothing.

SAM

It is a severed arm! Tess, did you cut up my girlfriend?

TESS

Yes, but Mitch and Ed helped.

MITCH

Hey, she never said anything about cutting people up when we started. Honest Sam, I didn't know we were going to cut her up.

SAM

Ok, Mitch.

MITCH

Why don't we forget about the light thing earlier and call it even.

SAM

I don't think the two are exactly parallel. Tess you can't keep killing my girlfriends like this. I really liked this one.

TESS
Technically, I didn't kill her, Mitch did.

MITCH
It was an accident. I swear I didn't mean to. It was just a back-up plan in case cutting her brakes didn't work.

SAM
You cut the brakes on her car.

ED
Oh, I did that. (Pause) My dad had a garage.

SAM
How much longer are you going to do this, Tess? Did you really think I wouldn't figure it out? Two thirds of the girls I have dated in the past eighteen months have either died or disappeared under mysterious circumstances. The only living one I know of changed her name and moved to England and won't return my calls.

MITCH
Still one out of three living, that's not bad.

ED
That's only 33%. 33% that were not horribly mutilated and killed. I think I am going to be sick.

TESS
Actually, I think those are the ones they can't find any record of.

ED
You think you met a nice girl, turns out she's homicidal maniac.

MITCH
The things we do for love.

TESS
That's why I did it, Sam. For love. I'm just not the same without you. And you're not the same either. I can see it in your eyes. They used to sparkle, now they're dull. I could help you, Sam.

SAM

Tess, this is why I left you in the first place. All this killing got to be too much. I never got to settle down or make any friends. You would usually kill them before they got too close.

TESS

I didn't want to see them hurt you. And you usually helped.

SAM

Tess, what are you doing?

TESS

In fact, as I recall, you were the one who would pick out the victims. Just like you picked out this one.

SAM

Stop it. This isn't what we rehearsed. What are you doing?

MITCH

Wait! Wait a minute! Hold the phone. Back the homicide train up! You've done this before? Sam, good old "I wouldn't hurt a fly if it were crawling on my dick" Sam is a cold-blooded killer?

TESS

Technically, Sam has never killed anyone. It is a game to him he sets up all the players. The young impressionable girl, me the hardened jealous bitch and himself the innocent bystander caught in the middle. Really, he has everything set up from the beginning.

ED

You think you know someone, you work with them every day. Talking and hanging out. Then you find out he is a homicidal killer. I have been spending the past six weeks sitting next to a homicidal maniac. And here I am trying to be nice to a homicidal maniac.

TESS

Shut up Ed.

ED

Will you stop saying that? You have been saying that all

evening. I think I have been very considerate. I haven't said how much it bothers me that you are still hung up on Sam. And I supported you in this little scheme of yours. All I ask is a little consideration in return. I mean, this is all—

SAM

Shut up Ed.

(Ed shuts up.)

MITCH

Hey Sam, why can't you do it? Why can't you kill anyone?

SAM

For the same reasons I am a vegan. I don't want to hurt any animal, not even one as useless as a human being.

TESS

Right, he just likes to watch. And he's afraid of blood.

ED

No kidding.

TESS

He gets nauseous, and his eyes roll back in his head, then he starts hyperventilating. It's kind of amusing, watching a grown man suffer so.

MITCH

I would have never guessed. Me, I'm scared of spiders and peanut oil. Bad experience at a Japanese diner. The ones where they cook at your table.

ED

I never would have guessed. Still, its comforting to know that even mass murderers have fears to over come. Makes them seem more like regular folks.

SAM

Tess is there any way to get rid of these guys?

(He motions to her.)

ED

Do you want us to go? We can leave you two alone if you want.

(Tess moves behind the two men. Slowly, in protest.)

TESS

No, Sam. I can't.

MITCH

My family was going out to eat one day. My mom was tired of tuna casserole and Dad had extra money since Tina quit and he hired Frank. I remember I was six. It was a clear autumn day and there was a crispness to the air. The leaves had just begun to turn red and orange. The colors mixed with the green, and I remember thinking--

TESS

Don't. Don't.

(Suddenly Ed drops to the ground. Tess has hit him in the back of the head with the arm. She stands over the body silent. Mitch stops talking.)

MITCH

What did you do? Did you kill him? Is he dead?

TESS

And now you are too.

(Before Mitch can move or scream Tess hits him with the severed arm. He falls over, dead. Tess stands over the fallen bodies. She says nothing. Sam's eyes are closed and turned away.)

SAM

Did you do it? Are they...? Are they dead?

TESS

I think so.

(She prods the bodies with her foot.)

SAM

You killed them.

TESS

You can check them if you like.

SAM

Tess you know I can't do that.

TESS

Sorry, I forgot. Murder. Blood. They tend to go together.

SAM

Still you did it. You said you wouldn't. You wouldn't kill anyone else. You always say that.

(Sam embraces Tess. He does something cute, like touch her nose or Eskimo kiss. She brushes him off.)

SAM

But here we are again. And here are three people who just moments ago were living, breathing and taking up space, albeit annoyingly. You are fabulous. Do you know that? Strayed from the script a little, but still fabulous. Even I thought you would never do it. Well maybe Mitch. But I was surprised to see you hit Ed like that. He must have really liked you to help you kill that girl. What did you see in him?

TESS

(melancholy)

He wasn't you.

SAM

See, I told you it would work out. And next time it will be bigger and better. We'll—

TESS

No.

SAM

What?

TESS

I said no. I'm not going to follow you around and murder anyone else. I am through. I quit.

SAM

Tess, don't be silly. You know as well as I do you can't quit. Not me, not this. You like it, more then I do sometimes. You like the rush, the thought that one day maybe you will get caught. You will never quit.

TESS

Fine. I retire. I'll be sure to send in my letter of resignation.

SAM

You disgusting whore. Who do you think you are? Where do you think you would be if I hadn't come along?

TESS

Stop it! You treat me like I hung the moon one minute and the next you push me down into the gutter. You tell me I am wonderful and beautiful only to show me later I'm no better then the dirt under your nails. Either way you're looking up my skirt or down my blouse. Goodbye Sam.

(She starts to exit)

SAM

I want it back.

TESS

What?

SAM

You heard me.

TESS

Yes, I heard you. And no. I can't kill them if you don't mark them. That's the way it works, you give them something they think is so wonderful then I come along and bash their heads in. I take it back and you know the job is done. Besides, it's mine.

SAM
I don't think the spirit in which it was given was the spirit in which it was received.

TESS
What does that mean?

SAM
The spirit in which it was given was not the spirit in which it was received.

TESS
How many girls have you pulled this on?

SAM
I just don't think I want you to have it anymore.

TESS
Good thing that is not your decision to make.

(Ed sits up. Rubs his head.)

ED
Ow. Tess, you didn't have to hit me so hard.

TESS
Ed--

ED
I think my brains are running out my nose.

TESS
Ed, what part of "stay down until I give the signal," did you have trouble understanding?

SAM
He's alive!?

ED
Of course I am. "He's alive." Well thank you Capt. Obvious.

SAM
Why is he alive? You said he was dead. You lied to me.

TESS

And you lied to that girl.

SAM

What girl?

TESS

The one I killed for you today. And every other one.

SAM

Oh right. Her. She was getting on my nerves anyway.

ED

So that makes it all right, then. I helped murder some poor young woman because she was getting on the boss's nerves. Now I have two questions and I want honest answers to both of them.

SAM

Yeah, ok.

ED

If you're afraid of dead bodies and blood how come you could wave that arm around? What did you do with the other women's bodies? And is Mitch going to be ok? He has been down for quite some time. And yes, I know that was three questions.

SAM

I have learned to control my emotions to an extent through meditation and breathing exercises. Besides that it's mostly the head that bothers me.

ED

And the other women?

SAM

Oh...uh..You know how it is. Time. Travel. One forgets things.

TESS

Sam you kept a diary.

SAM

I told you never to call it that. It was a journal. So what if I did, a journal is for writing not for reading.

TESS

You used to read it every night.

SAM

Oh come on its not like I kept it under my pillow or any thing.

(Tess and Ed stare at him.)

SAM

All right, so I did. And yes, it had one of those cheap locks on it too.

ED

Sounds like a diary to me.

SAM

It was a journal. A journal! If you call it a diary again I'll...I'll...I'll...

ED

(Singing)

Sam has diary. Sam has a diary.

SAM

(angry)

I swear Ed, if you don't shut up I'll--

(KRISTEN suddenly appears at the top of the staircase. SHE is brandishing a gun and now wearing a FBI uniform complete with utility belt, flack jacket and most importantly the baseball cap.)

KRISTEN

You'll do what, Sam Beckett? Or should I call you Rock E. Balboa VII, or would Kenneth Veal be more appropriate.

SAM

Tess, how many other people did you forget to kill?

TESS

Just two--no three. There was the girl in Crabapple Cove. Or was it Crab Rock? I forget. Anyway, she was just so nice. It would have been a shame. I got a letter from her last month-she's living in Phoenix and working as a systems analyst.

(Kristen glares at her.)

TESS

But I guess that isn't important right now.

KRISTEN

No. What is important is that you, Sam, are under arrest for conspiracy to commit and murder of 75 known individuals.

(She puts handcuffs on Sam.)

SAM

Kristen, can't we work this out. I was just kidding when I had Tess kill you.

KRISTEN

It's agent Starling to you.

(Mitch snickers to himself before remembering he is supposed to be dead.)

ED

If you're here, then who's chopped up into little pieces and stuffed in the set?

KRISTEN

A Genetically Engineered Android Lifeform. A GAL for short. Part human clone, part computer programming. Created to look and talk like an ordinary human complete with a set of implanted memories. Microphones imbedded in the skin work like a wire and a computer chip in the brain provides written and visual records of everything the GAL sees and hears.

ED

Fascinating.

KRISTEN

The best part is all the computer implants continue to work long after the body has ceased functioning, and apparently dismembered. Also the unit has a limited vocabulary specific to the assignment at hand. Of course each GAL has a limited functional time ratio.

TESS

What does that mean?

SAM

Excuse me...

KRISTEN

The computer chip gives out an electrical impulse at a specified, preprogrammed time, causing the brain and heart to stop functioning. In layman terms, it is programmed to die. This could be anywhere from a few hours to a number of days.

SAM

Excuse me. Sorry to hog all the attention, but are there not some rights I should be aware of?

KRISTEN

Oh, yes, you are right. You have the right to remain silent. You have the right to an attorney. If you cannot afford and attorney one will be appointed to you.

(She escorts Sam out as she finishes Mirandaizing him.)

ED

So I guess that about wraps things up.

TESS

There is still the trial. I'll have to testify. Wednesday there is a hearing for my conspiracy charges but they should be dropped.

ED

And Mitch?

TESS

He should be ok. I thought I heard him giggling.

ED

It's still early. You want to get a bite and catch a movie? I heard this new Chinese place is really good.

TESS

Sounds good.

(Tess kisses Ed on the cheek. They exit hand in hand. Mitch is left alone on stage. As the lights fade he looks up.)

MITCH

Uh...Guys...Can I get up now? Tess you never said the word. Um... I'm going to get up now, ok? I'm getting up? Ok? Ok.

END

Oh, Grow Up!

Written by
Ashley Johnson, Cole Lundquist, Erin McNamara, Jarrett Melendez, Larry Sawyer, Katherine Tardif

With concept assistance from
Delmore Adams, James Braun, Jim Gray, James Jones, John Jones, Erik Lutz, Tyler McAllian, Chris Pye, Shaw Smith, Ryan Woodward

Writing Advisor
Catherine Russell

SCENE I
(Prologue)

Play opens on a darkened stage.

Actors are frozen in various positions around stage, on platforms, standing, seated, some facing forward, some with backs to audience, etc., all with heads down. Each is dressed entirely in black, though costumes differ (mini-skirt with black tights, leggings and large overshirt, slacks and a t-shirt, etc.), and wears a wild, colorful hat. Each holds a high-powered flashlight, with the beam off at curtain.

In a coordinated sequence, each actor raises head and spotlights his or her own face while speaking lines. In some sequences a group of actors verbally "gangs up" on a single actor (particularly, on Doofus). The effect should be that of characters/scenes flashing into view then disappearing. Body movement or facial expression is only on a line, or in concert with another actor's line, per specific blocking. Otherwise, actors remain frozen.

The tempo is brisk, but it is important that every word and concept be communicated strongly by the actors and understood by the audience. The lines should not be monotone or mechanical, but read in flashes of full character, created by the actor, and played for the contradictions and the pairings. The overall effect should be that of fractured harmony, like visual elements flashing on a black screen.

SAM: Don't pick your nose.

KATE: Keep your hands to yourself.

CHRIS: Your face will freeze that way.

STATIA: Don't put that in your mouth...

JARRETT: You don't know where it's been.

ERIN: Don't play with that...

COLE: You'll break it.

KENNY: Don't sit too close to the TV...

ASHLEY: It'll ruin your eyes.

DELMORE: Don't touch a light switch with wet hands…

JOEY: You'll be electrocuted.

DOOFUS: (This actor's "doofus character" repeats; see subsequent lines.) Don't lick a battery.

ALL: (sloppy flash of lights at own faces, uncoordinated, as if accidentally falling out of pattern) Huh?…

Break in rhythm, then reestablish.

DANNY: You'll grow into it.

SAM: You'll grow out of it.

KATE: Put that down...

LARRY: You'll put your eye out.

CHRIS: Pick that up...

STATIA: Someone will trip over it.

JARRETT: Behave yourself.

ERIN: Play nice.

COLE: Don't run with scissors.

KENNY: Don't hold the scissors by the blade.

ASHLEY: Always hand scissors to someone else by the blade.

DOOFUS: Never put anything sharper than your elbow in your ear.

ALL: (actors click lights on and off in arbitrary directions) Whaa?…

Break in rhythm, then reestablish.

DELMORE: Hurry up.

JOEY: Don't run.

DANNY: **Don't slouch.**

WILL: **Stand up.**

SAM: **Sit down.**

KATE: **Eat your carrots.**

LARRY: **Eat your peas.**

CHRIS: **Chew your food.**

STATIA: **Swallow that.**

JARRETT: **Spit that out.**

DOOFUS: **(he lights his own shoes) Not on my shoes…**

Short pause. Resume.

ERIN: **Don't put that in the toilet.**

COLE: **You don't need all that paper.**

KENNY: **Lift the seat.**

DOOFUS: **Stand back or you'll be flushed down.**

ALL: **(all flashlights right on Doofus.) Shut up!**

Short pause. Resume.

ASHLEY: **Look at me when I'm talking to you.**

DELMORE: **Don't you give me that look.**

JOEY: **You're gonna get it.**

DANNY: **You need a nap.**

WILL: **You need a time-out.**

SAM: **Stand in the corner.**

KATE: **Sit on the naughty step.**

LARRY: **Get in.**

CHRIS: **Sit down.**

STATIA: **Shut up.**

JARRETT: Oh, grow up!

ERIN: **Stop that, people are watching…**

DOOFUS: **(he shines light all around) Oops!**

(All flashlights out)

All freeze, and, even though in darkness, they "notice" the presence of the audience. Actors are embarrassed, seemingly nervous and slightly confused, as if having been caught in the act. Tableau in darkness.

The following sequence takes place while crew/actors are beginning to set the stage for the subsequent scene. Lines should seem entirely unrehearsed. To the audience it should seem as if the actors are simply making it up as they work. Narrator 1 steps forward. Lights remain down.

NARRATOR 1: **(COLE) (in darkness) Good evening, ladies and gentlemen! Um, could I have just a little light please? (general stage lighting up) We were just, ah, working out some things. Pressures, anxieties, you know.**

What you have just witnessed is just some of what we hear every day. Day in, day out. Every... (choked pause, as if holding back an expletive) day. Do this, don't do that! Geez. Yak-yak-yak. Blah-blah-blah. We've heard it all. We're teenagers -- and let me tell you, as far as stations in life go, being a kid is really the sticky end of the lollipop. (sigh; general responses from other actors) But that's what we are. We're still kids.

Toward the end of this scene-setting sequence, actors playing roles of first letter characters in Scene 2 must exit the stage to prepare, though still looking as if their exits are just part of setting up the scene with the other actors. (Specifically: Chris, Ashley, Sam, Erin, Statia.)

CHRIS: **Speak for yourself! (exits)**

SAM: **No, think about it. We're not of age, most of us can't drive – (exits)**

KATE: (breaking in, wise-acre) Or shouldn't...

LARRY: We can't vote, we can't drink, we can't use credit cards...

DELMORE: We still have to get PERMISSION SLIPS to go anywhere, for crying out loud!

STATIA: Yeah, but look at the other side. We don't pay rent, we don't have bills, and we don't have a mortgage...(exits)

JARRETT: We don't have to go to jobs we hate every day...

DOOFUS: And best of all, we don't have kids!

Rejoicing all.

NARRATOR 1: Okay, so there are some advantages. But we want to take this opportunity to show you what it's like to be us.

DELMORE: We are fibbed to, lied about...

KENNY: Man, it's a wonder we get anything straight.

DOOFUS: (dramatically, being pathetic) All our young lives, we've been subjected to the electronic babysitter, and flooded with countless media images of what's right and wrong. Fairy tales, sitcoms, Mother Goose, radio, TV. All our lives. (sob) (other actors just sort of ignore Doofus when he does this stuff, or look at him like he's nuts; they're used to it)

DELMORE: Just think of what we have absorbed.

JOEY: Yeah, did you know that 33% of all night-shift workers are vampires?!?!

DANNY: Yeah, hey, I saw that in The Inquirer!

ALL: Ahhhh, The Inquirer!

DOOFUS: Yeah! The Bat-Baby!

KATE: (as a headline) My Friend's Mother's Best Friend's Cousin's Ex-husband's Stepsister's Babysitter Slept With Elvis.

All pause. Double-take.

ALL: Eeewwwwwwwww!

There is spreading confusion as everyone improvises lines, talking about tabloid headlines, celebrities, aliens being chased over the moon by trains, etc. Possible specifics to be featured during ad-lib: turtles mutating, animals that can talk, the Loch Ness monster, etc.

NARRATOR 2: (JARRETT) (breaking them off) Okay, okay. They get the point. (Indicates audience)

So, this is what it's like to be us. It's an inside look at our world.

The problems start early, with the simplest of ideas, the stories that you place in our heads when we are still very small. You mean well, but hey, a child has a very active imagination…

Oh, almost forgot … before we move on, we must introduce the sponsors of our program…

Narrator 2 gives stages, exits.

SCENE 2
(X, Y & Z)

NARRATOR 3: (CHRIS) (entering, taking on the character of ANNOUNCER) ... we'd like to remind you that this performance is brought to you by the letters X, Y, and Z, those stalwart sponsors of so many other fine programs for young people ...

X enters, breaking into Announcer's monologue. X is dressed like a classic B-movie thug, smarmy with dirty trench coat (closed) and a fedora. He is identified as X by the large "X" he wears on front and back of his costume, as designed.

X: STOP!

The X Babes, a '60s girl group, enter behind him quickly, singing. They are dressed as the letters S, Y and E, entering and taking position in that order.

BABES S, Y, E: (singing) ... in the name of love, before you ...

X: (cutting them off) Quiet! We'll get to that later, girls. (Directs his focus back to Announcer, and as a grand pronouncement, as if it were the answer to all life's questions...) Pants!

ANNOUNCER: (Puzzled; checks his zipper) Excuse me?

X: Pants. That's the new product we're promoting.

X rips open the trench coat to reveal sleazy black leather pants with studs, rips, etc.

ANNOUNCER: (trying to cover, as if X's entrance is a mistake) Um, I'm sorry, but you can't be out here. You're just the sponsor. You know, we talk about all the good things you do and you get credit for sponsoring the show. Get it? You don't just waltz out here ... Hey, wait a minute. What are you talking about? You're the good old alphabet, you know, (he sings) A-B-C-D-E-F-G... You're supposed to be promoting proper spelling and good grammar, strong character, the good things for the youth of America, not, well, pants.

X: Hey, I just wanna set the record straight. (taking stage, to audience) The world needs to know that the media have been lying to you. All of you. Misrepresenting us to the young people of the world. We're not just simple,

sweet letters that made up words like "sugar," "rainbows," "happy duckies" and "bunnies."

(turns attention to Announcer) Let me tell ya something, kid, where I come from, there's a whole big alphabet out there, just full of letters. Good letters ... and baaaad letters. (In the process of the argument, other letters enter the stage, including specifically the letters T, H, G, I, R and W, partying as they enter.)

Take the letter O, for instance. (O comes forward) You see O, and you probably think of "robins" (O pulls a stuffed birdie out of pocket while X shows a flashcard with the word "ROBINS"), "cookies" (O pulls a giant cookie out of pocket while X shows "COOKIES" flashcard), and "snowflakes" (O tosses fake snow from his pocket while X shows "SNOW" flashcard). O. Oh-ho-ho. Well, let me tell you, you just catch O on his down time and you'll also find him hanging out in words like "chaos" (O mimes chaos while X shows "CHAOS" flashcard), booger (O picks nose while X shows "BOOGER" flashcard; X, S, Y & E physically react to O's being gross, inadvertently rearranging themselves into "SEXY"), and --

O: (as O spots the girls and their provocative word) Yahoo! (O chases S, E, Y offstage left, much screaming; X remains)

X: (after O is out, to Announcer, deadpan, showing "YAHOO" flashcard) Yahoo.

ANNOUNCER: (embarrassed for X) But what about you? That outfit ...

X: Like it, huh? (strutting) Well, as you see, letters have different meanings sometimes, if you get my drift. I'm X, right? (elbow, elbow; jab, jab) And, I'd like to introduce you to one of my brothas in alphabets, the letter N! (N enters. He/she is two people tied back to back in a single costume. One side is Good N, other side is the Bad N; Good N faces audience first) By day, N's nice, the perfect choirboy from the church down the road. But by night, (N turns to show Bad N forward) N's as nasty as the bodily crevices of a large, sweaty man on a hot day. And at any moment, my buddy N can go either way... (Letter O shifts back and forth, back and forth)

The Babes, Y, E and S, reenter from left, in that order, scurrying, still being chased by O.

O: YES, YES, YES!

BAD N: (catches sight of the Babes as they position themselves center near

X, then conspiring with O, a la Jim Carey) Oooh! NASTY!

N Leans toward Babes with Bad N in the lead. Then, Good N places him/herself between S and O, pushing O away saying...

GOOD N: NO, NO, NO!

N spinning back and forth continues as they argue, (YES-YES-YES, NO-NO-NO) ad-lib.

X: (to audience) I rest my case.

In the process of the argument, the other letters begin partying more loudly. Chaos ensues. The Announcer has had it.

ANNOUNCER: Enough!

The letters sort of attempt to cooperate, drawing to attention, but in the scuffle and by the time they stand still they have inadvertently arranged themselves into S-E-X N-O-W. Announcer panics.

ANNOUNCER: Oh, no, no, no!

Letters scatter, finally settling down, but now they read S-E-X R-I-G-H-T N-O-W. Announcer panics again.

ANNOUNCER: Aaah! No, that won't do at all.

They scuffle again, and end up as W-H-Y N-O-T.

ANNOUNCER: Because, ah, this is a family audience! AHHHHHHH!!!

Announcer chases them all; some fall down, some exit (Specifically: Larry and Statia out for change), leaving N-O S-E-X standing.

ANNOUNCER: ENOUGH! (he's exhausted; sees N-O S-E-X) Okay, I'll accept that. Now, can we just stop?

BABES: (singing) ...in the name of love, before you break my heart...

General partying breaks out again, much singing and dancing among the letters.

ANNOUNCER: NO! Just shut up and get out of here, for the love of Mike!

X: OK, party at my house!

Letters exit, whooping it up, following X.

ANNOUNCER: (giving up) Oh, what the hell... (exits following letters)

(Set up for quick change for actors with letter roles who take first roles in Scene 3.) Narrator 4 steps forward to take over for the exhausted Announcer. This should be the same Actor playing the letter I.

NARRATOR 4: (DELMORE) Anyway, to get us back to the point -- which is, after all, US (indicates his "I") -- we'd like to show you what it's really like at BEDTIME!

SCENE 3
(Monsters in the Closet)

Behind last lines of previous scene, stage techs bring in set pieces for scene (dressed bed, stuffed animals, night table and lamp downstage right, room door center, and closet door downstage left). Scene opens with offstage live voices ad-libbing sounds of padding down hall to room, pre-bed chatter. Mother leads Boy into room and begins ritual of tucking him into bed. Boy is played by an adult actor, but played to the appropriate age. The effect should be convincing, not comic.

MOTHER: Did you brush your teeth, sweetheart?

BOY: Yes, Mom.

MOTHER: Because if you don't brush your teeth the sugarbugs will rot them! (She tickles him and makes silly noises about the "sugarbugs.")

BOY: (laughing) I know…

MOTHER: OK, goodnight punkin, sweet dreams …

BOY: 'Night, Mom.

Mother leaves room, closes door. Boy settles down. Suddenly, the closet door rattles sharply, loudly. Boy sits bolt upright, eyes open wide. Closet rattles again, louder, as if someone were having trouble with the knob. Finally, door flies open, and Sugarbug comes out. He's a tough customer, with a mean voice, but conversely, a sparkly and oozy-looking costume.

SUGARBUG: (ad-lib grumbles at doorknob on entrance) Hey kid, d'you brush your teeth?

BOY: (Abject fear) Y-Y-Y-Yeah…

SUGARBUG: Okay, never mind.

Sugarbug returns to closet and shuts door. Boy sits for a second, absolutely frozen with fear. He can't believe what he's just seen. Then from behind closet door…

SUGARBUG: Did you use toothpaste?

BOY: Umm ... I think so.

SUGARBUG: (sticking his head back out of the door) Sure about that kid?

BOY: (nods in assent, really big)

SUGARBUG: Okay. (returns to closet; then after a beat, from behind door) Hey, kid. Pleasant dreams! (demonic laugh)

Boy sits frozen in terror, mouthing words, but none come out. He finally musters up strength to say ...

BOY: MOOOOOOOMMMMMM!?!?!?!

Mother enters, aggravated.

MOTHER: (from behind gritted teeth) What IS it, punkin?

BOY: THERE'S A SUGARBUG IN THE CLOSET!

MOTHER: Now, we've been through this before. There is nothing to be afraid of, nothing in the dark, or under the bed, OR in the closet.

BOY: (almost crying) Yes there is, Mom ... I saw it. He asked me if I brushed my teeth.

Mother eyes him with growing impatience, turns to the closet and opens closet door. There is nothing in there but closet stuff.

MOTHER: See, nothing there. Nothing to be afraid of. Now, it's bedtime. No more foolishness. Next time it'll be Daddy who checks. Go to sleep, sweetie.

Mother kisses his forehead, leaves. Boy settles back down, warily. Suddenly, the closet door creaks open, and Cafeteria Lady steps out holding a plate.

CAF LADY: Hey, kid, ya didn't finish your lunch today.

BOY: I know, it tasted funny. (makes yuk face) What was it?

CAF LADY: I dunno. (picks up slab of something from plate, gray-brown and wiggly, handling it as if it were a poisonous snake, and dangles it, examining it closely) Same thing as yesterday. Mystery Meat, I guess.

BOY: **What IS Mystery Meat, anyway?**

CAF LADY: **(menacingly, advancing and waving 'meat' at Boy) Heh, heh, heh, heh...**

BOY: **(loud, not caring of the consequences) MOM!!!!!!!**

Cafeteria Lady ambles back into closet and closes door, disappearing just before Mother returns. Mother stomps in, very irritated.

MOTHER: What do you want now? This better be good!!!

BOY: **I don't want to go to school tomorrow.**

MOTHER: (sympathetic) What is it, sweetheart?

BOY: **(stuttering, whining, getting worse) MMMMM...MMMMM.... mystery meat!**

MOTHER: What?!?!

BOY: **(blathering and crying, trying to get it all out at once) Mystery meat ... She was there... And there... In closet... The... The... Cafeteria Lady (ad-libs continue)**

MOTHER: (fed up) That's enough. Now go to sleep, young man.

Boy stays upright in bed up, clutching blankets. Mother leans over his bed with her back to closet. Closet opens. Sugarbug, Cafeteria Lady, Mr. Potato Head, Elmo, Vampire, Hairy Spider, a sickeningly cute little girl, and various other terrors come out.

BOY: **Aaaaah! They're back, they're back! (he points; monsters dart back into closet) MOM, look!**

MOTHER: (she doesn't look) Stop it right this INSTANT!!!! You've been watching too much television, too much MTV. Those blasted Disney movies. Monsters aren't real. There is nothing to be afraid of. There is nothing in this room (she opens closet door with one hand, but keeps her visual focus on boy and doesn't look in, monsters wave from inside) and there is nothing in this closet!

BOY: **(sees monsters, screams) AAAAAAAHHH!**

Mother closes closet door on monsters, stomps to bedside.

MOTHER: Now, goodnight.

Closet opens. Monsters do line dance, partying. Boy panics, looks around for possible lines of defense, then musters courage to throw his stuffed animals at them. Monsters panic, scream, flee to the closet, closing the door behind them. Amazed that this has worked, Boy gets up the courage to go to the closet. Braces himself and opens door. Nothing is in there; no monsters.

BOY: Hey, they're gone. Maybe Mom was right. Maybe they really aren't real.

Boy returns to his bed. Pause. Closet opens. Priest enters from closet.

PRIEST: (comforting, gentle) Have peace, my child. You have nothing to fear, for these are only creatures of your imagination. Save your anxieties, son. Reality is frightening enough. (tone begins to change, more menacing) There are many real things to fear. Such as failure, financial collapse, missed opportunities, not getting into the right college, being a complete disappointment to your parents. And worst of all, well, (tone changes to that of game show host) young man, let me introduce you to the biggest fear of all, the Sultan of Sin, that Master of Mayhem, the Prince of Pain, friend to no one, enemy of all, that's right, you know him, El Diablo, Lucifer, Prince of Darkness, let's hear it for Theeeeeeeeeeeeeeeee Devillllllllllllllll!

Devil enters from closet. Goes to bed, assesses Boy.

DEVIL: I've been watching you for a long time. (pokes boy with pitchfork as if he were checking a roast)

BOY: DAAAAAAAAAAAAAAAADDYYYYYYYYYYY!!!!!!!!!!!!

PRIEST: (heading for closet) Get thee behind me, Satan!

Priest follows Devil into closet, closing door behind him. Father enters. He has complete patience because this is his first trip this evening.

FATHER: Having trouble getting to sleep, buddy?

BOY: Yeah... There's scary things in the closet...

FATHER: Well, lemme see if I can take care of things.

Father goes to closet, opens door; nothing there. Various bits as Father voodoos away the monsters for the benefit of Boy. He fusses everywhere but under the bed. Father returns to bedside.

FATHER: It's okay, I took care of everything. They're all gone now, pal. Now, you get some sleep, sport.

Father ruffles Boy's hair, leans over and kisses him on the forehead.

FATHER: Sleep tight, don't let the bedbugs bite.

Father leaves the room. Boy lies down. Pause. Suddenly Bedbug Walter pops up out from under downstage side of bed, near the foot.

WALTER: Whew, glad that's over. Hey, Herbie, coast is clear.

HERB: (popping up through the foot of the bed, right through the covers) Hey, how's tricks, Walter?

WALTER: Great, except for all the racket.

BOTH: Snacktime!

WALTER: So, what part do you want, Herb?

HERB: I want a drumstick, how 'bout you?

BOY: AAAAAAHHHHHHH!" ('Home Alone'-type scream.)

Bedbugs retreat into bed.

Blackout/Scene change.

As stage techs begin scene change, Boy gets out of bed to exit, then all the various monsters enter from closet with ad-libs, creating a monster dance number on the exit. An exasperated Mother enters the stage, trying to take control of things.

MOTHER: (MOTHER/STATIA) Will you guys get out of here?!?! You heard what I said, YOU'RE NOT REAL! (Monsters win, dancing her off stage)

KATE: Well, whether those monsters are real or not, unfortunately, not everything scary is just in our imaginations. What we are about to show you is something very different, something nearly every little kid has had to suffer

through -- the pain of humiliation, the pain of loss, and the pain of remembrance. When we're little, you tell us you'll always be there. And you mean it...but sometimes, it's just not true.

SCENE 4
(Triptych I)

Stage techs make changes, props in and out. Outside door downstage right, kitchen set center and left. Scene opens with mother (Barbara) making dinner. Outside/offstage right can be heard the sounds of children playing, created by offstage actors. Laughter, and cries of "Throw it to me!" This is followed by the sounds of a fall, and crying, "I want my Mommy!" Barbara shifts attention, goes to the door. Tommy comes clambering in, holding tattered knee. Tommy is played by an adult actor, but is played to the appropriate age. He wears a specific baseball cap that will also appear in the later scenes. The effect should not be comic. Barbara is dressed simply, slacks and a tunic or turtleneck so that the audience sees the locket she wears on a long chain around her neck.

BARBARA: (she stoops down to him, perhaps at a kitchen chair) Tommy, honey, what happened?

TOMMY: Mommy, I hurt my knee! (ad-lib incoherent jumble about the ball being thrown and how he fell)

Tommy continues whimpering. Barbara sits him on the chair and fixes his knee. He keeps crying.

BARBARA: There you go, all better!

TOMMY: But Mommy, they made fun of me. . .

BARBARA: What'd they say, honey?

TOMMY: They called me a sissy poophead.

BARBARA: Aw, Tommy, why'd they call you a sissy poophead?

TOMMY: 'Cause, 'cause, 'cause, when I fell I cried an', an', an' I, I said I ... I wanted my Mommy ... An', an' they said only a, a, sissy poophead would cry for Mommy...

BARBARA: Oh, now let me tell you something, and you remember this, Tommy. It's true no matter what they say: It's okay for you to need your mom.

And I'll always be here. OK?

TOMMY: It ... it is?

BARBARA: Yes, it is. Now, where's my sunshine? (smiles, removes cap and ruffles his hair)

She takes him into her arms and sings "You Are My Sunshine" first verse through, sweetly. He starts to relax, stops whimpering, starts sniffing. Mom gets a little bit silly with the song. Sings more, but more silly this time, cheerfully. Tickles and giggles. He smiles and starts to laugh. She hugs him.

BARBARA: Hey, Tommy, I'll tell you what! Let's go get an ice cream sundae!

TOMMY: With sprinkles?

BARBARA: Whatever you want, sweetie!

Brightness flashes across his face, then vanishes as he says...

TOMMY: But, Mom, we, we haven't had dinner yet...

BARBARA: How about we do things backwards tonight? We'll have ice cream, and then we'll have dinner when we come home!

TOMMY: Okay!

BARBARA: Okay!

She hugs him and sings the song cheerfully. They go out the screen door singing all the way.

Under following opening lines, stage techs change set and props to that of schoolroom. Blackboard downstage right, room door center. As scene change begins, Narrator 7 takes stage, in conversation with audience.

NARRATOR 7: (ASHLEY) But, we grow up. From preschool, to kindergarten, through the middle grades to high school, it just keeps going.

Other actors enter, one by one, each taking his or her place at a school desk/chair on the line, each in his/her own version of a dragged-out student entering class in the morning. Those with specific roles in the top of Scene 5 remain offstage until line entrances.

DOOFUS: **Yeah, it, it's like this big train chasing you down the tracks, an' it keeps comin' and you, you can't get out of the way! (dramatizes)**

KENNY: **(reacts to Doofus) Uh, yeah, growing up is tough, and school can be the worst of it.**

CHRIS: **God, I hated school! We get all this stuff thrown up in our faces about grades and rules and --**

DELMORE: **And some of the most useless stuff! Like having to memorize the entire periodic table of the elements! All 94 . . . no, 183. . . all of them!**

KATE: **And having to memorize a list of 32 prepositions! 32!**

DOOFUS: **I can't even memorize the seven dwarves!**

SAM: **No, no, no, some of the stuff IS useful, and some of the days are great. But some are just ROTTEN, from the get-go.**

Actors assume student postures at desks, slouching, horsing around, sleeping.

SCENE 5
(Myths of School)

Mr. Marone's homeroom. Marone enters the room with briefcase and brown lunch bag, getting situated behind his desk. Various other students filter in. Rob enters, limping. All students slowly settle into seats.

Marone is stiff, monotone, nerdish, but in command of class. Think Ben Stein.

MARONE: Good morning, class.

ROB: (as with subsequent 'commentary,' he breaks out of scene in monologue, directly to audience, as class freezes behind him; the odder the positions the better) Pffft... Good morning... This is where it starts. Lies, all of it lies. It is NOT a good morning. You wanna know how my morning went? I got up on the wrong side of the bed. I mean, I literally got up on the wrong side of the bed... stepped out, and what did I step on? My science project that I had worked on all night, a scale model of the entire known universe, made entirely of toothpicks and sugar cubes. That was how my day started. So, no matter what Mr. Moron says (in his face; Marone remains frozen), it is NOT a good morning.

CINDY: (has been raising hand frantically during end of Rob's monologue) Mr. Moron?

All giggle.

MARONE: The name is Marone, Ms. Pikowski.

CINDY: Yes, Mr. Marone... Uh, Mr. Moron (she's not being deliberately rude, just not too bright), have you seen my Spanish book? I think I left it here in homeroom yesterday.

MARONE: (pulling book out of his desk) Might this be your Spanish text, Ms. Pikowski? This book without a name, this book without a cover, this... NAKED BOOK??

CINDY: Uh-huh....

MARONE: Ms. Pikowski?....

Cindy shakes head indecisively, both yes and no.

MARONE: Was that shake a 'yes' or a 'no', Ms. Pikowski?

CINDY: (shakes NO and stammers YES) Yes?

MARONE: Well, exactly how am I supposed to know that? (resigned) Come get your text and take it to the art room to get a new cover.

Cindy creeps up to his desk, snatches the book and hurries out of the room.

MARTI: (she breaks out in monologue, directly to audience) Explain this to me. Someday, when I'm 30, and I'm piloting the Concord to Paris, will my flight manual NEED a lousy, paper book cover? NO! I'll still be able to fly without one! So why does it matter now? (sits down hard)

Marone is rifling through papers.

MARONE: (muttering to self) Well, well, what the, where the devil -- where DID the lunch menu go? (aloud) Well, people, I can't tell you what's for lunch today because I seem to have lost the lunch menu.

There is general gleeful commotion.

GEORGE: Too bad we can't lose the stupid lunch!

ERIC: Before we all lose our lunch. (makes barf face)

Laughter.

Door flings open with a WHAM! Lunchlady Doris appears in doorway. This is the same actor who played the Cafeteria Lady in Scene 3.

DORIS: Hi, kids!

ALL: (monotonous/mumbly, but scared) Hello, Lunchlady Doris...

DORIS: Mr. Moron, (she got the name wrong again; he sighs, shakes head) sorry about the delay, but the printer wasn't working this morning, so I bashed on it a couple times (she demonstrates, banging on his desk and in the process crushing Marone's neat little bag lunch) -- oh, sorry, guess you're gonna have to eat at my establishment ... again. Just like old times, heh heh heh... (she pinches his cheek)

Marone pulls away from pinch, breaks out in monologue, directly to audience.

MARONE: I can't believe that crazy old witch just did that! I have HATED that woman ever since I was a student amidst these hallowed halls. And she haunts me still…

Marone steps back to Doris, resets himself in pinch.

MARONE: It's Marone, Lunchlady Doris. (emphatically) It's always been Marone. Mah-rone.

DORIS: Oh, sorry, Mr. Moron.

Doris scratches herself in an unladylike fashion.

MARONE: Is there a reason you've graced my homeroom with your immaculate presence, Lunchlady Doris?

DORIS: Oh, yeah. So anyway, the printer's on the blink, so the menus weren't printed this morning, so I have come to announce today's exquisite gourmet menu. Uh, first we got yer choice cut prime rib au jus, garlic mashed potatoes, and a salad of baby greens...

ERIC: (breaks out in monologue, directly to audience) Allow me to translate. "Choice cut" equals: soggy, gray, cold, under- or over-cooked meat of an, uh, um, unknown source... (sits)

DORIS: Then we got grilled chicken with roasted red peppers and mozzarella cheese, on top of homemade sourdough bread...

CHERI: (breaks out in monologue, directly to audience, rolls eyes, smacks forehead, looks at audience) It's -- a -- stinking -- chicken -- sandwich. No, no, wait -- we're really not certain that it's chicken. What we do know, is that it's … beige. And, come to think of it … it tastes beige, too. In fact, it may very well be the only thing that actually tastes beige. (sits)

MARONE: What have you in the way of beverages?

DORIS: We got milk, chocolate milk, and low-fat milk.

GEORGE: (breaks out in monologue, directly to audience) Or, in other words, dishwater, muddy dishwater, and low-fat dishwater... (sits)

DORIS: And for dessert... eh heh heh heh heh heh...

ERIC: Oh, heaven help us ... no ... nooooo...

DORIS: Vanilla custard with cherry topping, blueberry cobbler, and tapioca pudding. Eh heh heh heh heh....

EMMA: (breaks out in monologue, directly to audience) You don't even wanna know what those are ... (sits, then stands again) ... no, no, no, I gotta tell you what those are. First, for custard with cherry topping, we've got eyeballs in bloody pus. The cobbler, well, that could be anything. We're pretty sure that it's organic -- and it might be intelligent, too. (shrugs) The tapioca, is, quite simply ... fish eyes.

DORIS: Thank you for your time, it's been lovely visiting. See ya later, Mr. Moron. Bye, kids! See ya at lunch! Eh heh heh heh... (exits cackling)

MARONE: And while we're on this whole food thing, class, let me remind you that the bathroom is no place for lunch. I mean, really people, how unsanitary is this? People defecate in there. (students snicker; Marone continues under his breath) and God only knows what else. Okay, kids, now it's time for algebra! And don't worry, class, this will be fun! (He turns to board)

Marone continues in background, scratching on board, entire class slowly falls asleep, one by one, heads plunking on desks, except for Edward, who is dutifully copying notes from the board.

MARONE: And these few simple notes should easily familiarize you with the Supersucromacroanalyzer Pastry Stress Theorem.

ERIC: (wakes up) The what?

MARONE: (ignoring him) Now, let us apply this theory. (Marone turns to find most of class asleep.) Ca-lass! (they bolt awake) We are now going to analyze the sugar content of a whoopee pie. Picking up where we left off, class, please go to page 326,475. And remember, everyone, lift with your legs.

Class all reach down and heave up tremendous, ridiculously large textbooks from beneath desks. (The bigger and more ridiculous, the better.) Books slam onto desks with thuds and poofs of dust.

GEORGE: (breaks out in monologue, directly to audience; freezes here should be in all manner of positions with students holding books in hand in all odd positions and with expressions of strain on faces) Yes. We have done ALL of

that, this semester. 326,475 pages! I have not slept since August 31. My hand won't stop shaking. And the dreams! The horrible dreams! (collapses sobbing, muttering)

MARONE: And let's look at word problem #215.

MARTI: AAAAHHHHHH!! (screams and runs out door)

MARONE: Well, I guess she's been hiding her issues all this time. Back to the word problem, class. Now pay attention. This will be useful for you in every day life...

Marone turns to board and begins elaborate equation as ...

ALL: (Marone freezes; group monologue) Riiiiiiiiight.

EMMA: (each, in turn, breaks out in monologue, directly to audience) Word problem. Let us illustrate a word problem.

ROB: Train A leaves from Detroit station at 4:26 AM.

ERIC: Explain to me why someone would even be AWAKE at said obscene hour, much less on a train ... in Detroit, for crying out loud!

ROB: At the same time, in Fenway Park, at the snack bar, three food service employees -- George, Mary and Lars -- are cleaning out the six 20-gallon beer keg taps. George can do it in <X-squared to the power of pi> -- 3.1415927 -- Mary can do it in <N + three>, and Lars, it takes 2 hours and 16.5 minutes.

EMMA: (in cheap Swedish accent) Because Lars is Swedish.

GEORGE: Meanwhile on a desolate, uncharted island, off the coast of Tasmania, a butterfly flaps its wings.

CHERI: Then, if Y equals the price of the double-fudge brownie that Jennifer is going to buy on the train from Detroit to Fenway Park, for your final grade, and to save natural habitat of said butterfly, find R...

CHRIS: ... in Euros.

All students express exasperation, except Edward.

EDWARD: (he has the answer, to Marone) OOH, ooh, OOH!

Marone turns to audience and smiles; students gang up on Edward. Freeze.

Blackout/Scene change. Actors exit. Narrator enters to cover scene change as stage techs switch props and set pieces.

NARRATOR 8: (KATE) And at the end of a horrible, horrible day like this one, after the harassment from the teachers, the primordial ooze served in the cafeteria, and (shudders and gets the heebie-jeebies) algebra, sometimes the only consolation you can count on is from your folks. But even that changes a bit as you get older. One day, Mom treats you to ice cream, and that's enough to make everything better. Remember how easy it was for Tommy to forget being called a sissy poophead? And that was okay -- those were simpler times, with simpler problems. But life doesn't stay simple. We grow up. Parents grow old. And, no matter how much it means to you or how much she loves you, Mommy can't always be there – as Tommy will learn.

SCENE 6
(Triptych II)

Under the previous monologue, stage techs have changed scene to hospital, room door downstage right, window center, bed downstage left. Scene opens with Barbara in a hospital bed. Barbara is (as obviously as possible) the same woman from Scene 4, but older, and should be played by the same actor. She appears to be sleeping. Doctor Ruston and Nurse are conferring over charts in ad-lib at bedside. Barbara wakes, raises arm weakly, calls...

BARBARA: Doctor Rushton?

RUSHTON: Hey, Barbara, how are you feeling?

BARBARA: (weakly) Well, I've been better. My throat's a little dry.

RUSHTON: (hands her some water) Here you go. Do you think you can handle some visitors?

BARBARA: I'll try… Have you told them yet?

RUSHTON: Yes.

BARBARA: Well, that's good.

Barbara starts shaking, unable to handle water glass. Rushton helps her, takes it, and returns it to table. Covers her hand with his.

RUSHTON: Are you in any pain at all, Barbara?

BARBARA: Well, I was, but I guess the medication has kicked in.

RUSHTON: Well, good. As I said earlier, we'll do everything we can to make you as comfortable as possible… (hesitates) for as long as you're here.

BARBARA: (sigh) May I see my son now?

Rushton nods to Nurse. Nurse goes out as she escorts Tommy into room. This is (as obviously as possible through costuming) the same little boy from Scene 4, grown to college age. He carries a backpack and wears the same baseball cap, this

time backwards. Ruston follows. Tommy puts down his bag by the door and crosses to the foot of the bed.

TOMMY: Hey, Mom.

Barbara doesn't answer. Fear is apparent in Tommy as he moves farther up the bed. Then he touches her on the arm.

TOMMY: Mom?

Barbara wakes, shifts around so she can sit up. He helps.

BARBARA: Hey, Tommy, how are you?

TOMMY: Um, I'm good.

BARBARA: How's Sarah?

TOMMY: Uh, she's good, she went to the mall to get some shampoo for you, she knew that you liked the stuff she got you last time. . . (he babbles on nervously)

Barbara shifts in the bed. Tommy helps her get situated.

BARBARA: Honey, sit here for a minute.

Tommy sits on edge of bed.

BARBARA: Listen, Tommy, I want you to do something for me.

Barbara reaches over to bedside table for a small jewelry case, which holds the locket she wore in Scene 4.

TOMMY: Yeah, Mom.

BARBARA: (taking the locket out of the box and handing it to him) This is the locket that Grandma gave me. That was a long time ago. She gave it to me the day I had you. When you and Sarah have a baby, I want you to give it to her.

TOMMY: Mom, we're not getting married until we're out of college, and besides you can give it to her yourself, Mom, then, uh, if we ever do have kids. (he tries to hand locket back to her; she doesn't accept)

BARBARA: Aw, honey, I don't think I'm going to make it to the wedding.

TOMMY: Of course you are.

BARBARA: No, I'm not, sweetheart. (she closes his hand over the locket, placing her hand over his) Okay, Tommy, now, c'mon, we all knew this was coming. Everybody has to die sometime; it's just my turn. (he reacts) I can't just take you out for ice cream and make it all better this time. Believe me, I wish I could. I'm sorry.

TOMMY: Yeah, but I just, I just can't handle this right now. (he turns away)

BARBARA: (smiles slightly) So, you still need your Mom, huh?

TOMMY: (turns back to her, looks up and starts to cry) Yeah, I still need my Mom.

BARBARA: Remember what I said, no matter what they say it's okay for you to need your mom.

TOMMY: It... it is? (he cries harder now)

BARBARA: Yes, it is. And no matter what happens, I'll always be with you. (She hugs him as best she can.) Now, where's my sunshine?

She reaches up to him and holds his arm, and sings "You Are My Sunshine," first verse through, sweetly. Towards the end of a verse, he is overcome, and turns away, toward the foot of the bed, but still holding her hand. She begins the second verse, lying back on the bed, but her voice trails off. He continues the song, but realizes she has stopped singing and turns back to her.

TOMMY: Mom? Mom?!?

No answer. He stands for a moment, and slowly finishes the second verse of the song to her, alone.

TOMMY: 'Bye, Mom.

Blackout/Scene change.

NARRATOR 9: (JOEY) And so, sometimes life takes a turn, and we have to learn to get along without part of our family. That's tough. Family is vital, whether it's Mom and Dad, Grammie and Grandpa, Aunts and Uncles, or just caring friends, our family is where we learn sharing, nurturing, love. As kids,

we're bombarded with contradictory images of what that family should be. But, in real life, there are all sorts -- dysfunctional families, and then there are the families in which there is no dysfunction at all... which sort of dysfunctional, come to think of it. You know, father knows best, siblings always get along, and, no matter what, Mom's cooking is always perfect.

SCENE 7
(Perfect Family)

Under the previous monologue, stage techs change set to two living rooms, side by side. Scene is split stage, dining room of TV Family at left, Real Family at right. Each family is around pre-set table. Action alternates between the two, with the non-featured family in full freeze.

Characters in the TV Family:
Dad (sweater vest, bow tie, short-sleeve dress shirt, pipe, "readers" and newspaper, tan dress pants, pocket protector)
Mom (floral Donna Reed dress, frilly little apron, beauty mark, perfect lipstick and Maybelline blue eye shadow, hairdo w/headband and little flip, little black pumps and pantyhose)
Son (12-13, side-parted hair w/cowlick, yellow gingham shirt tucked into belted pants, pocket protector, saddle shoes)
Daughter (8-9, mini-Mom with matching dress, saddle shoes, white tights)

Characters in Real Family:
Dad (Jabba the Hutt-size, tee shirt that only covers half of him, 3-day beard, beer-can hat, polyester pants showing butt-crack)
Mom (dirty fuzzy slippers, housedress, rollers, face cream, cat-glasses on a chain)
Son (12-13, Fonzie gone bad, leather jacket, tight pants, biker boots)
Daughter (8-9, cell phone, leather hot-pants, white go-go boots, feather boa, belly shirt)

Action begins with TV Family. Dad sitting at table, ready for dinner. Mom serving.

TV MOM: Jimmy! Suzy! Time for supper!

JIMMY & SUZY: (offstage) Coming, Mother! We were just doing our homework!

TV DAD: (sniff, sniff, sniff) Mmmm, honey, that smells wonderful! What's for supper?

TV MOM: Chicken croquettes with a warm spinach salad, Brussels sprouts and potatoes au gratin. It's the menu I got out of "Martha Stewart Living".

Freeze. Cut to.

Real Dad is drinking out of a bag, and scratching himself.

REAL DAD: (belch)

REAL MOM: (pulls out a megaphone) Dinner!

No response.

REAL MOM: Where are those little... poops?

REAL DAD: I dunno. They went out by the train tracks. I think they had rope.

REAL JIMMY: (offstage) Dad, how do you tie a double hitch knot?

REAL SUZY: HELP!!!

REAL DAD: Tie her up later, time for food.

Freeze. Cut to.

TV Jimmy and TV Suzy come trotting in. Suzy skips to her chair with doll in hand. Jimmy bounces in. They perfectly and quietly take their seats.

TV MOM: Did you wash your hands?

TV JIMMY: Yes, right after I took out the trash.

TV SUZY: Yes, I always wash my hands after I color.

TV DAD: How was school today, kids?

TV JIMMY: Oh it was swell, Daddy! I won the spelling bee! But someone stole my bicycle.

ALL: Awwww!

Freeze. Cut to.

Real Jimmy walks in, pulling along a brand, new, shiny bike. Real Suzy follows, ropes hanging off her, beating on Real Jimmy with her KISS Barbie. Real Jimmy kicks back his chair, flops down, and leans the chair back on its **back legs.** ***Real***

Suzy disentangles herself, throws the rope bits violently at Real Jimmy, sits down and starts brushing her hair at/on the table.

REAL SUZY: (noticing the bottle of Coke next to her) What is this? COKE? You want me to drink Coke with dinner?!?!

REAL MOM: Well, EXCUSE me. We're out of Mountain Dew!

REAL SUZY: (panic) We're OUT OF Mountain Dew!!!

REAL MOM: Yeah. Deal with it!

REAL DAD: (reaches over to cuff Real Jimmy on the head) Hey, butthead, where'd ya get the bike?

REAL JIMMY: Found it.

REAL DAD: That's my boy!

Freeze. Cut to.

TV DAD: Oh, this looks scrumptious, darling! But I thought we were going to eat later, when we go out?

TV MOM: No, dear, that's just dessert and coffee. I've made my crème brulee -- two cups of light cream, purchased from the market just this morning and mixed with five, lightly beaten, organic, free-range egg yolks, then there's a bit of vanilla, a dash of salt, and plenty of sugar. It's an amazing culinary masterpiece.

TV DAD: Oh, lovely! But, I thought you were going to make something special.

TV MOM: Well, I was, but I lost track of time when I was sorting through Jimmy and Suzy's old toys to take to the orphanage. Now, who wants more Brussels sprouts?

All three raise their hands.

ALL: I do!

Freeze. Cut to.

Real Mom is basically dealing out the plastic microwave dinners like a lazy airline

stewardess.

REAL MOM: Okay, who gets the chicken?

Real Suzy raises her hand. Real Mom tosses dinner at her.

REAL MOM: Meatloaf?

Jimmy gags. That's his "yes." Real Mom tosses his plate at him.

REAL MOM: Eat it, or else.

REAL JIMMY: Or else what?

REAL MOM: Or else y'ain't goin' with us after dinner.

REAL JIMMY: (obnoxious teenage boy thing) Yeah, great!

REAL DAD: Yeah, ain't we s'posed to bring somethin' to this?

REAL MOM: (pulls out a box of donuts) Whaddaya think I got these for?

REAL DAD: (disappointed) Oh. I thought those were for dinner.

REAL MOM: (contemplates the box for a moment) Aw, what the hell. Who wants a donut?

ALL: I do!

They all grab for the box.

Freeze. Cut to.

TV Family is happily wiping their mouths. TV Mom rises, starts to pick up dishes.

TV DAD: (looks at his watch) Look at the time! (notices Mom) Don't worry about that, sweetheart. The dishes can wait, just this once. We don't want to be late.

TV MOM: But really, I must insist . . .

TV DAD: (cuts her off) No, now we haven't seen these folks in ages. Let's not be late.

TV MOM: (setting down the plates) Yes, let's not be late. The sooner we get there the sooner we can come home.

TV DAD: Now, don't be ungenerous, sweetheart. They are my cousins.

TV MOM: (sigh) I know…

TV MOM: (resignedly) Ready?

Freeze in tableau. Cut to.

Real Dad stands and farts.

REAL JIMMY: Yeah, good one Dad!

They high five.

REAL DAD: My compliments to the chef.

Mom takes off outer housecoat to reveal second housecoat.

REAL SUZY: I'm takin' the cat!

REAL JIMMY: No you ain't!

REAL SUZY: Who says?!? I am so!

REAL JIMMY: No, you AIN'T. Cause the cat's in the dumpster. I know, cause I tossed 'em in there!

Jimmy and Suzy pester one another.

REAL DAD: I dunno how you talked me into this! You KNOW I hate goin' to these things.

REAL MOM: Oh, shut up.

Jimmy does that throat scratch cum mucus-clearing thing with his finger in his ear; Dad leans over and cuffs him. Then Dad does the same thing; Mom leans over and cuffs Dad.

Freeze in tableau. Cut to.

Cloth drop descends (or other actors carry in drop at back), "The Fogner-Bates Family Reunion." The two families converge down center.

TV MOM: (proffering casserole dish) Crème brulee?

REAL MOM: (proffering box) Jelly-filled?

Freeze.

Blackout/Scene change.

NARRATOR 10: (JARRETT) (entering) I'll take one of each thanks.
He stands there with donut as Moms break freeze and exit. Families follow.

NARRATOR 10: So, you recognize your family here? Aw, come on, you do. O.K., so real life is somewhere in between.

NARRATOR 11: (CHRIS) (entering swiftly, swiping the donut) Real life is like a jelly donut. One where you can't see the insides. It looks delicious, but you never know what's inside. Could be grape, strawberry, blueberry, apple – or prune. (bites donut; it's gross) Yuk. (exits)

NARRATOR 10: But unlike a jelly donut, life is what you make it -- or so you've taught us. Sometimes we make the best of it, do great things, but often we don't. We forget the good stuff and get stuck in the bad. Like Tommy – Tom – who forgot all the love and got stuck in the worry.

SCENE 8
(Triptych III)

Under the previous dialogue, stage techs change scene to home living room with desk center, front door downstage right. Tommy's old baseball cap is prominently displayed on the desk or wall. Scene opens with Tom at the desk on the phone, obviously in crisis. This is (as obviously as possible) the same Tommy from Scene 6, now an adult.

TOM: What're you talking about, late payments?!?! I sent it in weeks ago! (pause) Well, rather, my wife mailed it. (pause) What do you people expect of me? (pause) Hold on a minute, will you, I have another call. (switches lines) Hello? Oh, hi, Mr. Breedman, sir. (pause) Well, yes, I know I left early today… (pause) I had to be home to receive a couple of personal business calls. (pause) Yeah, I'm sorry, I know it's … but I've been under a lot of pressure at home. (pause) Mr. Breedman, could you please hold for a second? I have another call... (switches lines) Sorry. (pause) If I get the money in to you by the end of the week, will it hold off action against the house? (pause) Alright, thank you, thank you. (pause) Goodbye. (switches lines) Mr. Breedman, I'm really sorry, thank you for holding on. (pause) Let me go? But, I don't understand … I've been getting all my work done, on time! (pause) Doesn't that count for something? (pause) In your office, tomorrow, 8 a.m. (pause) Right, thank you. I'll see you first thing in the morning. (pause)Thank you, Mr. Breedman. (he hangs up)

Offstage, we hear his wife, Sarah, tucking in Tommy.

TOMMY: Mommy, can I have a bicycle for my birthday? One without training wheels?

SARAH: Well, we'll see. Now go to sleep, sweetheart.

Sarah comes out to Tom. She is dressed simply, with a plain turtleneck or tunic, and we can see that she is wearing Barbara's locket from Scenes 4 and 6.

SARAH: Tom, were you able to stop and pick up Tommy's bike?

TOM: Well, I tried to, Sarah, but apparently the credit cards are maxed out.

SARAH: How'd they get maxed out?

TOM: Well, why don't you tell me?!? And while you're at it, what the hell happened to the mortgage payment?

SARAH: Nothing, I mailed it. (almost under her breath) I only hope the check clears.

TOM: Oh my God, the checking account. You did transfer the money, didn't you?

SARAH: Me?

TOM: (angry at the world, directing it at her) Yes, Sarah, YOU! I told you you needed to do it. Geez -- We're up to our ears in debt, you don't work, our savings account is completely empty, our stocks are dying, and you tell me you FORGOT to transfer the money!

SARAH: (at a breaking point) What is the matter with you lately? You've done nothing but shout at Tommy, and at me, you won't tell me what's wrong, you're never home -- and when you are home you lock yourself in your office!

TOM: Don't you start on me! I haven't done a thing!

SARAH: Yes, I know, that's exactly the point!

TOM: Listen, Sarah, we've got the mortgage, two cars, I'm a husband, a father, we got married right out of college -- and how I ever let you talk me into that I'll never know!

SARAH: You're not a husband anymore, you're not a father anymore, you're not here for us, ever, and as for our marriage, we've been through this before, and there's nothing that says we HAVE to stay together. (pause) Maybe we should consider separating for a while, so you can get your head back on straight.

TOM: ME get my head on straight!

TOMMY: (offstage, breaking up the argument) Mommy, Mommy! My knee still hurts. . .

TOM: What's the matter with that kid? What's he whining about?

SARAH: He fell down today and hurt himself. You wouldn't have noticed,

because you barricaded yourself in your office.

Sarah hesitates, and then goes into Tommy's room.

SARAH: **Excuse me. I need to take care of our son.**

TOM: **(to himself, but aloud) Oh, God, what a horrible, horrible day.**

Tom fusses on desk, throwing papers about, while from offstage...

TOMMY: **Mommy, why were you and Daddy talking loud?**

SARAH: **Don't worry about it Tommy. Now, let me take a look at your knee.**

SARAH: **Now, you've got to cheer up, little man, because you've got a birthday coming up, and that means cake and ice cream and lots of good things! Now, let's see a smile.**

Sarah sings "You are My Sunshine" to Tommy. Tom, onstage, reacts to song, moves to doorway so he can hear it better. Sarah finishes the song, and comes out.

SARAH: **(resigned) Maybe that's what we should do; maybe Tommy and I should go stay with my mother for a while.**

TOM: **Sarah, where did you hear that song? I've never heard you sing it before.**

SARAH: **What, that song? Well, I just knew it when I was a little kid. Why?**

TOM: **Oh, nothing.**

SARAH: **(trying to be strong) I'll call my mother now and tell her I'm coming, we can stay there for a while – I imagine we'll be situated in a day or so, and you can have the house to yourself.**

TOM: **(collapsing) Sarah, I'm sorry. I know I've been a complete jerk. And I know all this crap with the bills and stuff doesn't matter – what matters is you and Tommy . . . and me. Look, let's not have any more talk about leaving. We can work it out.**

Sarah does not respond.

TOM: **What do you say we grab Tommy, jump in the car and go into town for an ice cream – like we used to when he was a baby.**

SARAH: But, Tommy's already in his pajamas.

TOM: So what? It doesn't matter. Let's try something different. Maybe we need to look at things from a different perspective. (he moves to her, joking, like they used to) Quick, to the BatMobile!

Sarah laughs, and absentmindedly plays with the locket she wears.

SARAH: I'll go get Tommy. (pauses; over her shoulder to Tom) I'm willing to try it if you will. (exits)

TOM: (speaking to the spirits) Thanks, Mom.

Blackout/Scene change.

SCENE 9
(Manifesto)

Quickly, stage techs and actors rest the stage as it was in Scene 1. Actors reset themselves in positions identical to those at the top of the play, this time wearing their basic black costumes and bright, wildly-colored vests, each of a different design.

SAM: So this is the way it goes.

KATE: This is life.

LARRY: Our life.

CHRIS: A life full of good things,

STATIA: Bad things,

JARRETT: And downright lunacy.

ERIN: That we can't predict

COLE: Or plan for.

KENNY: You have given us this life.

With each of the following lines, actors come forward, setting up in a loosely formed line downstage. They interact, as appropriate, on the lines. Together they are a force.

ASHLEY: You have brought me in to a world, where:

DELMORE: People kill each other over worldly goods.

JOEY: All people are equal.

DANNY: But some are more equal than others.

KENNY: You control my life by telling me what to do, what not to do, and how to do it.

ASHLEY: I can't chew gum in class.

DELMORE: I must raise my hand before speaking.

JOEY: I can't go to the bathroom without taking a big piece of painted wood with me.

DANNY: I must clean my room.

WILL: I can't change the color of my own hair.

SAM: I must like my relatives.

KATE: I can't get up in the morning on my own time.

LARRY: I must call so you know where I am.

CHRIS: You entrust us to the care of professional educators who fill our minds with. . .

STATIA: Latin.

JARRETT: Algebraic equations.

ERIN: Enough homework to make my eye twitch.

COLE: Historical facts of dubious accuracy.

KENNY: That probably won't be true when we graduate.

ASHLEY: The mass of an atom.

DELMORE: Physics.

JOEY: The Redcoats are coming! The Redcoats are coming!

DANNY: You have not decided whether my ancestors were monkeys …

WILL: Or whether we were all created in the space of seven days.

SAM: Six.

KATE: You have taught me...

COLE: How to tell my right hand from my left. (but he gets it wrong)

LARRY: How to put a condom on a banana.

KENNY: You have subjected me to detestable aunts and uncles and distant relatives and I have suffered through endless family reunions, weddings, church suppers, and funerals.

Subsequent lines run quickly, each actor creating a full character for each.

ASHLEY: Oh you are soooooo CUTE!

DELMORE: You're getting so big!

JOEY: Ain't you cunnin'

DANNY: You look just like your mother!

WILL: You look just like your father!

SAM: Why can't you be more like your brother?

KATE: What'd you do in school today?

LARRY: Why weren't you in school today?

CHRIS: When's the wedding?

STATIA: Are they divorced yet?

JARRETT: What number husband is this?

ERIN: You spoil that child rotten.

COLE: Did you SEE that dress she had on?

KENNY: Well, I NEVER.

Tone breaks, preparing to set-up the "attack" on two "victims".

ASHLEY: I have been pinched, patted, fondled, hugged, smooched, kissed, cuddled, tickled, patted on the head and spanked on the fanny.

DELMORE: It's a wonder I'm not bruised.

Subsequent lines come rapid-fire, sometimes overlapping, with group of actors mobbing and encroaching on a remaining pair, one male and one female actor (Ashley & Joey), being terrorized by the others. Fast.

DANNY: **Don't pick your nose.**

WILL: **Keep your hands to yourself.**

SAM: **Don't put that in your mouth...**

KATE: **Don't play with that…**

LARRY: **Put that down...**

CHRIS: **Pick that up...**

STATIA: **Behave yourself.**

JARRETT: **Play nice.**

ERIN: **Hurry up.**

COLE: **Don't run.**

KENNY: **Don't slouch.**

DELMORE: **Stand up.**

DANNY: **Sit down.**

WILL: **Eat your carrots.**

SAM: **Chew your food.**

KATE: **Swallow that.**

LARRY: **Spit that out.**

CHRIS: **Lift the seat.**

STATIA: **You need a nap.**

JARRETT: **Stand in the corner.**

ERIN: Get in.

COLE: Sit down.

KENNY: Shut up.

DELMORE: Oh, grow up!

SAM: I am just sick and tired …

F. VICTIM: (ASHLEY) (exploding under pressure) No! No more!

Victimizing actors freeze. Victimized pair joins forces, eventually clasp hands.

M. VICTIM: (JOEY) I am just sick and tired of being treated like a child. I can't take it anymore.

F. VICTIM: I'm getting out.

M. VICTIM: Now.

F. VICTIM: How?

M. VICTIM: I'm going to explode, do something radical.

F. VICTIM: Something never before done by someone my age.

KATE: (breaks freeze) Well, not really.

LARRY: (breaks freeze) O.K., it's close enough.

M. VICTIM: I'm gonna, I'm gonna, I'm gonna…

F. VICTIM: Grow UP!

M. VICTIM: I'm going to prove to you that I can be what you wanted.

All break freeze in turn, coming further forward, proudly.

CHRIS: Better than you expected.

STATIA: A beautiful butterfly.

JARRETT: Worth all the effort.

ERIN: And the heartache.

COLE: And the money.

F. VICTIM: And we'd just like to say thanks...

M. VICTIM: For all the times you yelled at me.

F. VICTIM: For all the times you held my hand.

M. VICTIM: For the encouragement.

WILL: For not repeating the story about how I wet my pants in the bowling alley when I was three.

SAM: Or how I was scared when you wanted me to sit on Santa Claus's lap.

KATE: Yes, it's been a long, bumpy road.

LARRY: A long, hard ride.

WILL: And that train still keeps coming.

STATIA: We're growing up.

JARRETT: We're almost there.

ERIN: Almost out of your hair.

COLE: Out of the house.

KENNY: Out of your checkbook.

DANNY: Well, at least until college.

Blackout.

Let Me Count the Ways

A Musical Comedy in Two Acts

By

Linda Britt

Score by Colin Britt

Prologue

(Stage is dark. Six women are scattered in various locations ... Specials come up on them, one by one, as they briefly tell their stories, and then the lights go down. Finally, a spotlight on KAREN, center stage, seated at her kitchen table. She looks up, out, says nothing. Spotlight goes out, stage to black.)

(Light up on Bette, with a glass of milk)

Bette: My husband went to the grocery store for a gallon of milk. I told him "Make sure it's one percent, or one and a half." Sometimes when he goes to the store, he comes back with whole milk. Whole milk! Do you know how much fat is in a glass of whole milk? Well, ... a lot, anyway. So I said 1 %, or 1 1/2% at most. And he said to me, he said "Sure, honey." I'll always remember those words. "Sure, honey." Those were the last words he ever spoke to me. ... Until they found him in Mexico, where he was living with this 19-year-old chick he'd run away with. I'll bet she doesn't drink anything but skim! (Light down)

(Light up on Laura, with shopping bags)

Laura: So, okay, I'd been shopping with my girlfriend. ... There was this great sale at Filene's? Well, I found all these gorgeous spring clothes at 75% off. 75%! You can't pass up a deal like that! So we had a great day, and I returned home with, like, a whole new wardrobe! Like this! (indicating bags) Well, it wasn't two days before I came home from work and found my favorite new outfit--a really pretty mint green suit--on my husband. I mean, the skirt was a little short, but otherwise, he looked pretty damned good! I know! Hard to believe. Yeah. Anyway, I moved out the next day. I might have handled it differently if he hadn't looked better than I did in my new suit. ... (Light down)

(Light up on Annie, with wine glass)

Annie: Billy took me out to dinner. He'd made a reservation, even. It wasn't the <u>best</u> restaurant in town, mind you, but it was one of those places that had tablecloths, anyway. And waiters who tell you their names ("I'm Matthew, and I'll be your server tonight")... and candles on the table, that kind shaped like a brandy snifter, only without the stem and with that netting stuff around it? Anyway, I ordered sirloin beef tips with rice. Billy had a steak and twice-baked potatoes. He said they overcooked his steak. They should have served it to him raw. We ordered dessert, but before it arrived, he told me he was leaving me. Out of the

blue! I mean, I didn't have a clue. I was sitting there, waiting for my strawberry cheesecake, and wham! Then my cheesecake came. Of course I couldn't eat it, not even a bite. That makes me so mad now! *(Light down)*

(Light up on Patricia, with wrench)

Patricia: Well, I left my husband, oh, about six years ago now. I paid the bills, packed up my stuff, my clothes, my jewelry, a few books, and the dog, and moved in with my mom. Oh, not for long. I rented an apartment a couple of months later. It's cute, and cozy. I like it a lot better than that big old lonely house ... Tom was never home. Or if he was, I never saw him. He was always working on that stupid house. Why, the plumbing got more attention than I did. Shoot, everything got more attention than I did. So I figured I'd rather just be alone. And you know what? I haven't been lonely since! *(Light down)*

(Light up on Rachel, with wreath)

Rachel: I just started celebrating Christmas again. I figure, hey, I'm not going to let that bastard ruin my holidays forever! I mean, for the first couple of years, it was rough. Really rough. How would you feel if your husband of 16 years, and the father of your two children, up and left you on Christmas Eve? Said "I don't love you any more" and left. He'd already packed his bags! Moved in with his "girlfriend"...I ask you! There I was, on Christmas Eve, having to play Santa for my kids, alone. I spent a lot of time that Christmas day fantasizing about what I wished Santa would bring my Phil. ... *(Light down)*

(Light up on Diane, wearing apron)

Diane: My first husband was just plain dumb. So I divorced him. Oh, I know; how smart does that make me for marrying him in the first place? Not very. But we were both young. And neither of us knew anything. But I thought I got it right with my second marriage. We had it all. ... the house, the kids, the dog. So okay. I admit it. I was not the perfect wife. (Remove apron). I was good at some things ... but when you come right down to it, dust bunnies need a place to live, too. And half the closet in the guest bedroom had more than enough space for Rick's clothes. ... And don't try to tell me you've never fantasized about that hot guy at work, the one with the beautiful blue eyes ... the end of marriage number two. You think one ex-husband is bad? Try two! *(Light down)*

(Spotlight on Karen, center. Light goes out, stage to DARK).

ACT I

Scene One

(Setting: Kitchen table in Karen's house, with four chairs. Spotlessly clean; Lights up on Karen, sitting at the table, smartly dressed, and staring into space. Knocking heard at kitchen door to outside. Enter Patricia, casually dressed, with newspaper)

Patricia: I've been knocking and knocking! Here's your paper...You look beautiful today! Are you on your way out? I came over for coffee (looking around). Oh, good, a full pot. Can I get you a cup? What do you take, one sugar or two? No milk, I know. Oh, here, I just gave you one and a half. *(Sitting, looking at newspaper)* Oh, my God, did you see this? *(Indicating story)* Gail's husband was arrested for embezzlement at the church. Do you believe it? *(Looks at Karen, who hasn't moved)* Karen? Karen!

Karen: *(silence)*

Patricia: Karen, honey, what's wrong?

Karen: *(finally)* Mike's gone.

Patricia: Gone! You mean gone, gone? Or just gone to work gone?

Karen: You get up, take a shower, get dressed, clean the house, pay the phone bill, make your grocery list, put the laundry away. ... and then you notice that none of your husband's clothes are in his closet.

Patricia: Now, don't jump to conclusions. There could be a logical explanation for it.

Karen: Sure.

Patricia: Like ... maybe he took a business trip and forgot to tell you.

Karen: Nice try .

Patricia: Or ... he had an emergency call from his mother. ... and he had to take an early flight and didn't want to wake you.

Karen: His mother's on a cruise in Alaska. She's doing just fine.

Patricia: Or ... he spilled something in the closet and took all his clothes to the cleaners so you wouldn't get mad, ... or ... maybe he's decided he

needs a whole new wardrobe and he donated all his old stuff to the Salvation Army! Yeah, that's probably it!

Karen: Uh huh ... a whole new wardrobe ... his suits and his summer clothes and his t-shirts and his sweaters ... and his underwear ... and his ties ...

Patricia: He joined the circus and doesn't need regular clothes anymore?

Karen: Patricia!

Patricia: Oh, Karen, I'm sorry. You've become a statistic! Look, here in the paper. Do you know I only take the paper for one reason any more? To read the divorce log. *(Turn to Karen)* See this?

SONG

"Why Get Married (in the First Place)? "

***(Spoken)* Did you know that**

After 16 years of marital bliss
Susan and Donald are calling it quits ?
And Charlie and Liz with lots of tears
Have ended their union of 28 years!
Bob and Natasha are singing the blues
And now are ones instead of twos !

So ... why get married in the first place?
What's the point if you end up here?
Mike leaving you is not the worst case.
Think what Henry VIII's wives had to fear!

***(Spoken)* Let's see, now--well, the details aren't here, but**

Janice and Tommy just sold the house
In a settlement that pitted spouse against spouse
She took her share and bought a small place,
Covered the windows in chintz and lace.
He took his and he said "up yours "
Hooked up with a band as a roadie on tour!

So ... why get married in the first place?

**What's the point if you end up here?
When he proposes just spray him with mace
You'll save yourself heartache and lots of tears!**

(Spoken) **And look at this! What on earth?**

**Who can explain why Sarah and Ed
After only four months say their marriage is dead?
When they said those words "till death do us part"
I guess what they meant was "till we see the warts! "
The ink on the lease they signed is still wet
And the wedding celebration has left them in debt!**

**So ... why get married in the first place?
What's the point if you end up here ?
Your husband has left, and maybe for good
(Karen): And I'd marry him all over if 1 could!**

Patricia: Tell me you didn't just say that!

Karen: He might have left me, but it's probably just for a few days. It's not forever. It can't be !

Patricia: I don't know how to tell you this, but from the looks of things in that closet, I'd say he's planning to be gone for quite some time ...

Karen: But how could he do this to me? And why? Mike loves me, I know he does!

Patricia: Oh, Lord, I need reinforcements! ***(Heads for phone, dials)*** **Hello? Rachel? Hey, it's Pat ... Listen, I'm at Karen's. Can you get over here right away? Yeah, and call Annie and Bette--I'll call Laura and Diane ...** ***(lights out).***

Scene 2

(Two hours later. Karen's house, now populated with several of her closest friends: Patricia, Bette, Annie, Rachel, Laura, Diane. At lights up, Bette and Patricia are comforting Karen, while others are telling divorce jokes.)

Karen: I don't understand it. I just don't understand it!

Bette: I can't believe Mike would do this to you. I mean, you just had your anniversary party last week!

Karen: Our fourteenth anniversary *(begins to sob).*

Patricia: He gave you that beautiful necklace.

Rachel: Trying to soften the blow, no doubt. I'll bet he had it all planned.

Bette: Rachel, you're such a cynic! ... Still, the timing is weird.

(in another part of the kitchen, the jokes get louder)

Laura: Hey, how many ex-husbands does it take to change a light bulb?

Others: *(ad lib)* I don't know/how many?

Laura: Just one: He holds the bulb while the world revolves around him! *(All around her laugh; Karen still in tears)*

Diane: No, wait: How many ex-husbands does it take to change a light bulb?

Others: *(ad lib)* Not another one!/groan!/How many?

Diane: None. They don't get the house anyway.

Rachel: Hold on ... If you saw your ex-husband and his girlfriend drowning in a swimming pool, would you … go to lunch or go to the movies?

(All laugh except Karen and Bette)

Bette: Come on, you guys! She's in pain here.

Laura: Sorry, Karen. Did it come as a shock?

Karen: *(Nodding and sobbing)*

Annie: Yeah. … I remember when Billy left me. I think I cried for two months. But it does get better, honey.

Rachel: That's right. … Give it time.

Others: *(ad lib)* Time heals everything/It'll be okay/don't cry, sweetie/ etc.

Karen: How can you say that? It'll never be better, ever! I LOVE HIM!

Bette: Of course you do, honey.

Laura: Right. Naturally you love him. He was the perfect husband.

Karen: Perfect *(agreeing)*

Diane: Sure … he never came home late.

Annie: He always called you.

Patricia: He always remembered your birthday and anniversary .

Rachel: Did his share of work around the house.

Laura: And he was thoughtful enough to leave you on a weekend, so all of us could come be with you!

(Karen dissolves in tears again)

Bette: Well, honey, he <u>did</u> leave you, didn't he, so I'd have to say he couldn't exactly have been <u>perfect.</u>

Karen: He certainly was ... until he left.

Diane: So why did he take off? Did he leave a note?

Karen: *(still sobbing)* I don't know.

Rachel: All right. Search the place. I bet we'll find one.

Annie: I'll take the bedroom.

Patricia: I'll go with you. *(exit with Annie)*

Diane: Honestly, we already know what the note's going to say!

Laura: Yep: "It's not you, Karen, it's me."

Diane: So predictable.

Bette: Don't listen to them, dear. I'm sure he has a good reason for ... his absence.

Karen: He was kidnapped! That's what happened!

Bette: Kidnapped.

Annie: *(Entering, waving a paper)* I found it! It's a letter, Karen!

Karen: Give it to me!

Bette: Don't you want us to read it to you, honey?

Karen: LET ME SEE IT!

Annie: Okay, okay!

Karen: *(Starting to read; others gather around; looking at each other apprehensively)* "My dear Karen. .." *(collapsing into tears again)*

Bette: *(asking others)* Should I read it?

All: *(ad lib)* Yes!/Read it!/Go ahead! (etc*).*

(Karen nods and waves her hand yes).

Bette:

SONG

"Dear Karen"

(spoken)	**My dear Karen**
(sung)	***I hope I've been a decent husband***
	Of course you've been a good wife.
	But now I find it's time to move on
	I'm ready to start a new life
(all women--chorus)	***He's ready to start a new life***

Thanks to you our house is neat
And you are an exceptional cook.
It isn't anything you have done
Although I know how things must look.

(chorus) ***He knows how things must look.***

You may wonder why I'm leaving
When I promised I'd be true.
Believe me when I tell you this:
The problem's me, it isn't you.

(chorus) ***The problem's him, not you.***

I must move on, must find myself
I'm feeling strangled here at home.
So off I go to find my future
Toward the horizon I must roam.

(chorus) ***Toward the horizon he must roam!***

So off I go to find my future.
I don't know if I'll be back.
I'll try to mail a current address
So send the stuff I didn't pack!

(chorus) ***So send the stuff he didn't pack!***

Bette: *(spoken)* "Sincerely, Mike."

Karen: SINCERELY!

All: *(ad lib)* If that doesn't take the cake/ what a jerk!/ how could he?/ He's worse than Billy!/ etc.

Rachel: Divorce him, Karen. Join the club.

Laura: It's nothing to be ashamed of. Hey, half of all marriages end in divorce.

Diane: That's the good news!

All: *(ad lib)* What?/ Huh?/ What are you talking about?

Diane: The other half end in death!

Laura: I've got it! What's the fastest way to a man's heart?

All: *(ad lib)* Through his stomach? / I don't know!/ What?/ etc.

Laura: Through the chest wall with a sharp knife!

Karen: *(wailing)* STOP! He might deserve it, but I could never do that!

Diane: I could.

Patricia: Me too.

Bette: So could I.

Annie: Remember that Paul Simon song, "50 Ways to Leave Your Lover"? I'll bet I could come up with at least that many ways to wound him mortally.

Rachel: At least ... Hey, there was that woman in Texas ... Didn't she run over her ex-husband with a Mercedes?

Karen: Twice! *(brightening a little)*

Patricia: Trouble with that is, it's kind of obvious, you know? That would be REALLY hard to get away with.

All: Yeah/ right/ it sure would/ they could trace the tires/ she probably had witnesses ...

Rachel: What we need ...

Laura: What we <u>really</u> need ...

Diane: Is a foolproof way to get rid of our ex-husbands, and get away with it!

All: *(stare)*

Patricia: There's no such thing. I mean, you can trace arsenic ...

Bette: And someone's bound to find out that you've cut the brake line of his car.

Laura: A woman went to K-Mart and said "I want to buy a shotgun for my husband:" The clerk said "Does he know what gauge he wants?" She said "No. He doesn't even know I'm going to shoot him!"

Karen: *(more interested)* No, that's way too messy.

Annie: There was that woman in North Carolina who hired a hit man to take out her husband!

Diane: And, yeah, the only reason you heard about that is because she got caught! Come on, you guys, we can do better than that.

Rachel: Did you see the TV movie about the woman who killed three husbands before she got caught?

Diane: Rachel, are you still watching those "Lifetime" movies?

Karen: "Lifetime, Television for Women."

Rachel: Listen, Diane, I'm not ashamed of watching "Lifetime," or for that matter, "Oprah." I always feel better seeing other women who are worse off than I am. At least I've never slept with my best friend's teenage son!

Laura: Wait! Have you seen your best friend's son lately? I'd be tempted ...

Annie: Hey, we weren't talking about sex. We were talking about killing our husbands.

Patricia: Not husbands. Just exes.

Laura: Right. So ... they don't count? Are we all crazy?

Rachel: Oooh! We could plead insanity. Yeah, that's it: Collective insanity.

Diane: Sure. Any judge would buy that defense.

Annie: I confess, girls. This whole topic really brings out my dark side.

Bette: Your dark side?

Annie: Oh, yeah.

SONG

"Temptation, or My Dark Side "

Temptation: It's my dark side.
It's been with me since I was a bride.
Temptation,. Even though I've tried,
I'm still living with my dark side.

When I'm lying in my bed at night
At the end of a normal day
My mind won't stop when I turn out the light

I think of ways to make him pay.

Like visions of sugar plums in olden days
Thoughts of sharp objects dance through my head
And pistols and shotguns and oozies and cannons
March in parade as I lie in my bed.

Temptation, etc.

I daydream of poisons and drownings,
Dark fantasies torture my nights.
I know that it's wrong, but still I go on
Imagining inescapable plights.

I think of him walking the plank
Or strangling to death with a string
He could fall down a muddy bank
Or choke on a fried chicken wing.

Temptation, etc.
I'm still living with my dark side.

Diane: Okay, that's pretty exotic. ... How many opportunities does a person actually have these days to walk a plank?

Rachel: I suppose someone <u>could</u> choke on a chicken wing, but I'd really rather <u>my</u> ex choke on his mother's meatballs.

Annie: Mine could choke on his own ego, it's so big.

Bette: I think I'd like to see my ex barrel-ride Niagara Falls. He's claustrophobic.

Annie: Now that's evil.

Bette: I know. I have had lots of time to think about it.

Patricia: Me too. Guess how I'd get rid of my ex.

All: How?

Patricia: He would get sucked into the plumbing and simply disappear.

Karen: Hey, did you guys forget why you're here?

All: *(ad lib)* Karen!/ sorry/ how you feelin '?/ etc.

Karen: Lousy! I feel lousy! And you're doing a horrible job of cheering me up!

Laura: Oh, come on! Doesn't it make you feel just a teeny bit better imagining all the awful ways Mike could disappear?

Karen: *(in tears again)* He's already disappeared!

Diane: Oh, Karen, you just don't know yet that you're better off without him.

Bette: Yeah. That's what we've all come to realize.

Laura: It's true, honey. Next year at this time, you'll be glad that he's gone.

Karen: I don't believe you!

Rachel: I know how you feel, sweetie. I was devastated. There I was, alone with my kids, that first Christmas. Crushed, humiliated. ... And you know what hurt most? Having to face that empty chair at Christmas dinner!

Diane: This is WAY too depressing.

Annie: I need some chocolate!

Patricia: Oh, yeah, now you're talking my language. Come on, I'll drive!

Karen: Where are you going?

Patricia: Chocolate run!

Annie: We'll be back in a flash.

Patricia: With Rocky Road, Mint Chocolate Chip, Double Fudge chocolate ...

Annie: Bye! *(exit, with PATRICIA)*

Bette: Okay, Karen, time for a plan. First we have to know. Where's your money?

Karen: My money?

Rachel: Well, yeah. When Phil left me, he cleaned out our joint accounts. I was penniless for months.

Karen: Oh, my God.

Rachel: Fortunately , since I'd already done my Christmas shopping, I could take back the presents I'd bought for him and get a refund.

Karen: Oh, my God!

Rachel: Sure. At least we could eat for a while.

Diane: I took half our money when I left Rick. I figured that was fair. And it was enough to pay my deposit and a few months' rent, while I got on my feet.

Bette: Well, I was totally cleaned out. It takes money to move to Mexico.

Karen: So what did you do?

Bette: I borrowed money and hired a good lawyer. Karen, please tell me you have your own bank account.

Karen: Ummnun ...

Diane: Okay. Call the bank now. *(Checking watch)* They're open until noon.

Karen: I can't! *(wailing).*

Laura: I'll do it. At least I'll dial the number for you. Of course, if his name's on the account, you can't stop him from taking all the money he wants.

Rachel: But if the money's still there, you absolutely should withdraw it before he gets the chance!

Diane: Yeah--maybe Mike didn't plan that far ahead.

Laura: Karen, where's your checkbook?

Karen: I don't know. Somewhere!

Bette: Think!

Karen*: (getting up)* Ummm. ... It's where I always keep it! In this drawer here.

(taking out checkbook)

Bette: *(grabbing the checkbook)* Karen! You only have $32 in this account!

Karen: Yeah so?

Diane: Oh, Karen, I don't think we're going to lose sleep over $32!

Laura: Where's the rest of your money?

Bette: A savings account, maybe?

Karen: *(searching through drawer)* I know it's here somewhere!

Diane: What? What are you looking for?

Rachel: This is just like Court TV! It's so exciting!

Diane: Rachel, get a life. Karen, are you looking for your passbook?

Karen: Uh huh ...Here it is! *(opening it)* So Mike didn't take it!

Laura: Well, that's something to be grateful for.

Karen: *(in tears again)* I told you he's a great guy.

Diane: *(taking passbook)* Sure he is. Karen, you and Mike have to have more than this. Where's the rest of it?

Karen: Mutual funds? No, wait, a money market account? I think.

Bette: You think!

Rachel: You don't know? Oh, Karen, no !

Karen: I didn't worry about money. ... That was Mike's department. I don't even know how much money we have !

Laura: Come on, Karen, I'm taking you to the bank. We're going to figure this out.

Diane: Okay. We'll stay here and wait for the ice cream! If you need us, call us.

(Exit Karen and Laura)

Rachel: She has no idea.

Bette: You can't blame her. How could she have known?

Diane: You would think she'd have learned something from us!

Rachel: Oh, Diane, you know no one can tell you what it's like. You have to experience it yourself.

Diane: All I know is, someday it's going to hit her, and she'll want to kill the S.O.B.

Rachel: Maybe she won't actually want to kill him ...There are other possibilities.

SONG

"Lorena Bobbitt "

I don't really want to tell you
What my deepest secret is
'Cause I know that you'll just call me
A radical feminist. But I'm really not at all that way
At least I never thought so
I'm actually quite conservative
In politics; I was taught so.

But here's the thing about me you should know tonight:
I think Lorena Bobbitt got it right.

Let's say your man's an awful cad
Let's say he's cheated more than twice
Let's say that what he did was bad
Let's say he screwed his best friend's wife!
What can you do to pay him back?
I have a thought! Pull out your knife!

(enter Patricia and Annie)

Asleep he won't put up a fight
I think Lorena Bobbitt got it right.

Oh dear, it seems I've shocked you.
You don't think I look the sort
Who'd be a butcher in disguise
Who wouldn't be the best of sports.
You ' d never dream to look at me
That I'd end up on Court TV!

I'm really not the murderous type
But 1 think Lorena Bobbitt got it right!

Patricia: Why, Rachel! I'm shocked!

Rachel: No, you're not. Don't tell me you weren't secretly cheering when you heard that story !

Bette: *(making face)* EWWWWWWWW!

Diane: I figured she must have just gone over the edge.

Annie: Yeah ... the knife's edge!

Patricia: Hey, guys, ice cream! Ummm Where's Karen? Is she

okay?

Rachel: Gone to the bank with Laura.

Annie: Her spoons must be here in one of these drawers ... Aha!

Patricia: Why the bank? ... Oh, no, he didn't take all their money, did he?

Bette: We don't know yet.

Diane: I learned two lessons from my first marriage that I applied to the second: One: I kept my own last name, and two: I kept a separate bank account. Of course, some things were in both names. We have joint custody of them.

Annie: Could somebody please explain to me why marriage is so hard?

Diane: You want a list?

Rachel: I didn't think it was, until Phil left me. I thought I had a pretty good marriage!

Annie: I thought I did too, but look what happened to us!

(Lights fade on kitchen, women still talking to each other)

Scene Three

(Lights up on proscenium: Two men with golf clubs surveying course, out: Billy and Phil)

Billy: So what are your kids up to these days?

Phil: I wish I knew. I don't get to see 'em much.

Billy: Man, that sucks!

Phil: Yeah, I really miss them. Jane started college this year, and I haven't even seen her dorm.

Billy: Oh, you see one dorm room, you've seen them all.

Phil: I suppose I did really screw Rachel over, but I thought the kids would have forgiven me by now.

Billy: Yeah. It's probably because the only side of the story they ever hear is her side.

Phil: Her side ...Well, it's not like my side is all that defensible. I should have waited until after Christmas.

Billy: Oh, come on! It's not like you just woke up one morning and said "the hell with this, I'm leaving!" You had your reasons.

Phil: I did. Of course I did. Things had been going from bad to worse.

Billy: That's how it was with Annie, too. I mean, she just didn't ... well, she didn't get where I was coming from.

Phil: No, I guess not. Rachel either. I think I'd been seeing Susan for about four months before I moved out.

Billy: Did she know?

Phil: Who, Rachel? Not until I left. Yeah, she was surprised.

Billy: So why DID you pick Christmas Eve?

Phil: Susan wanted me to spend Christmas with HER.

Billy: Uh huh.

Phil: But I kind of thought Rachel would be happy when I left. She'd been mad at me for years.

Billy: Why mad?

Phil: Oh, who knows? But I couldn't make her happy.

Billy: Well, Annie tried to tell me I didn't WORK hard enough at our marriage. Who the hell decided that marriage was supposed to be work?

Phil: That's what I'd like to know. When I go home, all I want to do is relax.

Billy: Yeah, but instead it never ends. Do this. Do that. Not THAT way. MY way.

Phil: God, yes. Never satisfied. And I know I have some good points.

Billy: Of course you do. We all do.

Phil: I was a good provider. I did chores. I washed her car at least every couple of weeks.

Billy: She was lucky to have you.

Phil: And I could have done a great job raising the kids, if I'd only had the chance.

Billy: Sure you could.

Phil: Hell, I went to their soccer matches. I went to parent-teacher conferences.

Billy: I'll bet she's forgotten all the good things you ever did.

Phil: Of course she has. Or if not, she'd never admit to them. I will forever be "The Bad Guy."

Billy: Naturally, if you only listen to her side!

SONG

"'Our Side "

Phil: ***If you listened to her and only to her***
You'd think I'm the scum of the earth.
Not only while I was married to her
But I've been this way since birth

Billy: *The scum of the earth, the mud of her shoe,*
The bacterium on her tooth plaque,
The mold on her bread, already turned blue
In the trash at the bottom of the sack.

Phil: *I'm the lowest of the low for sure*
I don't deserve to live any more

Billy: *I don't deserve to live, for sure,*
Because I 'm rotten to the core.

Duet: *If you'd only listen to our side*
If you'd please let us have our say
You'd realize then we have nothing to hide
And every dog deserves his day.

Phil: *Look: I know I left her on Christmas Eve*
Which perhaps was a dumb thing to do.
But once I'd made up my mind to leave
I had to get out--wouldn't you?

Billy: *My wife never did understand me*
I'm a man of incredible needs
I'm not superman, not made of steel
When my finger is cut, it bleeds !

Phil: *I hated the looks that she gave me*
When I walked in late or forgot to call.

Billy: *And I felt that she never forgave me*
If I left dirty clothes in the hall.

Duet: *If you'd only listen to our side*
If you'd please let us have our say
You'd realize then we have nothing to hide
And ever dog deserves his day.

Phil: *I couldn't be who she wanted me to*
Could not measure up to her ideal.
I did try my best, I swear it to you
But her version of me wasn't real.

Billy: *No one can be who they wanted us to be*
Perfection just does not exist.
No one can do it--least of all me.
I don't even make the short list.

Duet: *Now that you've listened to our side*
And you've kindly let us have our say
You must realize we have nothing to hide

And every dog deserves his day.

Phil: Ready to hit the links?

Billy: Absolutely.

(Lights down on Phil and Billy.)

Scene Four

(Lights up on Karen's kitchen/with Patricia, Bette, Diane, Annie, Rachel)

Bette: What if you did? What if you had great marriages? What if that's it, that's the best there is? You had good marriages, and they still ended!

Diane: So: Is there no hope? Is the entire world condemned to lousy marriages that stay intact or good marriages that fall apart?

Patricia: No, of course not ... I don't think so. We must know SOME couples who are happily married.

Rachel: Name one.

Patricia: Well. ... how about Keith and Charlotte? They've been married for, what, eighteen years?

Diane: Yeah, and for the last three she's been seeing a therapist.

Patricia: There's nothing wrong with therapy!

Diane: No. I mean "seeing" a therapist.

Annie: Okay. Then there's Eric and Jolene. They're, like, the perfect couple.

Bette: Until last month. He caught her with the pizza delivery guy.

Annie: Oh, no !

(Lights down on kitchen,. lights up on bank with banker, Karen and Laura).

Banker: So let me get this straight. You suspect your husband may have taken all your money.

Karen: Of course not. He wouldn't do that to me.

Laura: *(to banker)* Yes, that's right. Can you please check all the accounts held by Karen and Mike ?

Banker: All right. Do you have your account number with you?

Karen: Here's my passbook. But I don't have the info for any other accounts.

Banker: Well, we can check that for you, but I need two forms of

identification.

Laura: Get out your driver's license! ***(Reaching/or Karen's purse, pulling out billfold).*** **Here!**

Banker: Thank you. I'll be right back.

(Banker exit)

Karen: Wait! I'm sure this isn't necessary.

Laura: Karen! Wake up and smell the skunk!

(Lights down on bank; Lights up on kitchen)

Patricia: Amanda and Jim! They renewed their wedding vows last year. It was a beautiful ceremony.

Rachel: Sorry to tell you this, but he was already having an affair with the babysitter .

Patricia: Oh, no!

Diane: Why are you surprised?

Annie: How about Joe and Eleanor, over on Silver Street? Their grandchildren are almost grown, and they're still happily married.

(exchange of glances)

Bette: You could have us there.

Rachel: I don't know them. Are you sure he's not a closet gambler, or something? Maybe a serial killer?

Patricia: Absolutely. They are simply the perfect couple.

Annie: You see? I knew there had to be one somewhere!

Diane: So you're saying. ... there's hope?

(Lights down on kitchen; lights up on bank)

Karen: You 're sure?

Banker: Yes, ma' am. It's in black and white.

Karen: You haven't made a mistake?

Banker: No, ma'am.

Laura: When did this happen?

Banker: Let me check ... Just yesterday.

Karen: So ... I'm broke?

Banker: Not exactly. You have $683 in your savings account, and $32 in your checking.

Karen: But ...

Laura: And Mike has $73,000.

Banker: That's right. Unless he's spent it.

Laura: My ex would have bought out Filene's with $73,000.

(Lights down on bank; lights up on golf course, Billy and Phil)

Billy: So how much is child support setting you back these days?

Phil: Not a cent. My youngest turned 18, so I'm free and clear!

Billy: Well now, that's worth celebrating!

Phil: How about you? Still forking over the alimony?

Billy: Oh, yeah. I wish Annie would find a nice guy and get married again! Or even a not-so-nice guy. My girlfriend's not exactly thrilled about all that alimony.

(Lights down on golf course, lights up on kitchen)

Annie: I wish I could find a nice guy and get married again. Trouble is, if I did I'd have to give up my alimony.

Diane: Yes ..."Remember the Alimo-ny,"

Bette: Yeah, that's the downside.

Diane: *(dawning realization)* Oh, God. I didn't even think about that! If we killed our exes, we'd lose our alimony, child support ... everything!

Bette: Still, it might be worth it!

Rachel: Hell, yes. Listen, Phil got to the point where he wanted me to account for every dime of child support I got.

Diane: Screw that. If I want to spend my alimony on a trip to Mexico, by God, Rick's not going to stop me.

Bette: Anywhere but Mexico.

Annie: I hear you ... I even felt guilty when I bought a new refrigerator!

Rachel: Screw that, too! What, is your food supposed to rot?

Patricia: Control freaks, all of them. We should just take 'em out.

Annie: Are you guys really serious?

Rachel: Well, I'm serious. I don't know about anyone else!

Diane: Oh, man! This is scary!

(Lights down; then up on bank, Karen shaking her head; lights up on golfer;. lights up again on kitchen)

SONG: Trio

Billy	**Karen**	**Diane**
It's always her side	*What he deserves is*	*Could we afford it,*
Everyone hears	*Perhaps beheading*	*The loss of income*
It's never my side	*Or freezing solid*	*That we'd risk trying*
My hidden fears	*while he's out sledding*	*To murder the bum?*
They all believe her	*He could be strangled;*	*It sure would cost us*
They think I'm pond scum	*A rabid skunk bite*	*A pretty penny*
I might as well be	*A drive-by shooting*	*Like half his money*
An out and out bum.	*A kangaroo fight.*	*If he has any.*
Why is it always her side?	*I know that it's evil*	*How can we afford it?*
Why is it never mine?	*To talk about his death*	*Have we lost our heads?*
I'm not such a bad guy	*But he should suffer*	*Have we gone crazy*
Look at me, I'm fine!	*Until his dying breath!*	*To wish them dead?*
I'm not a bad guy	*He could take a fall*	*If we have to choose*
Let me tell you why!	*Off a horse or wall*	*What to save or lose,*
She's not right for me	*Have a parachute fail,*	*Would we pick the money?*
It's so plain to see	*Or be killed by hail.*	*Or death to an ex-honey?*
You have to believe	*Overdose on C-Span*	*We can make a plan*
I just had to leave	*Get locked in a trash*	*I know that we can*
I have nothing to hide	*Or fall from a boat*	*There is just one flaw*
I have my good side	*Sing too high a note!*	*It's against the law.*

(Lights out: Curtain. End Act I)

Act II

Scene One

(Lights up on Karen's kitchen, 2 weeks later; Karen pacing; Laura, Patricia, Rachel, and Annie seated at the table)

Karen: So, why hasn't he called, or written, or anything? ... I know! Maybe he's had a terrible accident! That's it! He was in an accident and has amnesia!

Laura: Yep--I'll bet he totally forgot about that $73,000 he took.

Patricia: Yeah, that's it. Poor guy.

Annie: Amnesia ... You have to feel sorry for him.

Rachel: I know I do.

Karen: *(Banging her head against the wall.)* He doesn't have amnesia, does he?

Patricia: Nope.

Laura: Not a chance.

Rachel: Let me think: NO.

Patricia: I'll take a wild guess as to what happened. Hmmmm ... he took the money, disappeared, and doesn't want to be found.

Laura: Could be. Probably left the country. Your $73,000 has gone "bye-bye."

Karen: *(sinking into chair)* Oh, God.

Patricia: *(brightly)* Or he could have amnesia!

Annie: So, Karen. ... how goes the job search?

Karen: I have a couple of leads ...plus I have an interview on Tuesday for a great job.

Patricia: Good for you! Who's it with?

Karen: Ed Stanley. Do you know him? He's a lawyer, looking for a

paralegal for his firm. He says he'll train the right person.

Rachel: I know that name from somewhere.

Annie: How'd you fmd it?

Karen: My attorney recommended me to him. He knew I was looking for a better job to cover his fees ...

Rachel: No--I'm wrong. That was Ed Stevens from Stuckeyville (you know, that bowling alley TV lawyer?)

Annie: Enough TV, Rachel!

Patricia: That job should be right up your alley, Karen! You're the most organized person I know.

Karen: I used to be ... Somehow it's all gotten harder.

Laura: Listen, Karen, if you need any money to tide you over, let me know. I have some saved.

Annie: Me too, hon. Not a lot, but what I have is yours.

Karen: Oh, thanks so much. I'll let you know.

Patricia: So, seriously, how are you doing?

Karen: Seriously? I feel like someone took my feet and shoved them down my throat until they came out the other end.

Laura: Ouch.

Karen: And like someone turned out every single light all over the world.

Patricia: Oh, sweetie.

Karen: And like global warming sped up and the polar ice caps melted and the waves are lapping at my chin.

Laura: Okay, okay, we get it!

Karen: You asked.

Annie: Don't make us sorry that we did!

Rachel: This is great dialogue, though. I feel like I'm in a TV movie!

Karen: *(exasperated)* You know what? I don't think I'll ever

understand why he did it. What did I do to him to deserve this?

Annie: Stop it right now. I mean it! Don't ever say that again!

Patricia: I can't tell you how much I hate those words!

Rachel: Sweetie, it wasn't you.

Laura: You did nothing. Nothing! AS IF ...

Karen: I just wish ...

Laura: Karen, my dad always said "Wish in one hand, shit in the other, and see which one gets full first! "

All: *(laughter, ad libs)*

Karen: But I thought I knew him!

Patricia: I still think I know my ex better than he knows himself. But did any of you ever feel like your husbands knew you?

Laura: I guess Brad knew my taste in clothes, anyway.

Annie: It's funny. I thought we were so close! Soul mates, even. And then Billy left me like that and it hit me: Maybe he never knew me. Maybe nobody ever knows anyone, really.

Patricia: My husband would have needed a manual. Unfortunately, I didn't come with one.

Karen: It's obvious now that I didn't know Mike. I would never have dreamed he could hurt me like this. But the opposite's true, too. I don't think he knew me at all.

SONG

"(He couldn't see) The Real Me "

Although I'm not a beauty queen,
I'm attractive in my way.
No one calls me Bonnie Jean
But there are men who look my way.

People say my smile is nice
People say I have good hair
One or two men might look twice
If I've dressed myself with care.

But what about what's inside?
What about the rest of me?

I don't look like Frankenstein's bride
But what's inside is the best of me.

You might think he'd know me well;
We were married for fourteen years.
And the marriage--it went pretty well
As marriages go, until the tears.

But the thing is, he never knew me,
Never cared what made me care,
Never saw my soul, never looked into me,
And I am more than what I wear.

So what about what's inside?
What about the rest of me?
I don't look like Frankenstein's bride
But what's inside is the best of me.

He doesn't know what's inside
Doesn't know what I'm feeling.
Maybe I am Frankenstein's bride
And he never knew the real me.

Karen: (sigh) Maybe he's had amnesia for our entire married life. I mean, it's not like I didn't <u>try</u> to tell him things.

Laura: Amnesia ... Speaking of which, where are Bette and Diane? Weren't they supposed to meet us here?

Annie: Yep. They're late.

Patricia: We're going to miss our movie!

Annie: Tell me one thing: Why do we want to see this movie, anyway?

Laura: Two words: Mel Gibson

Karen: He's married.

Patricia: Yeah. If he weren't, of course, he'd be oh so available to you and me. But who needs Mel?

Annie: That's right. Who needs him, when handsome, rich bachelors are already wearing our doors thin from all the knocking they're doing?

Laura: Speak for yourself. The last bachelor who knocked on my door was fourteen, and he wanted me to pay him to shovel my walk.

Karen: It hasn't snowed since last winter!

Laura: See what I mean?

Rachel: I think I'm technically a virgin again ...That's how long it's been for me.

Patricia: Actually, I've been meaning to tell you something.

Annie: What? Pat, are you seeing someone?

Laura: Details, honey! Don't hold out on us.

Patricia: Well, it's just someone I met at the coffee shop.

Karen: Who? What's he like?

Rachel: What an amazing coincidence! You were both in the same coffee shop at the same time!

Patricia: Don't get too excited. We're just having dinner.

Rachel: Oooooh! Where? When?

Annie: I want to be a fly on the wall.

Patricia: Look, there's nothing to tell yet. It's just dinner. Next Tuesday.

Laura: Is he hot? What was he wearing when you met him?

Patricia: He's just a guy! His name is Dave, and we're eating Chinese. Don't worry, I'll tell you everything ... when there's something to tell!

(Enter Bette and Diane, with shopping bags.)

Bette: Sorry we're late!

Diane: But look what we brought! *(taking hats out of bags)* Look at these great hats! We bought one for everyone!

Bette: A different color for each of us!

Diane: See, it's symbolic. We're all alike, but we're all different.

Laura: Okay, guys, that's deep.

Patricia: Oh yeah. Deep *(without enthusiasm)*

Rachel: That's really sweet of you. What inspired you?

Bette: Those "red hat" women. Except we didn't want people to think we're identical.

Annie: Right. Because otherwise we look exactly alike.

Karen: Well, I think it's a great idea. Kind of like a secret club.

Laura: *(unconvinced)* Yep. Now all we need is a clubhouse and a secret password.

Patricia: A password: How about "Thelma and Louise"?

Bette: Come on! Put them on!

Laura: Oh, no! Not me! This hat is definitely not me.

Annie: Here--I'll trade with you. This is your color.

Laura: I don't care what color it is! I would not be caught dead in that hat in public. I love you guys, but frankly, your taste in fashion sucks.

Diane: Now I'm hurt. We spent ages picking out the right colors. We even missed Mel Gibson for this .

Laura: You missed Mel Gibson!

Rachel: One problem: Wouldn't these hats kind of make us conspicuous?

Diane: Yeah ... and the problem with that would be?

Bette: Oh, I forgot! We're trying to stay undercover!

Rachel: Exactly: for when we put our plan into action.

Laura: What plan? We have a "password," but we don't have a plan!

Annie: We have a plan to make a plan. That's almost as good as having a plan.

Karen: No it isn't.

Annie: It's better than no plan at all.

Diane: Not really. Surely we can do better than planning to plan to make a plan!

Bette: This is ridiculous. Look--there's precedent here. We can just be a First Wives' Club, only with teeth.

Diane: The question is, *(wandering to kitchen knife set, perhaps taking one out)* which one do we start with? I mean, they all deserve it, but we can't exactly take them all out at once.

Annie: Right.

Rachel: I nominate Phil *(checking under the sink, taking out poisons).* If ever a man deserved to kick the bucket, it's him.

Diane: You 'd better check his will first, to make sure your kids are taken care of. If he changed his will so all his money goes to little miss "trophy wife," your kids are screwed.

Bette: *(Wringing a dishtowel)* I wouldn't care if we took out old Speedy Gonzalez. Between Charlie's move to Mexico and attorney fees, he hasn't got much left, anyway. Trouble is, I don't know how I'd get him to Niagara Falls for that barrel ride.

Annie: *(Opening fridge, taking out chicken)* I think we should invite all our exes to a nice chicken dinner. We could undercook the chicken, and they could all get salmonella poisoning and die.

Patricia: Not that that isn't a delightful image to ponder, but wouldn't that be a bit obvious? Can you imagine Tom's reaction if I invited him to dinner after all this time? And they'd "coincidentally" all get sick while we wouldn't ...

Annie: Okay, okay, so what's your brilliant idea?

Patricia: I didn't say I had one. ... It would be great if we could take care of all of them at once, but I just don't see that working.

Annie: Maybe ... maybe ... Maybe we could send them all letters, telling them they've won a prize, and they have to show up somewhere at a certain time, only when they all converge there, the car or the building or something could "accidentally" blow up!

Rachel: Oh, sure, this sounds doable for us--we just have to locate a building, get our hands on some explosives, and assume all our exes will show up on time for once.

Karen: Laura, you're being awfully quiet. Got some creative ideas bubbling?

Laura: I don't know ... I mean, it's easy enough for me to joke about it, but ...

Diane: Wait! I've been saving this one for you! What should you do if you see your ex-husband rolling around in pain on the ground?

All: *(ad lib)* I don't know!/What?

Diane: Shoot him again. ***(laughter all around)***

Laura: Right--But was it really Brad's fault that he preferred Lizwear to Tommy Hilfiger? I mean, does he deserve to die for that? That's kind of a case of the fashion police carrying things a bit too far.

Patricia: Are you backing out on us, Laura? What about all for one and one for all?

Laura: Hey, I'm here for you guys, but have a heart! ***(pause)*** **That's it!**

All: ***(ad lib)*** **Hunh?/what?/what are you talking about?**

Laura: You all know what that is, right? It's a trap, the humane kind, you know, the kind that doesn't actually kill the animal you're trying to get rid of, but just traps it, and then you have to take the trap a long, long way from your house, a long, long way, where you open the little door and set your squirrel or your groundhog free, never again to find its way back "home. "

SONG

"Have-a-Heart"

(Spoken) See, I guess I'm soft-hearted, 'cause what I'm really looking for is a giant-sized have-a-heart trap.

All (chorus):

Have-a-heart
Have-a-heart
She's looking for
A have-a-heart

(Spoken) Only what would I use for bait? Money? Beer? A younger woman? No--in my case it would have to be something by Gucci ... a new handbag ... sexy shoes ... leather...

(chorus)

Have-a-heart
Have-a-heart
She's looking for
A have-a-heart.

(Spoken) So I'd put out the baited trap, leave it there for him to find ... and ... SLAM! The door shuts, and then? And then? WHAM! Into the car, down the road, across the bridge, out of town, over the river and through the woods, a quiet country spot, release!

(Chorus)

Have-a-heart
have-a-heart
She's looking for
A have-a-heart.

(Spoken) He'd wander off, wearing his Gucci, and I'd hop back in my car and race away, not forgetting my have-a-heart trap. He'd be gone, out of my life! I'd be lighter, brighter, prettier, sweeter, a better person altogether. And since he would never stop to ask for directions ...

(Solo)

If I only had a have-a-heart
I'm still looking for a have-a-heart
All I need is a have-a-heart
It's what I need for a fresh new start.

(Chorus)

Have-a-heart
Have-a-heart
She's still looking
For a have-a-heart!

(Lights down on kitchen)

Scene Two

Lights up on Brad (actor could be doubled as one of the husbands from Act I, cross-dressed), on telephone.

Brad: Right. Right. I know, but ... Right ... I see. No. How long would I have to take the hormones? Forever?!? Even after the surgery? ... Uh huh. And the procedure itself ... how long does it take to recover? ...Very funny. And the total costs? ... I see ...Yeah. Well, I'll have to get back to you. That's a lot of money, and with the divorce ...Yes, that's right. Okay, then. Thank you very much. *(hangs up)*

SONG

"More Like Her"

***Women always say we should be more like them
Spend more time at the bookstore and less at the gym.
We should share our feelings and understand theirs
We should pay more attention to household affairs.***

***(Chorus) So I became more like her
How, then, can she complain?
I became a sensitive fellow
Not a macho bone remains.***

***I never could repair the engine of a car
But I could give the driveway a new coat of tar.
I thought that would please her; but I couldn't win.
She wanted less of yang, and much, much more of yin.***

***(Chorus) Yes, I became more like her
Why, then, is she upset?
I wear a dress, I've tried makeup.
How much more like her can I get?***

***I was head of my household for nearly ten years
Cut the grass, earned the bacon and drank lots of beer.
But I had to connect with my femjnine side
So I did to the point that my other side died.***

***(Chorus) And I became more like her
I completely changed my life
But in the end she wasn't happy
Said she didn't want a wife.***

(lights down on Brad. Lights up on kitchen)

Patricia: But, Laura, doesn't it make you crazy that he lied to you all those years? He didn't just become someone else overnight!

Annie: Yeah. That's what I was maddest about with Billy. As far as I knew, things were going great. But he must have known for a long time before he hit me with it.

Laura: I don't know. I guess I just have to look at the humor in the situation. Imagine all of your ex-husbands in heels ...

(Lights up on chorus line--the exes in .fishnet stockings and heels, all but Brad fidgeting and adjusting their stockings)

And I really think Brad *wanted* things to work out between us. Anyway, how easy can it be for him? He can't even figure out which restroom to go in any more!

Rachel: You'll forgive me if I don't shed any tears over Brad's problems.

(Lights down on kitchen; chorus does brief kick line to instrumental of "Have-a- heart." Men remove heels, rub feet. Lights down on kick line.)

Diane: Look: I don't feel sorry for any of them. Every one of us got married under the illusion that it would last forever. And I know that every single one of us worked our tails off to make our marriages work.

All: *(ad lib)* That's for sure/ right/ yeah.

Diane: And even if they wanted things to work out, they put more effort into improving their golf scores than into their marriages.

Bette: Charlie's handicap is down to 6.

Rachel: Phil's just emotionally handicapped.

Bette: They all are. Everyone knows we're more ... perceptive than they are.

Diane: I'm going to give you a prize for understatement of the year!

Annie: It's the whole "being from different planets" thing. Or different universes. Like, Billy thought he was being nice to me, taking me to a fancy restaurant to break the bad news. Like it matters where you are when your husband tells you he doesn't love you any more!

Bette: Still ... I could have sworn that Charlie loved me, that we

both thought we'd be married to each other forever.

Annie: So what went wrong?

Bette: Honey, I could write a book about what went wrong. He probably thought that I was a little anal about certain things. But jeez, I never would have left him for bringing the wrong kind of milk home.

Laura: I think some kind of weird chemical transformation happens to men when they get married.

Rachel: It's not chemical, it's orthographical. Just a couple of letters get changed: from m-a-n to m-o-r-o-n.

Patricia: Without warning me, too. And then it's too late!

Diane: You know what? Our mistake was not getting rid of our exes before they were our exes.

Patricia: That's right. Do you know how much sympathy widows get?

Annie: Divorcees don't get sympathy. We get shafted.

Karen: So what you're saying is that I should kill Mike before I divorce him.

Rachel: Too late. You'd be the prime suspect now. You have the motive.

Bette: Besides, you'd have to find him first.

Karen: I am going to find him, but I need help. Laura, can you lend me money for a private detective?

Laura: Sure, hon, if that's what you want.

Karen: *(determined)* It is.

Annie: I might know someone who can help you out.

Karen: Who?

Annie: My cousin, Mark. He's really good, and as a favor to me, he'll probably give you a break on his rate.

Diane: Good for you, Karen.

Karen: Do you have his number?

Annie: Just a second *(looking in purse, pulling out business card)* Yep. Here you go.

Karen: *(cross to phone, dial)* Hello? Ace Detective Agency? May I speak to Mark Alcott, please? *(lights down)*

Scene 3

(5 days later. Phone rings; lights up on Karen's kitchen. She enters, in bathrobe)

Karen: Yes ... What? You found him? That was fast. Where is he? ... He's where? You've got to be kidding! .... I can't believe it. Are you sure he's not dead? ... No, of course I believe you; I'm just stunned ... Uh huh ... You did? He said what? All right. Yes, I'll meet him. Where? ... Why? .. Oh, never mind. ... Uh huh. ... At six o'clock. All right, I'll be there. Thanks. *(Hangs up phone,. shakes head ... Perhaps picks up photo of Mike and looks at it. ... Then picks up phone and dials)* Hi, Bette, it's Karen ..."Guess who's coming to dinner ..."

(Lights down)

Scene Four

(Several hours later. Lights up on an empty park bench. After a brief interval, MIKE approaches. Well-dressed, but a little hesitant, as if he thinks the bench might jump up and bite him. Checks out bench, then sits. Waits. Enter KAREN, looking gorgeous. Maybe wearing white linen. Stands next to bench).

Mike: *(stands)* Hi, Karen. You look great.

Karen: *(nodding)* Mike.

Mike: You want to sit down?

Karen: No.

Mike: Mind if I do?

Karen: No.

Mike: *(sitting)* So ... How have you been?

Karen: *(evenly)* You bastard. Like you care. Disappear for three weeks and then ask how I've been?

Mike: *(standing)* I'm sorry, Karen.

Karen: Oh, sit down! And don't come any closer.

Mike: *(sitting)* I just thought ...

Karen: I don't care what you thought.

Mike: Come on, Karen. Give me a break here.

Karen: *(frighteningly calm)* You think I should give you a break.

Mike: *(backpedaling)* Well, yeah, I mean no, umm ...

Karen: You think you need a break.

Mike: No! Look, I just want us to be civil.

Karen: Let me get this straight. You walk out on me, taking our life savings with you, I have to hire a private investigator to track you down, and you want us to be civil.

Mike: Karen, please don't make a scene.

Karen: *(still eerily calm)* You don't want me to make a scene.

Mike: You're scaring me here.

Karen: *(pulling out a gun, still calm)* Am I?

Mike: *(standing)* Karen! Is that thing loaded?

Karen: Sit down, Mike.

Mike: *(sitting)* Karen?

Karen: That's better. Now, where's our money?

Mike: *(stammering)* Our mo ... Money. Right, that. Well, I did close out our mutual funds, but I really needed the cash.

Karen: You needed the cash.

Mike: Yeah, see, I had to have a stake, to get a place to live, and ...

Karen: A place to live.

Mike: *(standing)* But I'll ...

Karen: Sit down.

Mike: *(sitting)* But I'll split it with you if you want. I thought we'd ...

Karen: I've told you, I don't care what you thought.

Mike: *(standing)* Karen.

Karen: Sit down.

Mike: *(sitting)* What do you want from me?

Karen: Ah. Now you ask. What I want, Mike, is for us to go back to the way things were, for our marriage to work, for us to live happily ever after.

Mike: But that's impossible.

Karen: Did you not ask what I wanted?

Mike: Is it about the money? Because you can have the ...

Karen: Did I say it was about the money?

Mike: *(standing)* Damn it, Karen ...

Karen: Sit down.

Mike: ***(sitting, and finally silent)***

Karen: ***(examining the gun, looking at Mike, fiddling with her wedding ring, perhaps removing it, but remaining quiet. Perhaps she wanders a bit. Mike watches her apprehensively, but makes no effort to leave. Finally Karen speaks, but more to herself than to Mike)*** **What do I want? I want not to be standing here with a gun in my hand, actually thinking about using it. I want the last three weeks not to have happened. I want you to be the decent man I married instead of the asshole you've turned into. I want not to feel this awful. I want not to have to spend all day every day thinking about what went wrong, about what you did, about how I'm going to survive this. I want not to cry myself to sleep every night. I want my perfect world again.**

SONG

"My Perfect World"

In my perfect world
I wouldn't have to tell you,
You would know.
In my perfect world
I wouldn't ask you not to leave,
You wouldn't go.
I wouldn't wait beside the phone
I wouldn't lie awake and moan
And I would not be left alone
In my perfect world.

In my perfect world
I'd wake up with you beside me in my bed.
In my perfect world
I could trust that you would do
The things you said.
I would hear the birds again
I wouldn't be afraid of men
I'd live now as I lived then
In my perfect world.

In my perfect world
I could look at other couples and not cry.
In my perfect world
I would not have had to learn to say goodbye.
I would not be standing here
I would not be shedding tears
As I looked back on the years
In my perfect world,
In my perfect world.

Mike:

In my perfect world
I would not have caused the pain that you feel.
In my perfect world I would be the man you married, not a heel.
But I did the best I could
And you would have understood
In my perfect world,
In my perfect world.

Duet:

In our perfect world
We wouldn't have to share the blame for this mess.
In our perfect world
We'd have known to fan the flame of wedded bliss.

Karen:

But you do not love me now
You forgot your wedding vow.

Mike:

No, I do not love you now
And I broke my wedding vow

Karen:

In my perfect world
In my perfect world.

(KAREN and MIKE have approached each other during the duet, but at song's end they have turned away from each other.)

Mike: Karen?

Karen: *(turns to him)*

Mike: Look, here's my number *(writing it on a business card)*. We can get together and figure out the finances. We have equity in the house ...

Karen: Mike, I really didn't want to shoot you.

Mike: God, I hope not.

Karen: But I did think about it. And about poisoning you, or pushing you off a tall building, or locking you in a room with a pack of rottweilers ...

Mike: Oh, is that all ?

Karen: No, I also thought about how nice it would be if you got permanently lost in the Sahara Desert, or had a parachute fail, or ...

Mike: Okay, okay. I get it, Karen. I can't help the way I feel, but surely we can work out a reasonable arrangement.

Karen: Mike, "reasonable" just isn't in my vocabulary now, at least not where you're concerned.

Mike: I suppose I deserve that.

Karen: ***(starting to get upset again)*** **That and more ... There aren't enough hours in the day for me to ...**

Bette: ***(who has entered during Karen's last speech)*** **Karen? Mike! What a pleasant surprise! Mike, how are you? I haven't seen you for ages!**

Mike: ***(rather flustered)*** **Er, no, well ...**

Bette: Karen, remember you promised me we could go see that Rodin exhibit today. Do you still have time? I really don't want to miss it. Mike, you'll excuse Karen, won't you?

Mike: Yeah, sure, I guess.

Bette: I mean, I don't want to interrupt ... But we still have 90 minutes if we leave now.

Mike: No, that's all right. I should be going, too. Karen, you know where to find me.

Karen: Right. I'd completely forgotten about our date, Bette. Thanks for reminding me.

Bette: No problem. All right then, we're off. Bye, Mike! Let's do lunch sometime.

Mike: ***(startled by the last)*** **Yeah, sure ... Right. Bye, Bette. Karen.** ***(exits)***

Karen: ***(watches him leave)*** **Pretty good timing.**

Bette: Well, I didn't want to show up too soon. And you seemed to be handling things pretty well. Though if you'd actually pointed that gun at him, I might have spoken sooner.

Karen: It's not loaded. ***(points gun in the air, fires. It makes a loud bang. Looks at Bette).*** **Er. ..**

Bette: It's not loaded?!

Karen: *(still holding gun, very gingerly)* This was my father's gun. My mom's had it since he died fifteen years ago. She swore it had never been loaded!

Bette: *(stares, speechless, points at gun)*

Karen: Oh my God. *(sits))* Oh, Karen. You could have killed him.

(Lights down)

Scene 5

(An hour later, in Karen's kitchen. Lights up on KAREN, surrounded by her friends).

Karen: I thought I was gonna die when that gun went off.

Bette: I thought MIKE was gonna die when you pulled that thing out!

Karen: I don't know what made me do it. I guess I just didn't feel like I could face him alone, unprotected.

Laura: But the gun was loaded?

Karen: Umm, yeah. That wasn't part of the plan.

Bette: But did you notice how quickly you got his attention?

Rachel: You should have shot him while you had the chance!

Diane: I can't believe this!

Karen: Why are you so shocked? Isn't this what you all wanted?

Bette: Karen, YOU were shocked.

Karen: Well, yeah, sure, that the gun went off. But you've all been talking about how many ways you could kill off your ex-husbands.

Patricia: But actually taking a gun and doing it? You haven't seen any of us do THAT yet.

Rachel: Yet ...

Annie: Nobody's going to shoot anybody. Not even you, Rachel, or me. And Diane, you'd have to take out two ... And I know you're not a serial killer.

Diane: Who said?

Annie: I did. And I'm right, and you know it.

Diane: Maybe. I don't know. Oh, I guess. Besides, I don't really have the motivation some of you do. My first husband was just an idiot, and you don't kill people for that.

Karen: Thank God.

Diane: And my second husband ... I know I left him, but I used to love him, you know? I really did.

Bette: Of course you did. I loved my husband too. A lot ...

Rachel: Too bad.

SONG

"Let Me Count the Ways"

Bette:

Let me count the ways I used to love him.
I could fill a book
With used to bes.
I recall the days
Of love and longing
Now everywhere I look
Are memories.

Diane:

I recall the times
Of endless promise,
Of holding hands and saying
I love you.
But cardboard hearts and rhymes
Don't make real music.
The promise ended when
He said "I do."

Duet:
Let me count the ways
I used to love him.
Etc.

Bette:

He didn't have to say The word "forever."
He didn't have to promise
To be true.
Love and Peter Pan
Don't go together.
A lifetime's so much harder
Than "I do."

Duet:

Let me count the ways
I used to love him.
Etc.

Diane: *(giving Bette a hug)* Oh, honey.

Karen: All I can say is, it's a good thing I don't depend on you guys to cheer me up. You're a very depressing bunch. Maybe I need some new friends!

Laura: Sure. Friends who will understand you better, and tell funnier jokes.

Karen: No, your jokes are fine. And who could understand me better than you can? I didn't mean it.

Patricia: We know. *(Looking around)* Well, have we run dry? Doesn't someone have a joke?

Annie: Sorry, fresh out. Laura? Come on, you always have a joke.

Laura: Let me think ... Okay, how many divorcees does it take to change a light bulb?

All: *(ad lib)* Not another light bulb joke!/Oh no!/I don't know, how many?

Laura: *(counting)* 1,2,3 ... 7.

Bette: Seven!

Laura: Yep! One to change the bulb, and six to form a support group!

All: *(laughing, as lights go down)*

Scene 6

(Eight months later. Lights up on MIKE, sitting at bar. There is a BARTENDER, perhaps one of the ex-husbands. MIKE fidgets with drink, gets up, sits down. stands and paces, sits again, fidgets with a drink. Finally KAREN enters, looking great, fashionable, beautiful.)

Mike: *(standing)* Thanks for meeting me.

Karen: Sure.

Mike: I mean, I know you're busy, so I really appreciate it.

Karen: No, it's fine. I just got off work.

Mike: Oh, good ... Umm, can I buy you a drink?

Karen: Okay. *(to bartender)* I'd like a vodka tonic, please. *(to Mike)* So, how have you been? *(They sit.)*

Mike: Good. I've been good. Things are ... good.

Karen: Good.

Mike: Yeah. Real good.

Karen: Good.

Mike: How about you?

Karen: Oh, things are great! I love my new job. I've already been promoted!

Mike: Really! Well, congratulations. *(Unsure how to continue)* That's really great. I'm very happy for you.

Karen: Thanks ... Umm, so why did you ask me to meet you?

Mike: *(Clearing throat, hemming and hawing)* Well, actually, I, uh, I was wondering if, maybe, you might, um, consider letting me move back in, if maybe we could try again.

Karen: What! *(Looking at him for a long minute)* You're serious, aren't you? Good Lord, Mike, you left over eight months ago !

Mike: Look, I know I've made mistakes. But I've changed, really.

Karen: Have you? Well, so have I.

Mike: You sure look great. *(Realizing maybe this wasn't the right*

thing to say) **I mean, you always did. You just, umm, well, I mean, you look great.**

Karen: Yeah, thanks.

Mike: So, anyway, what do you think? About us getting back together, I mean.

Karen: I don't think so, Mike.

Mike: Well, take some time to think about it. Don't be hasty.

Karen: Mike, don't do this.

Mike: But ...Why not? I've changed, really, and ... Karen, we were married for a long time! Don't throw our fourteen years out the window!

Karen: You really don't need to tell me how long we were together. Perhaps I should just remind you that you're the one who left me.

Mike: I know, I'm sorry. I don't know what I could have been thinking.

Karen: Look, the point is, we're not getting back together. I've changed too, and I'm much happier.

Mike: Oh.

Karen: Mike, I was crushed when you left. But that was months ago now. I've moved on. And obviously our marriage wasn't working in the first place, or you wouldn't have left.

Mike: I was a fool.

Karen: Maybe. ***(Her cell phone rings ... she pulls it out)*** **Hello?** ***(To Mike)*** **Excuse me.** ***(To phone)*** **What? He did what? The bastard! Okay, I'll be right over. Bye!**

Mike: What is it?

Karen: Oh, more of the same. Ted and Michelle have split up. I need to get over there.

Mike: Let someone else go !

Karen: No, Mike. ***(Getting up)*** **Look, I appreciate the thought. I know it took a lot of courage to ask me.**

Mike: Please, Karen ...

Karen: No. You just keep looking for that new horizon you left me for. It's out there somewhere. Bye, Mike!

(KAREN exits. Mike is left at the bar, stirring his drink and staring after KAREN's shadow.)

Bartender: Can I get you a refill?

Mike: Yeah, sure. *(pause)* Hey, do you know how many ex-wives it takes to change a light bulb?

Bartender: No. How many?

Mike: Just one, but man, she really screws it over.

(Lights out; curtain)

INSIDE OUT

A PLAY IN TWO ACTS

By Peter S. Lee

CHARACTERS:

Guy Polatsky

Voice 1 (A voice inside his head)

Voice 2 (Another voice inside his head)

Jesus

Ivy (Guy's Angel)

Young Boy

Devil

Roll Caller

ACT I

Early morning.
A porch on a cabin in Maine, looking out on a lake.
Present: A man named Guy Polatsky, sitting alone on stage, with writing materials on his lap. Offstage: The voice of Jesus.

Offstage: Voice 1, the voice of Guy.

VOICE 1: What kind of freak have you made me? Are you happy with your handiwork? Maybe you were drinking. Maybe you will strike me down for being so ungrateful. Maybe a frank discussion is not an option.

JESUS: What is it that you are so mad about? What is it that you want?

VOICE 1: To find a way to make it happen.

JESUS: What's "it"? Writing?

VOICE 1: Yeah, writing. Because it seems to be the only way out. Haven't I thought hard enough about this?

JESUS: You've thought hard. But maybe you need to think some more.

VOICE 1: This is like therapy, right? You lead your patient on to his own discoveries.

JESUS: Yeah, something like that. Smart ass.

VOICE 1: Is it playwriting?

JESUS: Could be.

VOICE I: I know nothing about it.

JESUS: You know plenty. What's the setting?

VOICE 1: A porch somewhere, in a cabin, in Maine. Looking out at the lake, early morning. The water is still and the clouds are tinted with early morning reds and oranges, yellows.

JESUS: Right. Who's present?

VOICE 1: Me. But I'm not alone.

JESUS: Am I invisible? Just a voice?

VOICE 1: It depends. How long would it take for the audience to catch on?

JESUS: You could tell them a lot with the playbill.

VOICE 1: Yeah. I think they'd catch on, quick enough.

JESUS: What's the story?

VOICE 1: A middle-aged man, lawyer/writer, discovers he's a playwright during his early morning session.

JESUS: Is that it?

VOICE 1: No. It's about his struggle with his Maker. But if you go all Jesus, people will squirm.

JESUS: Right. You have to tone that down.

VOICE 1: But maybe it's just a play popping out, like a poem does, now and then. He wants to latch on to something that will help things make sense.

JESUS: It may be.

VOICE 1: There we go again.

JESUS: Look, just relax.

VOICE 1: Man. A playwright. The first think I think about is the guy whose father tried for ten years and then gave up.

JESUS: Maybe he didn't try hard enough. There are a lot of guys who want to be playwrights.

VOICE 1: Yeah. But they're not crazy enough. They don't have the voices inside their heads.

JESUS: It helps to be schizophrenic. Not everyone can handle that well.

VOICE 1: Makes me wonder whether you shouldn't be more than a voice, so people could read your face, see if you were kidding.

JESUS: Yeah. Maybe they could see me, but you couldn't.

VOICE 1: What about staging, lighting, movement on stage?

JESUS: Forget about that. It's not an action flick. People come for the dialogue. *(Little one comes in, says: " Hi Daddy. " Falls asleep on Guy's lap.)*

VOICE 1: Little one comes in, falls asleep on lap.

JESUS: Excellent.

VOICE 1: No dialogue there.

JESUS: I heard him talking.

VOICE 1: Right. O.K. Add that in when he comes in.

JESUS: Whatever.

VOICE 1: Can the guy be talking? If he's talking, then it's not an internal monologue.

JESUS: Right. It's like he's talking to himself.

VOICE 1: So, there's a voice for him, while he's writing.

JESUS: Yeah.

VOICE 1: Impossible to act. The guy's just sitting there, with a pad on his lap, pretending to write? It would look like the guys who pretend to play the guitar while they're singing. Foolish.

JESUS: Not necessarily. The audience would forget. They love to get sucked in.

VOICE 1: Maybe we could break it up with a cup of coffee?

JESUS: Fine.

VOICE 1: So, we have a guy pretending to write, with a kid asleep on his lap, and a Jesus figure that may or may not be visible to the audience, and an offstage voice for the guy.

JESUS: Jesus figure? Maybe I'm in a robe or something. You want the crown of thorns?

VOICE 1: Sorry. So, how do you get that undulating water effect of the lake?

JESUS: You take a long term video in the early morning and project it

onto the screen.

VOICE 1: Would have to be a movie theater, with a stage. *(pauses.)* So, how would you be dressed? What do you wear when you make visitations?

JESUS: I'm pretty hip. I have to be. Think John Lennon.

VOICE 1: Maybe you have a Starbuck's coffee.

Enter Jesus, dressed in jeans, black t-shirt with I luv NY and round wire-framed sunglasses. Entrance of Jesus unrecognized by Guy. However, Jesus directs his comments to the sitting Guy. Guy's responses still coming from offstage Voice 1.

JESUS: I don't have long, you know.

VOICE 1: Right. *(starts to worry.)* I'll have to wrap it up. Bring it home. A one-acter.

JESUS: Look, before I go there are a few things you should know.

VOICE 1: Okay.

JESUS: Trust in the process. Just like you've been doing.

VOICE 1: Right.

JESUS: You're doing fine.

VOICE 1: Okay.

JESUS: Relax a little. Enjoy it.

VOICE 1: I will.

JESUS: Have fun with it.

VOICE 1: Right.

JESUS: That's about it. Good luck.

VOICE 1: Thanks.

JESUS: I'll see you around.

VOICE 1: O.K.

JESUS: Peace. *(Walks offstage.)*

VOICE 1: Yeah. Peace.

PAUSE-Lights fade out and then in.

Still on porch.

Guy's Voice 1 still offstage. Voice 2 also offstage.

VOICE 1: So what do I do with it?

VOICE 2: The play?

VOICE 1: Yeah. And who are you going to be?

VOICE 2: Another voice inside your head.

VOICE 1: Great.

VOICE 2: It's funny.

VOICE 1: So; maybe you're a stage presence; too?

VOICE 2: I think I should be. *(enters, dressed in jeans, black t-shirt.)* For the audience to register facial expressions.

VOICE 1: And the guy, still writing, right?

VOICE 2: Yeah, the guitar player. He's writing his little ass off.

VOICE 1: And the kid. Still sleeping?

VOICE 2: Yeah. He's had a chance to relax, during the break.

VOICE 1: If it makes a long run, it would be the most boring part known to man.

VOICE 2: Yeah. But you can vary it with all the thousands of stage mom kids. *(Kid squirms. Guy pauses, thinks for a while.)*

VOICE 1: So, what do you do?

VOICE 2: You type it. You read it. You see if it plays. You produce it. It can't be that hard.

VOICE 1: Right. *(Another long pause.)*

VOICE 1: The pauses won't play.

VOICE 2: ***(gets up.)*** **Right. You've got to keep it moving. I think I should have a Starbuck's coffee.**

VOICE 1: ***(lifts his head; raises eyebrows.) (Motorboat goes by.)***

VOICE 1: What about the motorboats?

VOICE 2: I think that if you had one zip through it would be an aural sensation. I think it would be hilarious.

VOICE 1: Like a bee in a cartoon.

VOICE 2: Right.

VOICE 1: You couldn't overdo it, though. ***(Another boat.)***

VOICE 2: Right. Maybe twice.

VOICE 1: So, what's the point?

VOICE 2: The point? Of the story?

VOICE 1: Yeah.

VOICE 2: Does there have to be a point?

VOICE 1: I don't know. Maybe not.

VOICE 2: Maybe the point is that a hard-working guy makes a little headway.

VOICE 1: Can that be a play?

VOICE 2: Who knows. Why not?

VOICE 1: ***(Long pause.)*** **Maybe a playwright's knots come unglued and he starts writing plays.**

VOICE 2: Yeah. Come unfurled like a spinnaker.

VOICE 1: I think it might be time to run.

VOICE 2: Yeah, I think this one's over.

VOICE 1: What are we going to do? ***(pauses, thinking.)*** **A playwright** ***(reflectively.)***

VOICE 2: **Why not?**

VOICE 1: **Why'd it take so long?**

VOICE 2: **To figure it out?**

VOICE 1: **Yeah.**

VOICE 2: ***(shrugs .)***

VOICE 1: ***(laughs.)***

VOICE 2: **What?**

VOICE 1: **That's funny. A voice inside the head, shrugging his shoulders.**

VOICE 2: **This could play.**

VOICE 1: **What do we know? We don't know anything.**

(Pause.)

VOICE 2: **Maybe Jesus comes back.**

VOICE 1: **Let me do the writing.**

VOICE 2: **Right. *(pauses.)* So, do you think it was him?**

VOICE 1: **Who? Jesus?**

VOICE 2: **Yeah.**

VOICE 1: **Remember. We've got to tone that down.**

VOICE 2: **Right.**

VOICE 1: **Still, why not?**

VOICE 2: **Seemed like him.**

VOICE 1: **What'd you think?**

VOICE 2: **Pretty cool.**

VOICE 1: **Yeah.**

VOICE 2: **Sitting right there.**

VOICE 1: **He said to relax.**

VOICE 2: Have fun with it.

(A loon call out on the lake.)

VOICE 1: Right.

VOICE 2: Remember. It's entertainment.

VOICE 1: Right. Cute.

(Loon passes by out front.)

VOICE 2: The baby loon?

VOICE 1: Yeah.

VOICE 2: It's like the parents were calling you: "Come see our baby."

VOICE 1: Yeah.

VOICE 2: You know, it's probably the same pair that's been coming here for years.

VOICE 1: Yep.

VOICE 2: He can't be more than a couple of weeks old.

VOICE 1: If that. *(Guy gets up, gets binoculars, then camera.)* Have fun with it.

(Voice 1 still offstage. Guy sits.)

VOICE 2: It's got to be a newborn.

VOICE 1: That's why they're so proud.

VOICE 2: They came right over here to show him off.

VOICE 1: Amazing.

VOICE 2: It was the first thing they did when they woke up.

VOICE 1: What does it mean?

VOICE 2: What does it mean (*as if to say, "What do you mean, what does it mean?*)

VOICE 1: Yeah.

VOICE 2: Why does it have to mean anything? Why does everything always have to mean something? Maybe it doesn't mean anything. Maybe they like you.

VOICE 1: I know.

VOICE 2: You can't just enjoy it.

VOICE 1: Right. I'm going to. I'm going to let go.

VOICE 2: Don't come apart now. Don't freak out.

VOICE 1: Very funny. *(GUY gets up to check on his family, then comes back.)* Everybody's sleeping.

VOICE 2: (shrugs.)

VOICE 1: So, you think it could play?

VOICE 2: Why not?

VOICE 1: I don't know. Maybe. Maybe it's the big pretend.

VOICE 2: Maybe it's funny. Maybe it's heartfelt. Maybe it's engaging. About a guy, who tries his hardest in this fucked up world to do the right thing by his family and by himself. And, that every now and then in the chaos, he has a moment of peace where someone or something wishes him well, thinks well enough of him to visit him with their baby loon. Did you ever think of that? Did you, you moron?

VOICE 1: When you put it like that, no.

VOICE 2: Yeah. It could play. Maybe Jesus needs to come back and sit on your head, or take you by the hand, like Peter Pan, like the ghost from Christmas whatever, and fly you around a little.

VOICE 1: Yeah, yeah, yeah.

VOICE 2: Maybe you should keep coming out here, while your family is gone, and finish this play.

VOICE 1: How are we going to do the loons?

VOICE 2: The stills. From the photographs.

VOICE 1: Enlarge them. And project them on the screen.

VOICE 2: The women would Ooh, and the men would laugh.

(Guy buries his head in his hands.)

VOICE 2: Hey. It's okay. It's okay. Jesus.

VOICE 1: (laughs sadly, then collects himself)

Enter Ivy, wearing wings

***VOICE 1: Introducing*: Voice, this is Ivy, Ivy, Voice,**

(Ivy and Voice greet each other.)

VOICE 1. Do you think it will play, 1vy?

IVY: I don't know. It's worth a shot. Your stories are so leaden. They're like lead weights. It's a little lighter, that's for sure.

VOICE 1. Yeah.

IVY: You know, you think it should be easy. Everybody would write plays if it was easy.

VOICE 1: You know, I don't want to get into another fight.

VOICE 2: *(acknowledging that he's not really welcome, starts to back away)* - Maybe I'll let you two talk.

IVY: I don't want to fight, either. But just 'cause I don't want to fight doesn't mean that there aren't some things I have to say.

VOICE 1: Like what?

IVY: Like, give it a try. Go with it. Like Jesus said, "Have fun with it." God knows, you've tried hard enough.

PAUSE-Lights fade out, then in.

A day later, in his study, at home. Voice 1 still offstage. Onstage: Guy sitting, Voice 2.

VOICE 1. So, where do we go from here?

VOICE 2: You cannot direct the unconscious.

VOICE 1: Yes, yes you can. I think you can gently guide it.

VOICE 2: It brings to mind, then, why you don't guide it to finishing Edwin Drood.

VOICE 1: Right.

VOICE 2: So, you're the smart one. What do you say about that?

VOICE 1: I say it's complicated. On the one hand I want to direct all my energy into isolating the language for Drood. Yet, this dialogue pours out and I get the visitation thing. Ivy's right about the short stories; you wonder if you have made an advance past something, or whether it was preparation. You

wonder whether there are parallel fronts. You know, Dickens loved the theater.

VOICE 2: Oh yeah?

VOICE 1: Oh, yeah. He was passionate. Very theatrical. There's all this talk about how theatrical his dialogue is and it's true; he had the sense of it. I think he wrote one play, which was a flop. He acted, too.

VOICE 2: Really?

VOICE 1: Yeah. The guy was nuts about the theater. His descriptive genius would not play out in the theater, though. He had both gifts, and he fused them well. You wonder what would have happened if he hadn't died.

VOICE 2: Right.

VOICE 1: So, I guess the answer is: You write. You get it done. You pour it out. My Drood ending is so heavy, like my stories. It's leaden. People don't want to hang a weight around their neck when they read something. It's too much work.

VOICE 2: Right.

VOICE 1: I'm open to it, though. But, it's more from a feeling that I'm not a quitter. I'm not a jumper. I don't want it to be that I didn't finish because it was too hard, like Causabon.

VOICE 2: Who?

VOICE 1: The guy in Middlemarch who's writing this absurdly long opus that will never get done in a million years.

VOICE 2: Oh.

VOICE 1: You think about it, Causabon is damn funny. It's obvious to me now that he is a parody. I'm sure she meant it that way. He's a type. But he was so realistically portrayed, that you respond to him like he is a complete loser. You hate him. You feel for Dorothy all the way. Masterful.

VOICE 2: Hmmm.

VOICE 1: Right. The point is: Don't get stuck. There's a difference between quitting and getting stuck. With quitting there's nothing next; with not getting stuck, there's something after. You're moving onto something.

VOICE 2: Right.

VOICE 1: Like I said, it's complicated. You know, it's funny, but it makes me think of Edith Wharton again. Isn't it true, that she had a love affair once, and was happy and that her fiction went all blah. It melted.

VOICE 2: (shrugs.)

VOICE 1: Yeah. I think it was her. But Dickens fooled around all the time, and his fiction didn't suffer. I wonder what would happen ...

VOICE 2: Yes?

VOICE 1: Never mind.

VOICE 2: So, is this a "My Dinner With Andre" kind of thing?

VOICE 1: Yeah, so far. But I liked that. Did you?

VOICE 2: Yeah. It was okay.

VOICE 1: I was riveted. Except for the hoodoo voodoo part. I thought it faded a little.

VOICE 2: ***(looks at Guy puzzled, raises his eyebrows.)***

VOICE 1: I think you have to grab them by the balls right from the first word and not let go until the end. It's not meditation.

VOICE 2: Playwriting?

VOICE 1: Yeah, and I mean that in the attention-getting way for all you future biographers with limited imaginations. I'm not a closet anything.

VOICE 2: Maybe an action sequence?

VOICE 1: Right. Excellent. What do we do?

VOICE 2: The action should flow from the dialogue.

VOICE 1: Right. It can't be too obvious of a change.

VOICE 2: Right. ***(Both thinking.)***

VOICE 1: Is the guy still at the camp?

VOICE 2: No, he's home now.

VOICE 1: Still writing?

VOICE 2: Yeah, in his study.

VOICE 1: They should play catch.

(PAUSE-Both think)

VOICE 2: Yeah. Catch. I'll get the gloves and ball.

(exits stage to get gloves and ball. returns. Voice 1 still offstage.)

VOICE 2: ***(holding gloves and ball.)*** **You 're thinking.**

VOICE 1: Yeah.

VOICE 2: Of what?

VOICE 1: Of what to put in and what to leave out.

VOICE 2: Your doctor's visit?

VOICE 1: Yeah.

VOICE 2: Don't worry.

VOICE 1: I've got to go.

VOICE 2: Right.

(Guy gets up to leave. Ivy enters, passes Guy, picks up a glove and starts playing catch with Voice 2).

Lights fade out.

PAUSE (Guy and Voice 2 are in Guy's study again.)

VOICE 2: So, what about Causabon?

VOICE 1: What about him?

VOICE 2: Did he quit or was he stuck?

VOICE 1: You know, that's a really good question. ***(pauses.)*** **I think he got stuck. Yeah, Causabon got stuck. Maybe he should have moved on to something else. What was it that he was writing anyhow?** ***(gets up to reach for Middlemarch on a shelf)***

VOICE 2: Do you think you're stuck?

VOICE 1: I think I was stuck, in more ways than one. But that I'm not now. ***(pauses.)*** **You know, it occurs to me that if you're just talking to me and I'm writing on my pad, it's not very interesting to watch.**

VOICE 2: Right. Your ***(pause)*****, whatever it is, should be out here, too.**

Enter Voice 1.

VOICE 1: (His voice, from now on, is through Voice 1, onstage.) **It's like the good conscience/bad conscience thing.**

VOICE 2: Right. ***(pauses.)*** **So, how does it feel?**

VOICE 1: To be unstuck?

VOICE 2: Yeah.

VOICE 1: Feels good. I like it. It's a brave new world. *(pauses.)* Okay. *(Guy looks at the book)* She says that Causabon was understood for many years to be engaged in a great work concerning religious history; also, as a man of wealth enough to give luster to his piety, and having views of his own which were to be more clearly ascertained on the publication of his book.

VOICE 2: (affecting interest.) Huh.

VOICE 1: Yeah. I was stuck all right. Still, I worry.

VOICE 2: About what?

VOICE 1: Maybe I'm a jumper. That paralyzes me.

VOICE 2: Why?

VOICE 1: Because if you can't finish something, why aren't you just a pretender? I don't want to be a pretender .

VOICE 2: (nodding.) But it's not like you've given up on "Drood."

VOICE 1: Right.

VOICE 2: You've got to go with it, which you have one, consistently.

VOICE 1: Right.

VOICE 2: In the absence of some better information, like a merger of the right brain and the left brain, it seems like you're on the right track.

VOICE 1: Yeah.

VOICE 2: Keep running.

VOICE 1: Right. *(Pauses.)* You think about Shakespeare, all those historical plays. You know he had read Plutarch's Lives, or whatever it was. Still, how do you get the voices of Claudius, King Henry, Hamlet - get them so down? That couldn't be left brain.

VOICE 2: You wouldn't think so.

VOICE 1: He was a regular guy, too.

VOICE 2: *(nods.)*

VOICE 1: And Edmund and the other Tyrones. That was just O'Neill's family, right?

VOICE 2: ***(Shrugs.)***

VOICE 1: Yeah. It was. It's autobiographical. Think of it. It was his second to last play.

VOICE 2: ***(Nods.)***
(Lights fade.)

Next day. Study again. As the lights come up, Guy's voice -Voice 1 -enters stage. Voice 2 is already on stage.

VOICE 1: **(as if coming into consciousness.)** ***Maybe that's what it takes.***

VOICE 2: What?

VOICE 1: ***(through Voice 1, onstage.)*** **Being a writer.**

VOICE 2: Right. But maybe what is what it takes?

VOICE 1: Putting it all behind, and I mean <u>all</u>.

VOICE 2: All what?

VOICE 1: All earthly desire. The whole nine yards.

VOICE 2: I guess I don't understand you. You may be losing your audience, too.

VOICE 1: Right. I need to tie them in.

VOICE 2: The men get impatient. They didn't want to come in the first place.

VOICE 1: It's like golf. ***(pauses, looks over to Voice 2 with hands open, as if to say: "How's this?")***

VOICE 2: ***(nods.)*** **Good, but how so? Plus, now you're going to lose the women.**

VOICE 1: (nodding animatedly.) It's like golf because in golf, there's a moment of faith, a moment of truth, when you have to let go and give up control. That's the beauty of it and also the challenge. In order to hit a good golf shot, there is a moment of faith when you have to relinquish control.

VOICE 2: ***(nods.)***

VOICE 1: The things we attach ourselves to, to get by, the things we cling to, the secret wishes we hold most dear, we have to let go of.

VOICE 2: Wow.

VOICE 1: Is that heavy?

VOICE 2: No really.

VOICE 1: It takes practice. It takes time.

VOICE 2: You think you've gotten there?

VOICE 1: I don't know. I am famous for self-delusion. There might be someone this play appeals to. Still, the way I learn things, I have to come to it myself. Telling me doesn't work. I honestly wonder if it does for anyone.

VOICE 2: Like what, for instance?

VOICE 1: Like character development, for one. A teacher could tell me to develop my characters. But until I arrive at the same conclusion, such advice is meaningless.

VOICE 2: Is that something you need to do?

VOICE 1: Develop my characters?

VOICE 2: Yeah.

VOICE 1: Yes. And it's one thing to say develop them. It's another thing to do it. You don't just pull out a bag of tricks. That would be patently false.

VOICE 2: So, how do you do it?

VOICE 1: You let them breathe more. You let them out into the open. Let them look around. I think of what's her name, on the hillside.

VOICE 2: Maria?

VOICE 1: Yeah. Julie Andrews, singing her heart out, while the plane zips by. Was it Maria?

VOICE 2: I think so.

VOICE 1: So what is she all of a sudden, Italian? An Italian nun in Austria. I don't know. Is Maria a good Austrian name?

VOICE 2: ***(Shrugs.)***

VOICE 1: I see a panel of lights, like a light meter, that registers sound, like on a stereo and the louder it gets, the more lights come on. Maybe with a play, with writing, the more clever you are, the more lights, the more you're connecting with your audience. And, I don't know, maybe my panel is registering halfway up, doesn't quite get there.

VOICE 2: *(Slightly annoyed.)* You know, maybe you're over the fucking top, and you just don't see it.

VOICE 1: I hope so, Guy. Don't tell me you have to believe. I think that's a bunch of horse shit.

VOICE 2: I'm not telling you anything.

VOICE 1: It may come down to shit luck, like my old man says.

VOICE 2: *(Shrugs.)* So, you let them breathe on the mountaintop. What else.

VOICE 1: (Laughing.) You work 'em. You look around the bend. You see what's out there This "Voice" guy, for instance.

VOICE 2: You mean me?

VOICE 1: Yeah. Who is he? He's steady Eddy, right? Always there, loyal, but not very interesting.

VOICE 2: Thanks a lot.

VOICE 1: I don't know, maybe there's something there I haven't seen.

VOICE 2: Maybe there is.

VOICE 1: So, what do I have to do? Go mining?

VOICE 2: You know, Pal. That just must might be exactly what you have to do. Stop writing at the surface of things.

VOICE 1: *(Thinking it over.)* Okay. I'll try it.

VOICE 2: If I said you were halfway through, what would you think?

VOICE 1: I'd say there was a long way to go. And the audience, they'd either breathe a sigh of relief or get up at the next break to go.

LIGHTS FADE

END OF ACT I

ACT II

Early morning. In Guy's study. Present: Jesus, Guy (sitting in his chair), Voice 1.

JESUS: Not that again.

VOICE 1: That's right.

JESUS: Life's not good enough for you, you have to be a writer.

VOICE 1: So that's what this boils down to?

JESUS: You're treading on thin ice, babe.

VOICE 1: Now we're getting somewhere.

JESUS: Look *(pauses.)*

VOICE 1: Look what? Why don't you say it, for once.

JESUS: All right, big shot. I've saved both your kids, once each already, and I've saved you from cancer. Don't you get it, Pal? You're not even supposed to be here.

VOICE I: *(pauses, silent.)* I know you were there both times for my kids. I know you've been there for me.

JESUS: Okay. So you know. Now what? I've got to make you a writer?

VOICE 1: You know, you don't have to make me anything. It's not ungrateful of me to try and do something with my life besides being a real estate lawyer. You know what? I am more than that, with all due respect to my brethren at the bar, whose unfailing courtesy, intelligence and honor I acknowledge and respect. I am smarter than that; more clever. I have thought harder, deeper and longer. And you know it.

JESUS: You know, we consider you a problem case.

VOICE 1: You guys play tough, that's for sure.

JESUS: Do you think that anyone cares about you're little dramatic monologue or dialogue or whatever you want to call it? (gestures to audience.) Do you want a show of hands?

VOICE 1: *(thinking gets up, walks over to Jesus.)* Yeah. Let's have a show of hands. Let's do it right now. We'll settle it, once and for all, you and me. If it sucks, I quit.

JESUS: You know, this breaks all the rules.

Enter Ivy and Voice 2 to watch, both sit unobtrusively in the corner.

VOICE 1: Fine. Let's break 'em. Let's get it done with. Let's get it over with. How many of me do you have, who try so hard? You can't have that many. Are there enough of us so you can squander some of them? You get someone here who's willing to push it a little. Why are you going to squelch that? What does that show to my kids? Is this about you? Is that what this is all about? With all due respect, maybe it was you who wanted to write. Someone prevented you. (looks up.)

JESUS: No, it's not like that.

VOICE 1: You know, Jesus, I got something going here. I really do. You must see that. What is the problem with letting me write? Just what is the fascination with lawyers? Wait a minute, you didn't want to be a lawyer did you, like my old man?

JESUS: (laughs.)

VOICE 1: That's it. You wanted to be a lawyer!

JESUS: (heaves with laughter.)

VOICE 1: This will send shock waves through the New Testament scholars.

JESUS: *(holds up a hand; still laughing, turns semi-serious.)* Cool it, Pal. You're playing with fire. What are you trying to prove, anyway?

VOICE 1: Is that what you 're telling me, that you planned for me to become a lawyer.

JESUS: What we're telling you is that something went wrong when you were little. You know, there's a word for people like you.

VOICE 1: What is it?

JESUS: Never mind.

VOICE 1: It doesn't matter. If that's what you really want me to be, that's fine.

JESUS: What do you want, Guy?

VOICE 1: You think it'd be easy to say, after all this time. But you're thinking, it gets occluded. *(pauses.)* But I think I can safely say that I would like a chance to write.

JESUS: *(notices Ivy and Voice 2 looking at him)* What are you looking at?

(They quickly look away.)

VOICE 1: You know the word you were looking for - it's donkey.

JESUS: Could've been.

VOICE 1: I just figured a long time ago, that if I kept trying, that something had to change. I still believe that. Change for the better.

JESUS: I've got to go.

VOICE 1: All I ask is, that if I've got to go, you'll take care of my family.

JESUS: I will. ***(exits stage.)***

PAUSE.

Next day. Same place. Jesus and Guy.

VOICE 1: You knew that allowing me to be a writer would not change things.

JESUS: That's right.

VOICE 1: It wouldn't have made me feel better .

JESUS: We have no problem with you being a writer. That's not the issue.

VOICE 1: The issue is how do you deal with the things that you can't change.

JESUS: Right.

VOICE 1: The paralyzing self-consciousness around strangers.

JESUS: For one.

VOICE 1: It can only improve so far.

JESUS: And then what? Even poor people and sick people can sometimes be filled with joy. ***(pauses.)*** **The truth is hard.**

VOICE 1: Yeah.

JESUS: You're the hardest case I know. Good luck, Guy.

VOICE 1: Thanks. I'm going to try. I'm going to give it a try.

JESUS: It's a rough road ahead.

VOICE 1: I think I'll rest. *(puts his head against the back of the chair, closes his eyes.)*

Voice 1 and Voice 2 are now onstage.

VOICE 1: In the morning when I write is when I feel the best.

VOICE 2: You know, Guy, you talk about being stuck. This play is in the mud.

They look at each other, then say, in unison:

VOICES 1 & 2: Action sequence. *(Voice 2 gets ball gloves again.)*

Enter Ivy.

IVY: Can I play?

Voice 1 gets a bat, hands a catcher's mask to Voice 2.

VOICE 1: Here, wear this in case of foul tips. I got a split lip once playing this. Voice 1 stands across the stage, far enough for a pitch.

VOICE 1: We'll play balls and strikes.

IVY: How do you play?

VOICE 1: You just try and hit it. You have the fun part. Voice 2 will call the pitches.

Voice 1 pitches. Ivy swings.

VOICE 2: STRIKE!

Voice 1 throws a few more pitches. Ivy keeps swinging and missing. Voice 2 calling out each time: "STRIKE!"

VOICE 1: Boom, Boom. Goes down on three pitches. Now, it's Ivy Rodriguez at the plate.

IVY: Am I still up?

VOICE 1: Yeah. You can bat.

VOICE 2: I'm not so worried about ma as the audience.

VOICE 1: *(laughing.)* Right. She won't hit anything.

IVY: Hey!

VOICE I: Throws the change-up. Oh, Ivy, that was your pitch, right there.

VOICE 2: So what if you are a writer, Guy. What then?

VOICE 1: Good question. I've been thinking about that. (throws another one.)

VOICE 2: BALL!

IVY: Damn.

VOICE 1: I think there's something in the saying "There's nothing stopping you but yourself." And do you have the chutzpah, the huevos to do it? I run away from it?

VOICE 2: Why?

VOICE 1: Maybe I'm lazy. Maybe I'm scared. Maybe it's guilt, or shame, or habit. It takes balls to break with convention. You can't announce it. That will jinx it. It's a surreptitious moment. It is like enemy territory. I'm in there now. Dying to jump back, to run to safety. "On a quiet Wednesday morning in the middle of July, conditions were appropriate and Guy Polatsy stepped over the line."

VOICE 2: What's it like?

VOICE 1: Quiet. Calm. Don't worry, it will be all right. No one will notice, no one will care. I'll put a message on the machine. I wonder-do I have the balls to be a writer?

Guy gets up in a panic and leaves the room. Lights fade.

Lights come on again. Guy enters stage.

VOICE 1: Back again.

VOICE 2: Crisis?

VOICE 1: Yeah, but it will be okay. I thought I was a goner.

VOICE 2: There's no stopping you now.

VOICE 1: Only myself. My fears. Lack of talent. I think if I continued to get up early, but then got to write later after the kids went to school, say, then I'd take a shower. I'd treat it like a business day.

VOICE 2: Right.

VOICE 1: The time that you sit has to be without guilt or self-remonstrance. A whole host of conditions must obtain.

VOICE 2: Of course.

VOICE 1: I'm not going to put on a tie. But I will not dress like a slob. No

work shoes, either.

VOICE 2: Fine. *(pauses.) During this conversation, the mini-baseball game has continued.* Still, she might connect with one.

VOICE 1: Right.

Net drops between stage and audience.

VOICE 1: If it takes a lifetime, I will try and find an answer, Dear Jesus.

Jesus re-enters. The game pauses.

JESUS: Don't stop. I'll call the pitches. *(He calls them, interspersed with conversation. Ivy gets progressively more frustrated because she can't hit the ball, as sub-plot for comic relief. She is obviously not following the thread of the discussion.)* The answer to what Guy? There are lots of questions. The answer to life in general? It's easy. Family and service to others. The answer to writing? Directing the unconscious-at least for fiction. It's like directing a flashlight. You are not the light, but you control what it shines on.

VOICE 1: Sometimes, when I'm thinking about directing it, something else pops out.

JESUS: Right. When you shine a light in the darkness, you may illuminate something interesting. It's worth looking at, recording. STRIKE! *(Ivy taps the head of the bat on the ground)* Watch the ball, Ivy. If you strike a rich vein, mine it for all it's worth, it doesn't mean you give up on the rest of the gold mine.

VOICE 1: Right.

JESUS: If it's tapped out, then gently lead it on. STRIKE! *(Ivy gets a little more upset.)* It changes direction slowly.

VOICE 1: Like a tanker changing course.

JESUS: Then watch out for the swing back.

VOICE 1: Right.

JESUS: Happiness is fleeting. STRIKE!

IVY: Damn it!

JESUS: Ivy!

IVY: Sorry.

JESUS: Trust in me, Guy. I've got to go. *(playing stops. Jesus departing.*

Everyone looking at Guy. Jesus stops, looks around.) **But you've got something here, Guy. I think it plays. So long.**

Pause.

VOICE 2: So you've got a guy, sitting on a porch with his voice playing catch with an angel.

VOICE 1: Yeah. And Jesus calling balls and strikes.

VOICE 2: And giving the guy some advice.

VOICE 1: Right.

VOICE 2: *(sarcastically)* Sounds pretty interesting to me.

VOICE 1: I had a dream last night.

VOICE 2: Oh no. A dream sequence.

VOICE 1: No, really. I was living in the city, by myself, in a rented room. Two separate events happened: first, I went into a bar and had a drink. It was early morning and the bar was empty except for one guy and a hostess in a bikini top. The other thing that happened was that I was presented with some choices. I could take the subway to work, I could go fishing, or I could drive one of two VW Beetles that I had.

VOICE 2: Which did you choose?

VOICE 1: I chose to take the subway to work. It felt like a revelation.

VOICE 2: *(shakes his head.)* What does it mean, Guy?

VOICE 1: It's more like what it felt like. Presented with two types of choices, one constructive and one not, I felt like choosing the constructive one.

VOICE 2: I think you lost 'em, Guy.

VOICE 1: It was just a dream.

VOICE 2: I think you should shelve it.

VOICE 1: As an exercise.

VOICE 2: It's boring.

VOICE 1: It stinks. Forget it.

LIGHTS FADE.

Light is very dim in the study. Guy is alone. Ivy is onstage. Voice 1 is offstage.

VOICE 1: Ivy, are you there? I can hear you breathing.

IVY: It is I, Guy.

VOICE 1: Maybe it is that I am cracking.

IVY: You're fine. So what happens next?

VOICE 1: Maybe the guy dies right onstage. Goes out in a fit of convulsions. *(Guy grabs his neck).* Or maybe he falls asleep and dies, that would be more like it, in this play.

IVY: A comedy.

VOICE 1: Right. Jesus. What a piece of work I am.

JESUS: *(offstage)* You're okay.

VOICE 1: I hope that you can say I'm trying.

JESUS: Keep trying, Guy. Keep trying. You'll make it, somehow.

Lights fade,. Ivy exits stage.

Later, same day. When lights come on, Jesus and Voice 1 are onstage.

VOICE 1: You know, Jesus, the people want to know.

JESUS: Know what?

VOICE 1: There are a lot of burning questions.

JESUS: Like what?

VOICE 1: Who was the disciple that you "loved"?

JESUS: I think those are your questions, Guy.

VOICE 1: (laughs.) Yeah, I suppose they are.

JESUS: Does it really matter?

VOICE 1: I guess not.

JESUS: What else would you like to know?

VOICE 1: I guess I'd like to know how it felt on the cross.

JESUS: It hurt. When the world got dark, I knew there was something special going on.

VOICE 1: And the miracles?

JESUS: Which ones?

VOICE 1: The pigs.

JESUS: Yeah. Nasty little bastards.

VOICE 1: And the fish and the loaves?

JESUS: I've thought a lot about that. The shepherd and the flock stuff. I think that the world is mostly just a bunch of followers. They're all a bunch of followers. It's pathetic. The miracles were just the work of my father. I was just the instrument. Just like you are. He had a situation going on. He could see the whole thing with Caesar starting to slide. The Jews in Palestine were his only chance. He wanted to make the most of it. He sent me down to fire them up, to light a fire under their asses. To take Jerusalem. Pilate was a nobody. They were drunk all the time. But I was never any good at the big picture. I couldn't get past the suffering. When a beggar's been blind his entire life, it gets to ya. I think he saw that things were different on the ground. It started to get personal. We changed gears midstream. Don't worry, Guy, you're okay. You're fine. You're not the only one who believes. But we wanted to shake it up a little, get people moving. Get 'em off their asses.
What would happen if all the guys would turn off their stupid football games and all the women would stop painting their fucking toenails? And, instead, think about the Mideast crisis? This great country that gets things done. These men and women, so honest, sincere. What if 100 million men and women turned their attention to the Mideast problem? Food, phones, computers, infrastructure, politicians going, construction companies. Get the fucking job done. Move on to Africa. 100 million men and women. And you tell all the men there to wake up and smell the fucking roses. Do you want to kill the whole fucking continent? You're telling me they can't find Bin Laden? You get 100 thousand people to buy plane tickets to Kabul. You look for him like a missing child, which is all he is. I would get the airline industry going, that's for sure. You take 100 million people and go to Columbia. You stop burning all the rainforests. You're telling me you can't feed some of these people? France, German, England, Wales, you're telling me that these folks have nothing better to do than sit around and watch the tele? What we're getting at is the

people could do a whole lot better. Which is to say, they could do something. You could turn the whole place around. Make it fun. Even for the poor people and the sick people. The greedy bastards at the top of the pharmaceuticals wouldn't have to line their bloody pockets with gold. And the mordant cries of teenagers which bellow in our ears, maybe if they felt important, like they were doing something, making a contribution, maybe they wouldn't be so sad. I'm telling you, Guy, it's a mystery. The fishes and the loaves? They were hungry. What other questions? Am I such a mystery? To want people to forget about themselves for a moment. Have a drink. ***(Guy gets up and pours himself a drink.)***

VOICE 1: The efficacy of prayer?

JESUS: Very effective. Are you asking about yourself again, Guy?

Guy shrugs.

JESUS: What happens if you decide to keep going? Have you ever thought of that, Guy? Writing is like a foot soldier with a heavy pack on. That's what writing is. What happens if you decide to just keep going? You grind it out.

VOICE 1: I think of Norman Mailer.

JESUS: Right.

VOICE 1: You put the pack on. You start marching.

JESUS: It's where you end up, Guy, that people will remember.

VOICE 1: Right.

JESUS: It's like lobstering. You see a lobsterman on a crystal summer day, you think Now that's the life. You don't see him on the cold, rainy, foggy days. Do you want to crank out the words when you don't really feel like it? What will that do to your enthusiasm? Do you believe in writing? Or is it just a challenge? Will you hate it if you have to do it?

VOICE 1: It's the million dollar question, Jesus. I don't see the answer clearly. It has to do with faith.

JESUS: What does your faith tell you?

VOICE 1: It tells me, that even for a soldier who walks for weeks in the pouring rain, and even for the lobsterman, there come along certain moments, like the crystal summer day, when you say: I am at peace here. And even though they are few and far between, they are the standards by which we measure these decisions. There is no greater moment for me than when I make a connection in a plot, or a narrative twist occurs to me and I say to myself, "I could not have thought of that myself, but I sure am glad to be the one that found it." This is such a moment. The idea is that the measure, between competing ideas, is how we relate to the high point, to the moments of joy, no matter now far apart they are from each other. Based on that standard it is a slam-dunk for writing; no contest. Because it brings it all together, it is a flash

point, it's chemical and something new has been done which might have an effect on someone besides yourself, bring them through, and you are left with something lasting. That is my answer. It's the high points that we measure by, not the low ones. Then you do more, you try harder. You put it on, you keep marching forward, you hope for the best, you bring it on home.

JESUS: Yeah, like this play. Time to reel it in.

VOICE 1: *(pauses, thinking.)* Thanks for your time.

JESUS: No problem. I look forward to the show.

VOICE 1: Okay, then *(Voice 1 and Jesus shake hands.)*

JESUS: I've got work to do, just like you, Guy. We're all working for the same guy, just in different ways.

VOICE 1: Yeah.

JESUS: So long, for now.

Guy holds up his hand. Jesus exits stage. Lights fade.

Lights come back up, Jesus and the Devil are onstage, alone.

JESUS: What are you going to do to him? Are you going to kill him? Are you going to kill his kids? His wife? You think they're not going to meet up again, in Heaven? Face it, you lost him, he's mine.

DEVIL: We can always convert him.

JESUS: Yes, I suppose there is that possibility. Why don't you go ahead and try. Go ahead.

DEVIL: Maybe I will.

JESUS: You're a sore loser.

DEVIL: We haven't lost yet.

JESUS: Oh, yes you have. You've lost him.

DEVIL: For now, perhaps.

JESUS: Why don't you admit it. What's your fucking problem, anyhow.

DEVIL: Yeah.

JESUS: Because he was so sensitive, his brain got fried. He can't be a lawyer anymore. He's going to have to find a new way to make a living.

DEVIL: Funny how things happen.

JESUS: Not like you'd expect them at all.

DEVIL: And yet there's a similitude, a resemblance.

JESUS: Describe it for the audience.

DEVIL: Okay. Everyone has fatigue. Everyone has burnout. That's the resemblance.

JESUS: The first to be shocked will be his father.

DEVIL: Right. That might be a problem.

JESUS: Somebody's got to tell him.

DEVIL: He's got to know.

JESUS: He's blind to it.

DEVIL: Yeah. The thing that he grabbed is white hot.

JESUS: It would melt most people. You tried to break him, but you lost.

DEVIL: I haven't lost yet.

JESUS: Yeah, that's right. You just keep on trying.

DEVIL: I will.

JESUS: Good, 'cause it's not as if your energies couldn't be better spent elsewhere. Why did invest so much time in him? Did you really think you could flip him?

DEVIL: We thought he had potential.

LIGHTS F ADE.

When lights come back up, Guy and Voice 1 have joined Jesus onstage.

VOICE 1: Jesus, wait.

JESUS: Yes?

VOICE 1: What about the second coming?

JESUS: What about it?

VOICE 1: Well, we need help.

JESUS: You need to help yourselves. There is so much more you could do. You need to more organized. You could move mountains.

VOICE 1: We need a leader.

JESUS: No you don't. You need courage.

LIGHTS FADE.

Lights come back up, Ivy and Voice 2 have joined the others onstage.

VOICE 1: Hey, he's writing something.

VOICE 2: Yeah. Wow. Read it.

VOICE 1: It says: "The wind blew like an argument between the old oak trees and bent their limbs in silent gestures of earnest deprecation."

VOICE 2: Wow. Not bad.

VOICE 1: Yeah. Like a couple of old guys, pleading with each other. It must have been the muse that visited him, to give him the voice of King Henry.

VOICE 2: Shakespeare?

VOICE 1: Yeah.

Guy stands and reaches up for Shakespeare on the shelf.

VOICE 2: Oh, great. Here we go again.

VOICE 1: Oh, Jesus.

JESUS: What is it, Guy?

VOICE 1: What is it? It's the whole thing, that's all.

JESUS: What whole thing?

VOICE 1: The writing, you, the family, the business, the whole nine yards.

JESUS: *(nods)* So, what about it?

VOICE 1: It seems like too much sometimes.

JESUS: Yeah.

Offstage, voices. Someone reading roll call, and voices responding.

ROLL CALL READER: So, if you would please, as I call your name: Arnon (here), Aron (here), Abromsky (here), Aronson (here), Avermati (here), Boucher (here), Calthorpe (here), Carroway (here), Candide (here), Carter (here), Denton (here), Dalton (here), Dingham (here), Dettman (here), Cooper, that's a "C", Cooper, you here? (here), and Conway, another "C" (here),

Okay, Edwards (here), Elway (here), Feingold (here), Ferret (here), Gole (here), Gavin (here) ...

Voices fade into the background, still audible, as follows, below. At same time, Voice 1 talks.

VOICE 1: What's that?

JESUS: Roll Call.

VOICE 1: Yeah, but for what?

JESUS: The most recent crop?

VOICE 1: Holy shit.

JESUS: There's a spot for you, if you want it, Guy.

GUY: Ah, no thanks.

Continued roll call:

ROLL CALL READER: Galinsky (here), Garner (here), Hatwick (here), Hardwick (here),Hennessey (here), there's always a Hennessey, Horton (here), Halliday (here), Innis (here), Inman (here), Irving (here), Karruthers, with a "K" (here), Kaplan (here), Karamed (here), Kosinsky (here), Laban (here), Leventhal (here), Lassiter (here), Langdon (here), Langdorf (here), Lopez (here), Miller (here), Mackay (here), Malloy (here), Martin (here), Makowsky (here), Morriesette (here), Monroe (here), Nielsen (here)...

JESUS: Here come the "P's" Guy.

VOICE 1: No way, man.

ROLL CALL READER: Nevins (here), Nettles (here), Nissenbaum (here), Oleg (here), Orville (here), Polatsky..., Polatsky? Where the hell is he?

IVY: They're waiting on you, pal. What's it going to be?

Guy buries his head.

ROLL CALL READER: *(yells)* POLATSKY!

Guy's head pops up,. lights go off, silence.

After a brief pause, lights fade in. All characters, except Devil, onstage.

VOICE 1: Crap.

VOICE 2: Now what?

VOICE 1: I'm hungry.

VOICE 2: So eat.

VOICE 1: Yeah. Yeah, I think I will. I think I'm gonna. I'm gonna get some food.

VOICE 2: You do that, Guy. You go eat.

Guy and Voice 1 walk offstage. Voice 2 is shaking his head.

Guy comes back on, with a plain bagel and the complete Shakespeare. Voice 1 re-enters at same time. Guy sits down, opens volume. Voice 1 starts to recite.

VOICE 1: Dramatis Personae A collective sigh.

IVY: Just read it.

VOICE 1: Okay. I'll pick a passage (looks through.) Okay, here's one.

Reads King Henry's speech. As he reads, his voice gets softer and the lights fade.

VOICE I: "King Henry. Marry, if you would put me to verses, or to dance for your sake, Kate, why, you undid me. For the one I have neither words nor measure; and for the other, I have no strength in measure, yet a reasonable measure in strength. If I could win a lady at leapfrog, or by vaulting into my saddle with my armor on my back, under the correction of bragging be it spoken, I should quickly leap into a wife. Or if I might buffet for my love, or bound my horse for her favors, I could lay on like a butcher, and sit like a jackanapes, never off. But, before God, Kate, I cannot look greenly, nor gasp out my eloquence, nor I have no cunning in protestation: only downright oaths, which I never use till urged, nor never break for urging. If thou canst love a fellow of this temper, Kate, whose face is not worth sunburning, that never looks in his glass for love of anything he sees there, let thine eye be thy cook. I speak to thee plain soldier: if thou canst love me for this, take me; if not, to say to thee that I shall die, is true--but for thy love by the Lord, no; yet I love thee too. And while thou liv'st, dear Kate, take a fellow of plain and uncoined constancy, for he perforce must do thee right, because he hath not the gift to woo in other places; for these fellows of infinite tongue, that can rhyme themselves into ladies' favors, they do always reason themselves out again. What! A speaker is but a prater; a rhyme is but a ballad; a good leg will fall, a straight back will stoop, a black beard will turn white, a curled pate will grow bald, a fair face will wither, a full eye will wax hollow: but a good heart, Kate, is the sun and the moon, or rather, the sun, and not the moon, for it shines bright and never changes, but keeps his course truly. If thou would have such a one, take me; and take me, take a soldier, take a soldier, take a king. And what say'st thou then to my love? Speak, my fair-and fairly, I pray thee."

IVY: Wow.

VOICE 2: Lovely. A love declaration.

Lights Fade.

The End

TURNED TABLES

A One Act Play in Two Scenes
By Hugh Aaron

Cast of Characters

Bill - A salesman in his forties
Tall Skinny Man
Fat Squat Man
Bill's wife

Scene 1

(A plain room, gray walls, about 10 feet square, a single fluorescent light hanging from the ceiling, three folding chairs. Bill is seated alone as the scene opens, bending over, his face in his hands. After a few minutes a tall, skinny man and a squat, fat man enter through a door which they lock after them.)

TALL MAN: Are you finally ready to cooperate, my friend.

BILL: I don't know what you want.

TALL MAN: I want the right answers, just the right answers. Now, that's not asking too much, is it?

(The fat man doesn't speak, but his eyes and his body movements reveal what he is thinking. He is a mime. Bill constantly watches him to see whether he approves or disapproves of his answers.)

BILL: (rising) What do you mean the "right" answers? What in hell are the right answers?

TALL MAN: (firmly) Sit down, please. Of course you know the right answers. You've known them all your life, my friend.

BILL: Let's get one thing straight, I'm not your friend. And you're not my friend, that's for sure.

(The fat man appears hurt and turns sad.)

TALL MAN: Look into yourself, my friend. The answers are inside. Everyone knows the right answers if they look hard enough. (The fat man nods

vigorously.) I'm merely asking for your cooperation.

BILL: (muttering) Go to hell. You're nuts.

TALL MAN: I love nuts. (To the fat man) Don't you love nuts? (The fat man bursts into a wide grin and nods.) Now, now, my friend. Surely you must know that telling me to go to hell and calling me nuts would never qualify as the right answers.

BILL: This is unbelievable. Look, I'm just a computer salesman here in Buenos Aires on business. I hardly slept on the jet last night, and I'm beat. I'm supposed to be here only for the day then return home. So let's stop this nonsense. What do you say?

TALL MAN: (To the fat man.) Nonsense, he says. (The fat man shakes his head.)

BILL: You have the wrong man. I'm not political, I'm a threat to no one. When you approached me in the terminal then led me to your car, I assumed you were from the customer who was to meet me. This is simply a case of mistaken identity.

TALL MAN: Certainly not. We would never make such a mistake. (emphatically) Never! (The fat man shakes his head vigorously. Bill watches his every reaction.)

BILL: Then I'd like to know what I've done. I mean have I done something wrong? Are you the police? Have I unwittingly broken your law?

(The tall man and the fat man laugh, the fat man uncontrollably.)

TALL MAN: Broken our law? You arrived barely an hour ago and you've been under our protection the whole time. How could you possibly have broken the law?

BILL: That's right. I couldn't have. Then why are you holding me? Why this interrogation? I don't understand.

TALL MAN: (sympathetically) Bill, Bill don't you see? You keep asking questions. We are the ones who ask the questions, not you. You're here only to give answers - the right answers. (firmly) Your questions are most improper.

BILL: For Chrissakes, this is absolute madness.

TALL MAN: Madness? Well, well. (The fat man pretends to bang his head against a wall. Bill watches.)

BILL: Godamnit, I can tell you now you'll get nothing out of me. (screaming) Nothing, nothing!

TALL MAN: Come, come, my friend, calm yourself. Just give me the right answers and everything will be fine. Then you can go.

BILL: (leering) What if I don't? What'll happen then? Torture?

TALL MAN: Those are questions again, Bill. Most definitely not the right answers. Be advised that we're prepared to remain here indefinitely - perhaps forever. You must know that our patience has no end. (Gazes at the fat man whose eyes are teary with sorrow.)

BILL: Tell me what to say, and I'll say it.

TALL MAN: Tell you what to say? (He and the fat man burst into laughter again, the fat man uncontrollably.) If I told you to say that you despise your mother, would you say it?

BILL: That's absurd.

TALL MAN: Exactly. If I told you to say that you raped your daughter and wished your wife dead, would you say it?

BILL: Certainly not.

TALL MAN: Then you can see how ridiculous your request is. (The fat man giggles over the tall man's winning argument.)

BILL: Well, I can play your game, too. Actually I can say anything. It doesn't matter, does it?

TALL MAN: (He and the fat man smile at each other.) That was partly a question, my friend. But you're catching on.

BILL: I don't like what you're doing. That's my answer.

TALL MAN: And what is that? What do you think we're doing?

BILL: Well, victimizing people, controlling them, belittling them.

(The tall man and fat man stare in consternation at each other and leave the room.)

BILL: (to himself) Ah, now I've got them. I've struck a chord.

(After a few minutes the tall man and fat man return, and sit facing Bill, forming a closed triangle.)

TALL MAN: You must understand, my friend, that we're simply doing our job, nothing more.

BILL: I realize that. But I don't think you really believe in your job. You don't beat me or torture me the way professionals do. (The fat man screeches with laughter and rolls on the floor.)

TALL MAN: We have our principles. Our ethics.

BILL: I understand, and that's all you have. But you have no core belief, no belief in--in yourselves. You do what you're told to do like everyone else. You have souls of sawdust.

TALL MAN: Very clever. Yes, you're very clever. (The fat man stops laughing, gets up off the floor and sits on his chair, casting his eyes down.)

BILL: (confidently) I don't think there are any <u>right</u> answers. (The tall man joins the fat man staring at the floor.) Isn't that correct?

TALL MAN: That's a question.

BILL: Damn right it's a question. Now it's my turn. (Bill reaches for the tall man's chin and raises his head so their eyes meet. The tall man's eyes are filled with pain. Bill strikes the tall man's face with the flat of his hand. The fat man maintains his position.) Now it's my turn, you bastard, you with the sawdust soul. So now, you tell me. What are the right answers?

TALL MAN: (meekly) But you don't believe there are any. You just said so.

BILL: What has that got to do with it? What I believe has nothing to do with it. (stares at the fat man with contempt) You sonofabitch. (The fat man does not respond.) You're a coward, a weak, good-for-nothing coward. That's all you are. (Strikes the fat man on the side of the head with the flat of his hand, felling him to the floor, where he lies whimpering, his body slack. Turning to the tall man.) Okay let's have it, the right answer.

TALL MAN: Now you're just like one of us.

BILL: (frightened) What do you mean?

TALL MAN: Now you're one of us, but worse. You resort to profanity, and the worst of the worse, physical punishment.

<u>End of Scene 1</u>

Scene 2

(The stage darkens and when it lights up again the fat man and tall man have disappeared, and Bill is in his bed thrashing under the covers and screaming. His wife is lying at his side.)

BILL: No, no, no, no, no, no, no. (Writhing, he beats his pillow and whimpers.)

WIFE: (stroking Bill's hair) It's all right, Bill. It's all right.

BILL: (frantically) There's no right answer, is there? Is there?

WIFE: To what, Bill? What are you talking about?

BILL: (laughing with relief) For God's sake, I haven't the vaguest idea. (pauses, thinking) How long has it been since we've made love?

WIFE: How long...(startled) it's been months.

BILL: I'm sorry, very sorry. (The wife stares at Bill puzzled.) The question is do I have the courage to look into myself and find the key to my sawdust soul.

WIFE: You're sawdust soul? Who ever heard of such a thing? I love you, Bill, no matter what your soul is made of.

BILL: Do you know what the answer is?

WIFE: What answer?

BILL: The answer to the question.

WIFE: (holds Bill's hand) My dear, my darling. You must have had a bad dream.

BILL: The answer is I do have the courage, I do now.

WIFE: (humoring Bill) Good. Let's get up and I'll make you breakfast.

BILL: Breakfast? Forget breakfast. I'm hungry for you, for you, just you, let's make love.

WIFE: Oh, Bill! (They embrace.)

Curtain

THE LIEBESTOD

by Hugh Aaron

CAST OF CHARACTERS

S.H. Bronstein — a company chief executive
Loretta — his secretary
Cabbie — a taxi driver

(The Scene: Bronstein's office in the upper floor of a big city skyscraper. It is evening, and as the play progresses it becomes darker outside, visible through a large window behind Bronstein's desk. Lights from other skyscraper offices fill the window.)

BRONSTEIN: (In his late fifties. Leaning forward in his high back executive chair, he rearranges his pens, blotter, stacks of reports and paperweights on his already meticulous desk, a Queen Anne mahogany table. He presses an intercom button on his desk.) Will you come into my office, Loretta? (Loretta quickly appears with pad and pencil in hand. Bronstein glances at her casually.) Close the door, will you?

LORETTA: (In her mid-twenties. Perching on the edge of a chair beside the desk) I'm ready Mr. Bronstein.

BRONSTEIN: You've been here, let's see — how long has it been, Loretta?

LORETTA: Just over a month, Mr. Bronstein.

BRONSTEIN: Well, I think it's about time to start calling me Sam. (Loretta squirms in her seat.) Do you find that difficult?

LORETTA: The other girls —

BRONSTEIN: I know. They call me Mr. Bronstein. But you see, you don't have to.

LORETTA: But the executives call you S.H.

BRONSTEIN: That's their choice. Am I so frightening to you?

LORETTA: Well — (laughing nervously) yes, sometimes. I've seen you get angry.

BRONSTEIN: Only for effect, Loretta. It's how to get things done around

here. (frowning) When you get to know me, you'll find there's absolutely nothing to be afraid of. I'm quite harmless. You've been listening to the others, haven't you? (She nods.) Well, why don't you call me Mr. Bronstein in front of them. But when we're alone, it's Sam. OK? (She nods without conviction.) I'm very pleased with your work, y'know. You're the best I've ever had. Don't let it go to your head though.

LORETTA: (brightening) Thank-you Mr. Bron —, Sam.

BRONSTEIN: Now that wasn't so painful, was it? I'd like to get to know you better — on a professional level, of course. (He watches her face and finds it inscrutable.) After all, we spend more time with each other than we do with anyone else, don't we? (The phone buzzes. Loretta rises and heads for the office door.) Take it here.

LORETTA: (still standing, picking up the receiver) Consolidated Games. (After listening briefly, she covers the mouthpiece) It's for me.

BRONSTEIN: That's OK. Go ahead. I'll keep busy. (taking some documents from a pile, he pretends to be occupied but is listening.)

LORETTA: (into the phone) I can't talk now. I'm sorry. I can't help it. I'll see you tonight. Not now — please — we'll talk about it later. (raising her eyes to the ceiling) Yes, I should be there around six. (She hangs up, visibly agitated.)

BRONSTEIN: (loosening his tie) Why don't you sit down and take it easy? (motioning her to sit in the chair) What you need is a drink. (She stares into space, preoccupied. Bronstein snaps his fingers.) Hey, snap out of it. Are you OK?

LORETTA: (coming out of it) I'm fine, thank-you.

BRONSTEIN: It's none of my business, but as your employer I'm concerned. Who was that?

LORETTA: That — that was my husband.

BRONSTEIN: Your husband? But I thought you weren't married. Your application said —

LORETTA: I mean my former husband — really my husband who will soon be my former husband. Or whatever. (laughing)

BRONSTEIN: Now that's better. I take it you're getting a divorce.

LORETTA: Yes, I've filed. We're separated.

BRONSTEIN: I see. Separations, divorces, that sort of thing — they can be very painful.

LORETTA: Are you —

BRONSTEIN: No, no, (chuckling) but I broke up with a business partner once and they say that's like a divorce.

LORETTA: (her voice quavering) It's hard getting used to.

BRONSTEIN: I can imagine. (pausing) How long did you say it's been?

LORETTA: What? Oh, we've been married just two years.

BRONSTEIN: No, I mean how long have you been separated?

LORETTA: (wearily) Not very long. (lapsing into silence)

BRONSTEIN: (rising) Let's have that drink now.

LORETTA: I suppose I still love him but — (Her voice trails off.)

BRONSTEIN: Sure. It must hurt.

LORETTA: His abuse was too much. (Her eyes well with tears which she dabs with a handkerchief retrieved from her sleeve.)

BRONSTEIN: Life is very hard. (resisting the impulse to embrace her and stroke her hair) But you'll have no trouble finding someone else, a beautiful girl like you. (She smiles at him through her tears) If there's any way I can help —

LORETTA: I know you mean well, but I can handle this myself.

BRONSTEIN: Of course, of course. (Walking across the room to a hutch, he opens a cabinet door) Is there anyone else? I mean are you seeing —

LORETTA: I'm not ready, really. I'm still quite mixed up.

BRONSTEIN: I understand.

LORETTA: (Her eye catches a print of Degas's Prima Ballerina on the wall.) I've had it with men. For a while, anyway.

BRONSTEIN: (pouring wine from a decanter) This will make you feel better. (She looks at her watch. He smiles.) It's not five o'clock yet. The boss won't mind if you take a little wine. (handing her a full glass, then sitting on the edge of his desk, one leg dangling) But you've tried.

LORETTA: (puzzled) I'm sorry. Tried?

BRONSTEIN: You've tried others. You've gone out with some of the men in this office.

LORETTA: (blushing) Well, they asked me out. I thought it would help, but it only made things worse.

BRONSTEIN: (holding his glass high, toasting) To the right man.

LORETTA: (The phone rings. Without drinking, she places her glass on the edge of the desk and picks up the receiver.) Consolidated Games. Yes, Mr. Parker, he's here. I'll see if he's free.

BRONSTEIN: (Signalling that he would take the call, snatches the receiver from her hand and says gruffly) Bronstein. Yeah, now you listen to me, Parker. Either you get that production line going, or I'll get a new manager. Do you read me? (slamming the receiver into its cradle) Godamm ninny. (His back to Loretta, he stares out the window then turns to her.) I'm sorry. Sometimes you gotta be rough. (Lifting his glass, he swigs down the wine.) Now where were we? (Loretta, gazing at two other pictures on the walls, remains silent.) What were we talking about, eh?

LORETTA: It's getting rather late.

BRONSTEIN: Say, I just had a thought. How would you like — now, you don't have to if you don't want to — how would you like to join me for dinner tonight?

LORETTA: Oh, I'm sorry, Mr. Bron — I mean Sam — but I couldn't tonight. You know, my husband —

BRONSTEIN: Oh, yeah. I forgot. Some other time then.

LORETTA: I'm really not ready. It will take a while.

BRONSTEIN: Of course, of course. I do understand.

LORETTA: Thank-you. I appreciate your thoughfulness.

BRONSTEIN: But, as you admitted, you've gone out with other men.

LORETTA: Only once or twice.

BRONSTEIN: (demanding) So what's wrong with me?

LORETTA: (startled) Oh, it's not you. Believe me, it's not you. (casting about for words) May I ask you a question?

BRONSTEIN: (smiling) Of course, you can.

LORETTA: Did you select the prints for this office or —

BRONSTEIN: (breaking into a laugh) I sure did.

LORETTA: Really, they're quite beautiful. Sometimes I pass up lunch to visit the art museum down the street just to browse through its wonderful galleries. It's food enough for me. I dabble a little in acrylic, you know, but I'm not very good.

BRONSTEIN: Is that so? Then, maybe you noticed what my prints have in common.

LORETTA: (rising and studying each one closely) Music?

BRONSTEIN: Right you are. Music. There's Degas's Prima Ballerina, and there's Chagall's The Violinist, and over there's Manet's the Fifer.

LORETTA: I'm amazed, truly amazed, Mr. — Sam.

BRONSTEIN: (delighted) You are? But why?

LORETTA: You're a businessman dealing with practical, down to earth things every day. To appreciate art requires a certain sensitivity and —

BRONSTEIN: So you think being a businessman makes me insensitive, is that what you think?

LORETTA: Oh, I didn't mean that.

BRONSTEIN: I grant you, what you say may be true of other businessman, but as I said before, I'm quite harmless. So how about some more wine? (refilling his empty glass) Do you like music?

LORETTA: Oh, yes.

BRONSTEIN: Then you shall have some. (He rushes across the room to a stereo cabinet as she glances at her watch.) Isn't it terrific that we both love art, and music, too? (Handing her an album) Do you know this one?

LORETTA: (shaking her head) No, I'm afraid —

BRONSTEIN: No? I'm surprised.

LORETTA: Well, it's not my sort of music really. I — I, do you know The Beatles?

BRONSTEIN: Who?

LORETTA: Bruce Springsteen?

BRONSTEIN: I think I've heard of him.

LORETTA: Tina Turner?

BRONSTEIN: Well, no.

LORETTA: Dire Straits?

BRONSTEIN: (inserting the disc in the player) Listen to this. Listen to some real music. (The early strains of Wagner's Liebestod floods the room as she glances at her watch again. Bronstein glides to her, reaches for her hands, and passionately clasps her to him. As the music gathers momentum his mouth meets hers in a devouring kiss. He cups his hands on her buttocks. She struggles to wrench his hands away. The music reaches a crescendo as she tears herself from him.)

LORETTA: No, no. Please, no. (The music dies and the phone rings. She picks it up but is too frazzled to speak. He takes it away from her.)

BRONSTEIN: Yes? OK, I'm late tonight. So what? I have some problems. Of course, everything's all right. I'll be a while yet. Look, go ahead and eat alone. I'll grab a bite out before I get home. No, don't wait up for me. I don't know when I'll be done here. For Chrissakes you heard me.

LORETTA: (heading for the door) Good night, Mr. Bronstein.

BRONSTEIN: (covering the receiver with his hand) Wait a minute. Please wait. (lifting his hand from the receiver) It's nothing. Nothing's wrong. I'll be home when I get there. (hangs up)

LORETTA: (anxious) I'm late already. I have to meet my husband.

BRONSTEIN: Forgive me. I'm afraid my emotions got the better of me.

LORETTA: (opening the door) He'll be terribly angry.

BRONSTEIN: (shouting) So let him, godammit. You're getting a divorce. What do you care, or have you forgotten? Tell him to screw himself.

LORETTA: (pausing, as if seeing her marital situation clearly for the first time) I — I suppose you're right.

BRONSTEIN: Sure I'm right. Wake up! Tell me: why don't you like me?

LORETTA: (standing near the door) It isn't that I don't like you.

BRONSTEIN: (plaintively) Then what is it? Am I too old?

LORETTA: Oh, it's not that. It's just — I mean — aren't you a married man?

BRONSTEIN: (relieved) Is that all? Please sit down. I'd like to explain something. (She remains at the door while he sits on the edge of his desk.) I have my business, my passion and my family, see. I keep each separate, understand? One has nothing to do with the other. Am I a married man, you ask? That's a meaningless question.

LORETTA: I don't think it's a good idea to get involved with a married man, Mr. Bron — Sam.

BRONSTEIN: I'd be good to you. We'd have wonderful times together.

LORETTA: I — I'm sorry, Mr. Bronstein. I really need my space. I'm tired of being treated like some toy. I want someone who'll respect me. Do you know what I mean?

BRONSTEIN: You don't get it, Loretta. There are no strings attached. I'd treat you like a queen. You could have anything you wanted — a Jaguar

convertible, a fur coat, a fancy apartment. You'd have the best.

LORETTA: Thank-you, but I can't. I'm sorry, Mr. Bronstein.

BRONSTEIN: (angrily) For chrissake, I told you to call me Sam.

LORETTA: (moving into the doorway) Please excuse me. I'm terribly late.

BRONSTEIN: We can't go on this way, y'know Loretta. So don't come back unless — (His voice fades as tears well up in her eyes.) So you see it's your decision. I couldn't bear having you here every day without — (She begins sobbing as she rushes from the stage.)

LORETTA: (traffic noise offstage, shouting) Taxi! Taxi!

CABBIE: Where to, lady?

LORETTA: Take me to — to freedom.

CABBIE: Where's that, lady?

LORETTA: Anywhere but here.

BRONSTEIN: (He plays the Liebestod again, replenishes his wine glass, sits at his desk, buries his head in his arms, and begins to weep. After a few minutes he rises and goes to a wall cabinet, and opens its door which reveals a mirror. He speaks to his reflection) Bronstein, you've become an old, ugly bastard. You better wake up. Why would anyone young want you anymore? Maybe for your money, your power? What good's that? Hell, you may think you're a big shot, but you're not. Not where it counts. An old, ugly bastard, that's all you are. (He watches through the window as various office lights in the neighboring skyscrapers go out, then reaches for the phone and dials.) Parker? This is Bronstein. How's it going? You say you're back in production? You're a good man, Parker, a good man. I knew you'd straighten things out. We'll talk again in the morning, OK? (He walks to the stereo and plays the record again, stopping at the mirror.) Well, at least the business needs me. That's something. (He sits at his desk and laughs.)

Curtain

REGALIA

A One-Act Play

By

Rick Doyle

Notes on Setting

A small, northern New England town.
The anteroom of the Regimental Temple. White paint everywhere. Woodwork primitive but done with care and a great deal of skill. Closet space for hanging up winter coats, storage space for utensils.
Two doors lead out. One, the Outer Gate, leads to the exterior. The other, the Inner Gate, leads to the hall where meetings are held.
There is a wooden, straight-backed chair next to the Inner Gate. This is where the Watch might sit. Also a wooden bench, painted white.
Posted on the rear wall, an announcement, hand-lettered, black on white: information about the draping of the charter, oyster stew supper to follow at the firehouse across the road. Also prominent, the symbol of the Order: something reminiscent of the Masonic compass.
Regalia simple but unmistakable. It must include sashes and black crepe armbands, and it may also include derbies. At least one member has a drum. Others carry staffs or flags with simple designs.

Enter men in regalia, wearing black crepe armbands. They proceed through the Inner Door.
WATCH and SERGEANT MAJOR, carrying staffs, take up position by the door.

SERGEANT MAJOR
Worthy Watch, let none pass this Inner Gate but those who count themselves the Friends of Saul.

WATCH
None but Friends shall pass, Sergeant Major.

SGT. MJR.
Have you the challenge?

WATCH
Sergeant Major, I do.

Whispers in Sergeant Major's ear, steps back.

SGT. MJR.
Right. Password of the day?

WATCH
Worthy Sergeant, I do.

Whispers, steps back.

SGT. MJR.
Right, Faithful Servant. Let those not recognized by this word be barred from entry to the Regimental Temple of Saul, unless they can work their entrance using secret signs or be guided by a Brother in good standing.

WATCH
Right, Worthy Sergeant.

SGT. MJR.
Stand fast.

Sergeant Major goes in, Watch closing Inner Door behind him.
Silence.
Enter LATECOMER, wearing regalia.

Whispers password into ear of Watch, goes in.
Silence.
Enter SECOND and THIRD LATECOMERS, more or less together. Each whispers the password, then goes in.
Enter EDGAR DOLAN, wearing regalia of order, as well as armband.

EDGAR
Say, they haven't started, have they?

WATCH
Not yet, they haven't.

EDGAR
I'd better slip in before they do.

WATCH
Right, Worthy Brother.

EDGAR
High Commander gets touchy about latecomers.

WATCH
Right you are.

EDGAR
You'd think he'd cut the Old Man some slack -- not on your life! And the Old Man four times Past Commander, too! You'd think that might mean something, but it don't.

WATCH
Right, Worthy Brother. Password?

EDGAR
There's the gavel!

WATCH
Come again?

EDGAR
By Jesus, I think it was! I think I just heard the gavel.

Tries to slip in, but is prevented by body positioning of Watch.

WATCH
Right, Worthy Brother. Give us the word and I'll let you by.

Edgar whispers a word.
Watch checks to make sure he's heard right. Shakes his head.
Edgar shows surprise.

WATCH
Take your time, think about it!

Acting as if he's just remembered, Edgar whispers again.
Silence.

EDGAR
That's not it?

WATCH
Not it!

EDGAR
No?

WATCH
Afraid not!

EDGAR
I'll be damned! I could've sworn that was it. Are you sure?

Enter FOURTH LATECOMER, who whispers the word.
Edgar tries to eavesdrop. Latecomer goes in.

EDGAR
***(Not whispering now)* Labor?**

WATCH
Sorry!

EDGAR
Caul.

WATCH
Take your time! Think about it!

EDGAR

Inheritance?

WATCH

That was last year.

EDGAR

Kinship. Kingship!

WATCH

Two years ago

A gavel sounds from within.

EDGAR

Sweet South American Christ!

WATCH

Take your time! Think about it.

EDGAR

Seed.

WATCH

That's not it.

EDGAR

I know it! But it was the day they bombed Pearl Harbor.

WATCH

Is that so?

EDGAR

You want to know what it was on V-J Day? August, 1945? Flourishing.

WATCH

Isn't that interesting!

EDGAR

It's right on the tip of my tongue.

Gavel sounds.

EDGAR

If you hadn't asked me I could have told you!

WATCH

You'll think of it.

EDGAR

I've given every password back to the Great Depression, and you can't let me in that door?

WATCH

Not without the current password.

EDGAR

They're draping the charter for Frank Ginn tonight.

WATCH

That's right, they are.

EDGAR

Do you know who Frank Ginn was?

WATCH

He came to a few meetings.

EDGAR

Oh, he came to a few meetings, did he? Is that so?

WATCH

Like I said. Nice old gentleman.

EDGAR

Frank Ginn was a charter member of this Order. He did more than come to a few meetings, I'll tell you!

WATCH

I knew him to speak to. No more.

EDGAR

We chopped wood together, once upon a time. Chopped wood together, did Frank and me. Hemlock, a dollar a cord -- felled, limbed, bucked, barked, and stacked. We knew the meaning of work in those days. Knew how to lend a brother a helping hand, too, by God. Why, Frank boarded with me and my wife May! During the Great Depression, that was. Frank drove truck when

he could. If it hadn't been for that we would have starved.

Gavel sounds.

EDGAR

Later we worked together out at St. Regis -- Seaboard, it was, back then. First in the woodyard, unloading cars with a cantdog and a pickaroon. Then up in drum barking. Groundwood, up in the block-bins. Finally we ended up on the paper machines. Thirty years on those paper machines! Frank retired three months before I did. That's how it was with Frank Ginn and me.

Gavel.

EDGAR

We were like brothers. And now you're telling me I can't go in there?

WATCH

Of course you can go in! With the password.

EDGAR

Who are you?

WATCH

You know who I am.

EDGAR

Let me in!

WATCH

You're welcome to work your way in, same as anyone else.

EDGAR

I can't remember the damned password! How am I supposed to remember the Four Secret Knocks?

WATCH

Or you can get a member to verify you, as soon as there's a break in the meeting.

Gavel.

WATCH

According to the Bylaws --

EDGAR

Bylaws be damned! There won't be any break in the meeting! The only thing they're doing tonight is draping the charter for Frank! And they're hell bent for leather in there! Get him out of the way so we can go have some oyster stew! You think they give a tinker's damn what goes on out here at the Gate?

Inner Door opens, and the Sergeant Major leans out.
Greets Edgar silently.
Edgar acknowledges.

SGT.MJR.

How goeth the watch, Brother?

WATCH

All quiet on the Orient Gate, Sergeant Major.

EDGAR

See? They're starting!

SGT.MJR.

(Reporting to someone inside) **All quiet on the Gate, Worthy Commander.**

Response from within. Edgar tries to slip in, but the Watch prevents it.

SGT.MJR.

(To Watch) **Hold fast to your station, Worthy Watchman, and be ever steadfast in the fulfillment of your duties.**

WATCH

Right, Worthy Sergeant, steadfast to the final report.

EDGAR

(At the same time) **Right, Worthy Sergeant, steadfast to the final report.**

Sergeant Major goes back in. Watch starts to follow. Edgar grabs his arm.
Watch shuts door without going in.
Silence.

WATCH

There's any number of Brothers willing to vouch for you. Or I could ask the High Commander to come out.

EDGAR

No! Oh my God, no! Don't do that! He's running a meeting in there. Don't interrupt the Commander just because his old fool of a father can't remember the password. I cause him enough trouble, as is. Just the other day I drove my car into the river over to Bucksport. See this bruise? I'm lucky I didn't drown. Happened to be low tide. It was that damned hill by the Library. Could've sworn I was stepping on the brake. Wasn't Raymond pissed!

Watch goes through Inner Door

EDGAR

I knew he would be. I hated to have the sheriff call him to come get me, but who else was there?

Edgar notices the Watch has gone in. Makes as if to hammer the door with his fist, but stops himself. He turns and looks back toward the sign announcing his friend's memorial.
Behind his back, the Inner Door opens a crack. Sergeant Major peeks out. Sees Edgar, closes door again.
Edgar takes crepe off, puts it in a pocket.
Long silence.
Enter RAYMOND DOLAN from Inner Door.

RAYMOND

What's going on? Dad?

EDGAR

I told him not to send you out here.

RAYMOND

Well I'm not going to leave my own father out here in the anteroom.

EDGAR

As long as you know it wasn't my idea.

RAYMOND

I'm just surprised to see you.

EDGAR

Member in good standing!

RAYMOND
Oh, sure. But they're draping the charter for Frank!

EDGAR
(Putting the crepe back on)
What of it?

RAYMOND
You said you wouldn't have anything to do with it.

EDGAR
I'd like to know when I ever said such a thing!

RAYMOND
When I asked you if you wanted a ride out here tonight.

Pause.

RAYMOND
How did you get out here tonight?

EDGAR
The day I can't drive --

RAYMOND
I told you -- no more driving.

EDGAR
I guess I can still drive! I still got a license.

RAYMOND
That Nova's not even insured. What if you got into another accident?

EDGAR
Raleigh said I could use it.

RAYMOND
Oh, I'm sure he did!

EDGAR
Ask him Friday, you don't believe me.

RAYMOND
I don't doubt it a bit.

Door opens a little. Sergeant Major appears.
Raymond shrugs, grimaces.

EDGAR
If he's still coming, that is.

Sergeant Major disappears, Inner Door closing behind him.

RAYMOND
Well, you're here now, I might as well give you the word.

EDGAR
Oh, you haven't got to give me the word.

RAYMOND
Why wouldn't Raleigh be coming home on Friday?

EDGAR
No reason I know of.

RAYMOND
Not like he'd go to his mother's, is it? You bet he's coming home for the weekend! Why wouldn't he come home for the weekend?

EDGAR
Course he is. Don't mind me.

RAYMOND
Unless he told you something different.

EDGAR
He hasn't said anything to me.

RAYMOND
About what?

EDGAR
About nothing!

He sits.

EDGAR
He hasn't said nothing to me about nothing.

RAYMOND
You feeling all right?

EDGAR
I'm fine.

RAYMOND
Take your medicine?

EDGAR
Oh, yes.

RAYMOND
That's good.

EDGAR
I mark it down on the calendar, now, as soon as I give myself the shot.

RAYMOND
That's a good way to do it.

EDGAR
Helps me remember.

RAYMOND
Coming in?

EDGAR
Not according to that cross-eyed son of a bitch you've got on the door -- Who is he, anyway? What tribe is he supposed to belong to?

RAYMOND
He's just doing his job.

EDGAR
By God, Frank Ginn would have let me in!

Door opens. Sergeant Major sticks his head out.

SGT. MJR.
***(To Edgar)* How's Edgar? Haven't seen you up to the paper machines lately. How you been?**

EDGAR

Oh, I can't complain.

SGT. MJR.

Like the raccoon said.

EDGAR

When he fell in the Fourdrinier!

SGT. MJR.

***(To Raymond)* Your old man ever tell you that one? About the raccoon that fell into the paper machine?**

RAYMOND

Bet there wasn't much left of him.

SGT. MJR.

Shut us right down. Number Three, wasn't it, Edgar? I was just a fourth hand. You must have been back tender.

EDGAR

Number Three, that's right. Old Frank was machine tender.

SGT. MJR.

Why, that must be twenty years ago! Is that possible? How long have you been out?

EDGAR

Christ Bobby I got done five years ago.

SGT. MJR.

Where does the time go?

RAYMOND

***(To Sergeant Major)* Tell Zimri to do the Treasurer's Report.**

SGT. MJR.

Sure thing, Ray.

RAYMOND

We'll be right along.

Sergeant Major disappears. Door closes.

EDGAR

You haven't got to stay here on my account.

RAYMOND

Well I'm not going to leave you out here.

EDGAR

Forty years I been coming to this Temple.

RAYMOND

I know you have, and I imagine you'll be coming for another forty years after they drape the charter for this Watch. Now let's work you in.

EDGAR

I'd be surprised if I didn't swear his grandfather in.

RAYMOND

You haven't been to a meeting for a while.

EDGAR

(Indicating his own regalia)

What in the name of Hell is all this supposed to be about? What is he, blind? Who does he think he is?

RAYMOND

Here, here! You got to calm down, Father.

EDGAR

Well it just seems like the Watchman ought to recognize a Past Commander when he sees one. Not only a Past Commander, but a Past Commander four times over! And not only that, but the father of the presiding Commander!

RAYMOND

I won't be presiding if I don't get in there to preside over this meeting.

EDGAR

Haven't I held every office in this Regiment? Sergeant Major, Treasurer, Recorder, Keeper of the Charter, Chaplain -- only once, Chaplain -- you couldn't get me to take that one a second time.

RAYMOND

Too much religion in it.

EDGAR
Haven't I got a seat on the Board of Elders, right now?

RAYMOND
That's right! We better get you in there, so you can do your job.

EDGAR
Job? What job? You don't do a goddamned thing, that I can see, but take up space on a hard bench. Still, don't it seem like he ought to recognize an Elder?

RAYMOND
Oh, probably.

EDGAR
Some of these jokers ought to be blackballed.

RAYMOND
Can't blackball a member in good standing.

EDGAR
That's a shame. Some of these young fellows need to be weeded out, you ask me. They're no more interested in this Regiment than Raleigh is.

RAYMOND
Raleigh's got other interests.

EDGAR
They don't care how things are run around here. They don't know the ritual. They don't know the Lore. Why, they've got no more business in this Regiment than Willard Francis!

RAYMOND
Willard Francis? He was never in!

EDGAR
Give him the credit for knowing he didn't belong. The night he came for the Vote on Applications, he got right up and walked out the door. Didn't even wait to hear how the vote came out! "I am far superior to any man that would give me the black ball." Walked right out that door. Never came back. One thing you've got to say for old Willard, he knew where he didn't belong. He knew. But I'm telling you, some of these young snots! They don't know the ritual. They don't know the Lore.

RAYMOND
They know the password!

EDGAR
What's that?

RAYMOND
I say you're right, they don't know!

EDGAR
You should get them to put your name in again. You've only served two terms, haven't you? I served four!

RAYMOND
I'm moving to Florida.

RAYMOND
You're not moving to Florida.

RAYMOND
We close next week, I'm flying down.

EDGAR
Florida!

RAYMOND
I'm fifty, I'm divorced, I've got a chance to take early retirement. I'd be crazy not to go.

EDGAR
You can have the snakes.

RAYMOND
I'd be crazy not to go!

EDGAR
Heat, too. The snakes and the heat.

RAYMOND
You've never even been there!

EDGAR
Got no use for it. No, thanks.

RAYMOND
But you know, Dad, you ought to do like I said and come right along.

EDGAR
Sell the house? I built that house. Lived in it since your mother and I got married.

RAYMOND
You may not have any choice in the matter.

EDGAR
By God I will!

RAYMOND
You don't take care of your diabetes, you won't be staying there.

EDGAR
Who says?

RAYMOND
Well it's out in the middle of nowhere. What if something happened to you?

EDGAR
Mailman comes by every day.

RAYMOND
A lot that helped Bertie Gray. It's too much, anyway. You can't keep the house clean. You don't cook for yourself.

EDGAR
I baked an apple this morning.

RAYMOND
You can't live on baked apples. Especially with diabetes. You've got to eat right. You don't eat right. Never do your blood-sugar tests. Lie to the doctor.

EDGAR
I do not!

RAYMOND
Saw it myself, the last time I took you in there. Nurse asked about rashes, what'd you say? You said you hadn't had any in a year. Sitting right there with your shoes and socks off, rash on your feet just as plain as day. You

know what she wrote on your chart? "Denies symptoms referable." You don't take care of yourself, you lie about it, and everyone knows it. The only person you're kidding is yourself.

EDGAR

I won't go to some home where they tie you down in bed! You can't make me.

RAYMOND

No, I can't. Wouldn't want to.

EDGAR

I built that house.

RAYMOND

But there may come a time when you have no choice. And when that time comes, you'll have to move out. Nobody said anything about a nursing home.

EDGAR

They tie you down and leave you to rot in your own filth!

RAYMOND

Nobody said anything about a nursing home!

EDGAR

They drug you so you don't even know your own name!

RAYMOND

Will you listen to me! I don't want you to go to a nursing home! That's why I'm saying come to Florida with me. If you come south with me, you're less apt to have to go to one of them places.

EDGAR

Oh Christ yes, probably! But I can still drive!

RAYMOND

We all make mistakes.

EDGAR

The brakes let go!

RAYMOND
You're going to get yourself killed, one of these days. If you don't kill somebody else first.

EDGAR
They say that was Frankie's first mistake. Let them talk him into giving up his license, and from that time on he was done for.

Sergeant Major sticks his head out into the anteroom.

EDGAR
I'll tell you what -- nobody's going to take my driver's license away from me.

RAYMOND
(To Sergeant Major) **Have they done the Elders' Report already?**

EDGAR
How can they, I'm on the Board!

RAYMOND
(Gesturing for Edgar to be quiet)
We'll be right along.

Sergeant Major goes in, closing door.

RAYMOND
You haven't sat on a Board of Elders meeting for a year. Not since the first time you went to the hospital.

EDGAR
I know how long it's been.

RAYMOND
You said they were a bunch of old fools.

EDGAR
I ought to know, I'm the biggest fool of all!

RAYMOND
You sure you took your insulin?

EDGAR
Yes, I'm sure.

He starts to drop his pants.

EDGAR

You want to see for yourself?

RAYMOND

Put your pants back on!

EDGAR

I'm sure I took my insulin.

RAYMOND

Well that's good, I'm glad.

EDGAR

I'm not Georgie Colton, you know! Nobody dropped me on my head.

RAYMOND

Come on, let's work you in. Nobody said you were Georgie Colton. Don't be so darned thin-skinned. And let's just drop the subject of your driver's license.

EDGAR

I ought to know whether I took my insulin.

Raymond knocks on the Inner Door, an elaborate, ritualistic gesture. Four raps: knock-knock... knock... knock.

EDGAR

Treat me like an imbecile!

From within, one knock.

RAYMOND

Nobody's treating you like an imbecile.

Raymond knocks: knock-knock... knock-knock.

RAYMOND

And don't go dropping your pants in public, you don't want people treating you like a moron.

Last pattern of knocks repeated, from within.

EDGAR

I wasn't in public.

Raymond has trouble remembering this one, at first: knock... knock-knock... knock.

RAYMOND

You don't call the Temple public?

EDGAR

No, I don't!

Return knock, from inside: knock-knock-knock.

RAYMOND

You've got a funny notion of public, then, all I can say.

He knocks a little harder than necessary: knock... knock... knock... knock. Watch sticks head out.

RAYMOND

(As the Inner Door opens) **Anyway, I call this an ideal place for keeping your pants on.**

WATCH

Who's there?

RAYMOND

A Son of Saul, Worthy Watch, seeking sanctuary in the Regimental Chapel.

WATCH

Right, Brother. Stand fast.

Goes in, closing door.

EDGAR

One temporary slip of memory, by God, and it's a national crisis!

Turns to leave.

EDGAR

One time! One time I forget to take that goddamned insulin! Do you suppose I'll ever live it down?

RAYMOND

All I did was ask if you'd taken your medicine. The last I knew it wasn't a crime to be concerned about your father's health, or has that changed, too?

EDGAR

Well it isn't a crime not to be able to bring to mind a password, either!

RAYMOND

I never said it was. Where are you going?

Inner Door opens. Sergeant Major sticks his head out into the anteroom.

EDGAR

You don't think I might have had a lot on my mind? Taking care of the insurance and the service and the marker?

Sergeant Major goes in.

EDGAR

Not to mention the company. The company, Holy Christ! Nobody ever heard of a dooryard call, not in this day and age. Is it any wonder I forgot my shot?

RAYMOND

You haven't got to leave!

EDGAR

Willard and Molly Francis! How long do you think it had been since I'd seen that old gravedigger and his old chore of a wife? But they came, just like the rest, out of respect for your mother. Brought me a jar of pussy willow tonic!

Sergeant Major sticks his head back out.

EDGAR

Pussy willow tonic! What next? Be a cold day in Hell before I ever drank anything that came out of that one's kitchen, now I tell you. Old torment. Peddled her tonic all up and down the countryside. Now I'd like to know who would have paid for pussy willow tonic. I wouldn't have paid a plugged nickel for it.

RAYMOND

(To Sergeant Major) **Give us a minute.**

Sergeant Major goes in.
Silence.

EDGAR
What would you know about it, anyway? How would you know if I'd taken my shot?

RAYMOND
I'm the one that gets your prescriptions filled.

EDGAR
You won't have to do it anymore, I can promise you that.

RAYMOND
Nobody's complaining about picking your prescriptions up.

EDGAR
To hell with it, anyway, if it's only an excuse to spy on me.

RAYMOND
You aren't careful, you're going to miss Frank's memorial.

EDGAR
Not if I have to be led in by the hand. I won't be led around by the hand like poor Frank was at the last of it.

Silence.

RAYMOND
Big difference between being a little absent-minded and being what Frank was at the end.

EDGAR
Who's absent-minded?

RAYMOND
Do you have the damned password, or do you not have the damned password?

EDGAR
I said I wasn't going to be led in there, and by God I meant it!

RAYMOND
Then let me give you the password. Come back in here!

EDGAR
Don't break any rules on my account.

RAYMOND
I don't see how it would break any rules. I happen to be the presiding Commander of this Regiment. I'm the one who gives out the password in the first place. I happen to know that you are -- besides being my father -- the oldest living charter member.

EDGAR
Not I. I'm no charter member. Now Frank, he was a charter member. Wally Fulton was. Charlie Cole, too. You look at the charter, when you drape it, you'll see their signatures, you won't see mine. Christ, it's a wonder they let me in! I came that close to getting blackballed.

RAYMOND
You didn't either!

EDGAR
They were funny about religion, in those days.

RAYMOND
Did we ever have one to get funny about?

EDGAR
Methodist!

RAYMOND
Oh, is that right? What was the minister's name?

EDGAR
I was always a Methodist, too. They put us in the orphanage after Dad died, but that doesn't change the fact.

RAYMOND
Look. Everyone knows you are a dues-paying member --

EDGAR
Nobody knows nothing. Look how many years I put in on that Number Three Paper Machine. Senior Machine Tender, when I retired! You think that means something? It does not. Couple weeks back, I went up there. See how the old hands were getting along. Foreman meets me at the rereeler. "Can't come in," he says.

Pause.

EDGAR
"Not authorized."

Pause.

EDGAR
"Company policy. Liability."

RAYMOND
I didn't know that. I'm sorry, Dad.

EDGAR
What am I -- a raccoon in the Fourdrinier?

RAYMOND
Nobody's going to object if I give you the password.

EDGAR
I wager the Worthy Watch might.

RAYMOND
The Hell with the Worthy Watch!

Edgar has taken his wallet out, and now looks through its contents.

RAYMOND
I paid them.

EDGAR
I know you did. I knew you did. You pay my dues every year, don't you? That's what you've given me for Father's Day every year now for twenty years. I was just checking to see if you'd given me the receipt. Talk about forgetful! How many times have you forgotten to give me the receipt? I'm not finding fault. Normally it wouldn't matter, but once in a while the Treasurer slips up, and it pays to have a receipt with the seal on it.

RAYMOND
That makes sense.

EDGAR
Seen it happen to Frank.

RAYMOND

Is that so?

EDGAR

Christ, yes. Wally Fulton, he was the Treasurer. Poor old Wally. The way his wife ran around! I'm surprised he knew where anything was.

RAYMOND

You want the password, or not?

EDGAR

No. No, I don't. Keep your damn password to yourself. I'll remember it presently.

RAYMOND

Look, I can't stay out here all night!

EDGAR

Don't, then! Go back in. Who's stopping you?

RAYMOND

What's the password?

EDGAR

Ransom.

Silence.

EDGAR

Harvest.

Silence.

EDGAR

Hammer? Anvil?

RAYMOND

Let me give you a hint!

EDGAR

Don't give me no goddamn hints!

RAYMOND

Father.

EDGAR

What?

RAYMOND

Your sash is crooked.

EDGAR

Never mind my sash.

RAYMOND

Better fix it. Pretty important...regalia.

Edgar adjusts sash.

RAYMOND

Yes, a fellow has to look after his...regalia.

Edgar strains to remember, Raymond waits.
Inner Door opens, Sergeant Major looks out.

EDGAR

Endurance?

RAYMOND

No!

Sergeant Major retreats, closing door.

RAYMOND

I am trying to help you!

EDGAR

Don't you raise your voice at me.

RAYMOND

I'm sorry. I'm sorry. You're right. But you don't want the word. You don't want me to vouch for you. You don't want a hint.

EDGAR

You don't need to raise your voice at me.

RAYMOND

Just tell me one thing. What did Frank ever do to you, that you would refuse to pay your respect?

EDGAR

Don't you ever raise your voice at me. What have I done to you, that you would raise your voice at me like that?

Enter ALICE VIOLETTE, from Outer Door.

ALICE

Well, look at this! Hello, Boys!

RAYMOND

Evening, Alice.

EDGAR

Alice.

ALICE

What have we got, there, a break in the meeting?

She busies herself gathering utensils for the oyster stew.

RAYMOND

Not just yet, Alice, no.

ALICE

Well, when there is a break, send someone across to the fire station, before Jenny Millett puts her back out trying to set those tables up by herself, will you?

RAYMOND

All right. Will do.

ALICE

Don't forget, now.

RAYMOND

I won't forget.

ALICE

(To Raymond) **Don't you let him, Edgar. Keep him straight.**

RAYMOND

He will. He'll keep me straight.

ALICE
I imagine! *(To Edgar)* How you been feeling, dear? You looking more like your old self.

EDGAR
Me? I'm fine.

ALICE
You are?

EDGAR
Never better.

ALICE
***(To Raymond)* Me and Mum seen him out to the IGA, there, last Spring. We was worried about him.**

RAYMOND
He give us a scare, but he's fine, now.

ALICE
There, that's right. Awful good to see you getting around again, Edgar. You didn't look like yourself, in the Spring.

EDGAR
No, I don't imagine I did.

ALICE
I said to Mum, I go, "Mum, that poor old Edgar Dolan's been through the wringer, judging by the looks of it." I could see.

RAYMOND
He's tough as a boiled owl.

ALICE
There, course he is. Well, Edgar, you're lucky, you got your boy here to look after you.

EDGAR
I guess I don't need much looking after.

RAYMOND
So you say you got enough help over there?

ALICE
Oh, land, yes. More than enough. Like I said, we just need help with those tables. Other than that, we've got more help than we know what to do with.

RAYMOND
I'll send a couple of the boys over.

ALICE
Don't forget!

RAYMOND
He won't let me!

ALICE
***(On her way out)* I hope you brought your appetites!**

RAYMOND
Count on it!

She exits.
Silence.

EDGAR
Old sow!

RAYMOND
What did Frank ever do to you?

Silence.

EDGAR
Maybe I could think if everyone would just leave me alone for one minute.

RAYMOND
Stubborn!

EDGAR
Christ! Is it any wonder a man can't think straight, with all the distractions around here?

Raymond buries his face in his hands.
Silence.

EDGAR
What did I say before?

RAYMOND
How in the Hell am I supposed to know?

EDGAR
And he calls me forgetful!

RAYMOND
A word slipped your mind, so what? You think nothing ever slips my mind? I'm not the one making a mountain of trouble out of this, Father.

EDGAR
I'm sure I'm not.

RAYMOND
Good, then. Come in. Come on in so we can get this meeting started.

EDGAR
I don't want to come in.

RAYMOND
Then why are you here?

Silence.

EDGAR
I don't know why I'm here.

Silence.

RAYMOND
Look, Dad, maybe you ought to go across the road. Go wait for us there. Alice will give you a nice bowl of oyster stew and some crackers. The rest of us will be along shortly. This won't take long, if I can just get back in there.

EDGAR
How many days was it? I forget. Was it fifteen, or was it sixteen days after I retired?

Pause.

EDGAR

The biggest fight we ever had was about life insurance. People didn't buy life insurance. Not like they do now. Didn't we fight! This scar? She threw a lard can at me. I had to cash in the policy to pay for the funeral. Thirty years I put into that paper mill! Planning for retirement. Planning for the future. Planning for May's future, really. If only I'd known! Oh, the thought crossed my mind, sometimes, maybe I'd drop dead before I turned sixty-five. But I had a policy -- I knew your mother would be provided for, whatever happened to me.

RAYMOND

You're as healthy as a horse.

EDGAR

Then I needed it, didn't I? Christless life insurance.

Inner Door opens, Sergeant Major sticks his head out. Pulls it back in, after gesture from Raymond, closing the door behind himself.

EDGAR

I never would have guessed she'd go first.

RAYMOND

Sometimes things don't work out the way we plan --

EDGAR

Would you?

RAYMOND

Sometimes --

EDGAR

I've got diabetes, for Christsake!

RAYMOND

Watch your diet, you'll live to be a hundred.

EDGAR

What would I want to live to be a hundred for?

Silence.

EDGAR
There wasn't any work for a long time. I don't know what we would have done, if Frank hadn't been paying board.

RAYMOND
I'd forgotten he was our first boarder!

EDGAR
May didn't want him at first. I had a hard time talking her into it.

RAYMOND
He drove for Alton Pierce.

EDGAR
Sometimes that was the only money we had in the house.

RAYMOND
I remember he gave me a ride down to Portland.

EDGAR
That's right, he did!

RAYMOND
Thought I was king of the world, up in the cab of that old Ford. Hauling smoked alewives. Left from Orland Village, still dark. Houses dark, down through Belfast. Smell of the fields all around in the dark. The woods. Saw deer, I don't remember where. Houses dark, down through Camden. Along the salt water. Route One, all the way down to Moody's Diner, stopped there for lunch. Baked beans and yeast rolls. Frank telling jokes to the waitresses at Moody's, then again in Portland, at the Fishermen's Market. Same jokes, both places. I pretended to understand. Now I've forgotten. But that old Frank sure knew how to make people laugh.

Pause.

RAYMOND
What was it he made Mom so mad about that time?

EDGAR
Christ knows!

RAYMOND
All I remember is her sitting at the table crying.

EDGAR

Could have been anything. Those weren't very good times.

RAYMOND

I have good memories!

EDGAR

What did you know? You were a kid! You might have good memories, but those were hard times. There wasn't any work. Not like there had been. Many's the day we didn't know where the next meal was coming from. We lived on potatoes and deer meat. Why, if Tim Smith hadn't been game warden, we would have starved. He was always willing to turn a blind eye. One day a bunch of us come out of the swamp down behind the Grange Hall, just as Tim came by. So he stops to talk. Doesn't even get out of the car. "Any deer hanging out down in the Swamp?" We'd just killed two. They were in the woods. So were the rifles. We were waiting while somebody went to get a wagon. "Any deer hanging out down in the Swamp?" "Well," Frank says, "not as many as there were before."

RAYMOND

Why'd Frank move out?

EDGAR

I don't remember.

Silence.

EDGAR

We were like brothers.

RAYMOND

What did Frank Ginn ever do to you, that you'd betray his memory like this?

EDGAR

He never done nothing to me.

RAYMOND

You just got done saying you don't know what you would have done without him, during the bad times.

EDGAR

Yes, well, I'll tell you -- since the Great Depression, Raymond, a lot of milk

has spilled under the bridge.

RAYMOND

Let me give you the password!

EDGAR

I know the password!

RAYMOND

What is it?

EDGAR

Ashes.

RAYMOND

No!

EDGAR

Sickle!

RAYMOND

No!

EDGAR

Monument. Winter. Harrow.

RAYMOND

Look at you. Too stubborn to admit you don't know the word, even if it means you can't go in and pay your respect to the best friend you ever had. You ought to be ashamed of yourself.

He turns to knock on the Inner Door.

RAYMOND

And by the way, I promise you, I am going to Florida -- I don't care if you can't remember your own name.

EDGAR

Oyster stew!

Enter Sergeant Major.

SGT. MJR.

Ray?

Sergeant Major closes the door, remaining in the anteroom.

RAYMOND

Time to fish or cut bait!

SGT. MJR.

It won't take long. We've really got to get going, here.

RAYMOND

Oh, sure! Sure! Of course we do! We don't want to hang around here all night. *(To Edgar)* You ready?

EDGAR

Go ahead. I'm not myself tonight. It's nothing serious -- go ahead, go on in there. I'll just sit and rest awhile. Go on, go on!

RAYMOND

If you say so.

He nods to the Sergeant Major, who will work them in with the Four Secret Knocks used by Raymond above.

RAYMOND

Give me the keys.

EDGAR

There's no need --

RAYMOND

(Keeping his back to the Sergeant Major)

Keys.

EDGAR

This is what they did to Frank.

RAYMOND

You brought me up the best you could, the least I can do is keep you from killing yourself on the highway. After I go South, you can do what you want to. Until then, no driving. You hear? You drove out here, after I told you not to, fine. I've offered to help you get into the meeting, and you don't want to be helped. Fine. Sit here. Sulk. But I have to go in there, and you can't be trusted, so let's go.

EDGAR
(Hands them over)
But I want them back after the meeting.

RAYMOND
You sit tight.

Door opens. Watch appears.

SGT. MJR.
Sons of Saul, Watchman, seeking sanctuary in the Chapel.

WATCH
Right, Brother. Stand fast.

Goes in, closing door.

RAYMOND
Or go! Go right on over across the road, if that's what suits you. Go sit with the old sows!

Watch at door.

WATCH
You may enter, Brother. Brothers. The High Commander --

SGT. MJR.
(Prompting) **Regimental Chaplain.**

WATCH
The Sergeant Major --

SGT. MJR.
Chaplain!

WATCH
You may enter, Brothers. The Regimental Chaplain awaits the word.

EDGAR
(To Raymond) **Go ahead! Go on! You've got a meeting to look after.**

Sergeant Major waits for Raymond, then follows him in. Door closes.

Silence.
Edgar remembers the password.

EDGAR

Regalia!

Silence.
Enter Watch. Takes up position at the door.

EDGAR

I haven't been feeling like myself lately.

WATCH

Do say.

EDGAR

I'm sorry about getting ugly with you earlier.

WATCH

It's just people don't have any respect these days.

Pause.

WATCH

They don't care about doing the ritual like they ought to. I call it a lack of plain, old-fashioned respect. You won't believe it, but I was over in Searsport, at the flea market, this summer, and I seen regalia.

EDGAR

Regalia!

WATCH

Twenty-five cents for a Commander's sash! Fifty cents for the derby! You see those things laid out on the table, it breaks your heart. Some people just don't care, one way or the other.

Inner Door opens, Sergeant Major sticks his head out.

SGT. MJR.

Watchman, are the gates fast?

WATCH

They are, Sergeant Major.

SGT. MJR.

Stand by while the charter is draped to mourn the passing of our Brother, Franklin Wallace Ginn, to the Higher Realm.

WATCH

Right, Worthy Sergeant.

Sergeant Major goes in.

EDGAR

Password? Password's the least of it! I'm surprised I know my own name, sometimes. Sometimes I just stand there with the refrigerator door open, wondering what I'm looking for. Quart of milk. Orange. Plate of mackerel. Insulin. Like things right out of your wildest dreams! It's the damnedest thing! I don't know I'm looking for the butter dish until I happen to notice the knife in my hand. Or I'll be making a phone call, and right in the middle of dialing the number not know who I'm calling. Or you'll be talking to somebody, and not know who they are. Know the voice. Know the face. But to put them together with a name... you can't remember, to save your soul!

Sounds of ceremony from inside: drumbeat, which continues under the following.

EDGAR

You have car keys in your hand. Don't know where you got them. Don't know where you think you're going. Don't know what you have to go for.

Pause.

EDGAR

Blackballed. That's what I am. Blackballed by my own memory. Or blackballed by my own lack of memory, I should say. Blackballed for life. Just like poor old Willard Francis.

Pause.

EDGAR

You must have known him! Gravedigger. Welldigger. Water witcher. Don't tell me you didn't know him! Willard gets himself nominated somehow. Nobody knows how. Old gravedigger! Can you imagine? But he's going to get blackballed. Charlie Cole will blackball him. Eddie Fish will. Frank will. Everyone knows it. Like Charlie Cole says, what's the sense? Why put yourself through the misery? But Willard won't withdraw his name. "I'm as

good as any man in the Regiment of Saul," he says, "Goddamn me if I ain't." Right here in the anteroom. First he's got company - maybe four or five applicants. One by one, the others get called in. Then it's just Willard and the Watch. In there, the Regiment is voting on his nomination.

Pause.

EDGAR

Why not? Why wouldn't they let him in? Didn't they let Georgie Colton in? Poor old Georgie! They let him in the Regiment, just like they gave him a job out at the mill. You see him in Groundwood. He cleans up the cordwood they pick out of the magazines. He isn't fit for nothing else. They give him a little blue wagon to haul around.

Pause.

EDGAR

But Willard Francis? That dirty bugger? That goddamn gravedigger? Who in his right mind is going to cast a vote to admit him as a member of this Temple? And Willard knows. He's sitting there, sweat pouring down his face. White as a sheet. You can hear the voices from inside, but you can't make out what they're saying. They've been talking for a while. They keep talking. The gavel pounds. Then not a sound. Not a sound. Willard stands up. He turns to the Watch, he's stiff as a pickpole. Puts his hat on. "I am far superior," he says, "to any man that might want to give me the black ball." Turns around, walks out that door.

Pause.
Slips crepe armband off.

EDGAR

What about you? How's your memory? Oh, I know, I know -- you're young, you're clever, you've studied the Bylaws, you've learned the ritual by heart, you know the Lore. But how's your memory?

Drum stops.

EDGAR

And I'll tell you another thing!

Enter Sergeant Major.

SGT. MJR.

Watchman, well done. Thy labors are at an end.

EDGAR

I'll tell you another thing --

WATCH

Thanks, Worthy Sergeant.

EDGAR

(Dropping crepe at Watch's feet)

Don't think I don't know who you are!

Enter officers and members from the meeting, including Raymond, on their way out for oyster stew, peeling off regalia as they go.

Curtain

Appendix

Production Notes, Cast Lists:

Standing Just Outside the Door

Ugly Ducklings

Oh Grow Up!

Let me Count the Ways

Piano and voice score for *Let Me Count the Ways*

Standing Just Outside the Door

Standing Just Outside The Door was commissioned by my Orono High School colleague and drama teacher Chris Luthin as Orono's entry for the annual one-act play contest of the Maine Principals' Association Drama Festival in 2002. The produced play had to run less than 40 minutes according to contest rules. Thus, we had to cut the Introduction and Scene 7. The first presentation was at Skowhegan High School on March 8, 2002. On March 19-20, there were two evening performances at Orono High School; and a special presentation during the school day soon after for the entire Orono High School student body and faculty.

The judges at the drama festival in Skowhegan presented Jonathan Bailey with an All-State Acting Award for his role as William Kinney and made the following comments about the play: "A provocative play presented with sensitivity and emotion;" "Very good subject matter performed with great energy and enthusiasm;" "A brave investigation of a delicate topic, not an easy one for any generation;" and "There were captivating moments, especially realized in Jon Bailey's performance which enhanced the ensemble's performance in the difficult presentation of the subject matter."

ORONO HIGH SCHOOL
PRODUCTION

Directed by Christopher Luthin

Technical Director Elliot "the Doctor" Wilcox

Cast of Standing Just Outside the Door:

Andrew Harrison	**Evan James**
Paul Dean	**Zack Pike**
Luise Werner	**Joelle Clingerman**
William Kinney	**Jon Bailey**
Bob Day	**Andrew Breece**
Doreen McIntire	**Savana Leveille**
Tucker Sherman	**Josh Thompson**
Fletcher Coombs	**Sam Walton/Griff Lambert**
Laura Fennelly	**Nicole Barclay**
Linda Coverly	**Lauren Onsrud**
Librarian	**Rebecca Bailey**
Tony	**Ian Averill**
Stage Manager	**Alycia Delaney**
Lighting	**Josh Hale**
Sound	**Kyle West**

Stage hands :
Rachel Smith
Nadja Blagojevic
Rebecca Bailey
Ian Averill
Joe Hallman
Krystal Grady
Chris Eason

UGLY DUCKLINGS

Ugly Ducklings
A Lesbian Drama

- **2004 world premiere, Venus Theatre, Washington, DC.**
- **Made in Maine, Maine Writers and Publishers Alliance (reading), Bangor.**
- **Workshop production, Bates College, Lewiston, Maine.**
- **Second Place, Celebration Theatre's New Play Competition, LA.**

"If it is possible that a piece of theatre can be both gritty and sublime at the same time, then Venus Theatre has achieved it in their world premiere production of Carolyn Gage's *Ugly Ducklings.*"

- *Metro Weekly Review*, Washington, DC.

" . . . deserves a central place in the lesbian feminist literary canon . . ."
- *off our backs,* Washington, DC.

". . . refreshingly well told tale that while raising all the issues that this anti-homophobic company and playwright want to raise, does so with an admirable restraint, avoiding the obvious traps of sensationalism and titillation and striking an admirable balance of theatricality and realism."

- *Potomac Stages,* Washington, DC.

"... Radically redefining beauty ... *Ugly Ducklings* reveals how notions of homosexuality can shatter the souls of girls and women ... an impressive work ... a brutally honest examination of what it means to be a young lesbian ..."

- *The Washington Blade*, Washington D.C.

" . . . a play about coming of age and homophobia and how people deal with emerging understandings about sexuality. It's a tough, tough, tough topic, and it's handled here with a great deal of raw energy, but also with a great deal of subtlety . . . a very, very nice piece . . . definitely worth seeing."

Peter Fay for WAMU
(NPR affiliate station),
Washington, DC.

Ugly Ducklings **picks up where *Tea and Sympathy* and *The Children's Hour* left off. Set in a girls' summer camp, the play explores the dynamics of homophobia in a same-sex environment.**

A gothic thriller, *Ugly Ducklings* examines the unhealthy turns that relationships between girls can take when they are not allowed their natural expression. The so-called "Ophelia Syndrome" comes alive as the cabin of younger girls, their self-esteem still reinforced by the primacy of their relationships, comes into contact with the older girls who have begun to turn against themselves and each other in their attempts to conform to the pressures of compulsory heterosexuality.

Angie, a middle-class college student, is falling in love with another counselor at the camp, Renée, who is a working-class "out" lesbian. Against this backdrop of intense homophobia, the young women struggle with their feelings for each other and the problems of defining themselves in a society that insists they be invisible. The camp legend about a monster in the lake parallels the adult phobias about lesbianism, and, confronted with an attempted child suicide, campers and counselors are compelled to face their worst fears in the microcosmic world of the summer camp.

Ugly Ducklings **breaks ranks with male-centered queer drama in foregrounding the experience of women and girls who are survivors of sexual violence and shattering romantic and sentimental conventions about the "gentle sex."**

Nine girls, four women
Two hours
Single set

Oh Grow Up!

CASTING

The total number of actors required for this script is flexible, but for purposes of the original production a total of 14 actors were used. Specific roles should be assigned as actors are cast, and certain connections can be made through casting and doubling. However, in certain scenes the repetition of a given actor within a scene indicates an extension of the prescribed characterization. Names of actors cast in the original production have been retained here as a guideline to distribution of lines in group scenes.

SET

The basic set for the production requires three operating doors, one of which needs to operate like a Dutch door (for Scene 3). The original production employed nine 4x8 flats, arranged in three sets of three, each set of three with a door flat at its center. The nine flats made a traditional upstage wall with two side walls, one angled toward DSR, one toward DSL. All were painted entirely black.

With the exception of the bed in Scene 3 and Scene 5, and the desk chairs in Scene 5, virtually all set furnishings can be basic black boxes of various sizes. In fact, such black boxes provide great utility in scene changes, and require and allow great imagination from both the performers and the audience. The original production used two 1.5'x 1.5' cubes and two 1.5'x 3' cubes.

COSTUMES

Basic all-black "under costumes" are worn throughout. The original production relied on close-fitting t-shirts, turtlenecks, and slacks for the men, and close-fitting tops and leggings for the women. The convention of "not seeing" the blacks is readily accepted by the audience, and allows actors to make rapid character changes by simply adding costumes pieces and not having to strip down.

LIGHTS

General stage lighting is sufficient, and all of the blackouts can be eliminated, if desired, by directing the actors in tight scene changes.

SCENE CHANGES
The integration of the work of stage techs helps make this a true ensemble piece. There is no interaction between actors and techs on stage, and the work of the techs should be a seamless underpinning to the action. It is necessary, then, that all techs are dressed in full stage blacks in order to "disappear" from view while they work. Similarly, when actors are required to help move set pieces, they must do so as unobtrusively as possible, unless they are specifically called to do otherwise in the stage directions.

SCENE-SPECIFIC PRODUCTION NOTES:

SCENE 1
-- Flashlights are used both for effect and in order to easily control lighting conditions (the original production was mobile). If your stage has the ability to light the actors with theatrical instruments, these could be used instead of or to augment the flashlights. Without the flashlights, however, the self contained effect would be lost.
-- Each actor wears an additional "formal" black costume piece. These included long cardigans and over-shirts, sports coats, tux jackets, leather jackets, etc., all black on black.
-- Stage furnishings included enough black boxes of various sizes to allow the actors to sit or stand at different levels.

SCENE 2
-- Announcer is costumed in a flashy sports jacket, like something out of a game show, worn over actor's basic blacks. Sequins work nicely.
-- The various letters were created by simply cutting large letters out of cardboard to be worn front and back, facing these with a thin layer of foam (for depth), decorating them, and making "jackets" of each by attaching elastic to the shoulders and around the sides. Letters were worn over basic blacks. Each letter's decoration reflects the character of the letter.
-- The changing "N" was created by loosely tying the two actors together back to back at the waists, then suiting them in their "N" together. Each side of the "N" was decorated reflect the character of "good" or "bad".
-- All entrances were around flats, not through doors.

SCENE 3
-- Closet was SL door; room entrance was CTR door, bed was against SR door.
-- Various monsters were created using simple masks and more elaborate costumes. Devil was a cape and a mask, as was Vampire. Sugarbug was created by using painted egg-crate foam to form wings and a tail that fit in one piece over the actor's head, on which he wore a wildly colored top hat with antennae. Bedbugs were created using wildly painted foam headdresses

and matching foam pincers.
-- Mom and Dad clothes were simply a jumper and a sport shirt, respectively, put on over the actors' basic blacks.
-- Cafeteria Lady was played by a male actor in female dress, including prosthetic breasts, wig and uniform over basic blacks. Casting a male proved particularly effective because he was able to distort his voice to make Cafeteria Lady even more creepy and overbearing.
-- The bed was simply a shallow plywood box with legs, cut to bed height and dressed with little-boy bedclothes and bed skirt. It was positioned with its "headboard" against the SR door.
-- In order to allow bedbugs to appear under and through the bed, the SR door was designed in Dutch-door fashion, with the bottom section swinging to backstage, breaking just at the height of the bed. Similarly, a hole large enough for the second Bedbug's head and shoulders was cut in the DSR foot of the bed, and that hole was disguised by the bedcovers until the Bedbug popped through, throwing back the covers. During the opening of the scene, the actors playing the Bedbugs swung back the lower section of the door and quietly positioned themselves under the bed, ready for entrance. They disappeared in reverse of the way they entered.

SCENE 4
-- Supporting the concept of the same actor playing Tommy in all three scenes is important, and a challenge for the actor playing the role. We found it most supportive to costume this first Tommy in overalls, and blocked him to be curled up on his knees as soon as possible so that his being younger than the young woman playing his mother was more believable.
-- Tommy's entrance was through SR door, as if it were an outside door. Barbara entered through the SL door.

SCENE 5
-- Each of the students wore only one carefully select additional piece of costume (sweatshirt, athletic jacket, letter sweater, flowered blouse, etc.) over their basic blacks. Edward is costumed especially according to his character.
-- One of the larger cubes became Mr. Marone's desk.
-- In the original production, folding desks with armrest were brought in on rolling platforms for the classroom. This might prove too unwieldy, and these could easily be replaced with a collection of simple black benches.
-- Lunchlady Doris was played by the same actor, and in the same costume, as in Scene 3.
-- The books were created each by gluing three or four old encyclopedia volumes together, and covering the whole, huge book with brown paper. Each was then decorated by the "student" to whom it belonged, and preset under each desk before they were brought on stage.
-- Student entrances were through CTR door. Marone's desk and

"blackboard" were positioned in front of SR door. SL door was not used.

SCENE 6
-- The hospital bed was created by over-dressing the little boy's bed from Scene 3 with white sheets, and placing it with its "headboard" against the SL door.
-- One of the large black cubes became the bedside table.
-- Tommy's attire has now changed to jeans and a college sweatshirt, again over basic blacks.
-- Barbara wears a hospital gown and cap, over basic blacks.
-- Ruston and Nurse wear medical uniform jackets over basic blacks.
-- Entrances to the hospital room were through SR door. Bed was positioned in front of SL door. CTR door was not used.

SCENE 7
-- The two very different dining room tables were brought on SR and SL, each on a rolling platform, entirely preset with tableware and chairs.
-- The Real Family table was covered with a ripped blue tarp, had mismatched glassware, and the family was seated on upturned milk crates.
-- The TV Family table was impeccably dressed with lace tablecloth, candlesticks, cloth napkins, and perfect fake food.
-- The Real Family father's costume was a constructed fat-suit built so that the actor was able to step into it in one piece.
-- All other costumes were created by simply adding the appropriate pieces over basic blacks.
-- Real Family kids entered through SR to SR table. TV Family kids entered through SL door to SL table.

SCENE 8
-- Tom's desk was made using one of the large black cubes.
-- The offstage dialogue between Sarah and Tommy could be seen through a scrim created in the door at center, or could simply be audible from offstage.
-- Entrances to Tommy's room were made through SL door. CTR and SL doors were otherwise left unused.

SCENE 9
-- Stage is reset to the same cube arrangement as was used in the Prologue.
-- Actors now wear their basic blacks, each with the addition of a wild, crazy and/or brightly colored vest.

Let Me Count the Ways was first presented in the February 2004 Bangor staged reading with the following cast members:

Karen: Amy Roche
Patricia: Jennifer Groover
Bette: Amey Feeley
Rachel: Cheryl Reynolds
Diane: Ellen Peters
Annie: Sharon Young
Laura: Linda Britt
Mike, Phil: Roger Philippon
Billy, Brad: Scott Powers

In its first fully staged production, at Community Little Theatre in Auburn, July 9, 2004, the cast was:

Karen: Amy Roche
Patricia: Carol Griffiths
Bette: Deb Kramlich
Rachel: Cheryl Reynolds
Diane: Ellen Peters
Annie: Sharon Young
Laura: Mary Turcotte
Mike, Phil: Roger Philippon
Billy: Gary Starzynski
Brad: Michael Litchfield
Banker: Anna Cyr

1. Why Get Married in the First Place?

Patricia, Karen

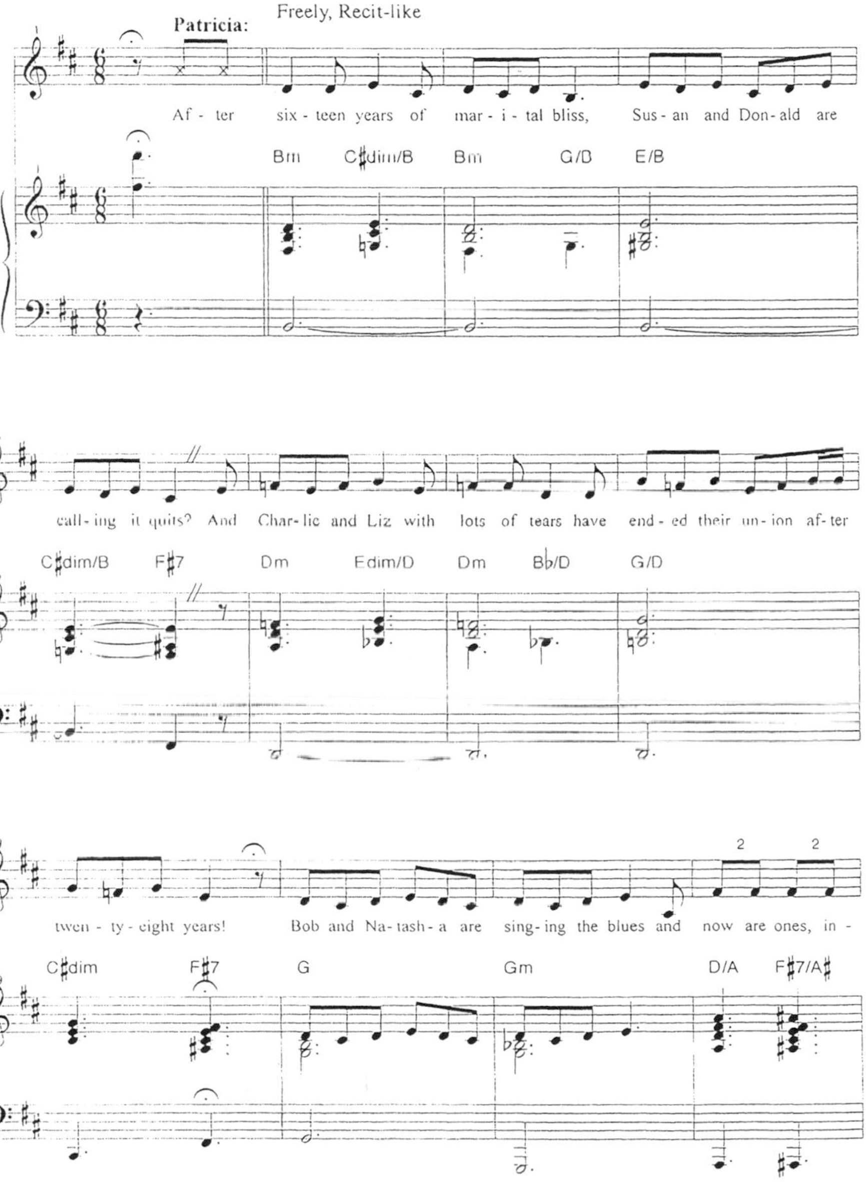

5
call - ing it quits? And Char - lie and Liz with lots of tears have end - ed their un - ion af - ter

C♯dim/B F♯7 Dm Edim/D Dm B♭/D G/D

9
twen - ty - eight years! Bob and Na - tash - a are sing - ing the blues and now are ones, in -

C♯dim F♯7 G Gm D/A F♯7/A♯

Moderato ♩.=122
13
stead of twos! So, why get mar- ried in the
Bm F♯7 Em F♯sus4 F♯7 GM7 F♯
18
first place? What's the point if you end up here?
Bm Bm/A Em C♯dim F♯sus4
23
Mike leav - ing you is not the worst case.
F♯sus4 F♯ G Em A D G

Think what Hen-ry the Eighth's wives had to fear!
Em
C♯dim/E
F♯7
Bm
A
G
F
E♭
D
G
Jan-ice and Tom-my
Cm
Ddim/C
just sold the house in a set-tle-ment that pit-ted spouse a-gainst spouse
A♭/C
F/C
Ddim/C
G
Ddim/F
G

41
She took her share and bought a small place, cov- ered the win- dows in chintz and lace.
E♭m Fdim/E♭ E♭m C♭/E♭ A♭/E♭ Ddim G7
45
He took his and he said, "Up yours!" Hooked up with a band as a
G7 A♭ A♭m E♭/B♭ G7/B
49
road- ie on tour! So why get mar- ried in the
Cm G7 Fm Gsus4 G7 A♭M7 G

54
first place?
What's the point if you end up here?
Cm
Cm/Bb
Fm
Ddim
Gsus4
59
When he pro - pos - es, just spray him with mace You'll
G
Ab
Fm
Bb
Eb
Ab
64
save your-self heart - ache and lots of tears!
Fm
Ddim/F
G7
Cm

69
Slow, like a dirge
rit.
Who can ex- plain why
Bb Ab F#m Em Dm F#7 Bm C#dim/B
73
Sa- rah and Ed af- ter on - ly four months say their mar- riage is dead? Whe
Bm G/B E/B C#dim/B F#7 Em F#
77
they said those words, "till death do us part," I guess what they meant was, "till
Dm Bb/D Bdim/D Bb/D Ddim

80
A tempo
we see the warts!" The ink on the lease they signed is still wet, and the
C♯dim F♯7 G Gm
84
wed - ding cel - e - bra - tion has left them in debt!
D/A F♯7/A♯ Bm F♯7 Em
87
So why get mar- ried in the first place?
F GM7 F♯ Bm Bm/A

92
What's the point if you end up here? your hus - band has
Em
C♯dim
F♯sus4
F♯sus4
F♯
G
Em
97
Karen:
left and pro - ba - bly for good And I'd mar - ry him all
A
D
G
Em
C♯m7(♭5)
102
o - ver if I could!
(Dialogue)
F♯7sus4
F♯7sus4

2. Dear Karen

Bette, Women

All:
rea- dy to start a new life He's rea- dy to start a new life.
tr
Bette:
Thanks to you our house is neat, and you are an ex- cep- tion- al cook. It
is - n't a - ny - thing you've done, al - though I know how things must look. He
All:

Bette:
knows how things must look. You may won - der why I'm leav - ing
when I pro - mised to be true. Be - lieve me when I tell you this: The
All:
pro - blem's me; it is - n't you. The pro - blem's him not you.

Bette:
Slow March Tempo
I must move on, must find my - self. I'm feel - ing stran - gled here at home. So
off I go to find my fu - ture Toward the ho - ri - zon I must roam.
All:
Toward the ho - ri - zon he must roam.
Bette:
As Before
So off I go to find my fu - ture.

rit.
I don't know if I'll be back. I'll try to mail a cur- rent ad- dress, so send the stuff I did- n't pack!
All:
So send the stuff he did - n't pack.

3. Temptation, or My Dark Side

Annie

been with me since I was a bride. Temp-ta-tion: Ev-en though I've
Am/E
B/E
Em
tried, I'm still liv-ing with my dark side.
F♯/E
Am/F
B7sus4
Em
When I'm ly-ing in my
Em

21
bed at night, at the end of a nor-mal day My
Em(maj7)
Em7
A/E
24
mind won't stop when I turn out the light I think of ways to make him pay.
Am
Em
Am
Bsus4/A
27
Like vis - ions of su - gar- plums in old - en days, thoughts of
Bsus4
C
Dsus4
D

30
sharp ob - jects dance through my head And pis - tols and shot - guns and
Am
Em
C
33
oo - zies and can - nons march in pa - rade as they dance through my head!
A7/C♯
Bsus4
36
(Opt. 8va)
Temp - ta - tion: It's my dark side. It's
B7(♭9)
Em
F♯/E

39
been with me since I was a bride. Temp - ta - tion: Ev - en though I've
Am/E B/E Em
42
tried, I'm still liv - ing with my dark side.
F#/E Am/E B7sus4 Em
45
I day - dream of poi - sons and drown - ings, dark
CM7 Em

48
fan - ta - sies tor - ture my nights. I know that it's wrong, but still
Am/
Bm7
F♯m
51
I go on im - a - gin - ing in - es - cap - a - ble plights. I
D
Bm7
D♭sus4
54
think of him walk - ing the plank or strang - ling to death with a
D♭
Fm
D♭

57
string He could fall down a mud - dy
Csus4 C Am
59
bank or choke on a fried chick- en wing. Temp -
Em C Am7 Dsus4 D
62
ta- tion: It's my dark side, it's been with me since I was a
Gm A/G Cm/G

65
bride. Temp - ta - tion: Ev - en though I've tried, I'm still
D/G
Gm
A/G
68
liv - ing
with my
Cm/G
Dsus4
D
70
dark side.
Gm
Cm
3
3
D

74
Gm
74

4. Lorena Bobbitt

Rachel

Rachel:
I don't real - ly want to tell
Am
you what my deep - est se - cret is 'cause I
F

11
know that you'll just call me a ra - di - cal fe - mi- nist.
11
Dm
G
14
But I'm real - ly not at all that way at
Dm
Dm(maj7)
Dm7
14
17
least I ne - ver thought so I'm ac - tual - ly quite con - ser -
G7/D
B♭
E♭
17

20
va - tive in po - li - tics; I was taught so.
Bb Asus4 A
23
But here's the thing a - bout me that you should know to - night: I
A Gm C Am Dm
26
think Lo - re - na Bob - bitt got it right.
Bb Csus4 C

30
30
34
Let's say your man's an aw - ful cad
Let's say he's cheat - ed more
34
Am
F
37
than twice
Let's say that what he did was ba
37
Dm

40
ad.
Let's say he screwed his
Dm Dm(maj7)
G
43
best friend's wife!
What can you do to pay him back?
Dm7 G7/D
B♭ E♭
46
I have a thought!
Pull out your knife!
A - sleep he won't put
B♭ Asus4 A
Gm C

49
up a fight I think Lo - re - na Bob - bitt got it
Am Dm Bb Csus4 C
52
right!
56
Oh

60
dear, it seems I've shocked you. You don't think I look the sort
8va
63
Who'd be a butch - er in dis- guise, who
(8va)
66
would- n't be the best of sports. You'd ne- ver dream to look
(8va)
loco
B♭

69
at me that I'd end up on Court T V! I'm
F/A
Gm7
Asus4
73
real - ly not the mur - der- ous type but I think Lo - re - na Bob
Gm
C
Am
Dm
B♭
Csus
76
bitt got it right. Yeah,
C
B♭

79
I'm really not the mur - der- ous type, but I think Lo - re - na Bob-
Gm C Am Dm B♭ Csus4
82
bitt got it right!
C Dm

5. Our Side

Phil, Billy

17
on - ly while I was mar - ried to her but I've been this way since
Am7
Em7
C
23
Billy:
birth The scum of the earth, the mud of her
D/C
GM7/B
D7/A
GM7
Em7
28
shoe, the bac - ter - i - um on her tooth plaque, the
CM7
Em7

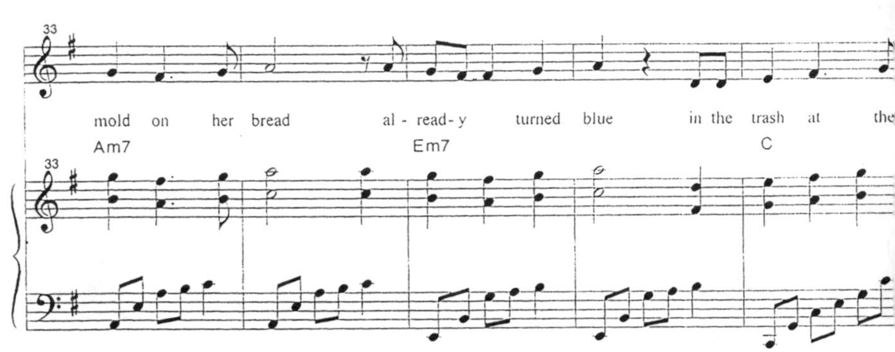
33
mold on her bread al - read - y turned blue in the trash at the
Am7
Em7
C

38
Phil:
bot - tom of the sack. I'm the low - est of the
D7
Bm

43
Billy:
low, for sure, I don't de - serve to live an - y more. I
E7
Am
Am/G
D7/F♯
D

49
don't de - serve to live, for sure, be - cause I'm rot- ten to the
Bm Bm/A G D C
55
Both:
core. If you'd on - ly lis - ten to our side if you'd
D E7 A A/G♯ F♯m F♯m/E
60
please let us have our say, you'd re - a - lize
DM7 C♯7 F♯m F♯m/E D9

65
(mel.)
then we have noth - ing to hide and ev - 'ry dog de - serves his
E7
A
F♯m
D
E7
70
day.
A
C
D7
75
Phil:
Look: I know I left her on Christ - mas
G9
Em7

79
Eve, which per - haps was a dumb thing to do. But
CM7
Em7
84
once I'd made up my mind to leave, I had to get
Am7
Em
CM7
89
Billy:
out-- would-n't you? My wife ne - ver did un-der -
D/C
GM7/B
D7/A
GM7

94
stand — me, I'm a man of in - cre - di - ble needs.
Em7
C
Em7
99
I'm not Su - per - man, not made out of
8va
Am7
loco
Em7
103
Phil:
steel when my fin - ger is cut, it bleeds. I
C
D

108
hat - ed the looks that she gave — me when I walked in
Bm
E7
Am
108

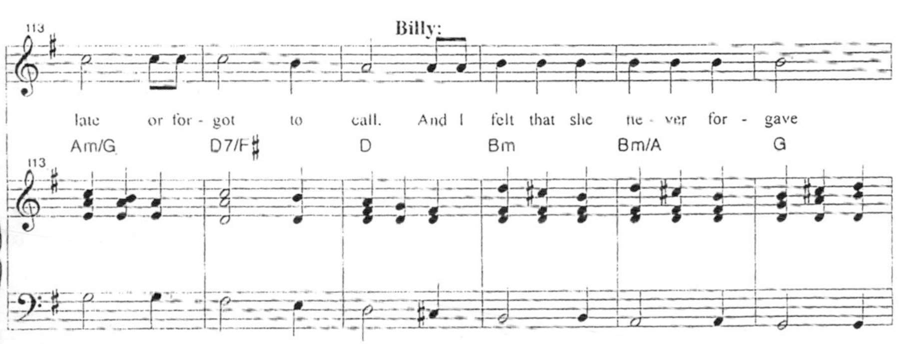
113
Billy:
late or for - got to call. And I felt that she ne - ver for - gave
Am/G D7/F♯ D Bm Bm/A G
113

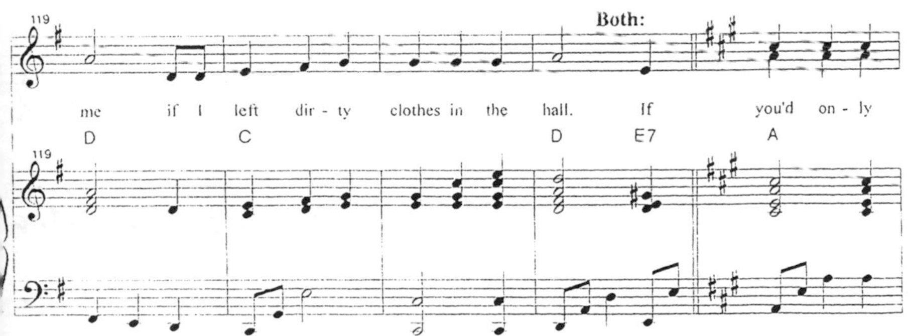
119
Both:
me if I left dir - ty clothes in the hall. If you'd on - ly
D C D E7 A
119

124
lis - ten to our side if you'd please let us have our
A/G♯ F♯m F♯m/E DM7 C♯7
129
say you'd re - a - lize then we have noth - ing to
F♯m F♯m/E D9 E7 A
134
Billy: his day.
hide, and ev - 'ry dog de - serves
Phil: I could-n't be who she
F♯m D E7 D9

138
want- ed me to could not mea- sure up to her i - deal. I
F♯m7/C♯
Bm7
D9/F
sim.
141
did try my best, I swear it to you, but her ver- sion of me was- n't
D9
F♯m7/C♯
F♯m7(♭5)/C
144
real
B: No one can be who they want us to be Per -
P: I could- n't be who she want- ed me to
Esus4
D9
F♯m7/C♯
sim.

147
fec - tion just does not ex - ist.
Could not mea - sure up to her i - deal
FM7/C
Gsus4
G
149
No one can do it— least of all me. I
I did try my best, I swear it to you
C9
G6/B
151
don't e - even make the short list. Now that you've
But her ver - sion of me was - n't real.
A
Gm/B♭
Dsus4
D

154
lis - tened to our side and you've kind - ly let us have our
A/G♯ F♯m F♯m/E DM7 C♯7
159
say, you must re - a - lize then we have noth - ing to
F♯m F♯m/E D9 E7 A
164
rit.
hide, and ev - 'ry dog de - serves his day.
F♯m D E7 A

6. Trio

Billy, Karen, Diane

8
head - ing or freez - ing so - lid while he's out
8
in - come that we'd risk try - ing to mur - der the
8
hears It's ne - ver my side My hid - den
8
Gm
Eb
Ebm(add2)
Ebm
Bbsus4
12
sled ding. He could be stran - gled,
12
bum? It sure would cost us
12
fears They all be - lieve her They
12
Bb
Bbm
Eb

15
K
a ra - bid skunk bite a drive - by shoot - ing
D
a pret - ty pen - ny like half his mo - ney,
B
think I'm pond scum I might as well be an
Pno.
C Fsus4 F D7 Gsus4 Gm
19
3
K
a kan- ga- roo fight.
D
if he has a - ny.
B
out and out bum. Why is it al - way
Pno.
E♭ F7sus4 B♭ F/A

23
I know that it's ev - il.
How can we af - ford it?
her side? Why is it
Gm
Gm/F
E♭
26
To talk a - bout his death.
Have we lost our
ne ver mine? I'm
D7
Gm
Gm/F

29
K
But he should suf - fer un - til his
D
heads? Have we gone cra - zy
B
not such a bad guy, look at me, I'm
Pno.
E♭
F7
B♭
B♭/A
32
K
dy - ing breath! He could
D
to wish them all dead? If we
B
fine! I'm not
Pno.
Gm
E♭7
A♭

take a fall off a horse or a wall
have to choose what to save or lose,
bad guy let me tell you
Eb/G
Fm
Fm/Eb
Have a pa - ra - chute fail. Or be
Would we pick the mon - ey or an ex -
why! She's not right for me, it's just so plain to
DbM7
C7
Fm

41
K
killed by hail. Ov - er- dose on C - Span
D
ho - ney? We can make a plan
B
see. You have to be - lieve I
Pno.
Fm/E♭
D♭△9
E♭7
44
K
get locked in a trash can, or fall from a
D
I know that we can. There is just one
B
just had to leave I have noth - ing
Pno.
A♭
A♭/G
Fm
D♭M7

rit.
Presto
boat or sing too high a note!
flaw: It's a - gainst the law!
hide; I have my good side!
Eb7
Db
Eb7
Ab

7. The Real Me

Karen

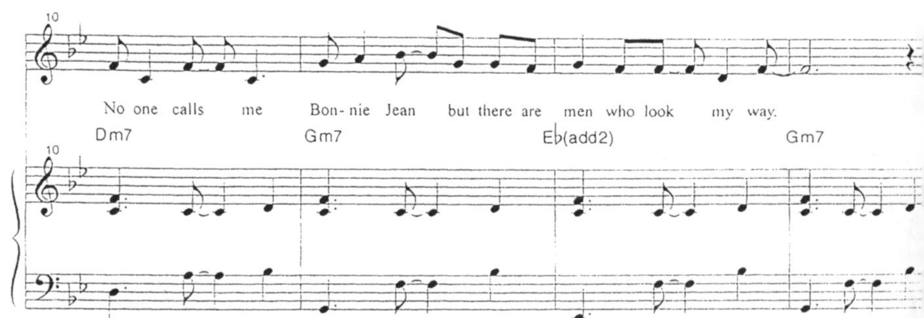

Moderato con moto
poco accel.
Peo - ple say my smile is nice. Peo- ple
Eb(add2) F7sus4 BbM7 Gm7
say I have good hair. One or two men
Eb(add2) BbM7 Dm7
accel.
might look twice if I've dressed my- self with care.
Gm7 Eb(add2) F7sus4

24
But what a - bout what's in - side? What a - bout the
Gm7
26
rest of me? I don't look like Frank - en - stein's
E♭M7
B♭M7
B♭M7/A
28
bride But what's in - side is the best of
Gm7
Cm7
F7sus4

30
me.
Gm7
30
Cm7
32
Gm7
32
34
You might think he'd know me well; we were mar- ried for four- teen years.
B♭△9
34
E♭M7
B♭△9

36
And the mar - riage— it went pret- ty well as mar- riag- es go, un- til the tears.
Dm7
Gm7
E♭M7
Gm7
38
But the thing is, he ne - ver knew me, ne- ve
Gm7
F7sus4
B♭△9
40
cared what made me care. Ne - ver
E♭M7
B♭△9

41
3
saw my soul, ne - ver looked in - to me, and
Dm7
Gm7
42
Less
I am more than what I wear. So what a - bout
E♭M7
F7sus4
F7sus4
44
what's in- side? What a - bout the rest of me? I
Gm7
E♭M7
Gently

46
don't look like Frank - en - stein's bride but
B♭
Dm/A
Gm7
48
what's in-side is the best of me. Yes, what a-bout
Cm7
F7sus4
B♭M7
B♭M7/A
50
As before
what's in-side? What a-bout the rest of me?
Gm7
E♭M7

52
don't look like Frank - en - stein's bride but
BbM7
Gm7
54
what's in- side is the best of me.
♩=144
Cm7
F7
57
He does - n't know what's in - side

61
Does- n't know what I'm feel - ing.
65
May - be I am Frank - en - stein's
69
Freely
bride
and he ne- ver real- ly knew the real
rit.
Cm7
F7sus4

73
me.
Bb(add2)
Gm7
Eb(add2)
Bb(add2)
73

8. Have-a-Heart

Laura, women

(Vamp)
All:
Cue: (1)...sexy shoes... leather...
(2)...quiet country spot, release!
Have - a- heart,
B♭m
F7
B♭
have - a- heart, she's look - ing for a Have - a- heart.
To Coda
E♭m
B♭
B♭/A
Gm
G♭
Fsus
F
B♭
D.S. al Coda
Have - a- heart.
B♭m

24
(Vamp)
Laura:
Cue: (3) ...never stop to ask for directions...
If on - ly I had a
C7/B♭
B♭m
F7
E♭m
28
Have - a - heart, I'm still look - ing for a have - a- heart
B♭
E♭m
B♭
31
All I need is a have-a- heart It's what I need for a fresh new start.
D♭m
A♭
D♭m
G♭m
C♭
A♭7

All:
Have - a heart, have - a- heart, she's look - ing
Db
Gbm
Db
Db/C
Bbm
A
for a Have - a heart.
Absus
Ab
Db
Db/C
Bbm7
A7
Ab
Db
Db+9

6. More Like Her

Brad

Freely
Wo- men al- ways say we should be more like them.
A
AM7

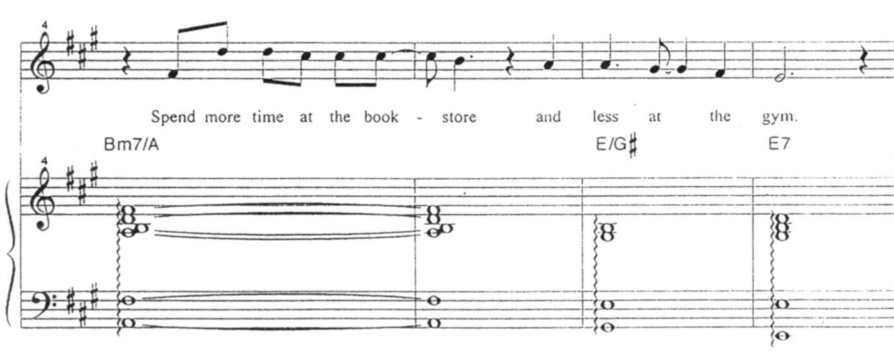
Spend more time at the book - store and less at the gym.
Bm7/A
E/G♯
E7

We should share our feel - ings and un - der - stand theirs.
A
A6
Bm7
E7

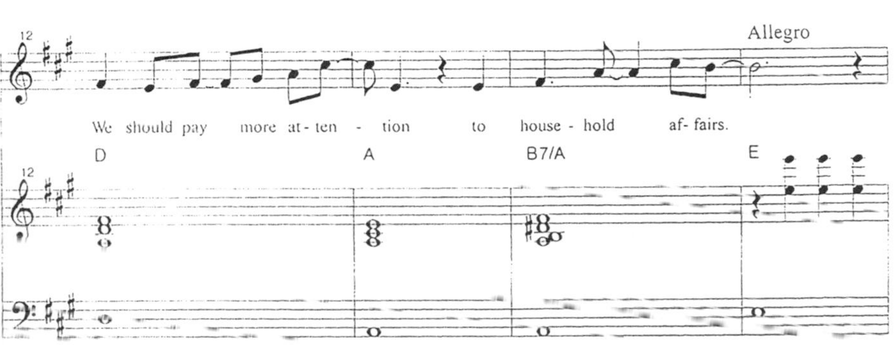
Allegro
We should pay more at- ten - tion to house - hold af- fairs.
D
A
B7/A
E

So I be came more like her
A(add2)
A
gliss.

How, then, can she com- plain?
I be- came a
AM7
C♯m
F♯m

22
sen - si - tive fel - low
Not a ma- cho
bone re- mains.
B7
G
E7
A
25
I ne - ver
could re -
D
E
A
gliss.
28
pair the en - gine
of her car
But
A6
AM7
A6

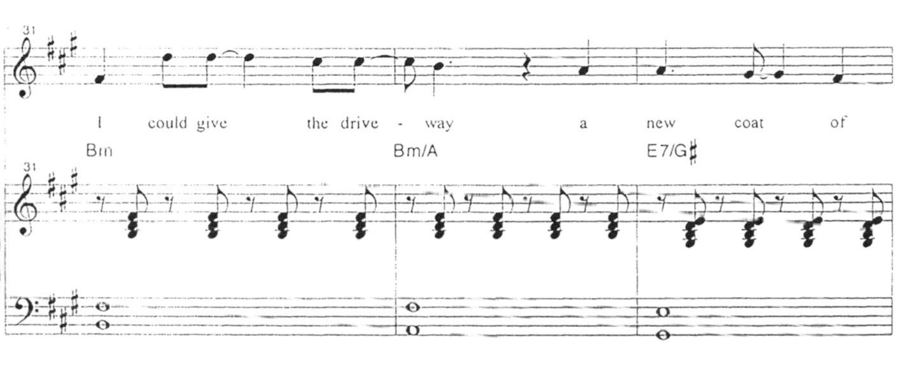
31
I could give the drive - way a new coat of
Bm
Bm/A
E7/G♯

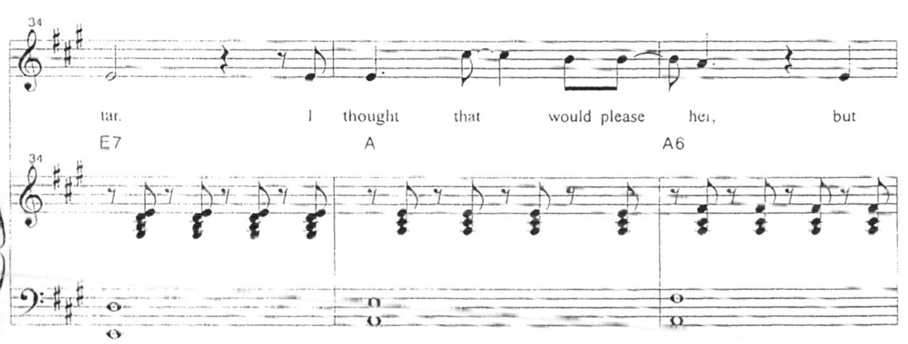
34
tar. I thought that would please her, but
E7
A
A6

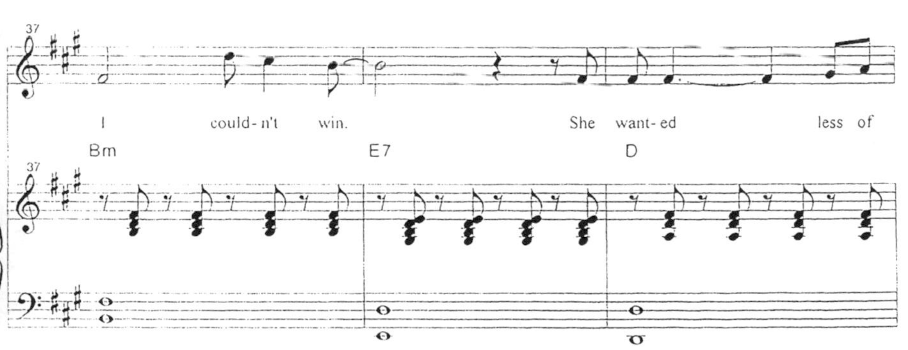
37
I could-n't win. She want-ed less of
Bm
E7
D

40
yang, and much, much more of yin.
A
B7
E7
43
So I be-came more like her
E7
A(add2)
A
gliss.
46
Why, then, is she up - set? I wear a dress, I've
AM7
C♯m
F♯m

49
tried make - up. How much more like her can I get?
B7 G E7 A
49
52
D E A B♭ B♭6
52
55
I was head of my house - hold for
B♭M7 B♭6 B♭ B♭6
55

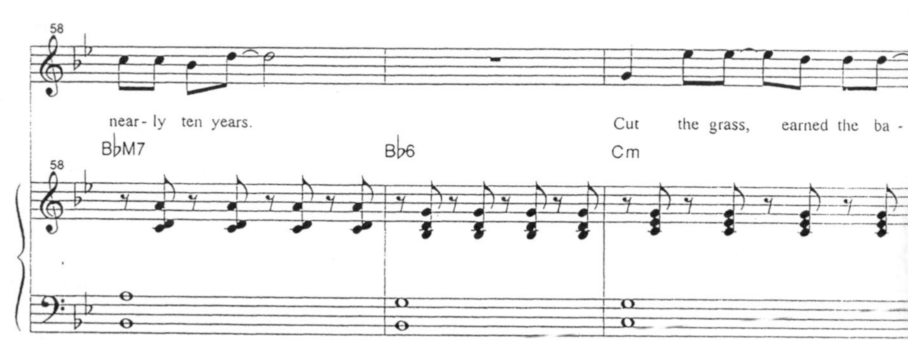
58
near- ly ten years.
Cut the grass, earned the ba -
B♭M7
B♭6
Cm

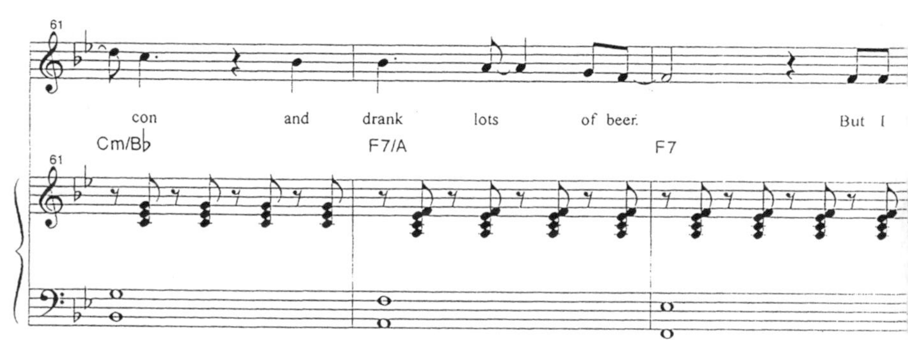
61
con and drank lots of beer. But I
Cm/B♭
F7/A
F7

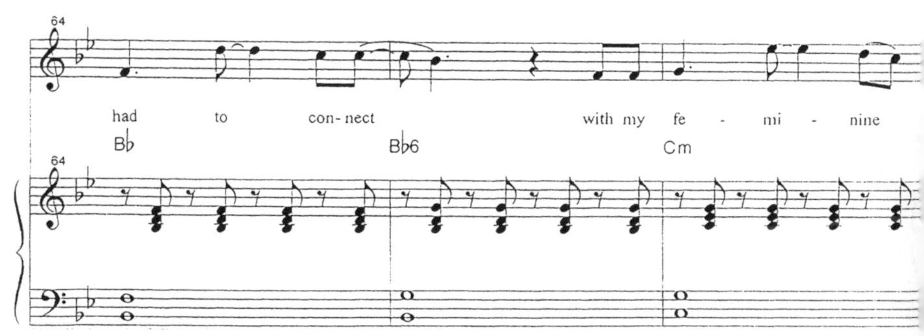
64
had to con- nect with my fe - mi - nine
B♭
B♭6
Cm

67
side so I did to the point that my
F7
Eb
Bb
70
oth - er half died.
So I be-came more like her
C7
F7
F7
Bb(add2)
gliss.
74
I com - plete - ly changed my life
But
Bb
BbM7
Dm

77
in the end, she was - n't hap - py So I be - came
Gm
C7
F♯
gliss.
80
more like her I com - plete - ly changed my
B(add2)
B
BM7
83
life But in the end she was - n't hap - py
D♯m
G♯m
C♯7

(opt. falsetto)
86
said she did - n't want a wife.
A
F#7
B
B6
89
BM7
B6
B
gliss.

10. My Perfect World

Karen, Mike

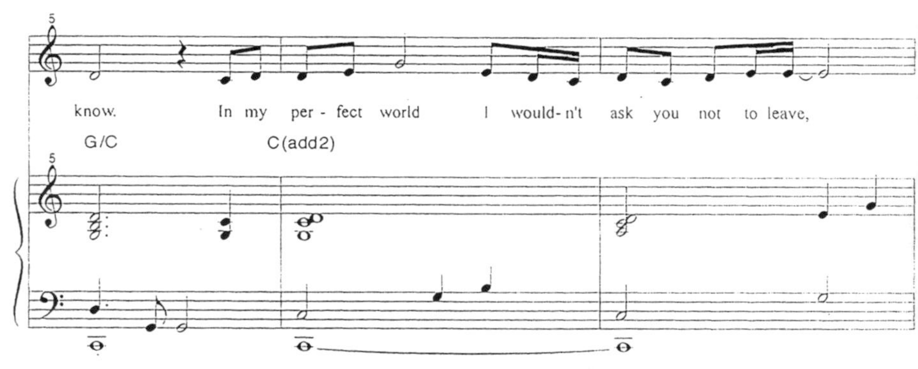

poco rit.
A tempo
would-n't lie a-wake and moan and I would not be left a-lone in my per-fect world.
Em/G
FM7
C△9
In my per-fect world I'd
FM7
CM7
FM7
CM7
wake up with you be-side me in my bed. In my
Dm7/C
G/C

21
per- fect world I could trust that you would do the things you
CM7
Dm7
24
said. I would hear the birds a- gain I would-n't be a- fraid of men
G7sus4 C/G E7/G♯ Am
Em/G
27 poco rit.
A tempo
I'd live now as I lived then, in my per- fect world. In my
FM7
CM7
FM7

30 A little stronger
per - fect world I could look at oth - er cou - ples and not
CM7
Dm7/C
33
cry. In my per - fect world I would not have had to learn
G/C
CM7
36
to say good - bye. I would not be stand - ing here
Dm7
G7sus4
C/G E7/G♯
Am

39
poco rit.
I would not be shed - ding tears as I looked back on all the years, in my
Em/G
FM7
41 A tempo
per - fect world. In my per - fect world.
CM7
FM7
Am7
44
Piú mosso
FM7
Am7
FM7
Am7

48
Mike:
In my
Dm
B♭
F
Gsus4
52
per- fect world I would not have caused the pain that you
FM7
Gm7/F
55
feel. In my per- fect I would be the man you mar - ried
C/F
FM7

58
not a heel. But I did the best I could
Gm7 C7sus4 F/C A7/C♯ Dm
61
I did what I thought I should and you would have un - der - stood in my
Am/C B♭M7
63
poco rit.
per - fect world. In my per - fect world.
FM7 B♭M7 Dm7

Meno mosso
Mike:
Karen:
In our per - fect world we would-n't have to share the blame
B♭M7
Csus4
F(add2)
m.d.
m.s.
for this mess. In our per- fect world we'd have known to fan the flame
Gm7/F
C/F
F(add2)
of wed - ded bliss.
Karen:
But you do not love me now
C7sus4
F/C
A7/C♯
Dm
Gm7

Mike:
76
You for- got your wed- ding vow. No, I do not love you now and I broke my wed- ding vow.
Am/C
B♭M7
Dm

79
Karen:
rit.
A tempo
In my per- fect world, in my per - fect world.
B♭M7
F△9
B♭M7
C7sus4
FM7

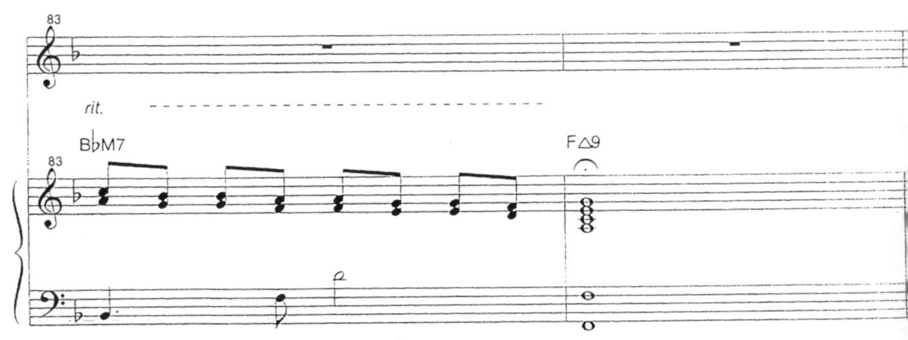
83
rit.
B♭M7
F△9

11. Let Me Count the Ways

Bette, Diane

Poco piú mosso
12
ev ev - 'ry- where I look are me - mo - ries.
16
Diane:
days days days days days . of end- less pro - mise.
19
of hold - ing hands and say - ing I love you.

But card-board hearts and rhymes don't make real mu - sic
Ped.
The pro-mise end - ed when he said, "I do."
Diane and Bette:
Let me count the ways I used to love him. I could fill a book with

30
used - to - bes. I re - call the days of love and long - ing
33
Now ev - 'ry- where I look are me - mo -
Ped.
36
Bette:
ries. He did - n't have to say the word "for - ev - er."

39
He did- n't have to pro- mise to be true. Love and Pe - ter Pan don't go to -
39
42
ge - ther. A life- time's so much hard - er than "I do."
42
46 Bette and Diane:
Let me count the ways I used to love him. I could fill a book with
46

49
used - to - bes. I re - call the days of love and long - ing.
52
Now ev - 'ry - I look are me - mo -
Ped.
55
Bette:
rit.
A tempo
ries. Now ev - 'ry- where I look are me - mo - ries.

59
59
rit.

Funded in part by a grant from the **Maine Arts Commission**, an independent state agency supported by the National Endowment for the Arts, and the **Maine Humanities** Council, a private agency